Kamichama Karin Chu ❤ 1

KOGE-DONBO

TRANSLATED AND ADAPTED BY ALETHEA NIBLEY AND ATHENA NIBLEY
LETTERED BY FOLTZ DESIGN

Ballantine Books ✱ New York

A Del Rey Manga/Kodansha Trade Paperback Original

Kamichama Karin Chu volume 1 copyright © 2006 by Koge-Donbo
English translation copyright © 2008 by Koge-Donbo

Published in the United States by Del Rey Books, an imprint of The Random House Publishing Group, a division of Random House, Inc., New York.

DEL REY is a registered trademark and the Del Rey colophon is a trademark of Random House, Inc.

Publication rights arranged through Kodansha Ltd.

First published in Japan in 2006 by Kodansha Ltd., Tokyo

ISBN 978-0-345-50403-6

Printed in the United States of America

www.delreymanga.com

3 4 5 6 7 8 9

Translator/adapter: Alethea Nibley and Athena Nibley
Lettering: Foltz Design

CONTENTS

A WORD FROM THE AUTHOR

Hello! This is Koge-Donbo. The new *Kamichama Karin* series has started, with a completely new story—and a new rival for Karin's love! Also, all the characters from the previous series play a big part, so if you're already a fan, this new series will be fun for you, too. Please enjoy *Kamichama Karin chu*!

HONORIFICS EXPLAINED

Throughout the Del Rey Manga books, you will find Japanese honorifics left intact in the translations. For those not familiar with how the Japanese use honorifics and, more important, how they differ from American honorifics, we present this brief overview.

Politeness has always been a critical facet of Japanese culture. Ever since the feudal era, when Japan was a highly stratified society, use of honorifics—which can be defined as polite speech that indicates relationship or status—has played an essential role in the Japanese language. When addressing someone in Japanese, an honorific usually takes the form of a suffix attached to one's name (example: "Asuna-san"), is used as a title at the end of one's name, or appears in place of the name itself (example: "Negi-sensei," or simply "Sensei!").

Honorifics can be expressions of respect or endearment. In the context of manga and anime, honorifics give insight into the nature of the relationship between characters. Many English translations leave out these important honorifics and therefore distort the feel of the original Japanese. Because Japanese honorifics contain nuances that English honorifics lack, it is our policy at Del Rey not to translate them. Here, instead, is a guide to some of the honorifics you may encounter in Del Rey Manga.

-san: This is the most common honorific and is equivalent to Mr., Miss, Ms., or Mrs. It is the all-purpose honorific and can be used in any situation where politeness is required.

-sama: This is one level higher than "-san" and is used to confer great respect.

-dono: This comes from the word "tono," which means "lord." It is an even higher level than "-sama" and confers utmost respect.

-kun: This suffix is used at the end of boys' names to express familiarity or endearment. It is also sometimes used by men among friends, or when addressing someone younger or of a lower station.

-chan: This is used to express endearment, mostly toward girls. It is also used for little boys, pets, and even among lovers. It gives a sense of childish cuteness.

Bozu: This is an informal way to refer to a boy, similar to the English terms "kid" and "squirt."

Sempai/
Senpai: This title suggests that the addressee is one's senior in a group or organization. It is most often used in a school setting, where underclassmen refer to their upperclassmen as "sempai." It can also be used in the workplace, such as when a newer employee addresses an employee who has seniority in the company.

Kohai: This is the opposite of "sempai" and is used toward underclassmen in school or newcomers in the workplace. It connotes that the addressee is of a lower station.

Sensei: Literally meaning "one who has come before," this title is used for teachers, doctors, or masters of any profession or art.

-[blank]: This is usually forgotten in these lists, but it is perhaps the most significant difference between Japanese and English. The lack of honorific means that the speaker has permission to address the person in a very intimate way. Usually, only family, spouses, or very close friends have this kind of permission. Known as *yobisute*, it can be gratifying when someone who has earned the intimacy starts to call one by one's name without an honorific. But when that intimacy hasn't been earned, it can be very insulting.

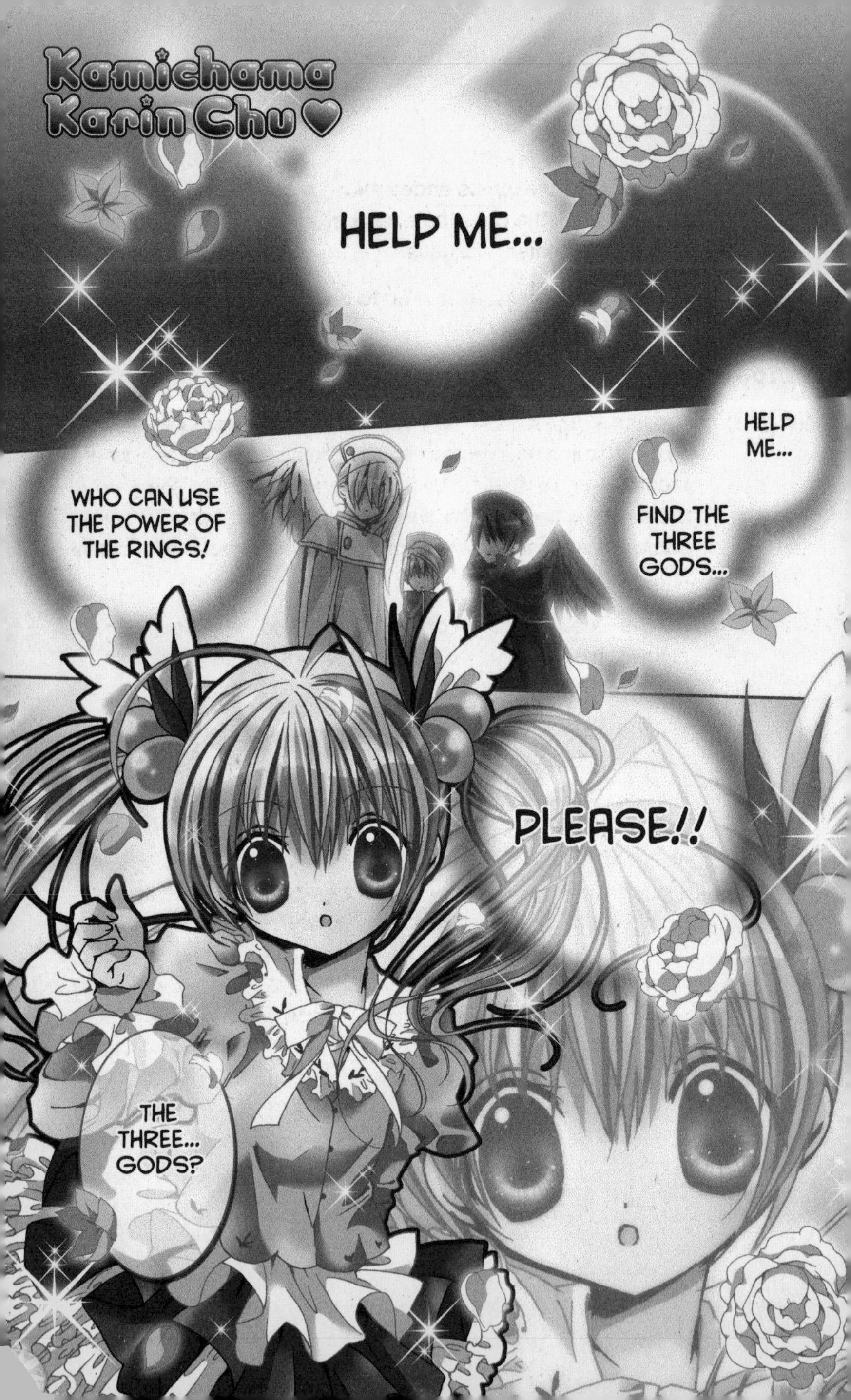
Kamichama Karin Chu♥
HELP ME...
HELP ME...
FIND THE THREE GODS...
WHO CAN USE THE POWER OF THE RINGS!
PLEASE!!
THE THREE... GODS?

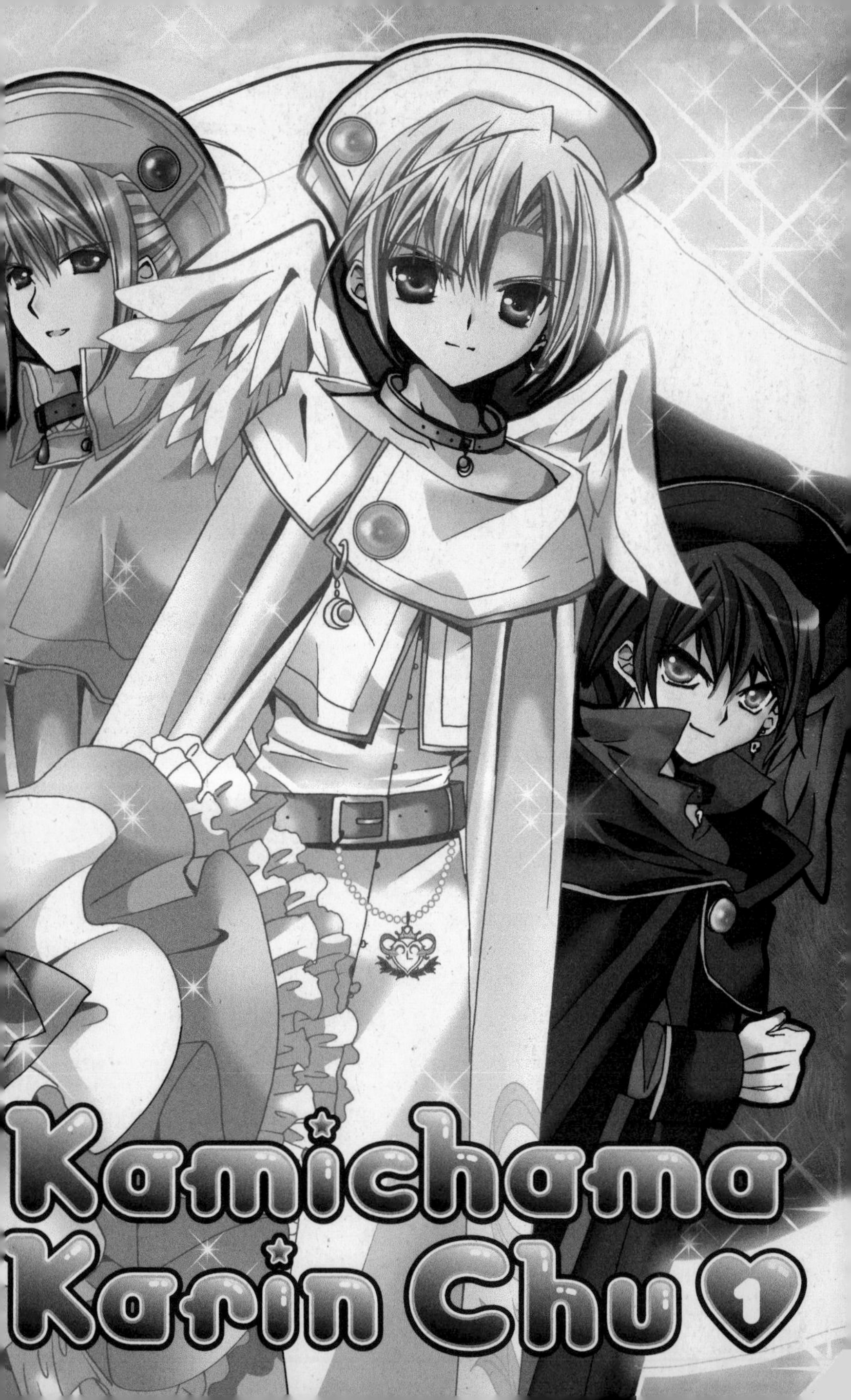
Kamichama Karin Chu 1

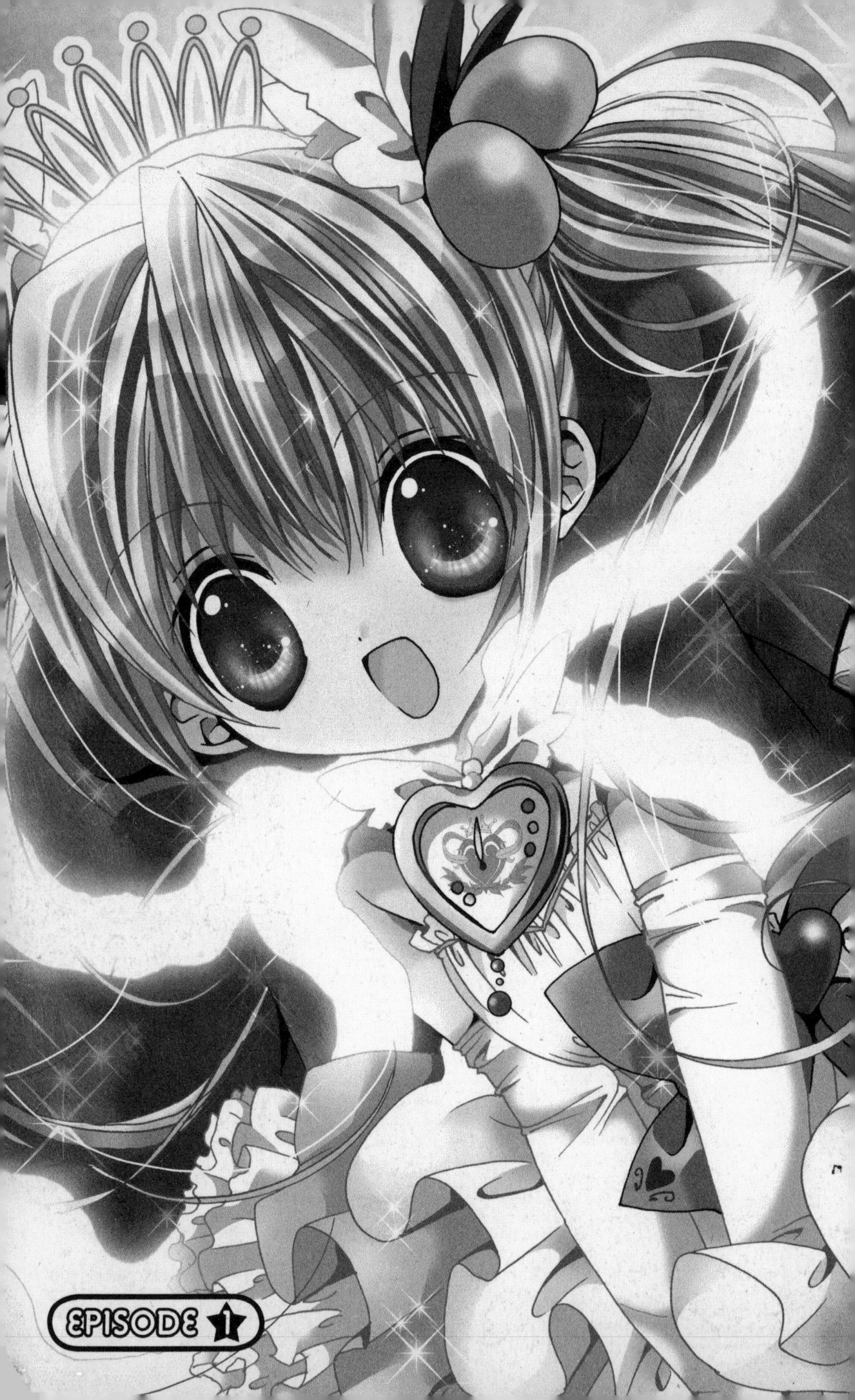
EPISODE 1

KAMICHAMA KARIN CHU IS THE SEQUEL TO KAMICHAMA KARIN. LET'S LEARN ABOUT WHAT HAPPENED IN THE FIRST SERIES!

STORY

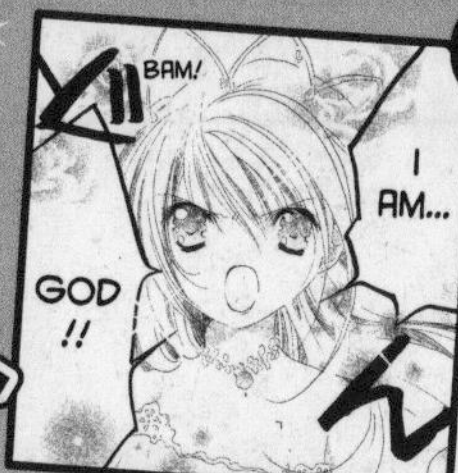
BAM!
I AM...
GOD !!

KARIN-CHAN IS GIFTED WITH THE POWER TO TRANSFORM INTO A GODDESS BY THE RING THAT WAS LEFT TO HER BY HER PARENTS. THIS RING SETS THINGS IN MOTION. KARIN-CHAN MEETS KAZUNE-KUN AND HIMEKA-CHAN, AND HER DESTINY CHANGES DRAMATICALLY....

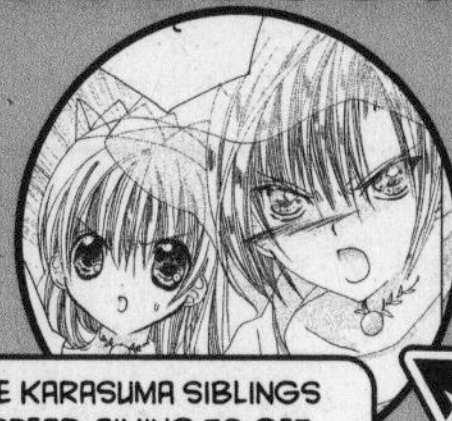

THE KARASUMA SIBLINGS APPEAR, AIMING TO GET HER RING, AND THE BATTLE GRADUALLY GROWS FIERCE.

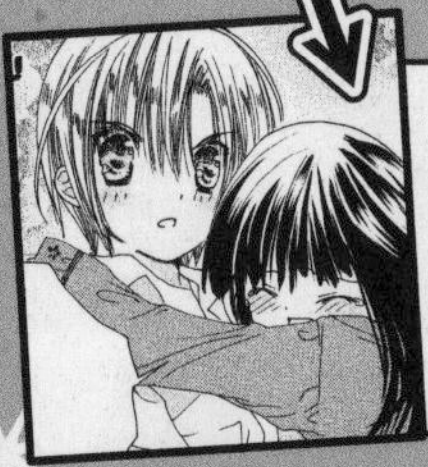

IN THE MIDST OF THE BATTLE, A SECRET IS REVEALED. THE SECRET: LONG AGO, KARIN-CHAN AND KAZUNE-KUN WERE MARRIED, AND HIMEKA-CHAN WAS THEIR DAUGHTER.

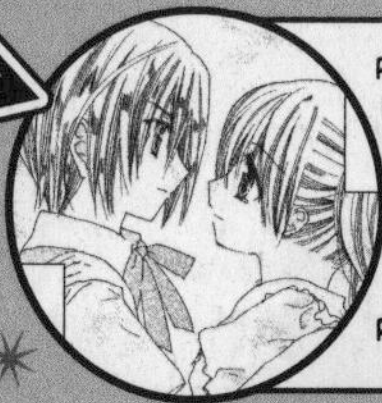

AFTER THAT, KARIN-CHAN AND THE OTHERS LIVED A PEACEFUL LIFE, BUT KAZUNE-KUN SET OFF ALONE FOR ENGLAND TO LOOK INTO THE SECRETS OF THE RINGS....

THE PEOPLE OF KAMICHAMA KARIN WORLD

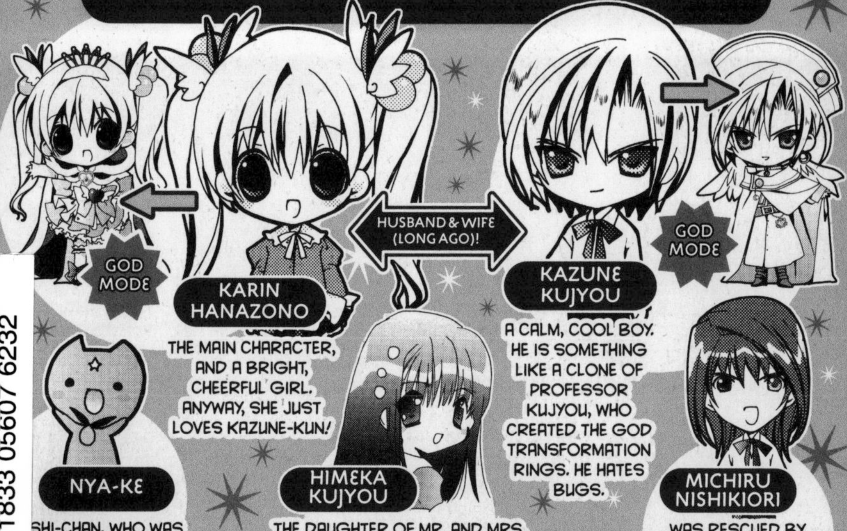
GOD MODE
HUSBAND & WIFE (LONG AGO)!
GOD MODE

KARIN HANAZONO

THE MAIN CHARACTER, AND A BRIGHT, CHEERFUL GIRL. ANYWAY, SHE JUST LOVES KAZUNE-KUN!

KAZUNE KUJYOU

A CALM, COOL BOY. HE IS SOMETHING LIKE A CLONE OF PROFESSOR KUJYOU, WHO CREATED THE GOD TRANSFORMATION RINGS. HE HATES BUGS.

NYA-KE

SHI-CHAN, WHO WAS KARIN-CHAN'S PET CAT, TRANSFORMED INTO A GODDESS AND WAS REVIVED.

HIMEKA KUJYOU

THE DAUGHTER OF MR. AND MRS. KUJYOU. WHILE STUDYING ABROAD IN ENGLAND, SHE OBTAINED THE KEY TO UNDOING THE SEAL OF THE RING OF ZEUS. SHE LOVES BUGS.

MICHIRU NISHIKIORI

WAS RESCUED BY PROFESSOR KUJYOU WHEN HE WAS IN A BIG ACCIDENT. KARIN-CHAN AND KAZUNE-KUN'S ALLY.

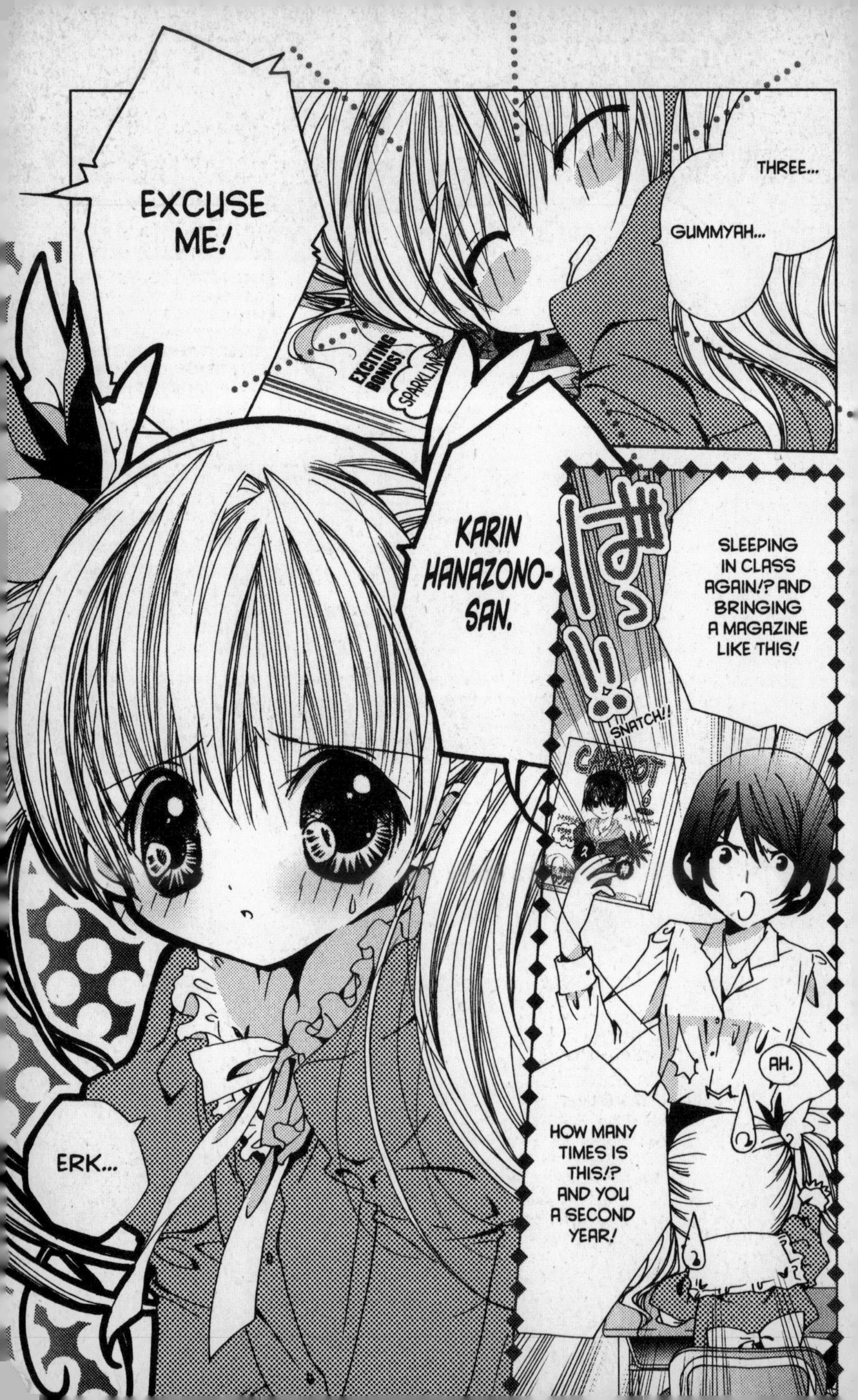
THREE...
GUMMYAH...
EXCITING BONUS!
SPARKLIN
EXCUSE ME!
KARIN HANAZONO-SAN.
ばっ!!
SNATCH!!
CARROT
SLEEPING IN CLASS AGAIN!? AND BRINGING A MAGAZINE LIKE THIS!
AH.
HOW MANY TIMES IS THIS!? AND YOU A SECOND YEAR!
ERK...

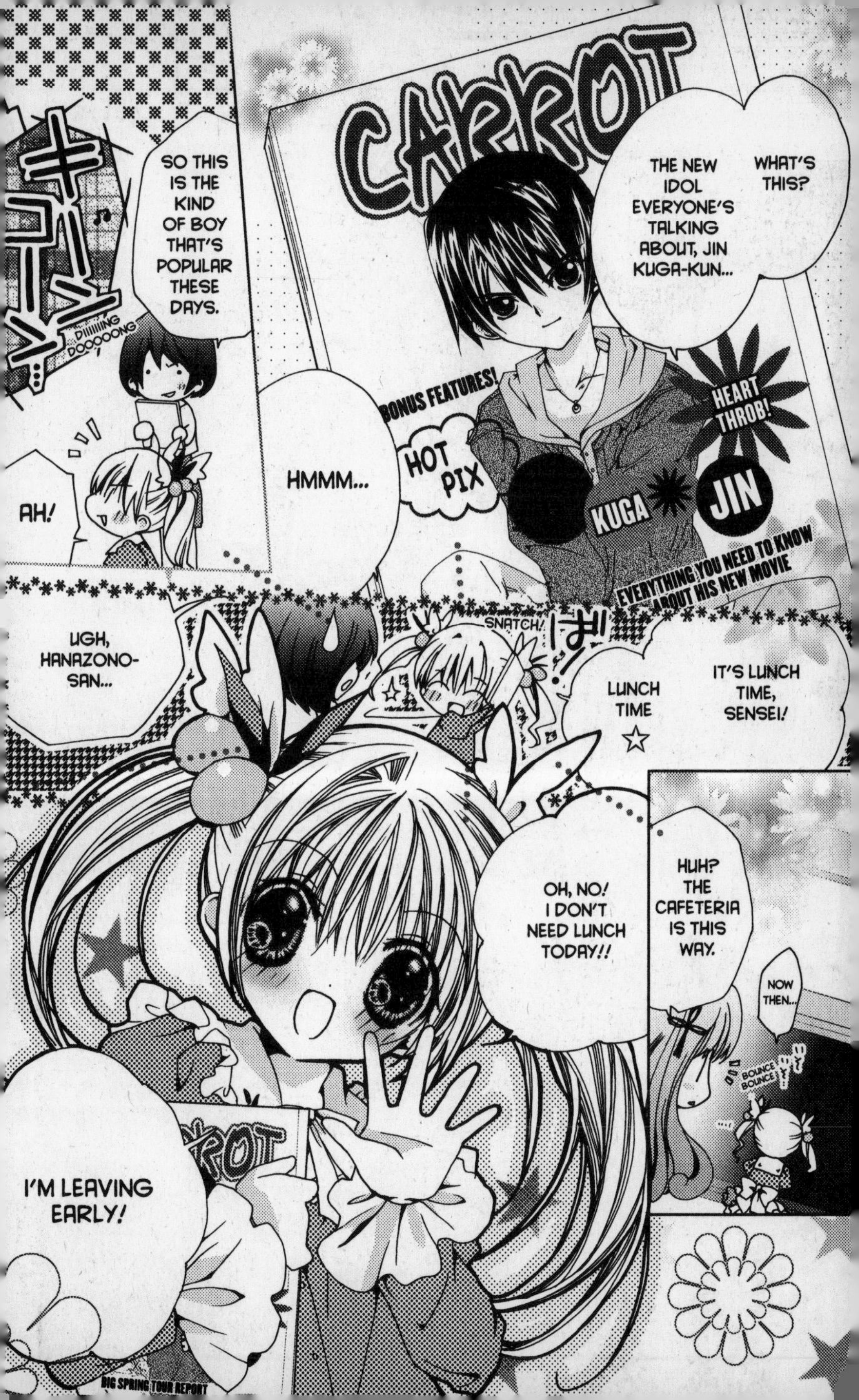
CARROT
WHAT'S THIS?
THE NEW IDOL EVERYONE'S TALKING ABOUT, JIN KUGA-KUN...
BONUS FEATURES!
HOT PIX
HEART THROB!
KUGA JIN
EVERYTHING YOU NEED TO KNOW ABOUT HIS NEW MOVIE
HMMM...
SO THIS IS THE KIND OF BOY THAT'S POPULAR THESE DAYS.
DIIIIIIING DOOOOONG
AH!
IT'S LUNCH TIME, SENSEI!
LUNCH TIME ☆
SNATCH!
UGH, HANAZONO-SAN...
HUH? THE CAFETERIA IS THIS WAY.
NOW THEN...
BOUNCE BOUNCE
OH, NO! I DON'T NEED LUNCH TODAY!!
I'M LEAVING EARLY!
CARROT
BIG SPRING TOUR REPORT

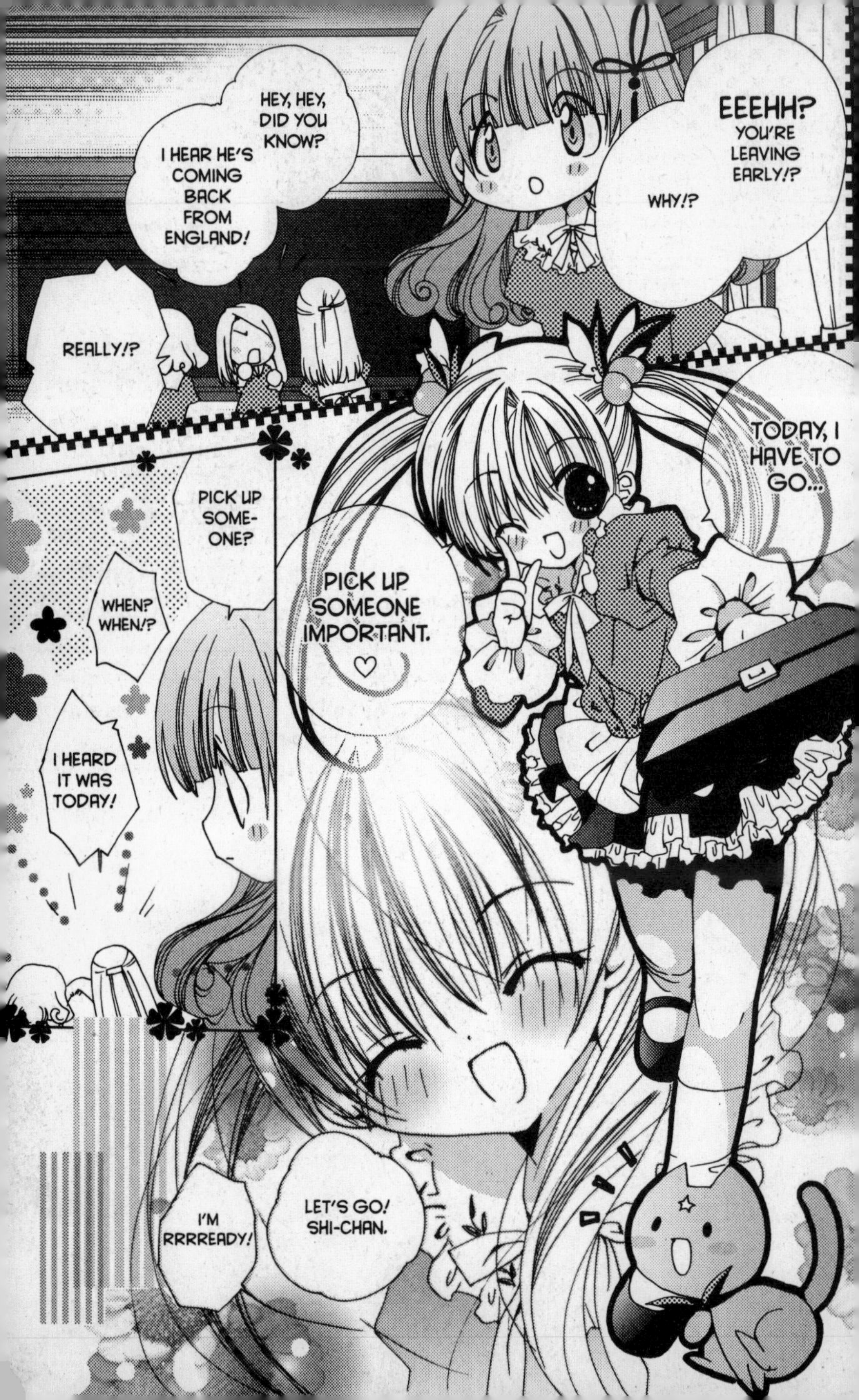
EEEHH? YOU'RE LEAVING EARLY!?
WHY!?
HEY, HEY, DID YOU KNOW?
I HEAR HE'S COMING BACK FROM ENGLAND!
REALLY!?
TODAY, I HAVE TO GO...
PICK UP SOMEONE IMPORTANT. ♡
PICK UP SOME-ONE?
WHEN? WHEN!?
I HEARD IT WAS TODAY!
LET'S GO! SHI-CHAN.
I'M RRRREADY!

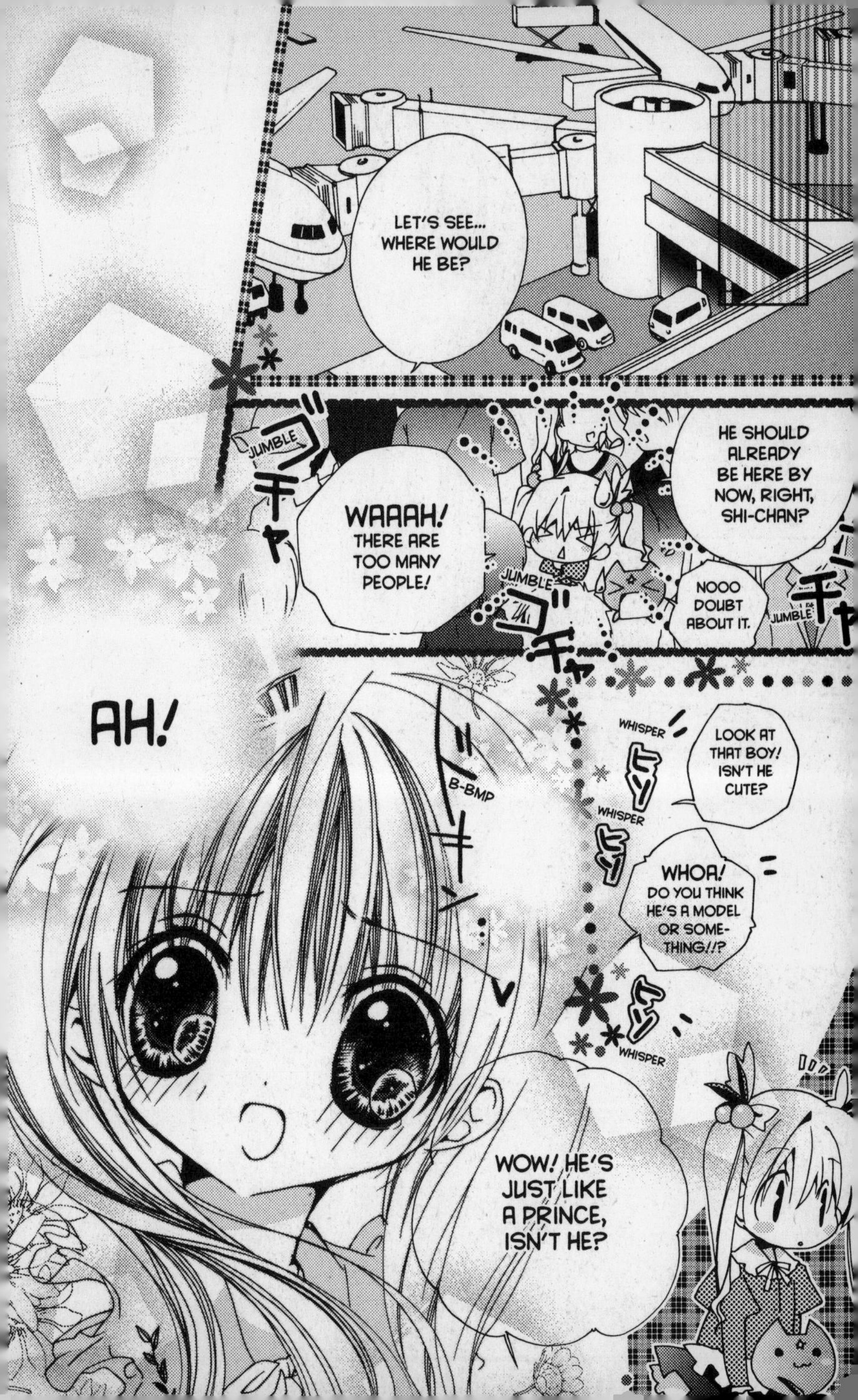
LET'S SEE... WHERE WOULD HE BE?
HE SHOULD ALREADY BE HERE BY NOW, RIGHT, SHI-CHAN?
JUMBLE
NOOO DOUBT ABOUT IT.
JUMBLE
WAAAH! THERE ARE TOO MANY PEOPLE!
JUMBLE
WHISPER
LOOK AT THAT BOY! ISN'T HE CUTE?
WHISPER
WHOA! DO YOU THINK HE'S A MODEL OR SOME-THING!?
WHISPER
B-BMP
AH!
WOW! HE'S JUST LIKE A PRINCE, ISN'T HE?

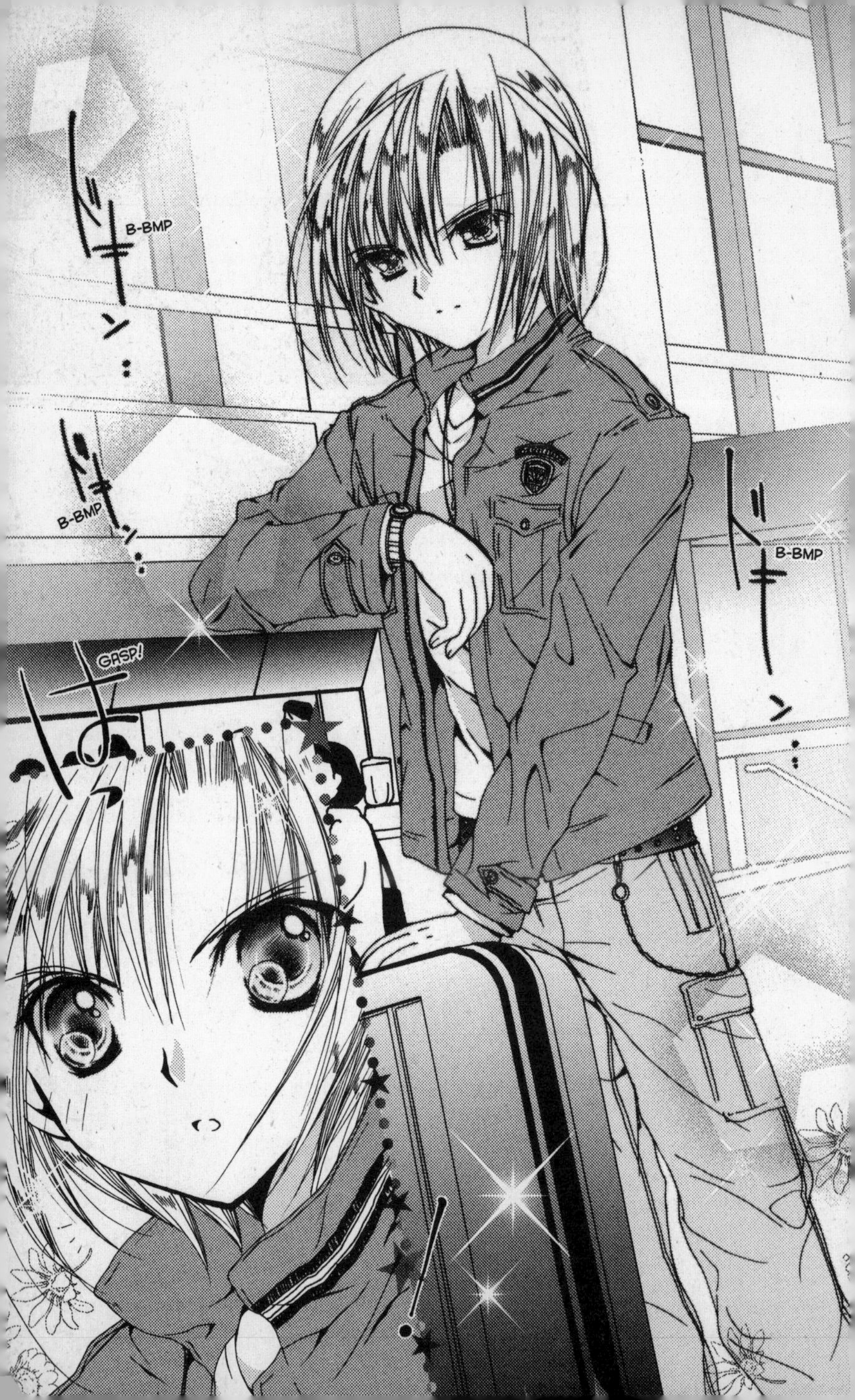
B-BMP
B-BMP
B-BMP
GASP!

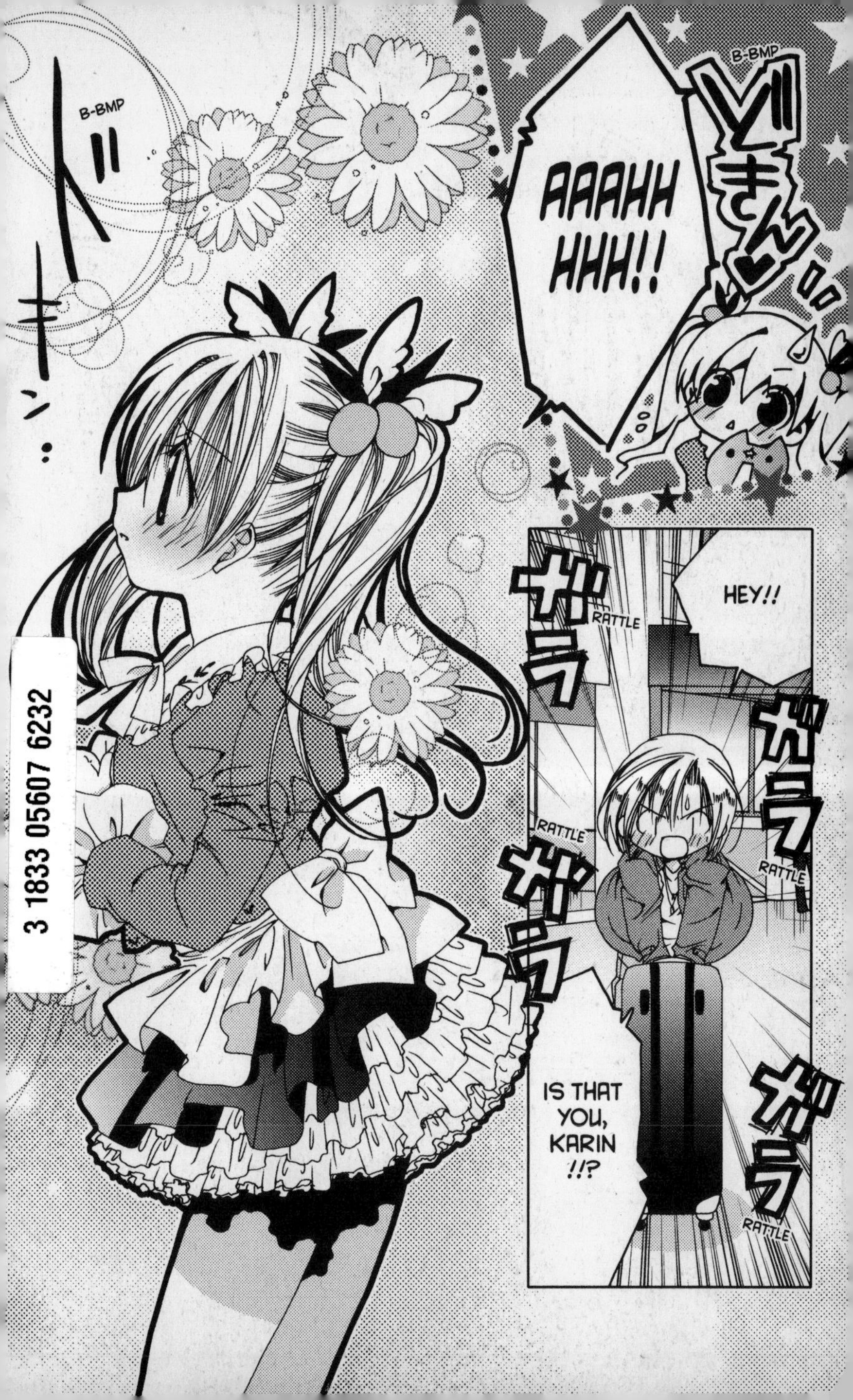

B-BMP
AAAHH HHH!!
RATTLE
RATTLE
HEY!!
RATTLE
RATTLE
IS THAT YOU, KARIN !!?
B-BMP

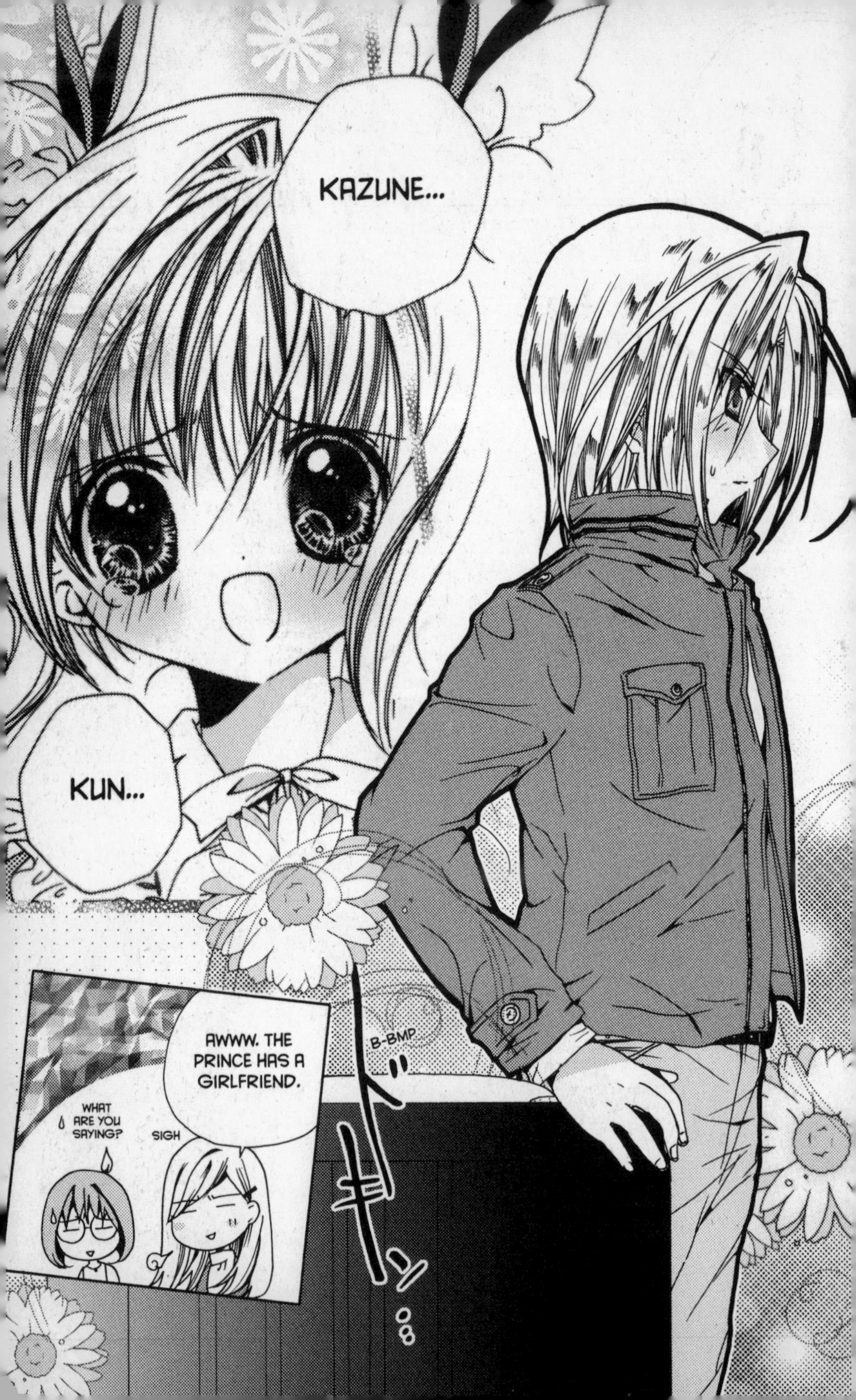
KAZUNE...
KUN...
B-BMP
AWWW. THE PRINCE HAS A GIRLFRIEND.
SIGH
WHAT ARE YOU SAYING?

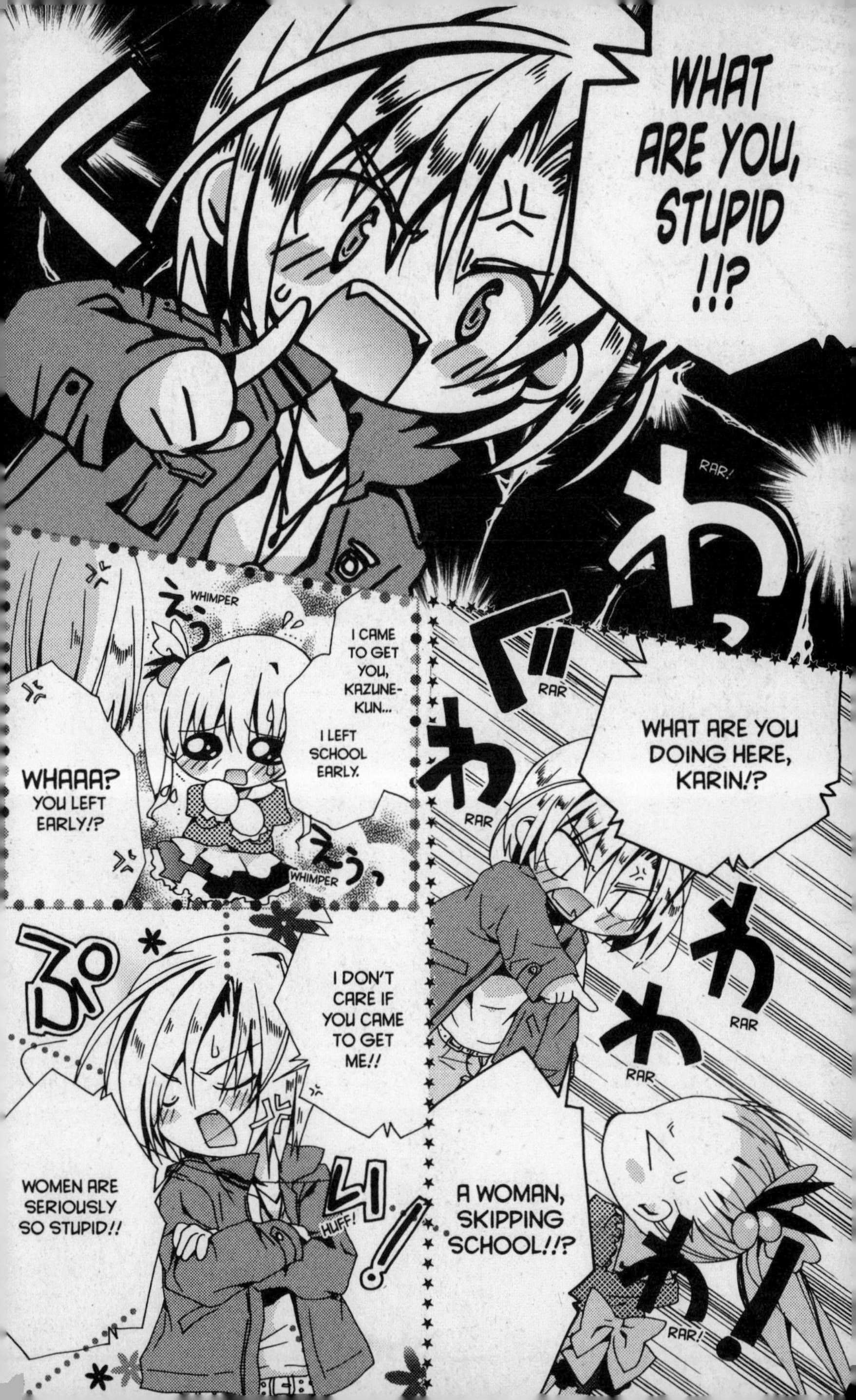
WHAT ARE YOU, STUPID!!?
わ
RAR!
ぐ
RAR
わ
RAR
WHAT ARE YOU DOING HERE, KARIN!?
わ
RAR
わ
RAR
A WOMAN, SKIPPING SCHOOL!!?
わ!
RAR!
えう
WHIMPER
I CAME TO GET YOU, KAZUNE-KUN...
I LEFT SCHOOL EARLY.
WHAAA? YOU LEFT EARLY!?
えう
WHIMPER
I DON'T CARE IF YOU CAME TO GET ME!!
ぷい
HUFF!
WOMEN ARE SERIOUSLY SO STUPID!!

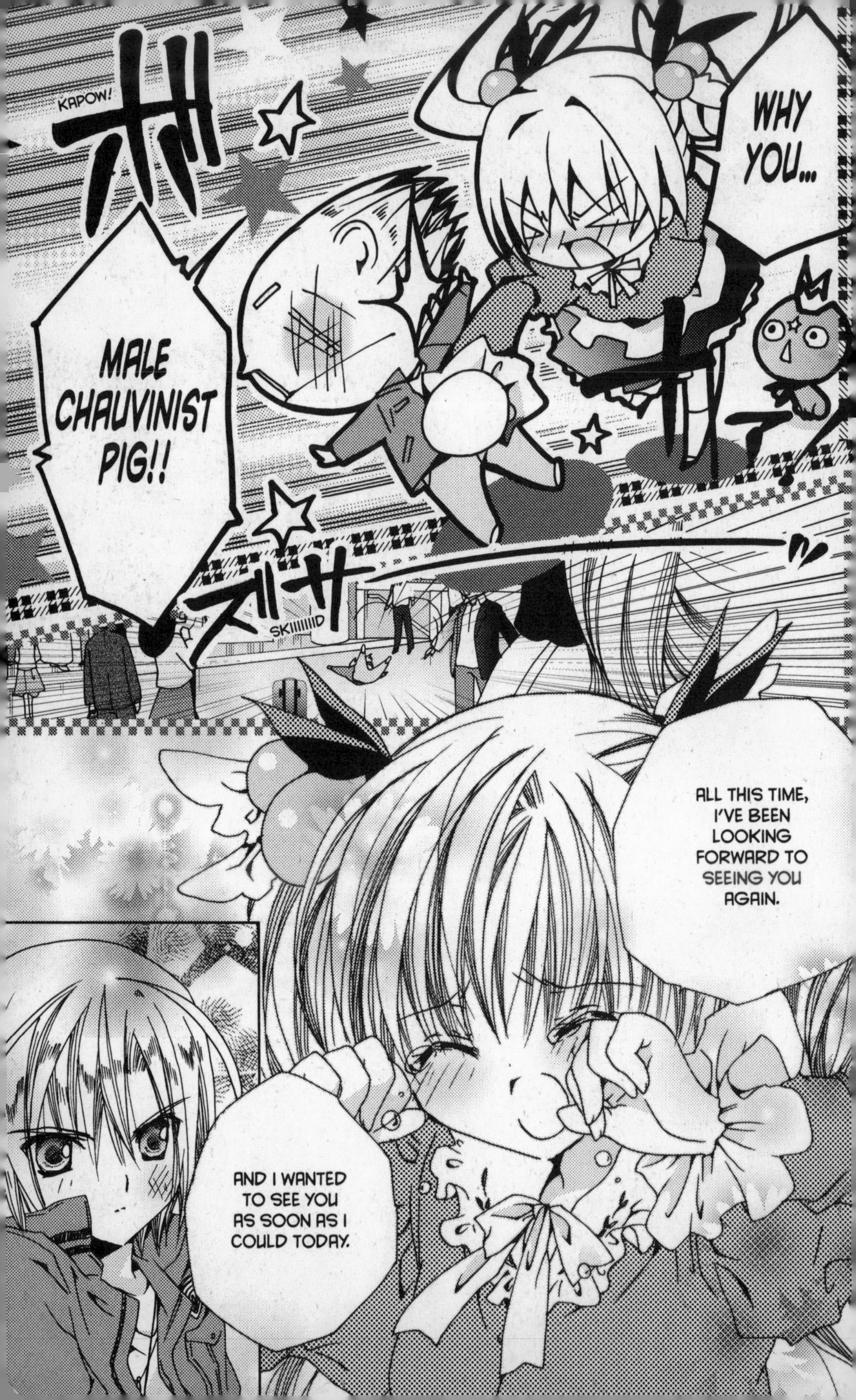
WHY YOU...
KAPOW!
MALE CHAUVINIST PIG!!
SKIIIIIID
ALL THIS TIME, I'VE BEEN LOOKING FORWARD TO SEEING YOU AGAIN.
AND I WANTED TO SEE YOU AS SOON AS I COULD TODAY.

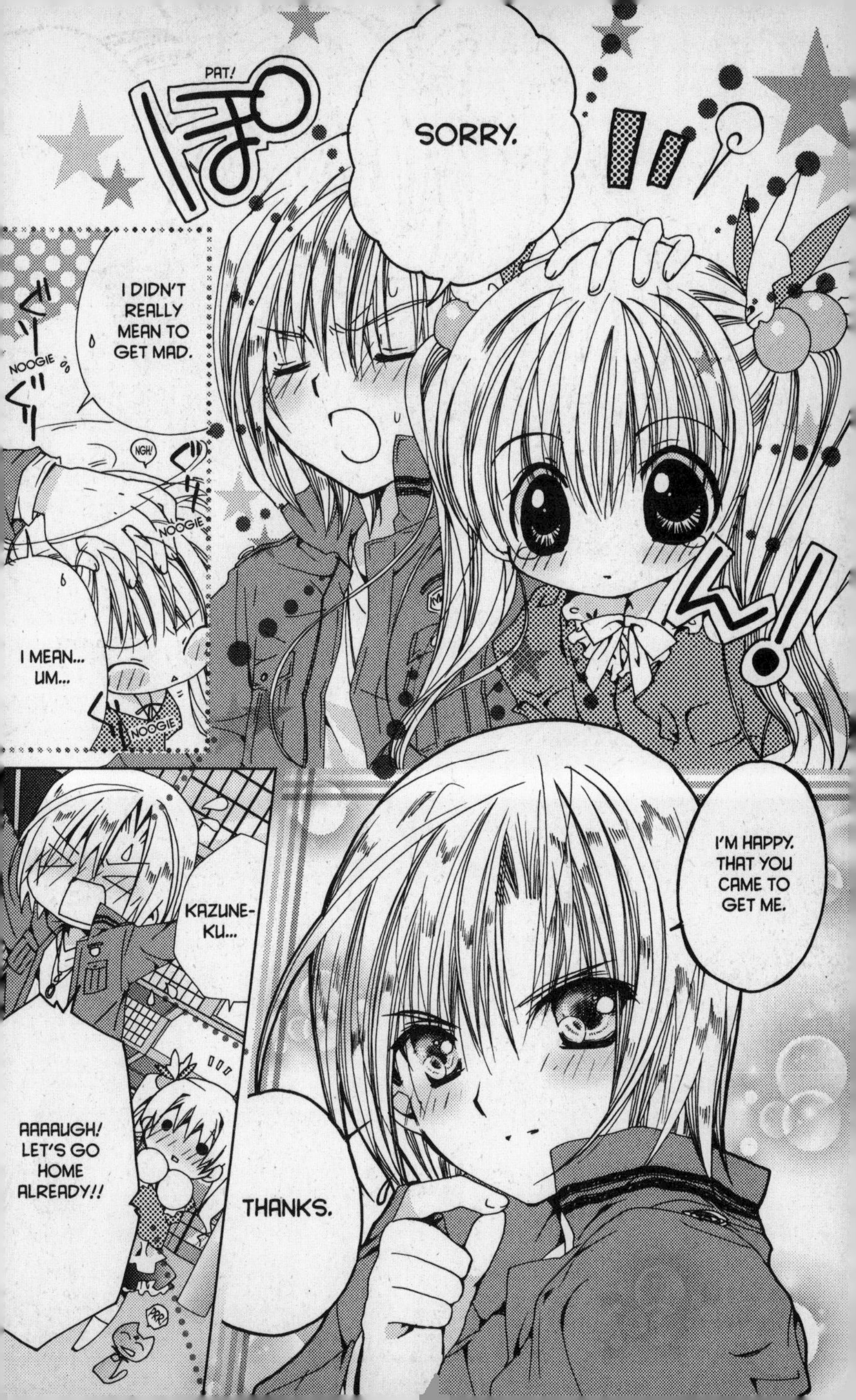
PAT!
SORRY.
I DIDN'T REALLY MEAN TO GET MAD.
NOOGIE
NGH!
NOOGIE
I MEAN... UM...
NOOGIE
I'M HAPPY. THAT YOU CAME TO GET ME.
THANKS.
KAZUNE-KU...
AAAAUGH! LET'S GO HOME ALREADY!!
PRR!

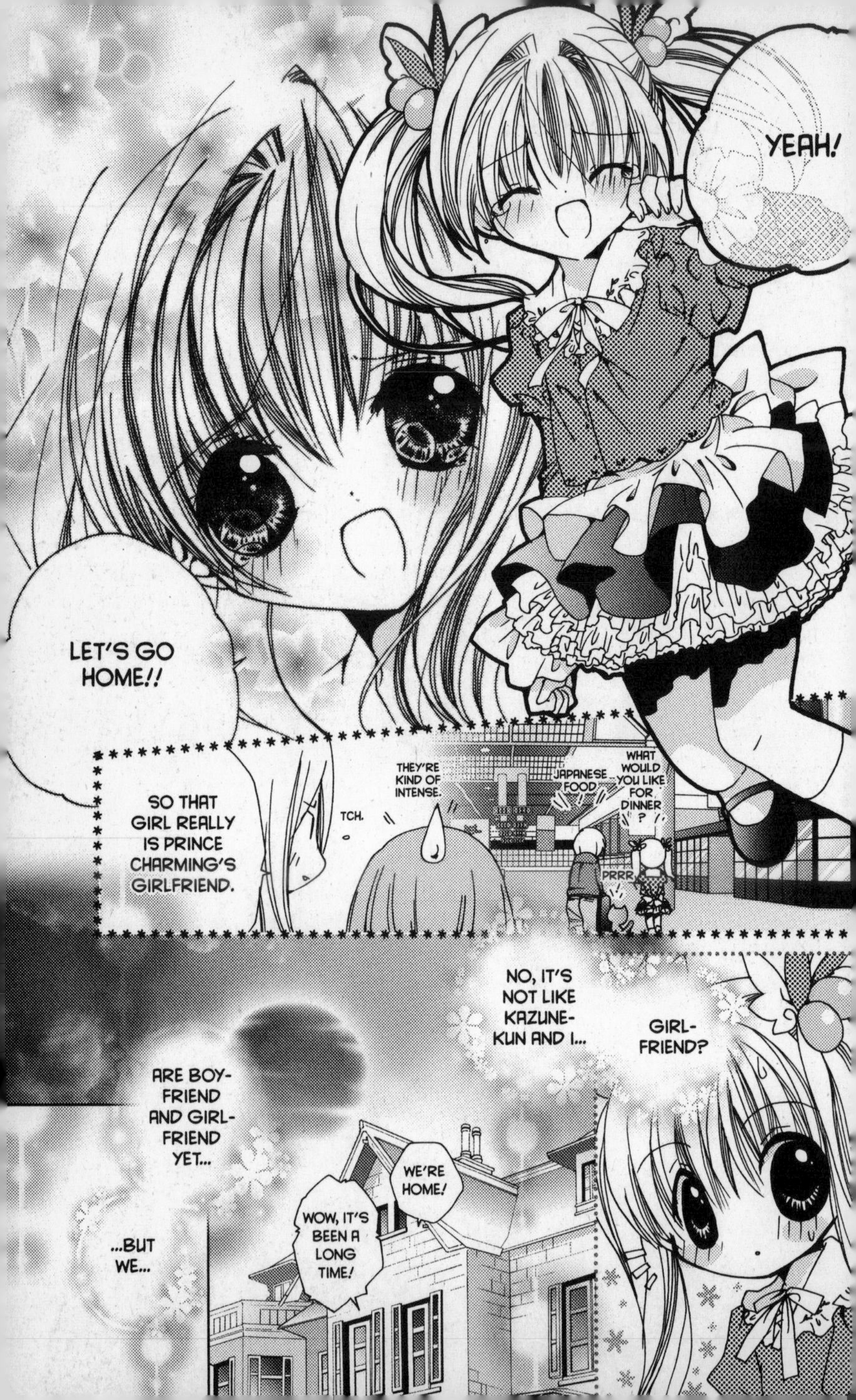
YEAH!
LET'S GO HOME!!
WHAT WOULD YOU LIKE FOR DINNER?
JAPANESE FOOD!
PRRR
THEY'RE KIND OF INTENSE.
TCH.
SO THAT GIRL REALLY IS PRINCE CHARMING'S GIRLFRIEND.
GIRL-FRIEND?
NO, IT'S NOT LIKE KAZUNE-KUN AND I...
ARE BOY-FRIEND AND GIRL-FRIEND YET...
WE'RE HOME!
WOW, IT'S BEEN A LONG TIME!
...BUT WE...

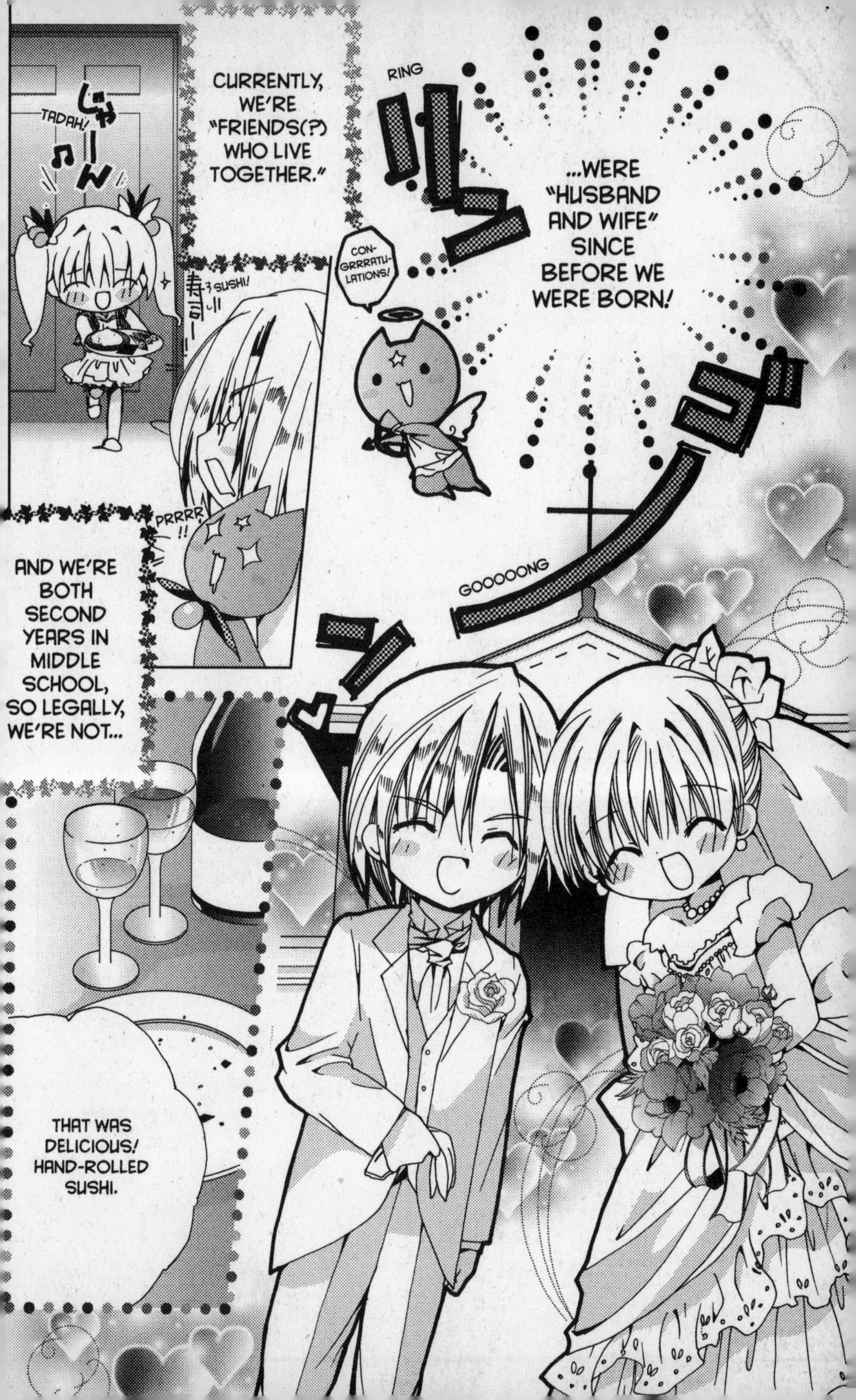
CURRENTLY, WE'RE "FRIENDS(?) WHO LIVE TOGETHER."
TADAH!
SUSHI!
PRRRR!!
AND WE'RE BOTH SECOND YEARS IN MIDDLE SCHOOL, SO LEGALLY, WE'RE NOT...
THAT WAS DELICIOUS! HAND-ROLLED SUSHI.
RING
CON-GRRRATULATIONS!
...WERE "HUSBAND AND WIFE" SINCE BEFORE WE WERE BORN!
GOOOOONG

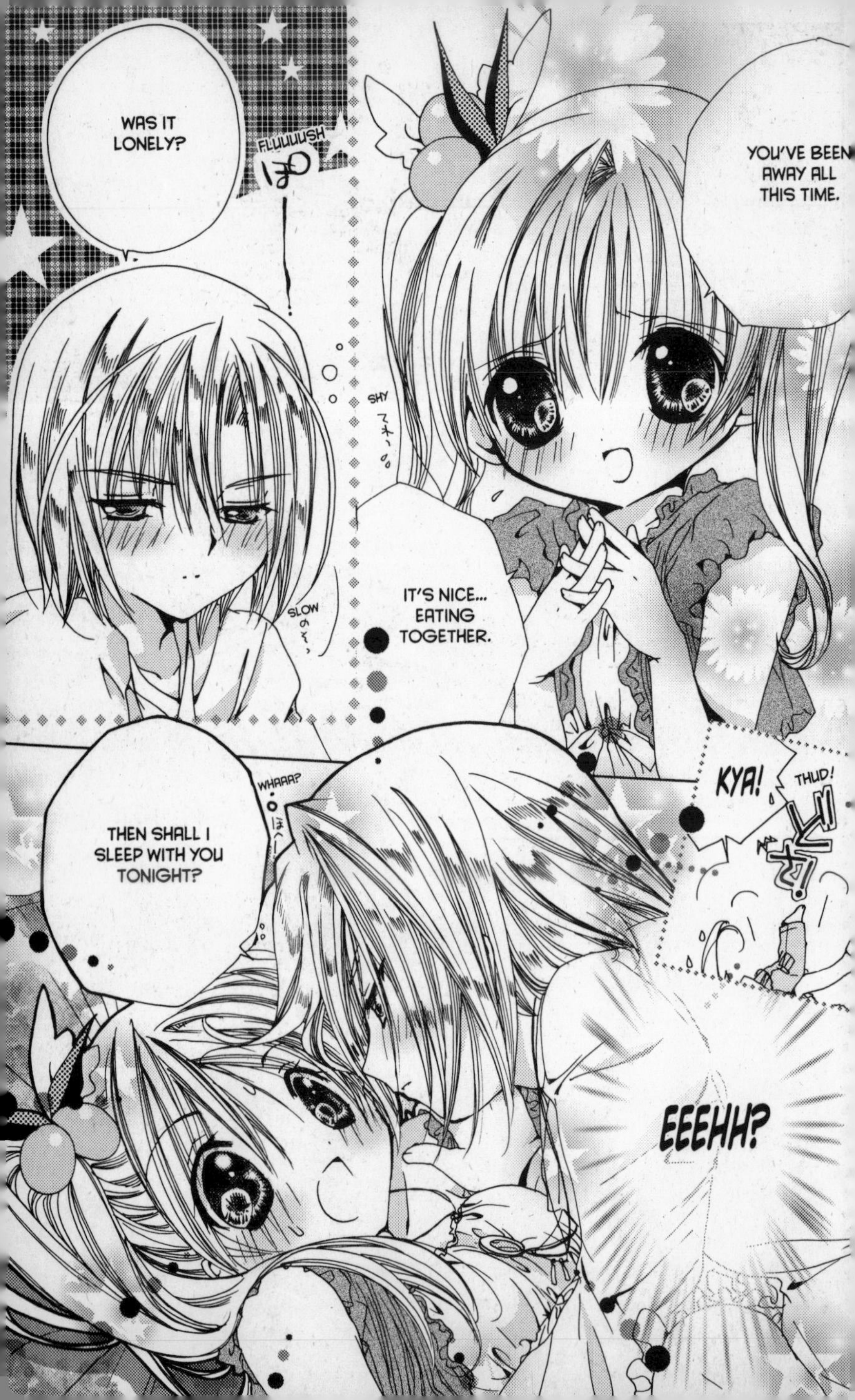
YOU'VE BEEN AWAY ALL THIS TIME.
SHY
IT'S NICE... EATING TOGETHER.
WAS IT LONELY?
FLUUUUSH
SLOW
KYA!
THUD!
WHAAA?
THEN SHALL I SLEEP WITH YOU TONIGHT?
EEEHH?

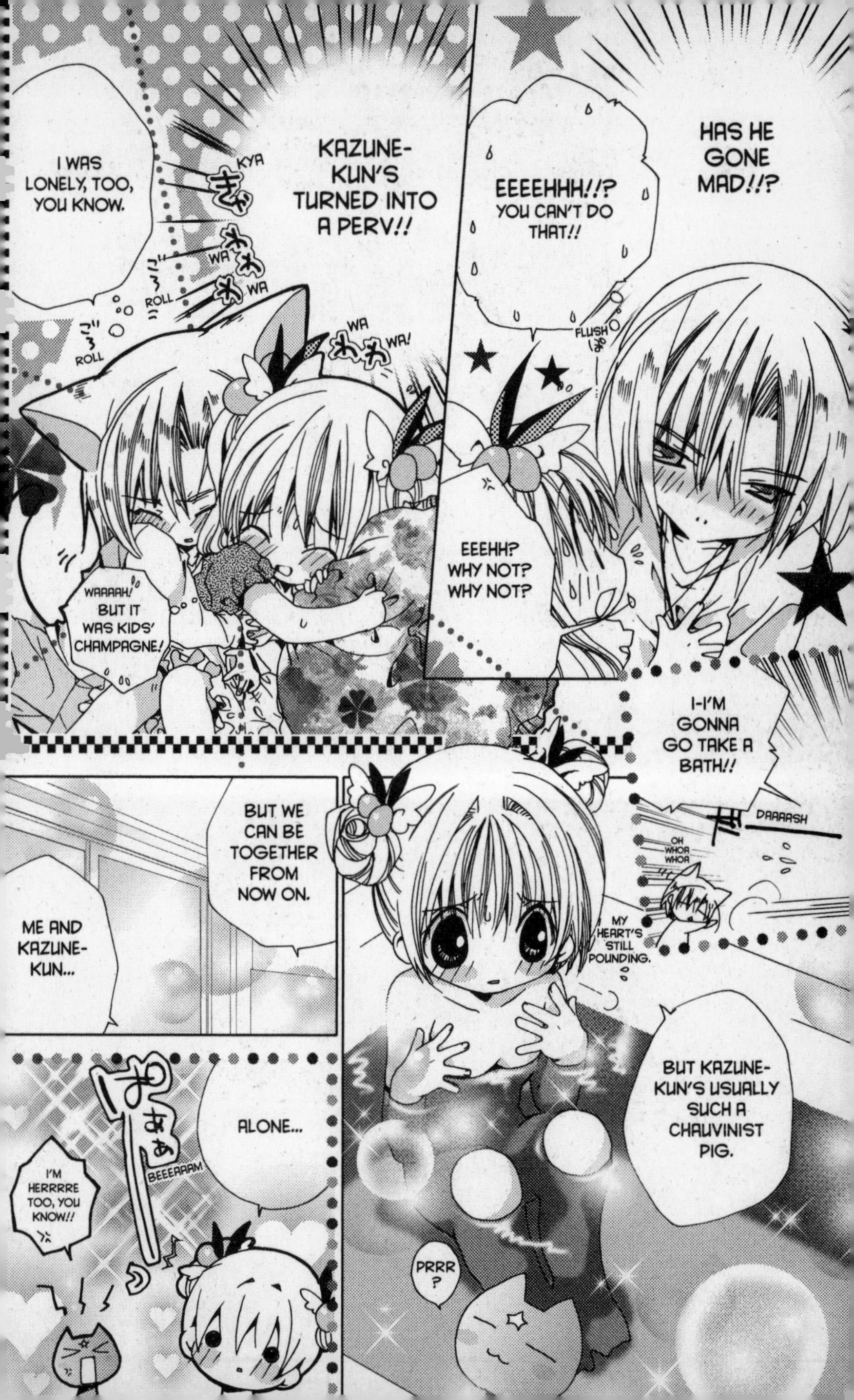
HAS HE GONE MAD!!?
EEEEHHH!!? YOU CAN'T DO THAT!!
FLUSH
EEEHH? WHY NOT? WHY NOT?
KAZUNE-KUN'S TURNED INTO A PERV!!
I WAS LONELY, TOO, YOU KNOW.
KYA
WA
WA
ROLL
ROLL
WA
WA!
WAAAAH! BUT IT WAS KIDS' CHAMPAGNE!
I-I'M GONNA GO TAKE A BATH!!
DAAAASH
OH WHOA WHOA
MY HEART'S STILL POUNDING.
BUT KAZUNE-KUN'S USUALLY SUCH A CHAUVINIST PIG.
PRRR?
BUT WE CAN BE TOGETHER FROM NOW ON.
ME AND KAZUNE-KUN...
ALONE...
BEEEAAAM
I'M HERRRRE TOO, YOU KNOW!!

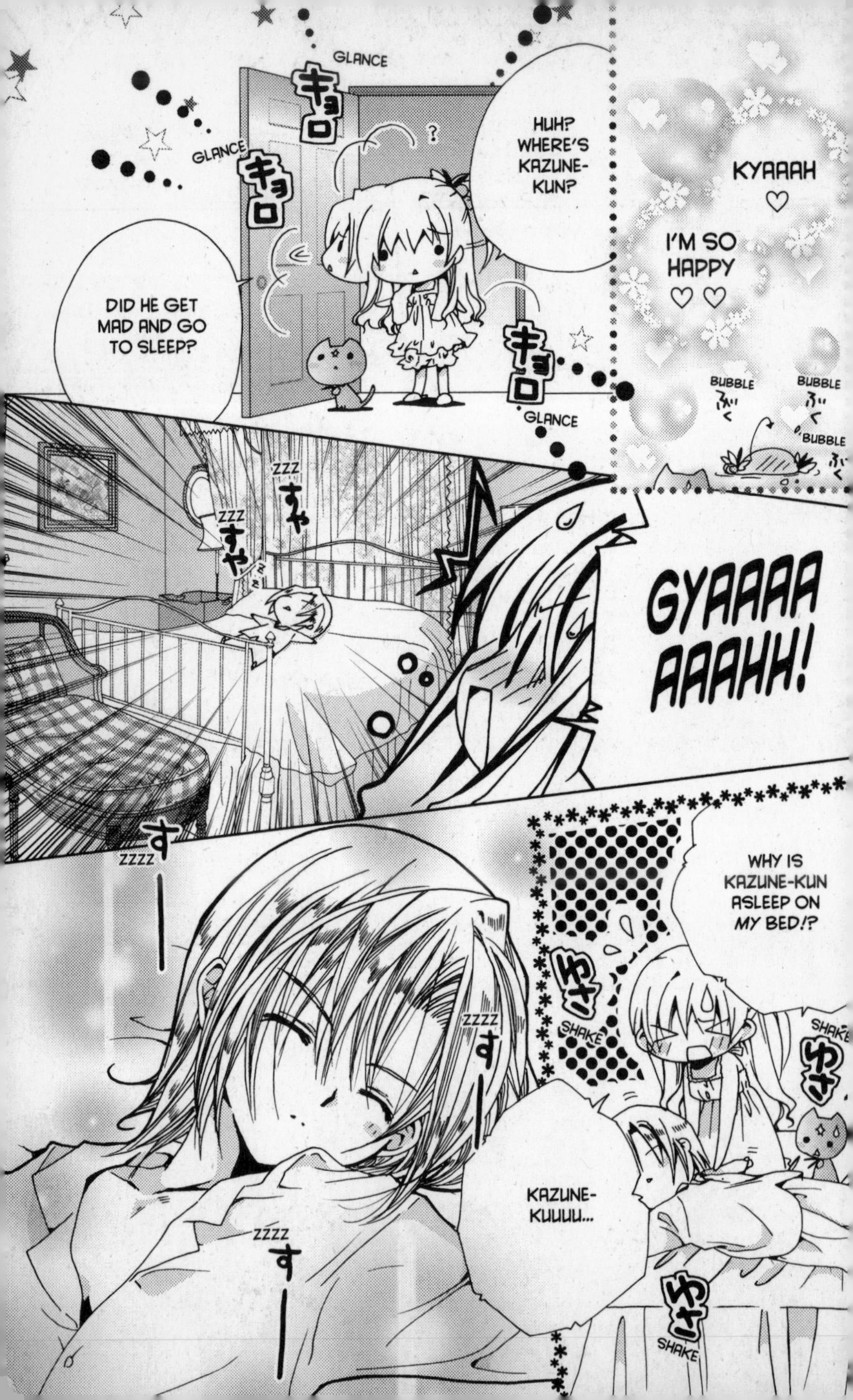
KYAAAH ♡
I'M SO HAPPY ♡ ♡
BUBBLE ぶく
BUBBLE ぶく
BUBBLE ぶく
GLANCE キョロ
GLANCE キョロ
HUH? WHERE'S KAZUNE-KUN?
GLANCE キョロ
DID HE GET MAD AND GO TO SLEEP?
GYAAAAAAAAH!
ZZZ すや
ZZZ すや
WHY IS KAZUNE-KUN ASLEEP ON MY BED!?
SHAKE ゆさ
SHAKE ゆさ
KAZUNE-KUUUU...
SHAKE ゆさ
ZZZZ すー
ZZZZ すー
ZZZZ すー

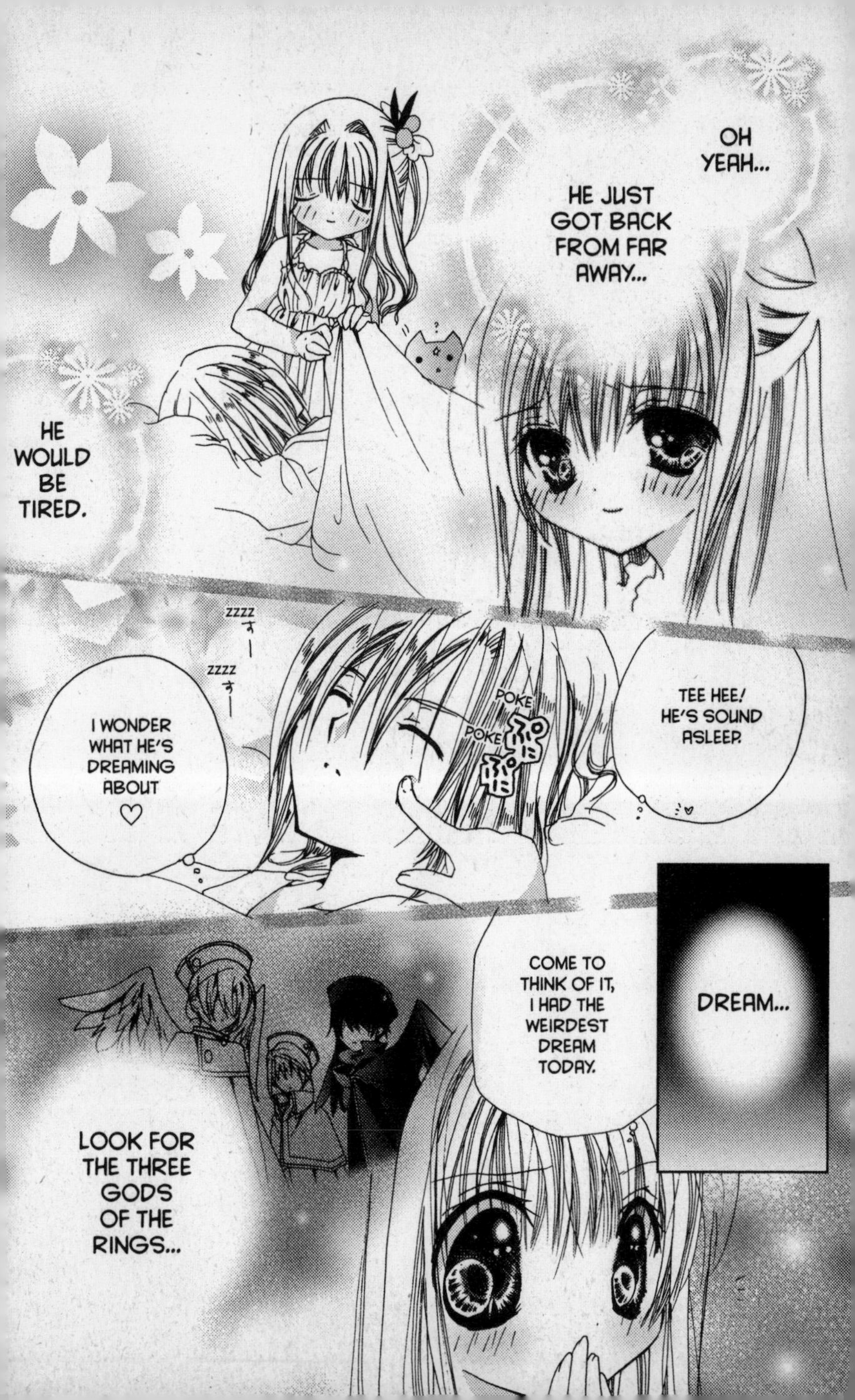
OH YEAH...
HE JUST GOT BACK FROM FAR AWAY...
HE WOULD BE TIRED.
TEE HEE! HE'S SOUND ASLEEP.
POKE POKE
ぷにぷに
ZZZZ すー
ZZZZ すー
I WONDER WHAT HE'S DREAMING ABOUT ♡
DREAM...
COME TO THINK OF IT, I HAD THE WEIRDEST DREAM TODAY.
LOOK FOR THE THREE GODS OF THE RINGS...

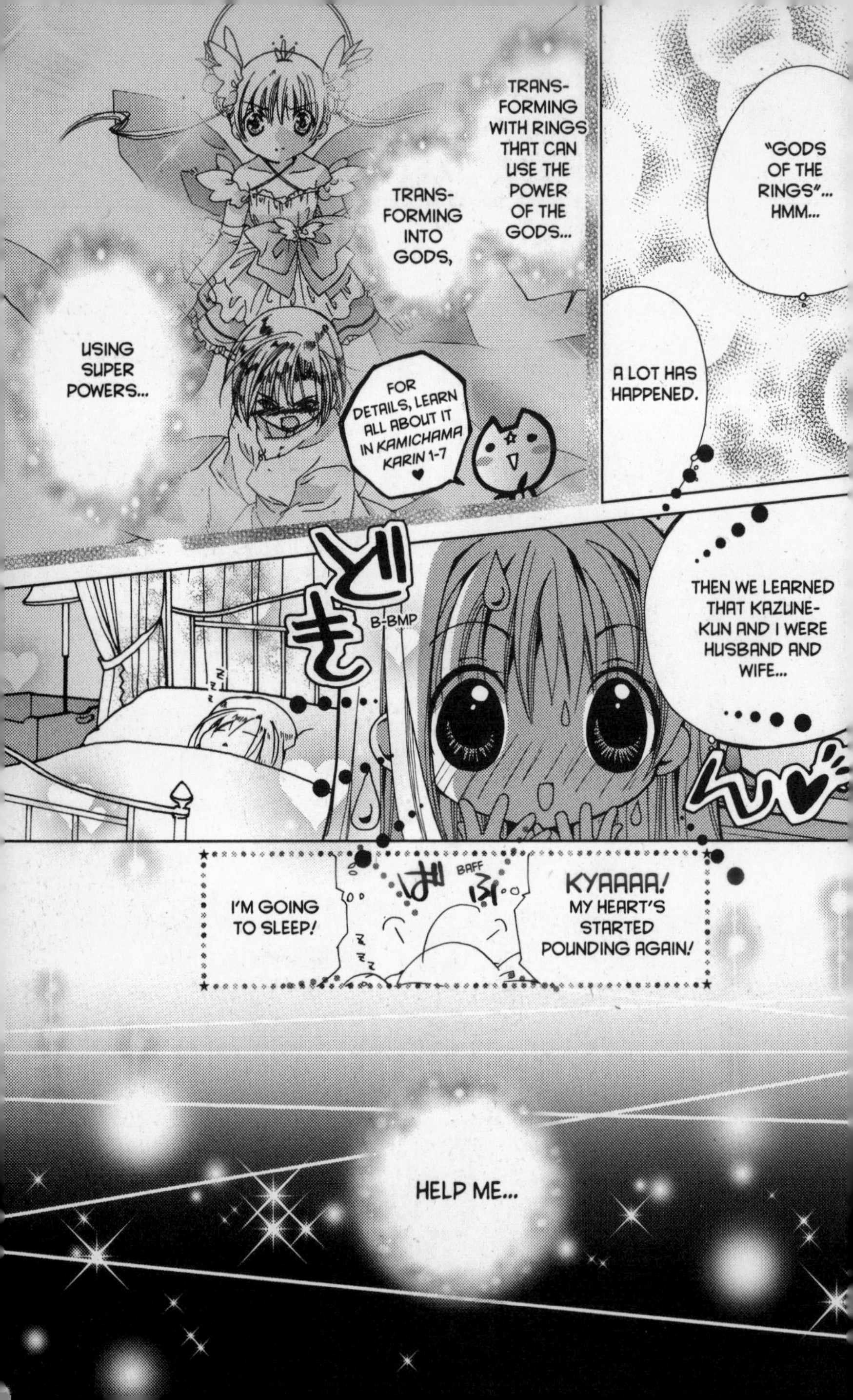
"GODS OF THE RINGS"... HMM...
A LOT HAS HAPPENED.
TRANS-FORMING WITH RINGS THAT CAN USE THE POWER OF THE GODS...
TRANS-FORMING INTO GODS,
USING SUPER POWERS...
FOR DETAILS, LEARN ALL ABOUT IT IN KAMICHAMA KARIN 1-7 ♥
THEN WE LEARNED THAT KAZUNE-KUN AND I WERE HUSBAND AND WIFE...
ん♥
どき
B-BMP
KYAAAA! MY HEART'S STARTED POUNDING AGAIN!
ぱふ
BAFF
I'M GOING TO SLEEP!
HELP ME...

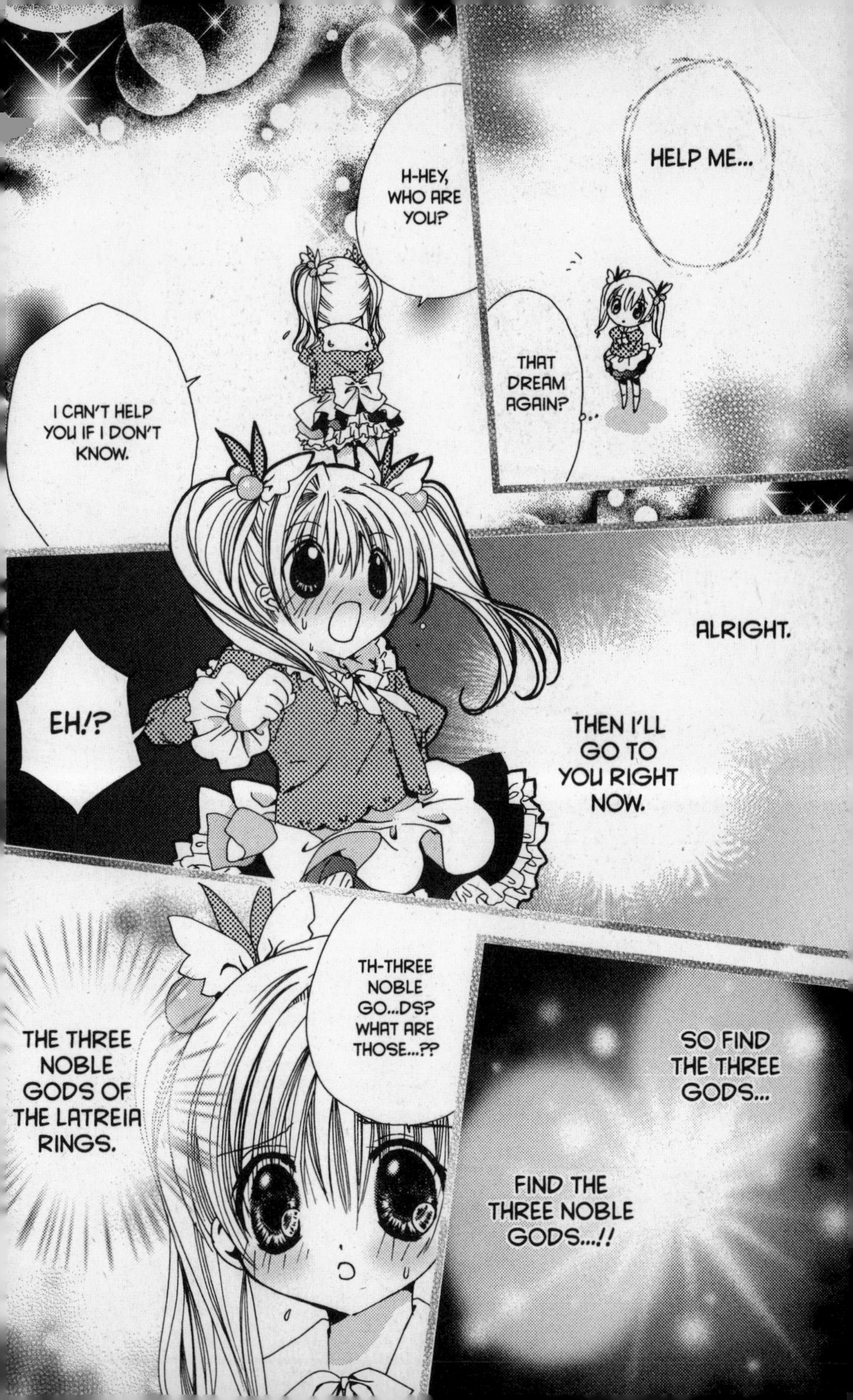

HELP ME...
THAT DREAM AGAIN?...
H-HEY, WHO ARE YOU?
I CAN'T HELP YOU IF I DON'T KNOW.
ALRIGHT.
THEN I'LL GO TO YOU RIGHT NOW.
EH!?
SO FIND THE THREE GODS...
FIND THE THREE NOBLE GODS...!!
TH-THREE NOBLE GO...DS? WHAT ARE THOSE...??
THE THREE NOBLE GODS OF THE LATREIA RINGS.

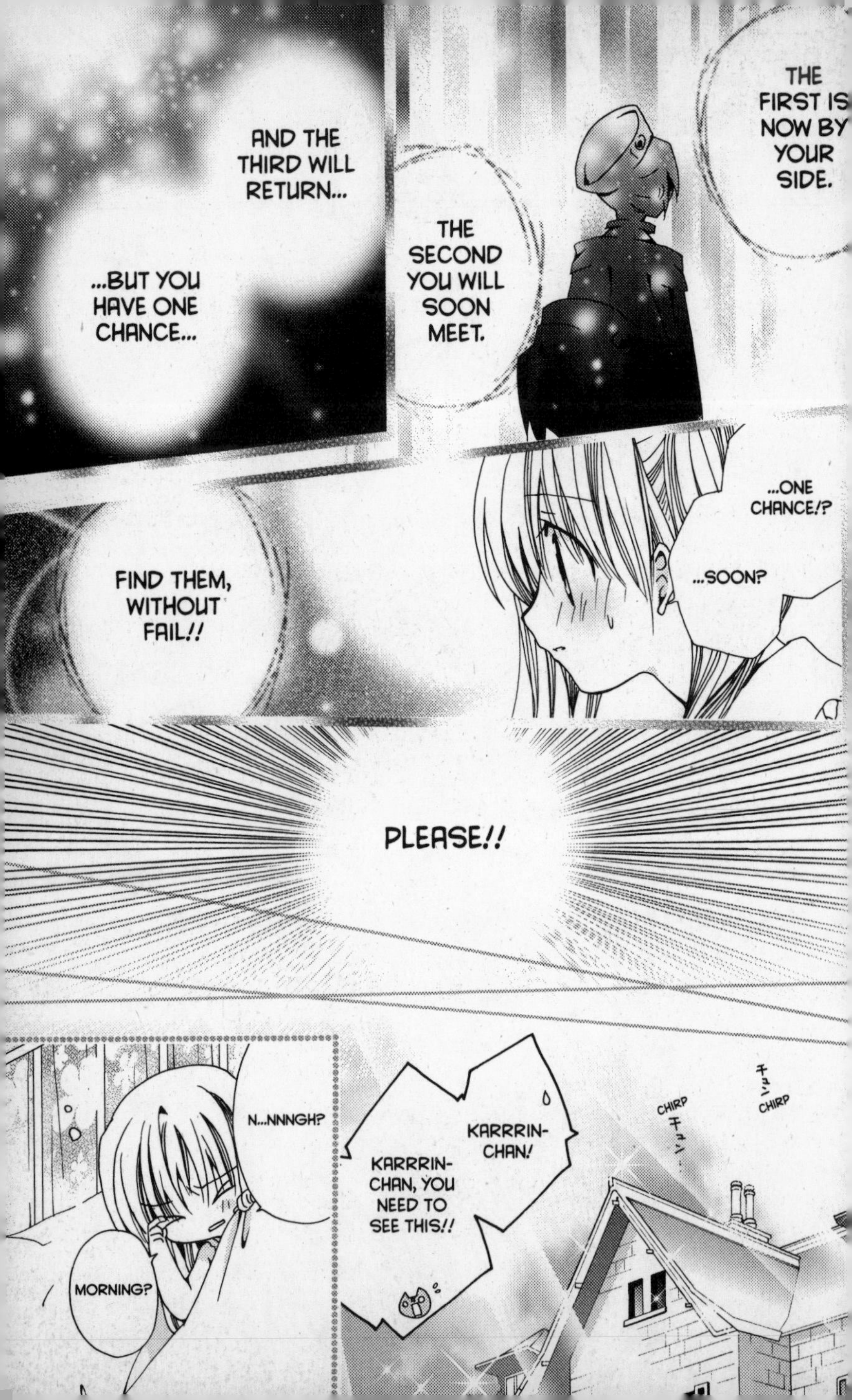
THE FIRST IS NOW BY YOUR SIDE.
THE SECOND YOU WILL SOON MEET.
AND THE THIRD WILL RETURN...
...BUT YOU HAVE ONE CHANCE...
...ONE CHANCE!?
...SOON?
FIND THEM, WITHOUT FAIL!!
PLEASE!!
CHIRP
CHIRP
KARRRIN-CHAN!
KARRRIN-CHAN, YOU NEED TO SEE THIS!!
N...NNNGH?
MORNING?

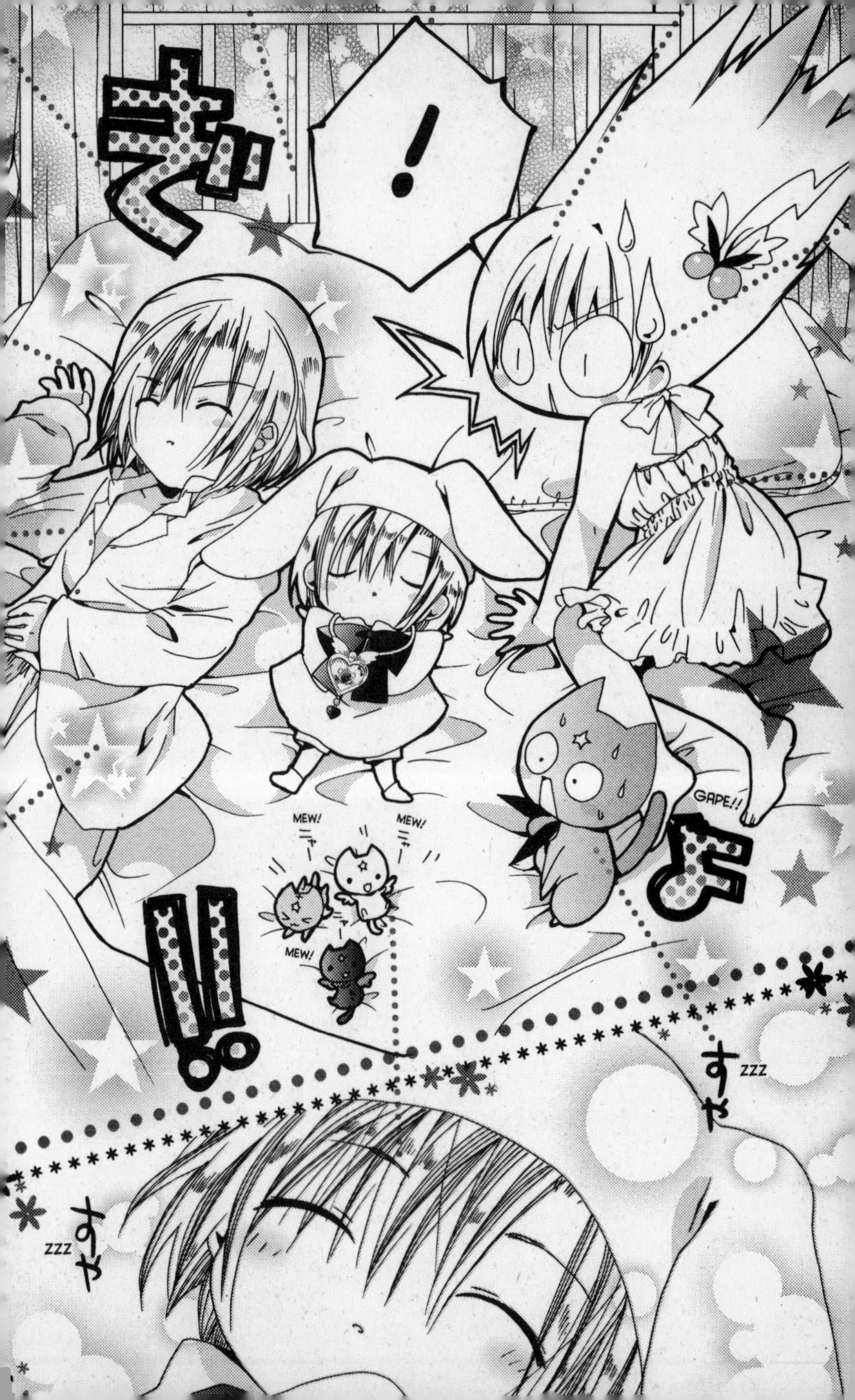
!
GAPE!!
MEW!
ニャー
MEW!
ニャー
MEW!
ニャー
すや
ZZZ
すや
ZZZ

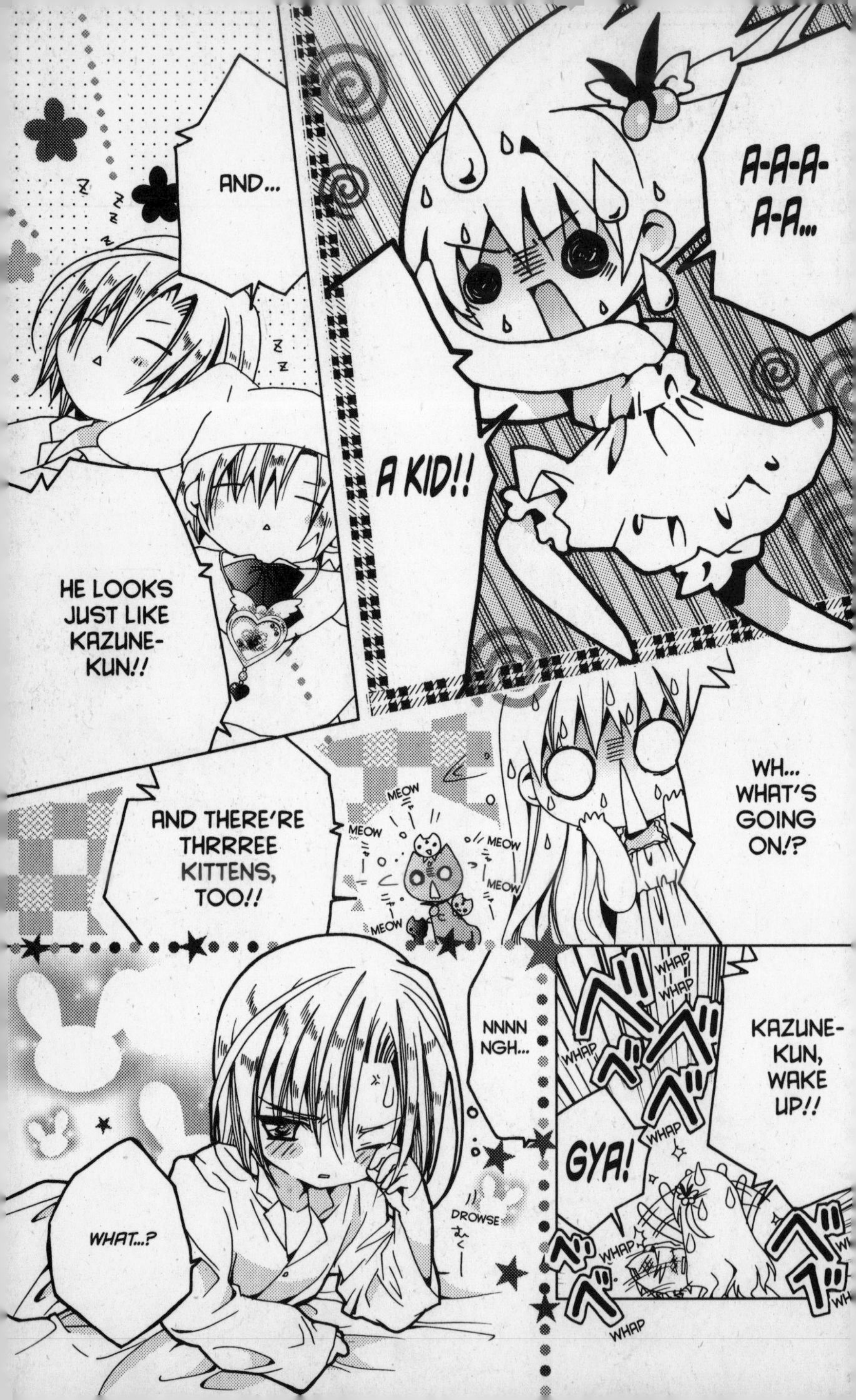
A-A-A-
A-A...
A KID!!
AND...
HE LOOKS JUST LIKE KAZUNE-KUN!!
WH... WHAT'S GOING ON!?
MEOW
MEOW
MEOW
MEOW
MEOW
AND THERE'RE THRRREE KITTENS, TOO!!
KAZUNE-KUN, WAKE UP!!
WHAP WHAP
WHAP
WHAP
GYA!
WHAP
WHAP
NNNN NGH...
DROWSE
WHAT...?

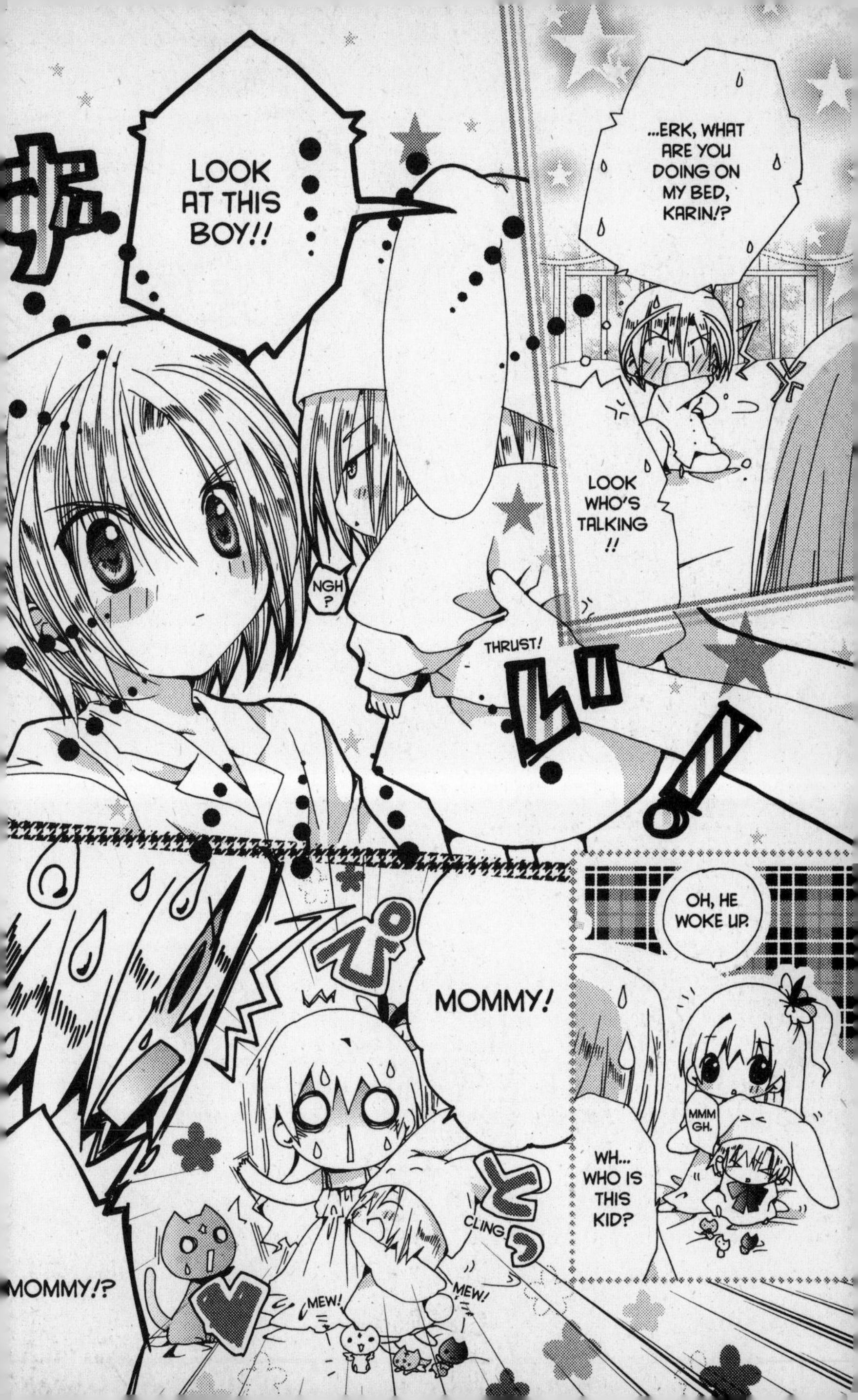
...ERK, WHAT ARE YOU DOING ON MY BED, KARIN!?
LOOK WHO'S TALKING !!
LOOK AT THIS BOY!!
NGH ?
THRUST!
OH, HE WOKE UP.
MMM GH.
WH... WHO IS THIS KID?
MOMMY!
CLING
MEW!
MEW!
MOMMY!?

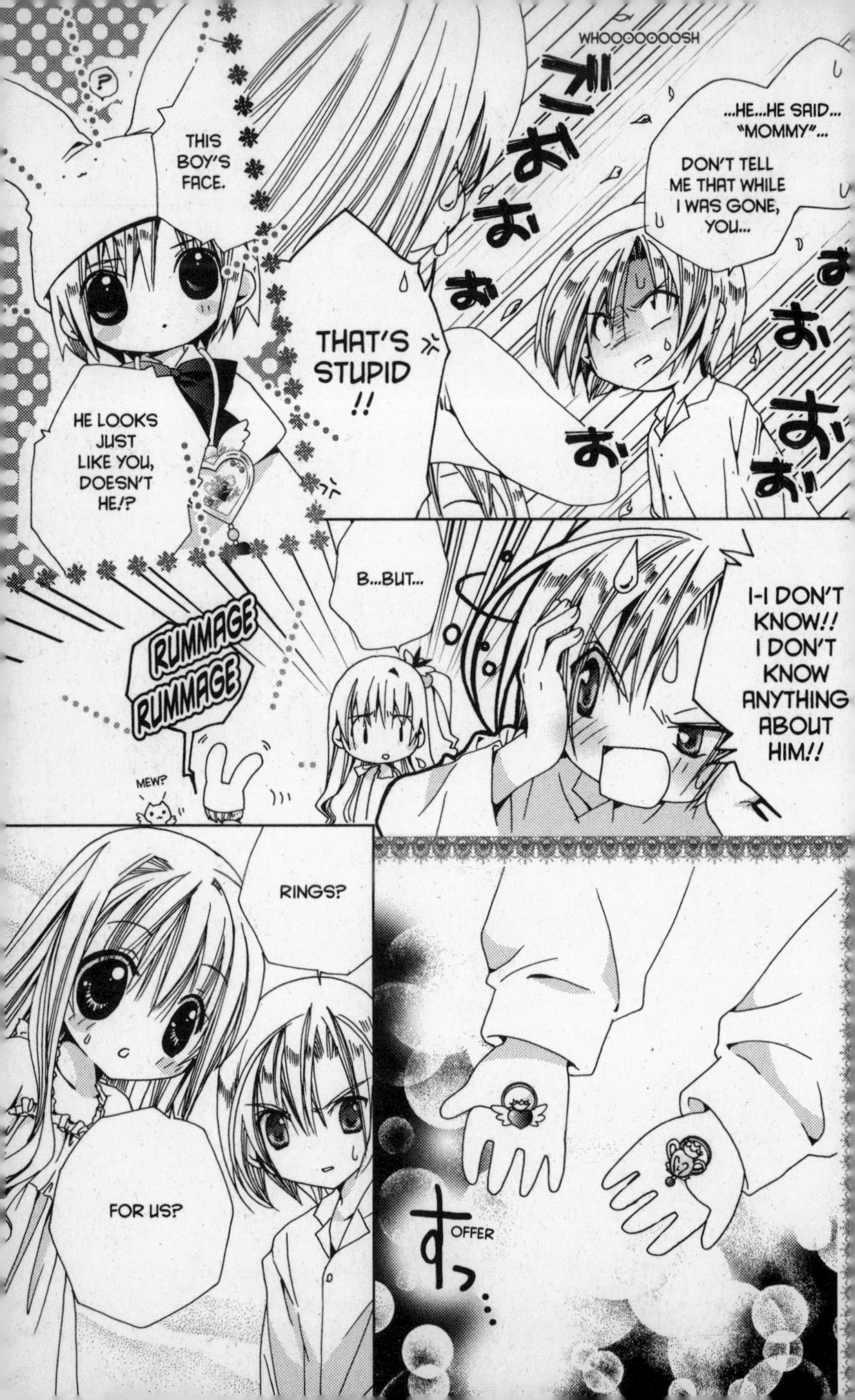
WHOOOOOOOOSH
...HE...HE SAID... "MOMMY"...
DON'T TELL ME THAT WHILE I WAS GONE, YOU...
THAT'S STUPID!!
THIS BOY'S FACE.
HE LOOKS JUST LIKE YOU, DOESN'T HE!?
I-I DON'T KNOW!! I DON'T KNOW ANYTHING ABOUT HIM!!
B...BUT...
RUMMAGE RUMMAGE
MEW?
OFFER
RINGS?
FOR US?

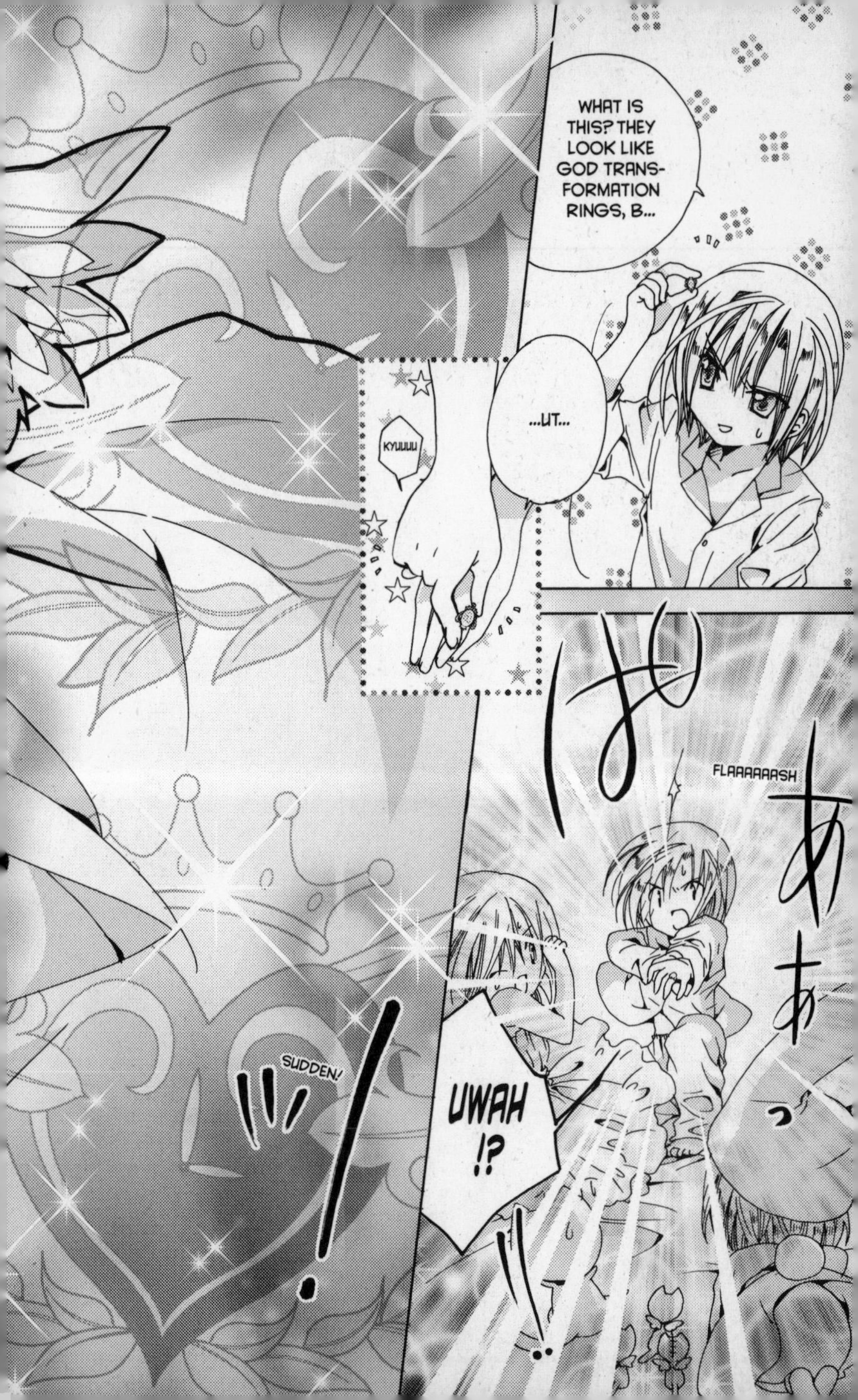
WHAT IS THIS? THEY LOOK LIKE GOD TRANS-FORMATION RINGS, B...
...UT...
KYUUUU
FLAAAAAASH
UWAH!?
SUDDEN!

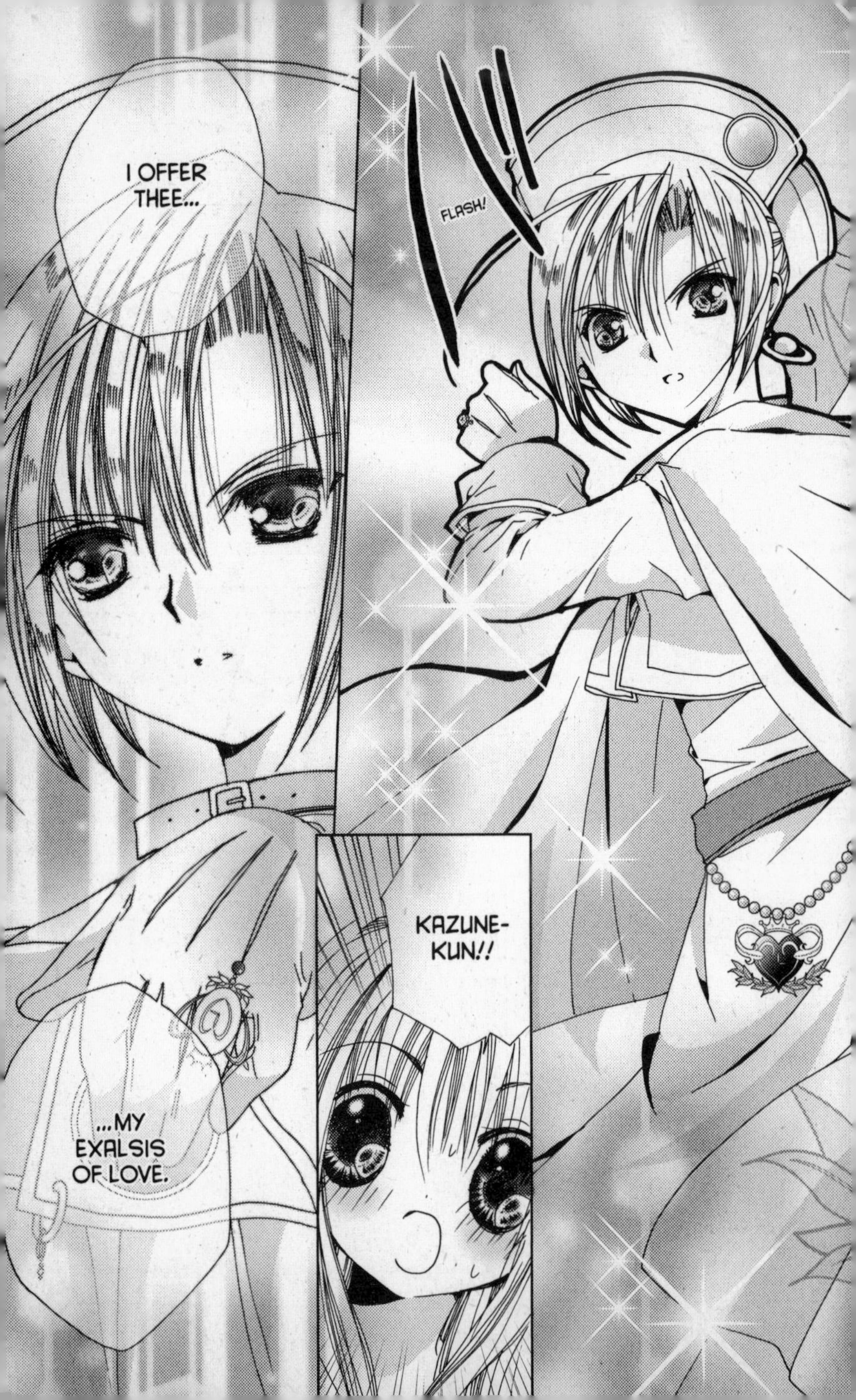
FLASH!
KAZUNE-
KUN!!
I OFFER
THEE...
...MY
EXALSIS
OF LOVE.

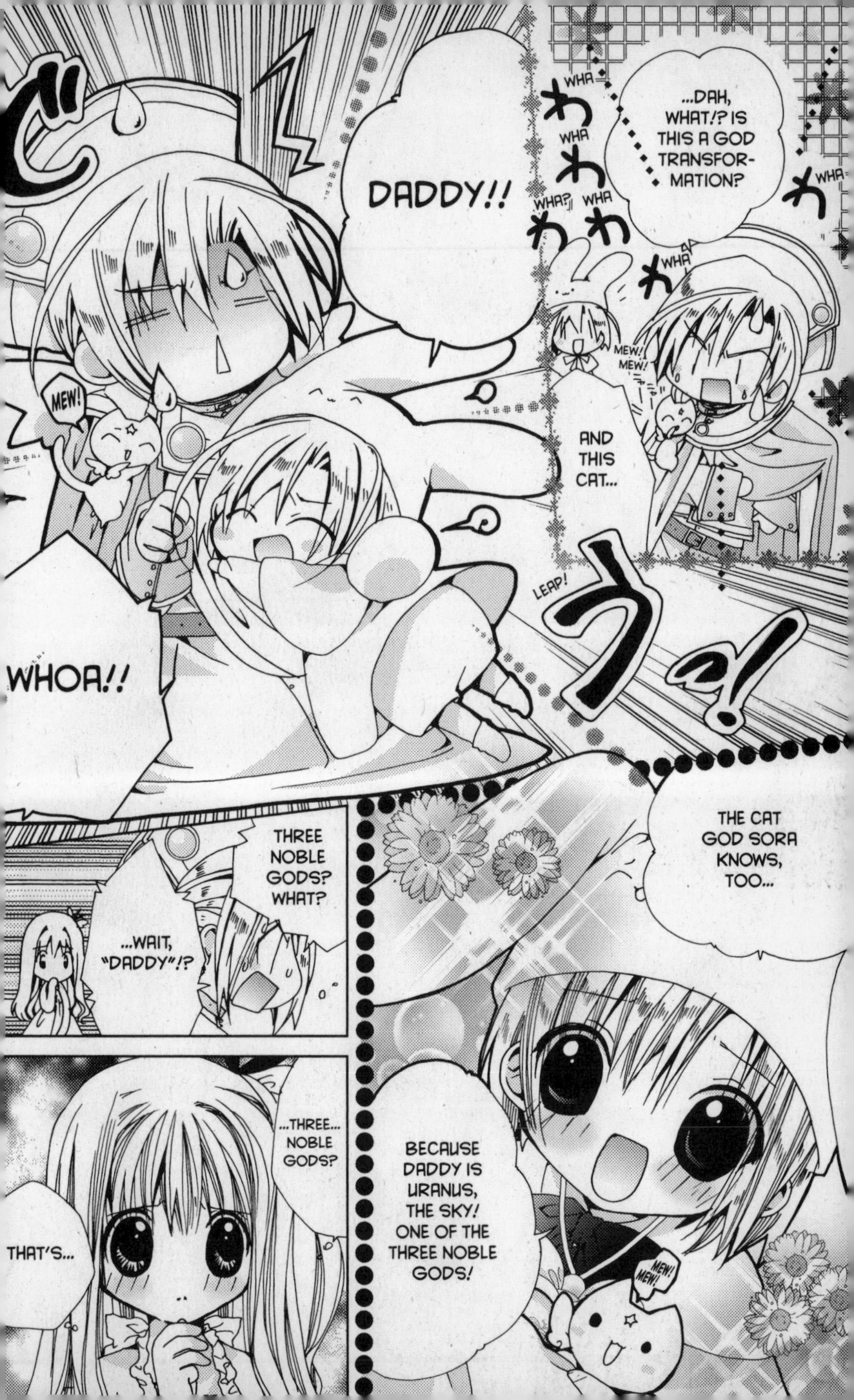
WHA
WHA
WHA?
WHA
WHA
WHA
...DAH, WHAT!? IS THIS A GOD TRANSFORMATION?
MEW! MEW!
AND THIS CAT...
LEAP!
DADDY!!
MEW!
WHOA!!
THE CAT GOD SORA KNOWS, TOO...
BECAUSE DADDY IS URANUS, THE SKY! ONE OF THE THREE NOBLE GODS!
MEW! MEW!
THREE NOBLE GODS? WHAT?
...WAIT, "DADDY"!?
...THREE... NOBLE GODS?
THAT'S...

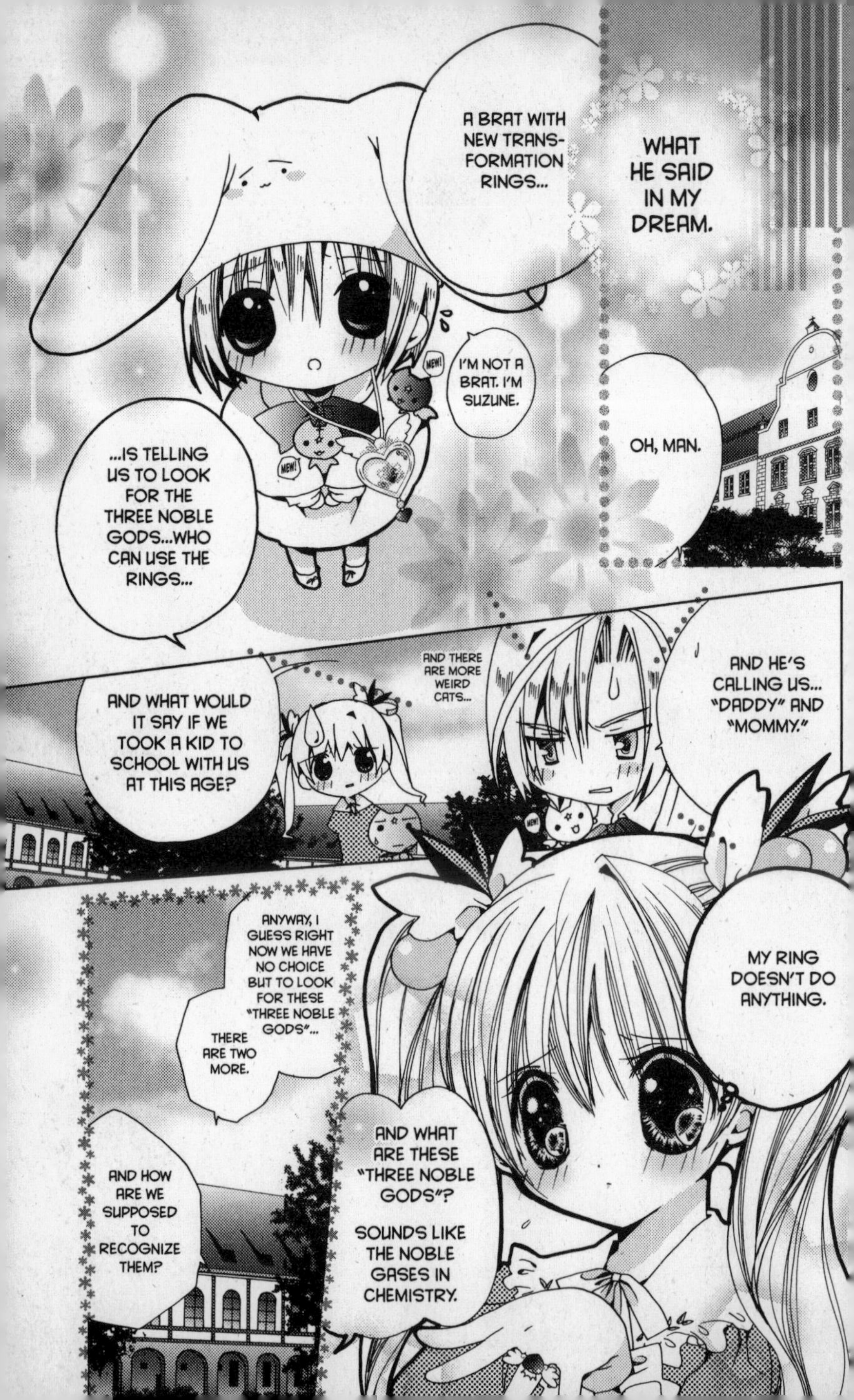
WHAT HE SAID IN MY DREAM.
A BRAT WITH NEW TRANS-FORMATION RINGS...
MEW!
I'M NOT A BRAT. I'M SUZUNE.
MEW!
...IS TELLING US TO LOOK FOR THE THREE NOBLE GODS...WHO CAN USE THE RINGS...
OH, MAN.
AND HE'S CALLING US... "DADDY" AND "MOMMY."
MEW!
AND THERE ARE MORE WEIRD CATS...
AND WHAT WOULD IT SAY IF WE TOOK A KID TO SCHOOL WITH US AT THIS AGE?
MY RING DOESN'T DO ANYTHING.
AND WHAT ARE THESE "THREE NOBLE GODS"?
SOUNDS LIKE THE NOBLE GASES IN CHEMISTRY.
ANYWAY, I GUESS RIGHT NOW WE HAVE NO CHOICE BUT TO LOOK FOR THESE "THREE NOBLE GODS"...
THERE ARE TWO MORE.
AND HOW ARE WE SUPPOSED TO RECOGNIZE THEM?

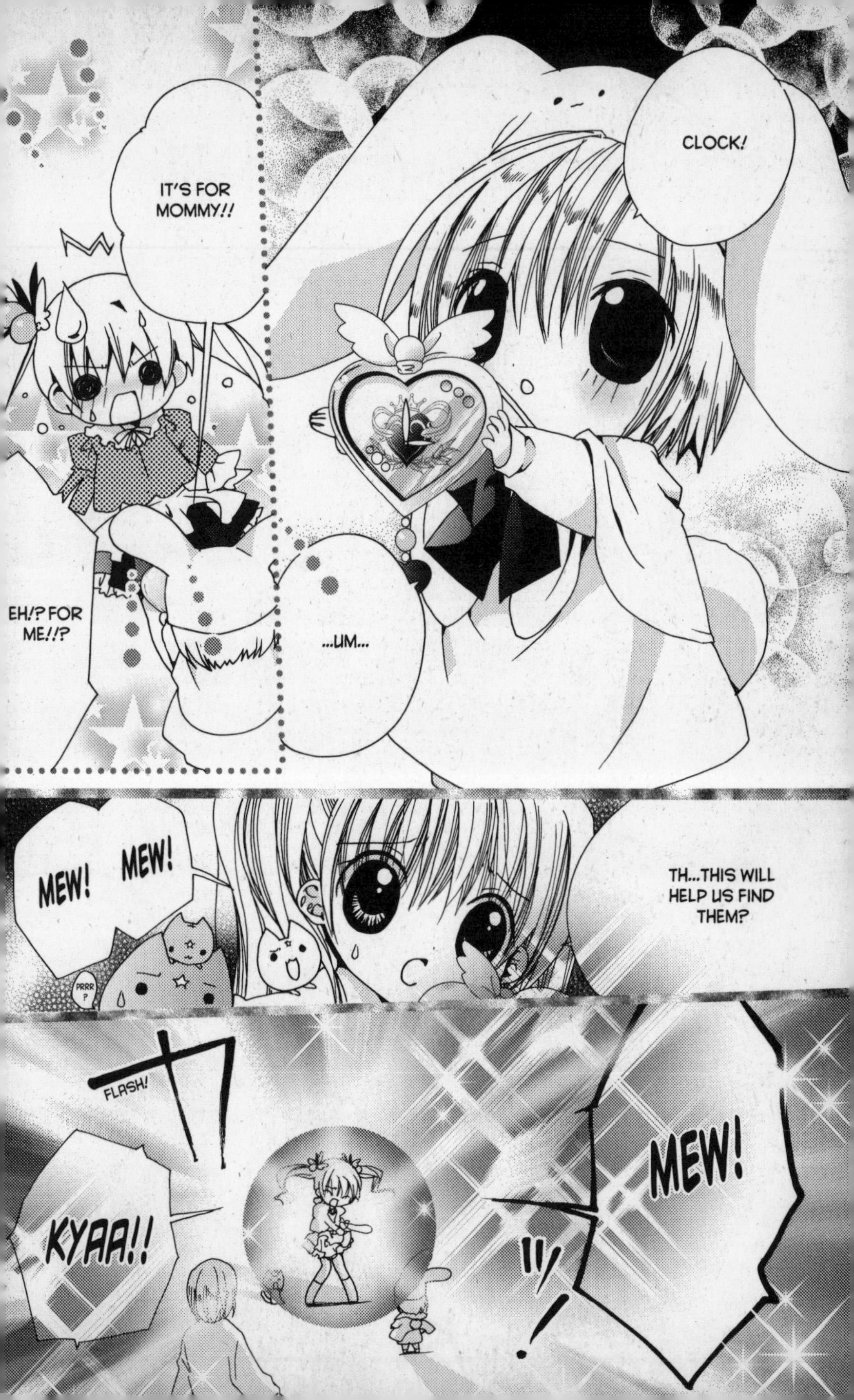
CLOCK!
...UM...
IT'S FOR MOMMY!!
EH!? FOR ME!!?
TH...THIS WILL HELP US FIND THEM?
MEW! MEW!
PRRR?
MEW!
FLASH!
KYAA!!

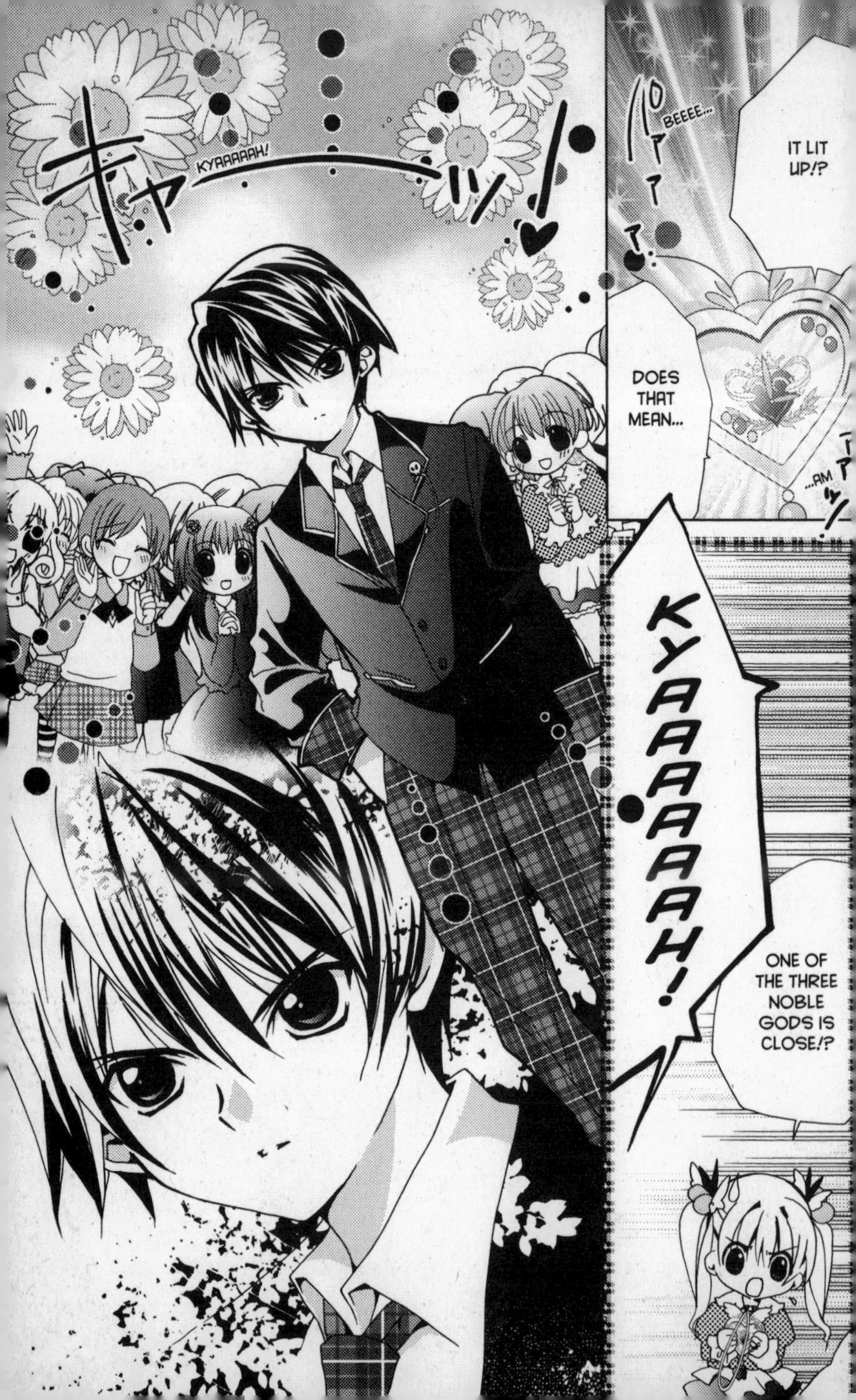
IT LIT UP!?
BEEEE...
DOES THAT MEAN...
...AM
KYAAAAAAAAH!
ONE OF THE THREE NOBLE GODS IS CLOSE!?
KYAAAAAH!

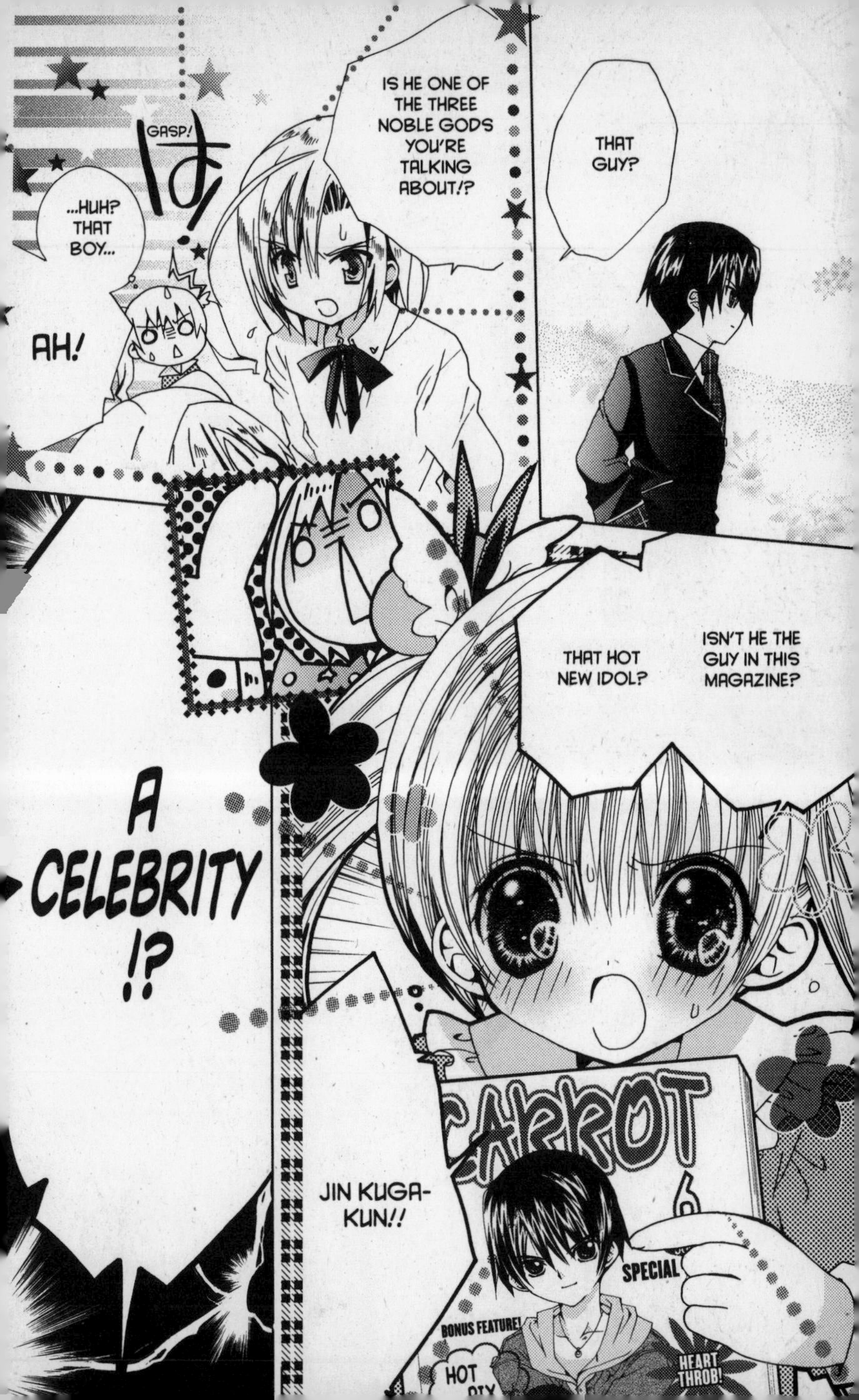
THAT GUY?
IS HE ONE OF THE THREE NOBLE GODS YOU'RE TALKING ABOUT!?
GASP!
は
...HUH? THAT BOY...
AH!
ISN'T HE THE GUY IN THIS MAGAZINE?
THAT HOT NEW IDOL?
JIN KUGA-KUN!!
CARROT
6
SPECIAL
BONUS FEATURE!
HOT
HEART THROB!
A CELEBRITY !?

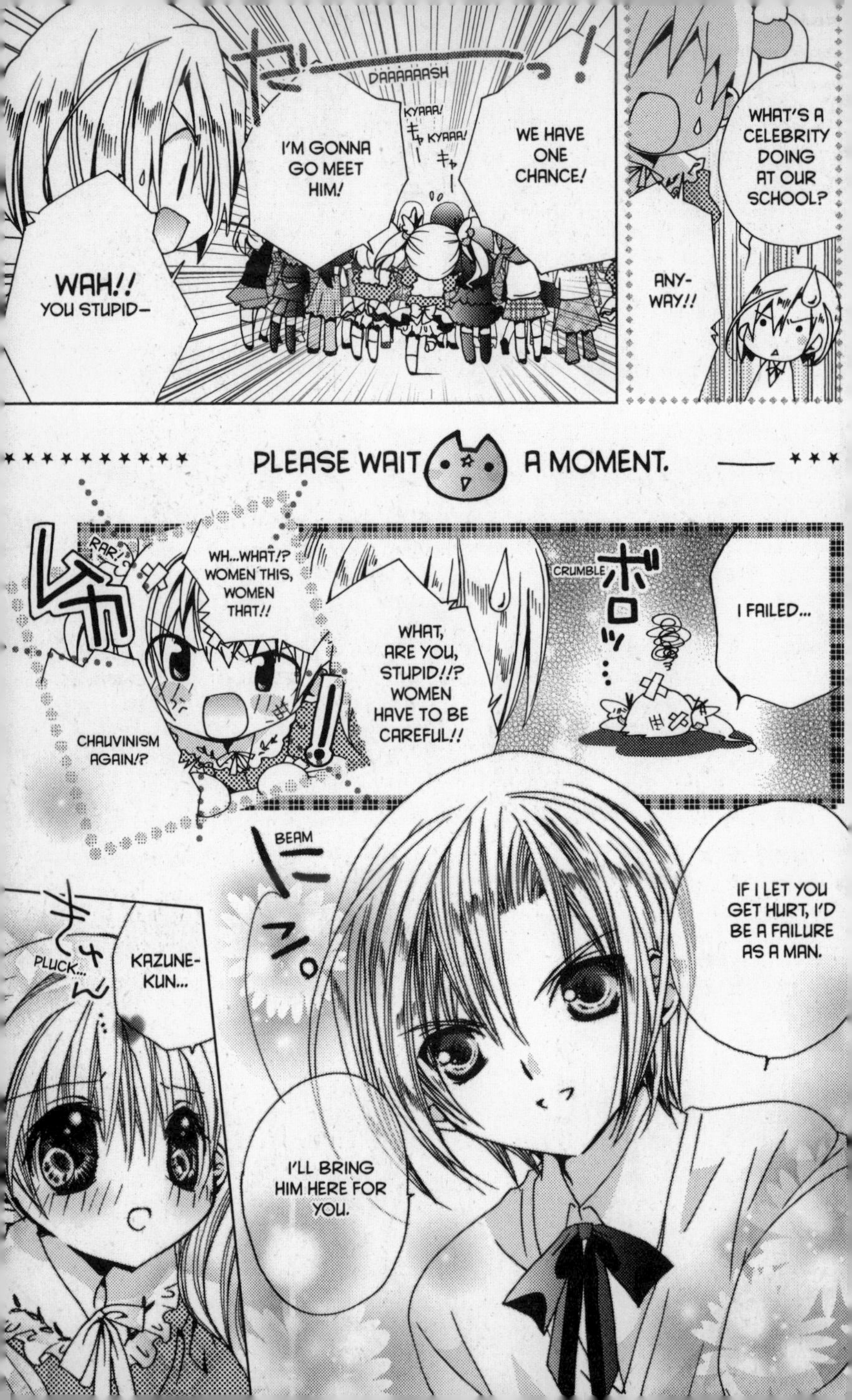
WHAT'S A CELEBRITY DOING AT OUR SCHOOL?
ANY-WAY!!
WE HAVE ONE CHANCE!
KYAAA!
KYAAA!
DAAAAAASH
I'M GONNA GO MEET HIM!
WAH!! YOU STUPID—
PLEASE WAIT A MOMENT. —
I FAILED...
CRUMBLE
WHAT, ARE YOU, STUPID!!? WOMEN HAVE TO BE CAREFUL!!
WH...WHAT!? WOMEN THIS, WOMEN THAT!!
RAR!?
CHAUVINISM AGAIN!?
IF I LET YOU GET HURT, I'D BE A FAILURE AS A MAN.
BEAM
I'LL BRING HIM HERE FOR YOU.
KAZUNE-KUN...
PLUCK...

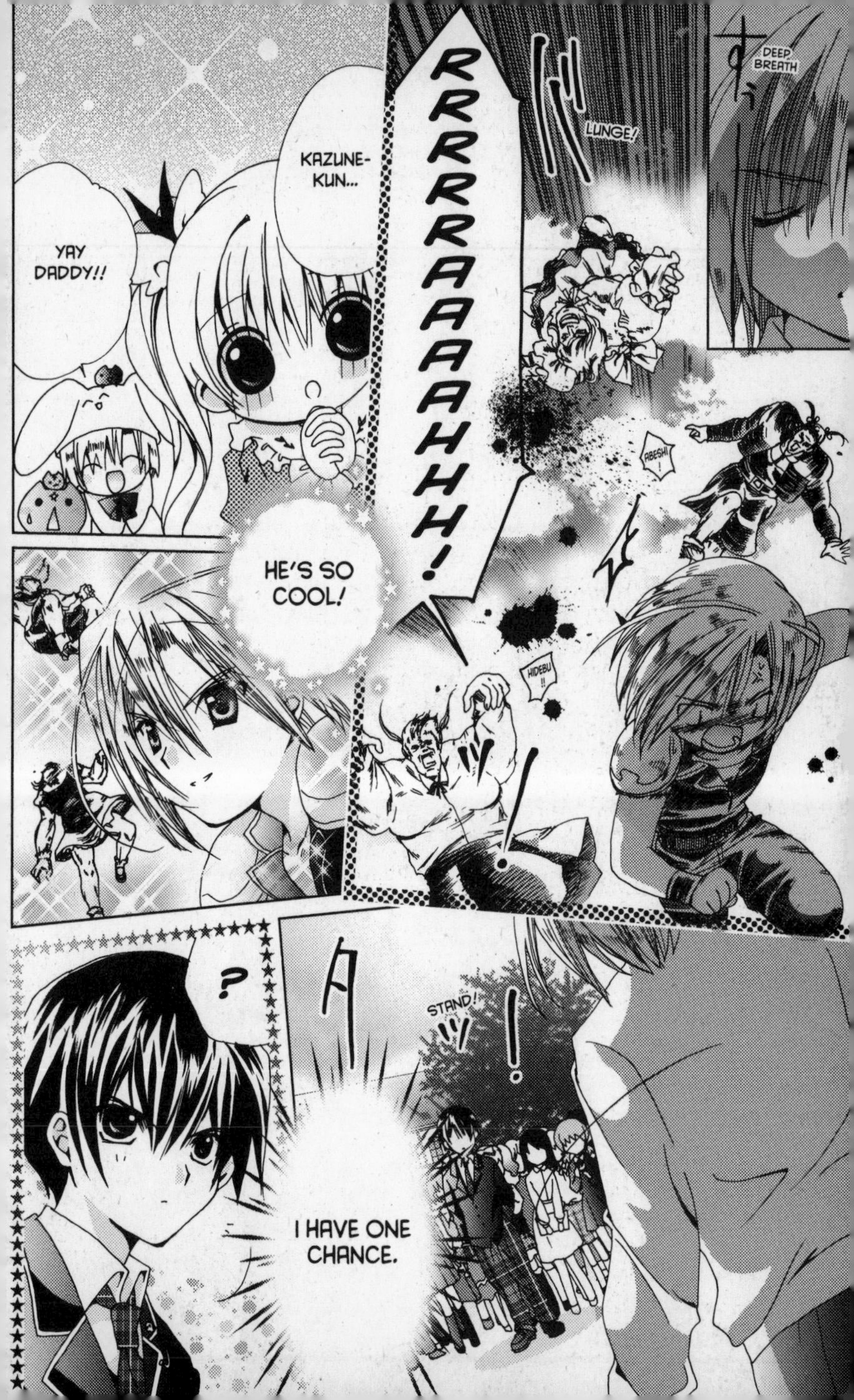
DEEP BREATH
LUNGE!
RRRRRAAAAHHH!
KAZUNE-KUN...
YAY DADDY!!
ABESHI!
HIDEBU!!
HE'S SO COOL!
STAND!
?
I HAVE ONE CHANCE.

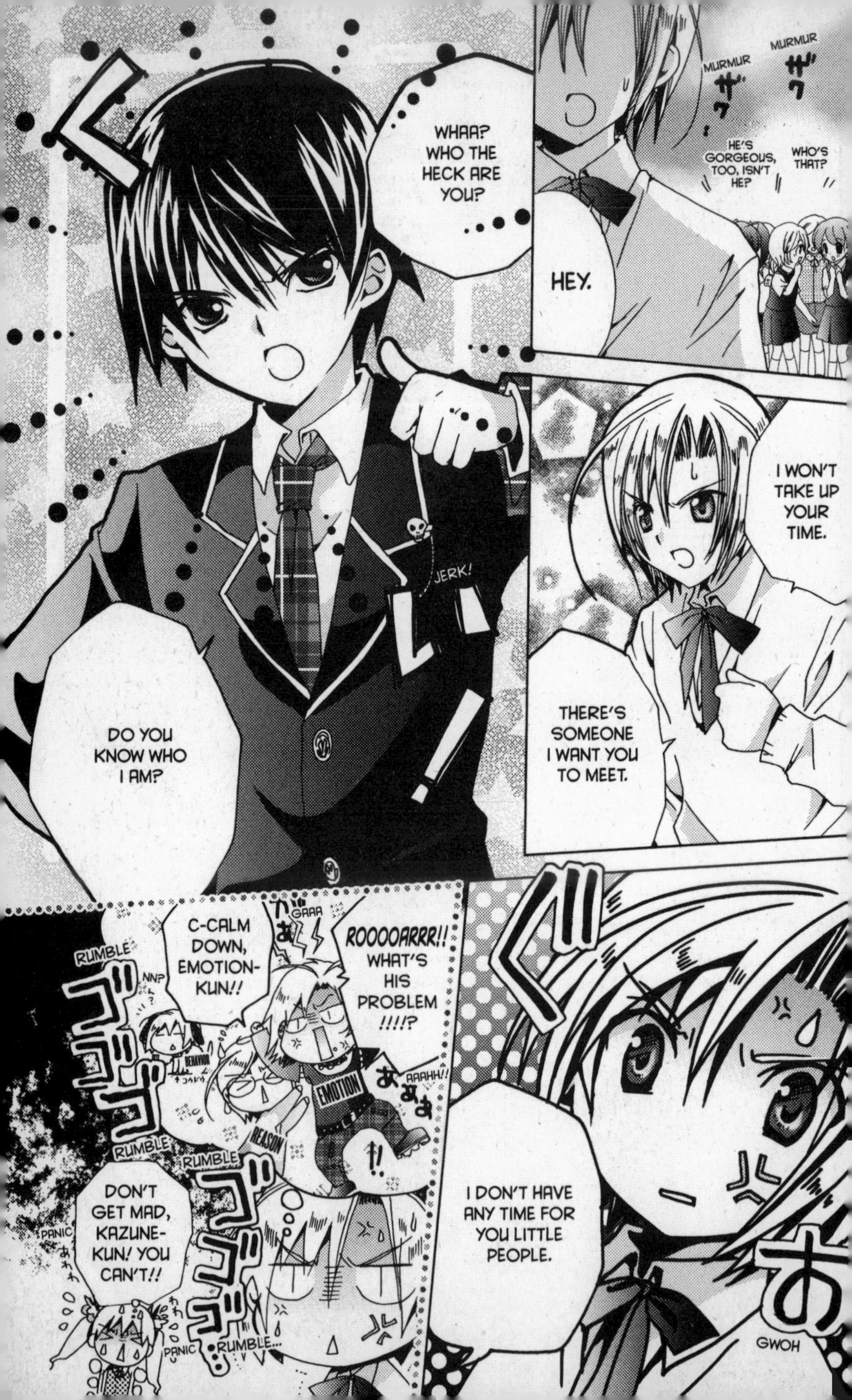
MURMUR
MURMUR
WHO'S THAT?
HE'S GORGEOUS, TOO, ISN'T HE?
HEY.
I WON'T TAKE UP YOUR TIME.
THERE'S SOMEONE I WANT YOU TO MEET.
WHAA? WHO THE HECK ARE YOU?
JERK!
DO YOU KNOW WHO I AM?
I DON'T HAVE ANY TIME FOR YOU LITTLE PEOPLE.
GWOH
ROOOOARRR!! WHAT'S HIS PROBLEM !!!!?
GAAA
C-CALM DOWN, EMOTION-KUN!!
RUMBLE
NN?
BEHAVIOR
EMOTION
AAAHH!!
REASON
RUMBLE
RUMBLE
!!
DON'T GET MAD, KAZUNE-KUN! YOU CAN'T!!
PANIC
PANIC
RUMBLE...

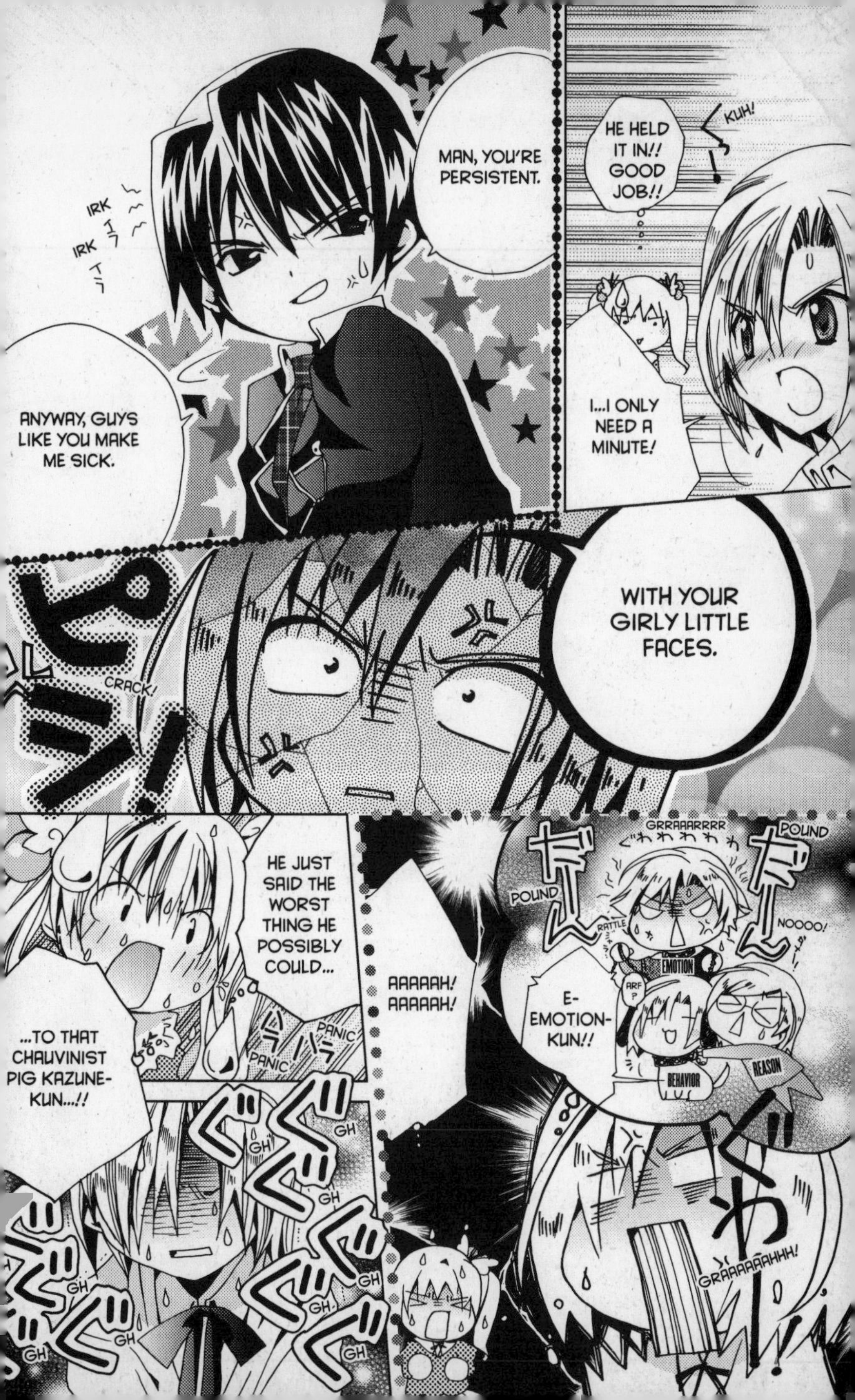

KUH!
HE HELD IT IN!! GOOD JOB!!
I...I ONLY NEED A MINUTE!
MAN, YOU'RE PERSISTENT.
IRK
IRK
ANYWAY, GUYS LIKE YOU MAKE ME SICK.
WITH YOUR GIRLY LITTLE FACES.
CRACK!
POUND
GRRAAARRRR
POUND
RATTLE
NOOOO!
EMOTION
E-EMOTION-KUN!!
ARF?
BEHAVIOR
REASON
GRAAAAAHHH!
AAAAAH! AAAAAH!
HE JUST SAID THE WORST THING HE POSSIBLY COULD...
...TO THAT CHAUVINIST PIG KAZUNE-KUN...!!
PANIC
PANIC
GH
GH
GH
GH
GH
GH
GH
GH

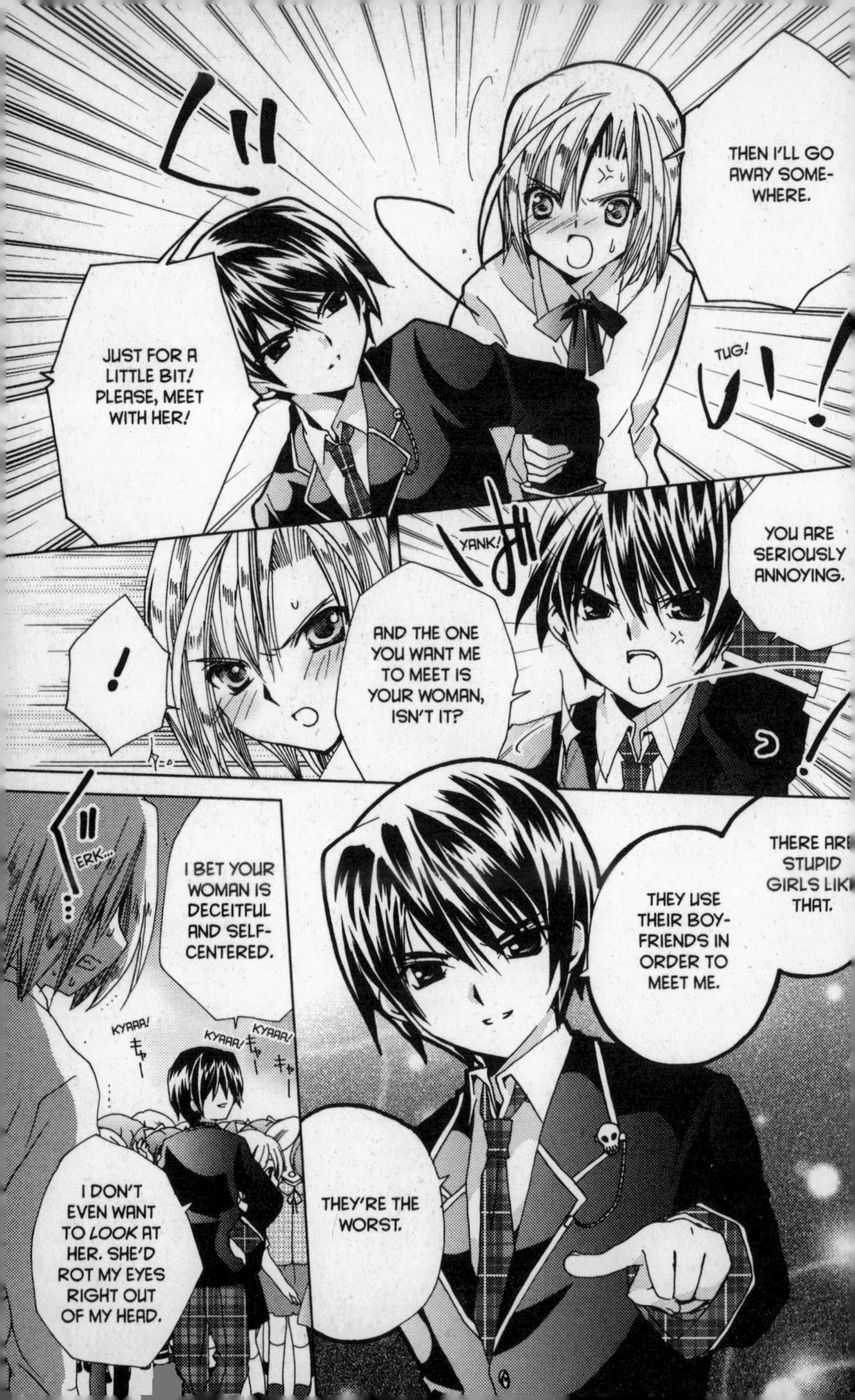
THEN I'LL GO AWAY SOME-WHERE.
TUG!
JUST FOR A LITTLE BIT! PLEASE, MEET WITH HER!
YOU ARE SERIOUSLY ANNOYING.
YANK!
AND THE ONE YOU WANT ME TO MEET IS YOUR WOMAN, ISN'T IT?
!
THERE ARE STUPID GIRLS LIKE THAT.
THEY USE THEIR BOY-FRIENDS IN ORDER TO MEET ME.
THEY'RE THE WORST.
I BET YOUR WOMAN IS DECEITFUL AND SELF-CENTERED.
ERK...
KYAAA!
KYAAA!
KYAAA!
I DON'T EVEN WANT TO *LOOK* AT HER. SHE'D ROT MY EYES RIGHT OUT OF MY HEAD.

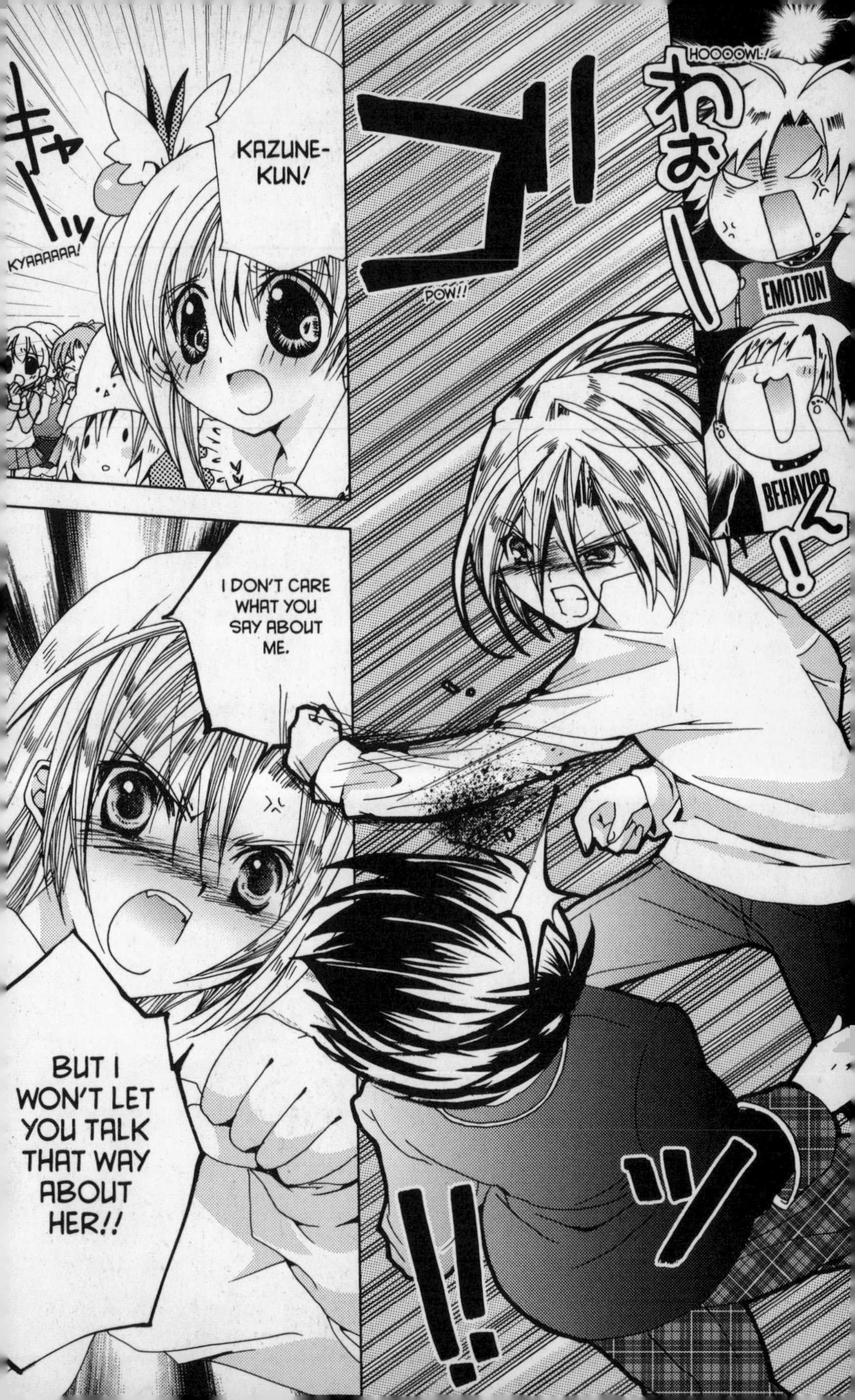
HOOOOOWL!
EMOTION
BEHAVIOR
POW!!
KYAAAAAA!
KAZUNE-KUN!
I DON'T CARE WHAT YOU SAY ABOUT ME.
BUT I WON'T LET YOU TALK THAT WAY ABOUT HER!!

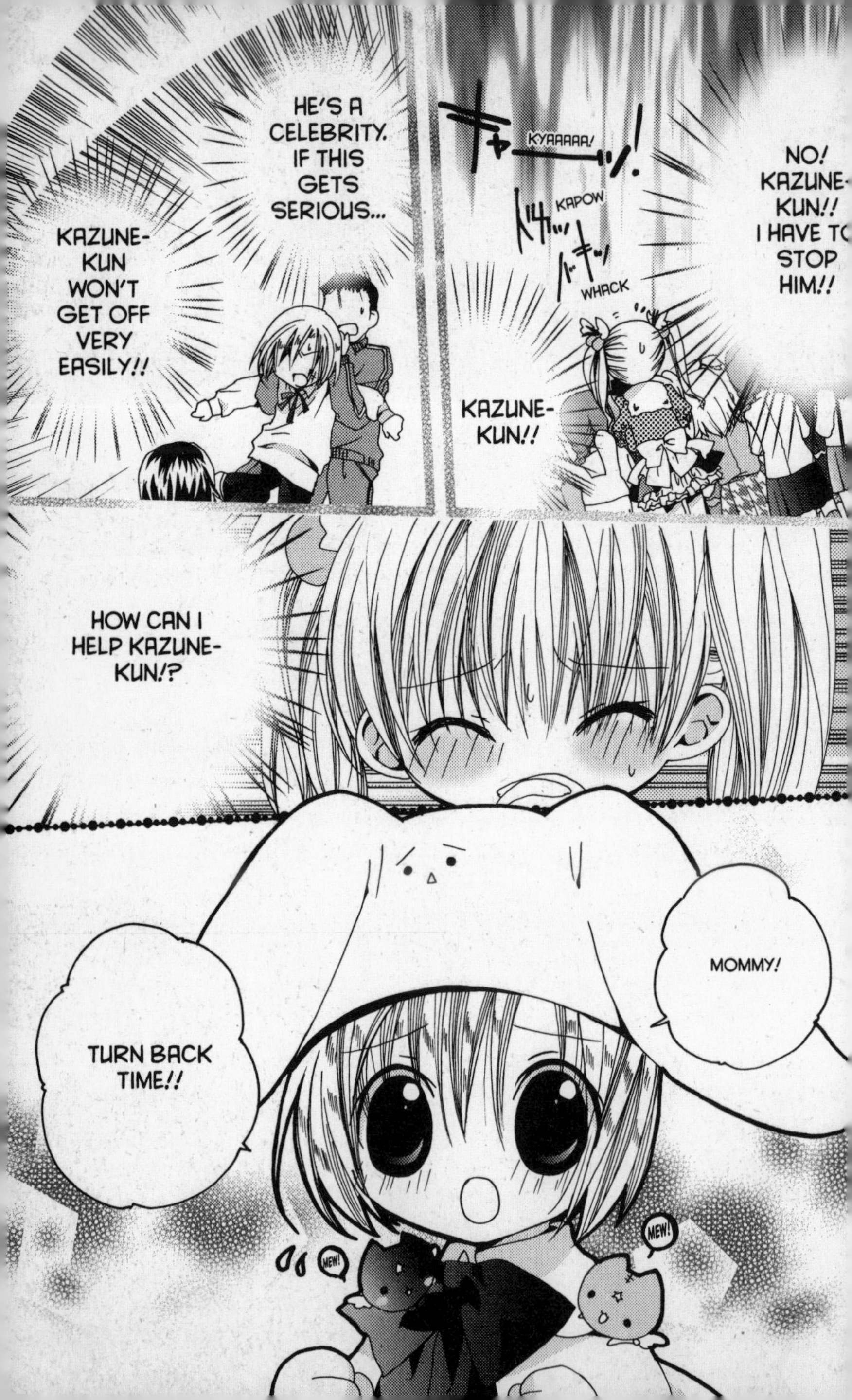
NO! KAZUNE-KUN!! I HAVE TO STOP HIM!!
KYAAAAA!
KAPOW
WHACK
KAZUNE-KUN!!
HE'S A CELEBRITY. IF THIS GETS SERIOUS...
KAZUNE-KUN WON'T GET OFF VERY EASILY!!
HOW CAN I HELP KAZUNE-KUN!?
MOMMY!
TURN BACK TIME!!
MEW!
MEW!

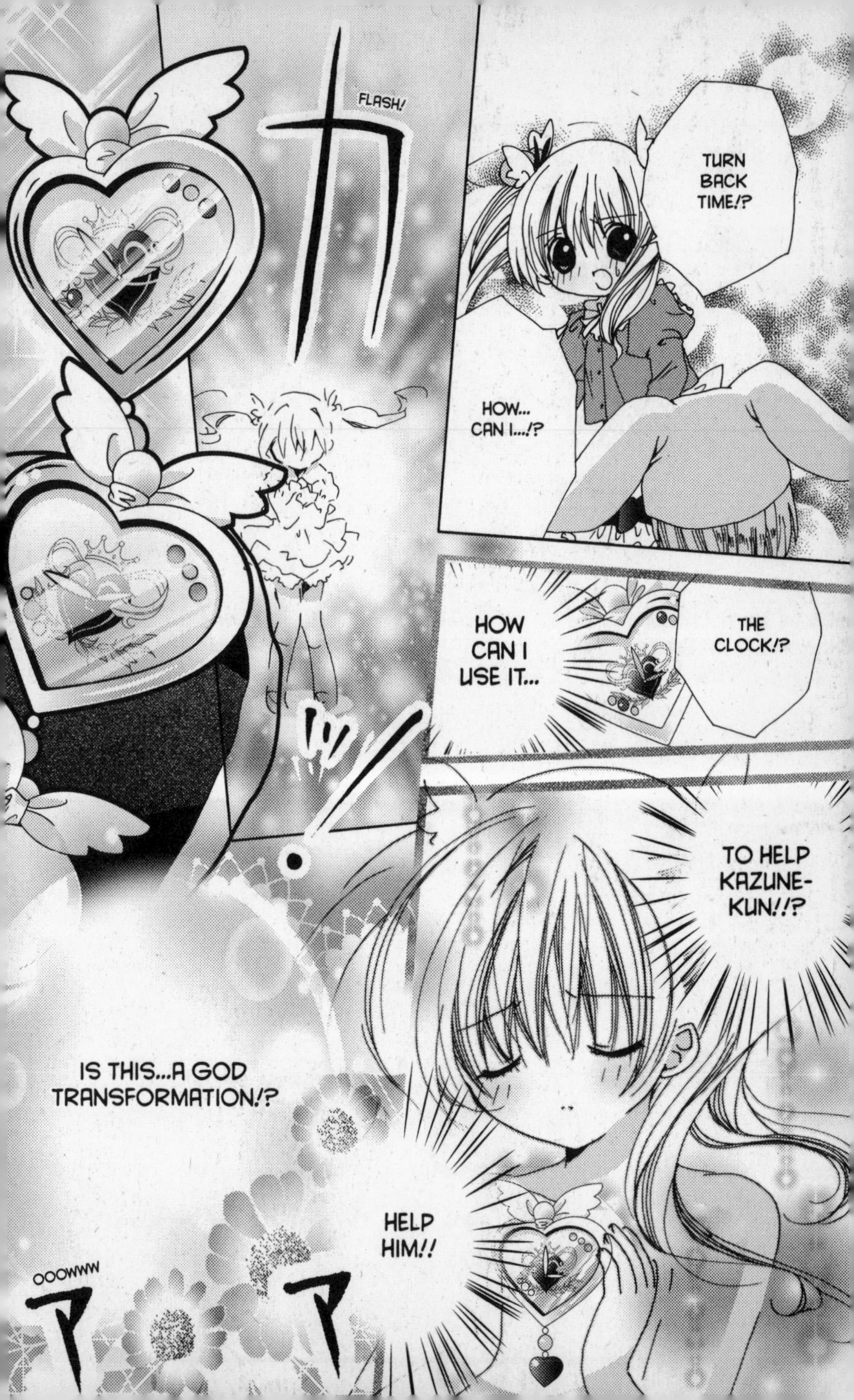
TURN BACK TIME!?
HOW... CAN I...!?
THE CLOCK!?
HOW CAN I USE IT...
FLASH!
TO HELP KAZUNE-KUN!!?
HELP HIM!!
IS THIS...A GOD TRANSFORMATION!?
OOOWWW

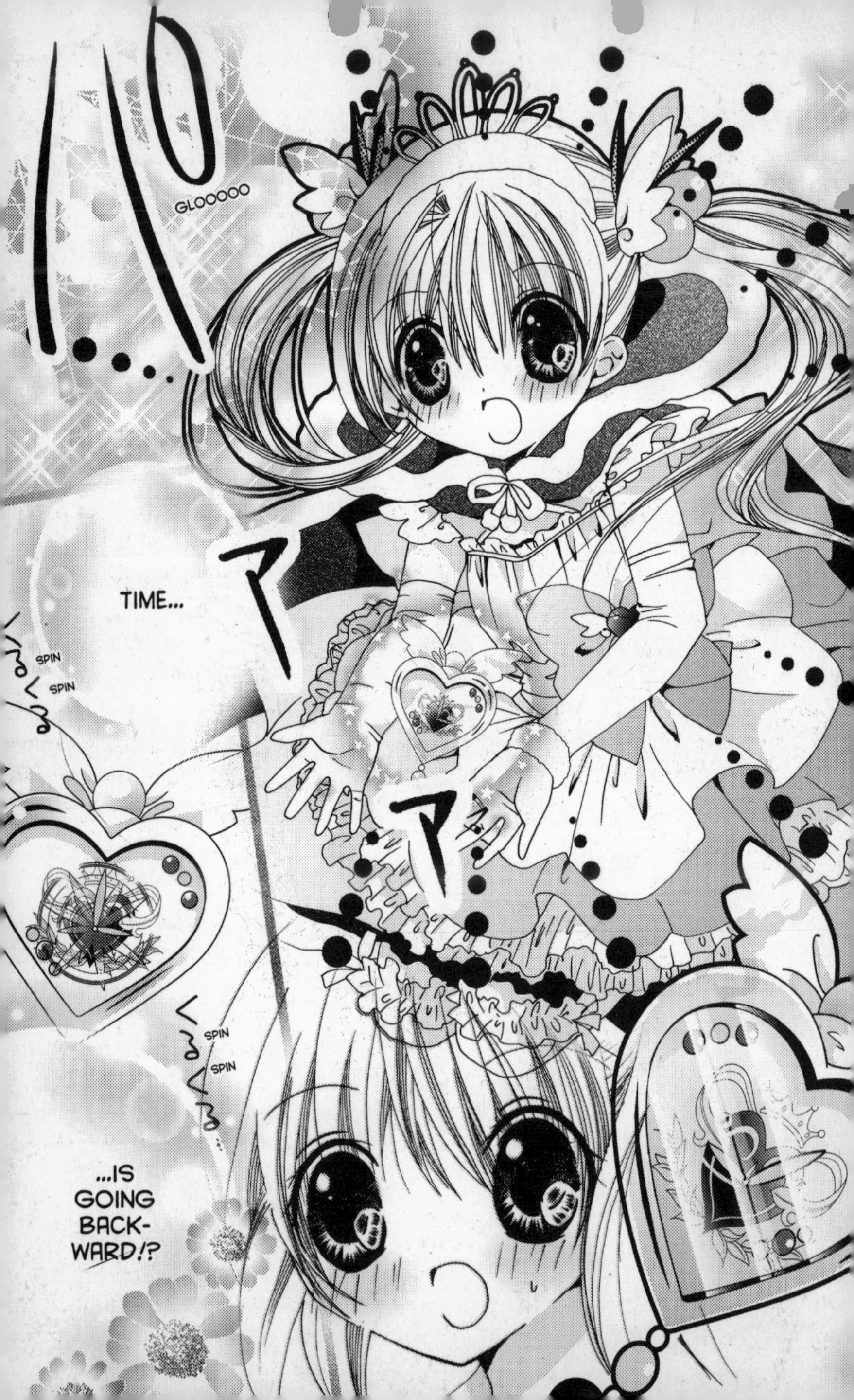
GLOOOOO
TIME...
SPIN
SPIN
SPIN
SPIN
...IS GOING BACK-WARD!?

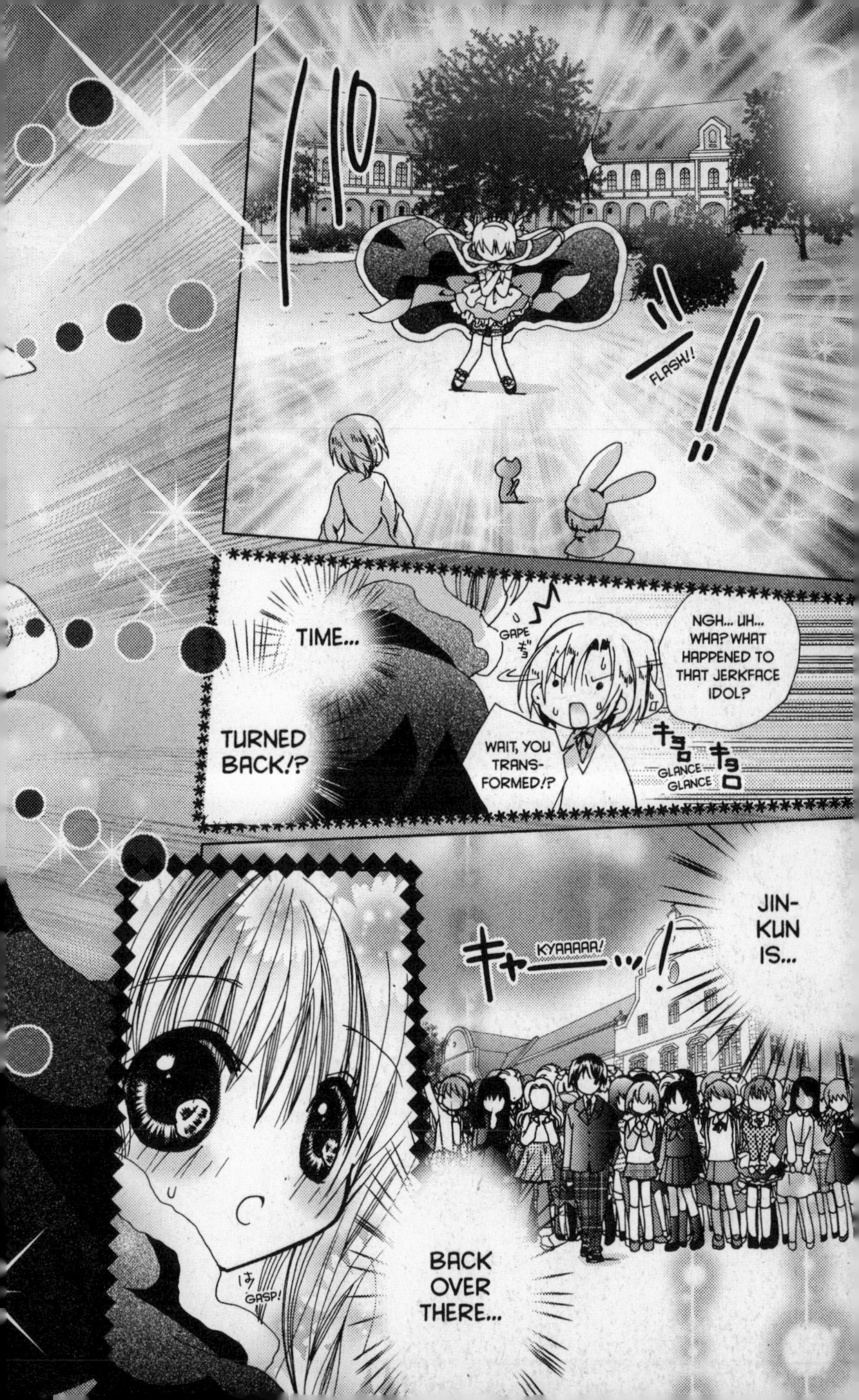
FLASH!!
NGH... UH... WHA? WHAT HAPPENED TO THAT JERKFACE IDOL?
キョロ キョロ
GLANCE GLANCE
GAPE
WAIT, YOU TRANS-FORMED!?
TIME...
TURNED BACK!?
JIN-KUN IS...
キャーッ!
KYAAAAA!
BACK OVER THERE...
GASP!

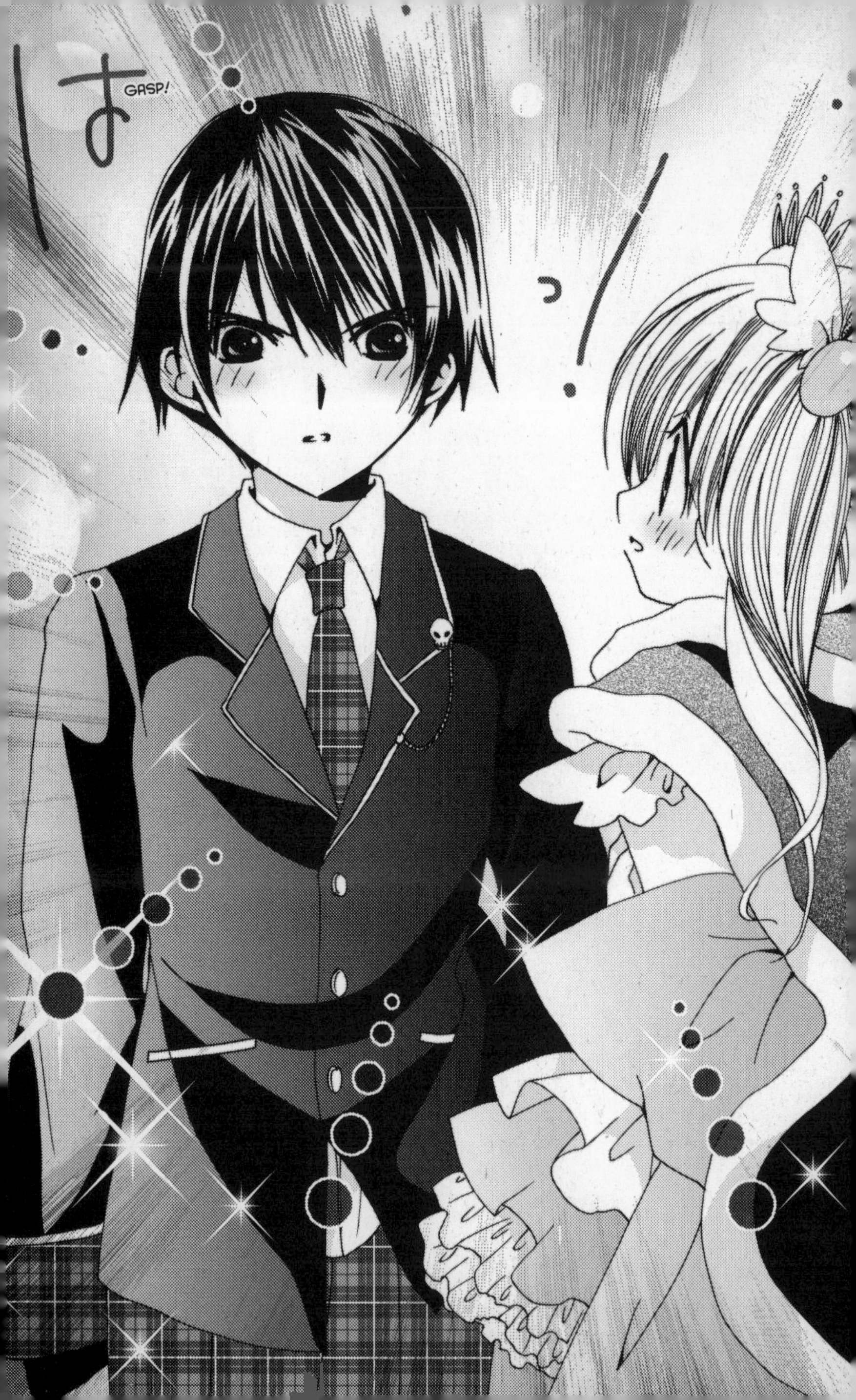
GASP!

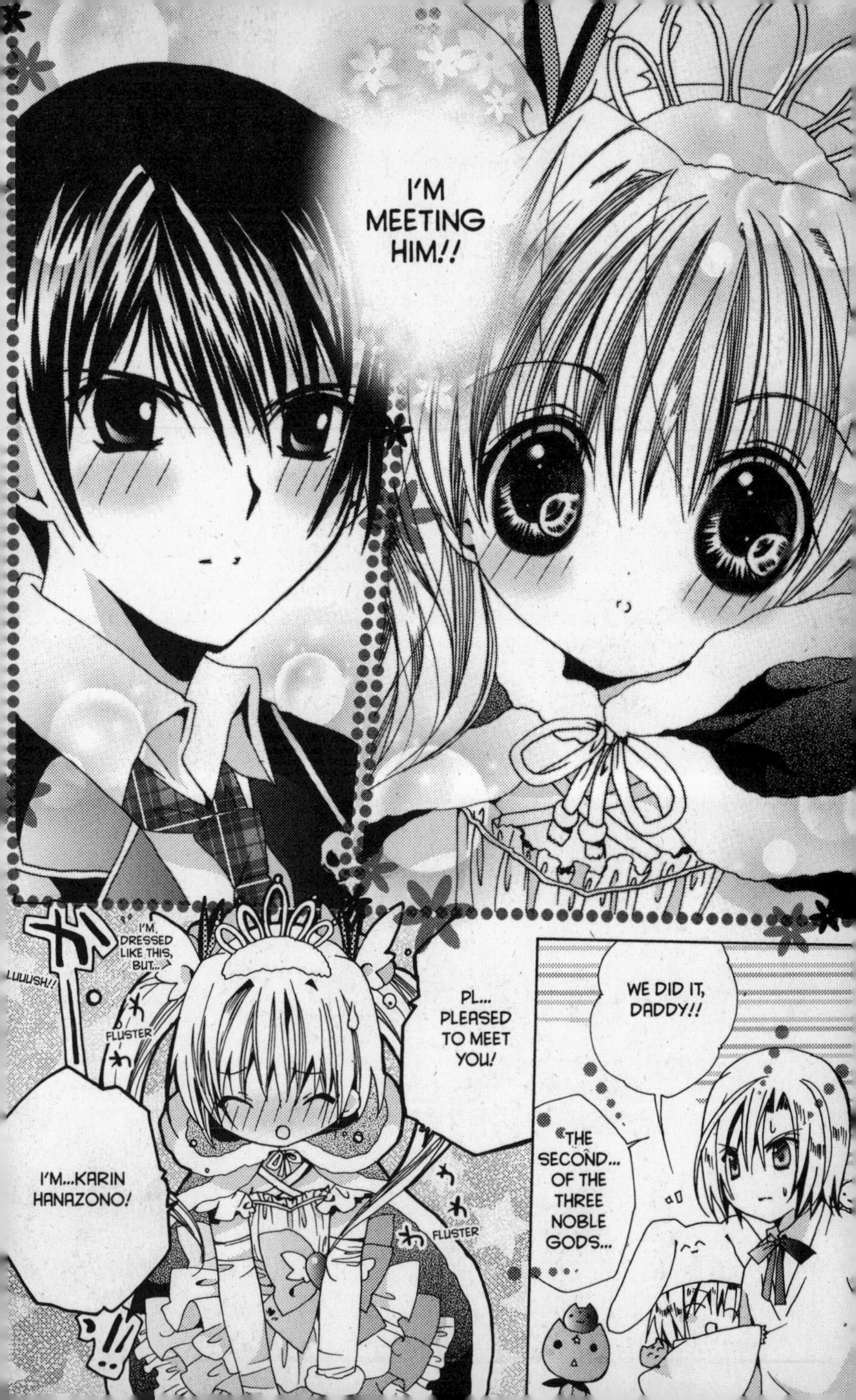
I'M MEETING HIM!!
WE DID IT, DADDY!!
THE SECOND... OF THE THREE NOBLE GODS...
PL... PLEASED TO MEET YOU!
I'M DRESSED LIKE THIS, BUT...
LUUUSH!!
FLUSTER
I'M...KARIN HANAZONO!
FLUSTER

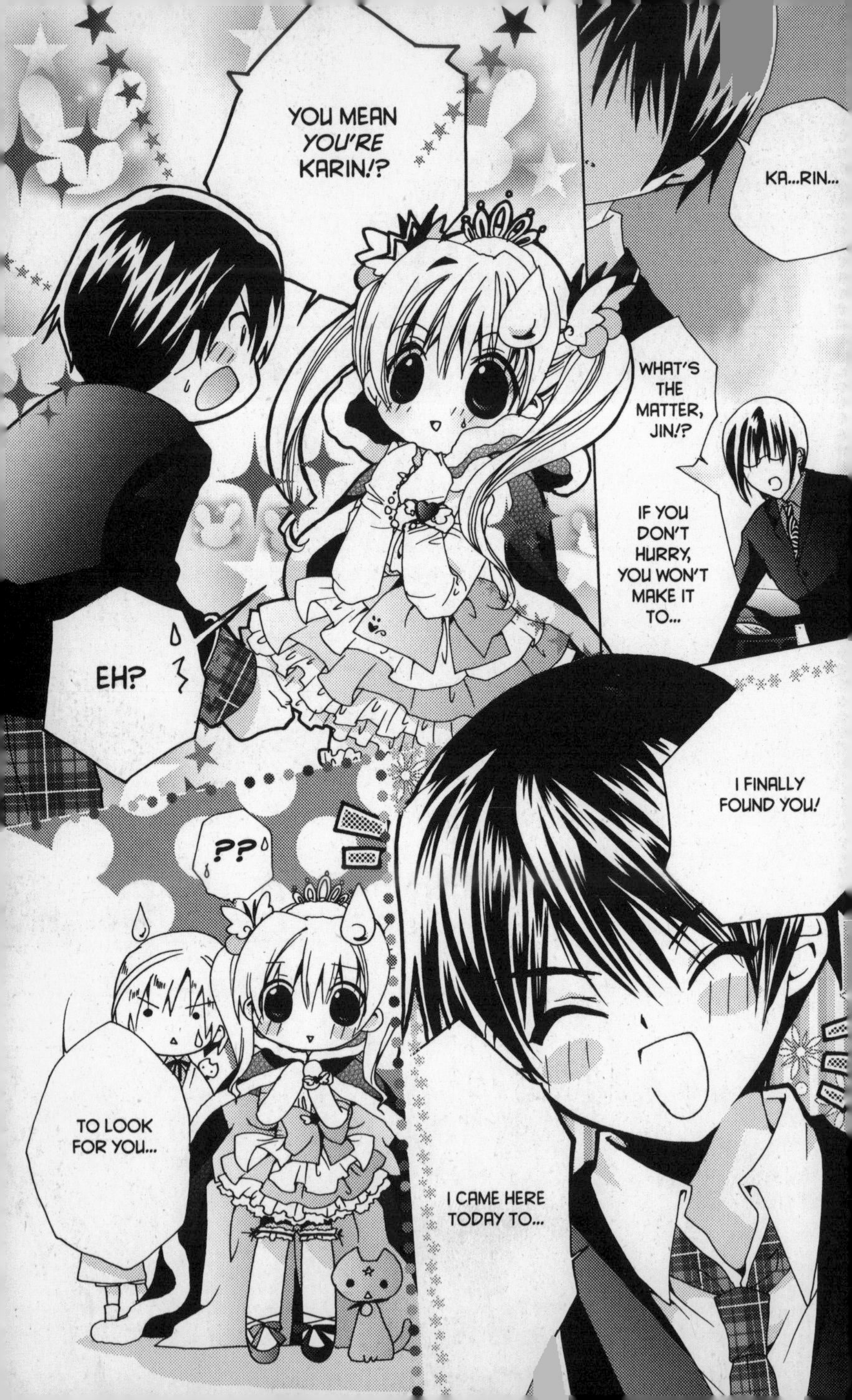
KA...RIN...
WHAT'S THE MATTER, JIN!?
IF YOU DON'T HURRY, YOU WON'T MAKE IT TO...
YOU MEAN *YOU'RE* KARIN!?
EH?
I FINALLY FOUND YOU!
I CAME HERE TODAY TO...
??
TO LOOK FOR YOU...

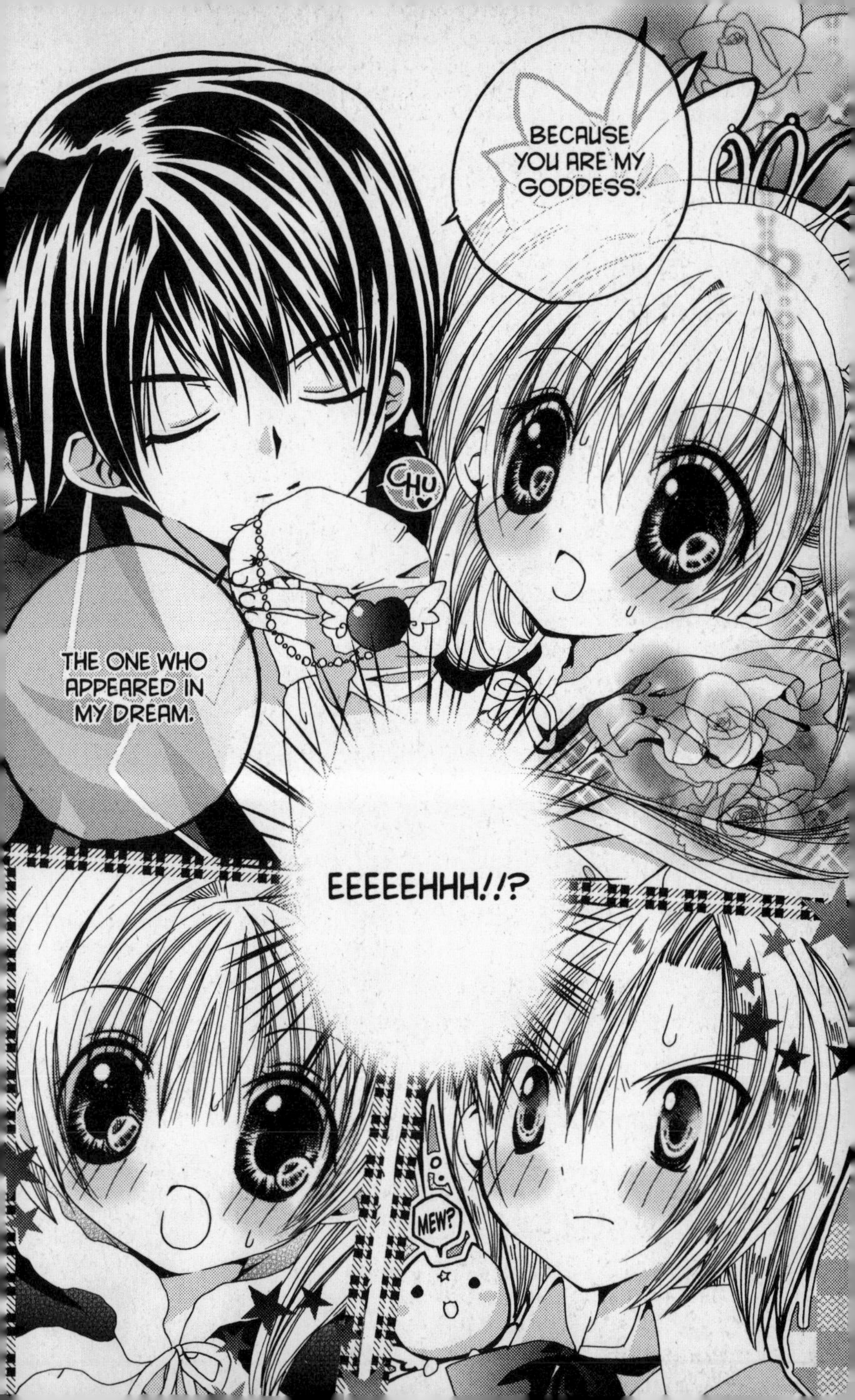
BECAUSE YOU ARE MY GODDESS.
CHU
THE ONE WHO APPEARED IN MY DREAM.
EEEEEHHH!!?
MEW?

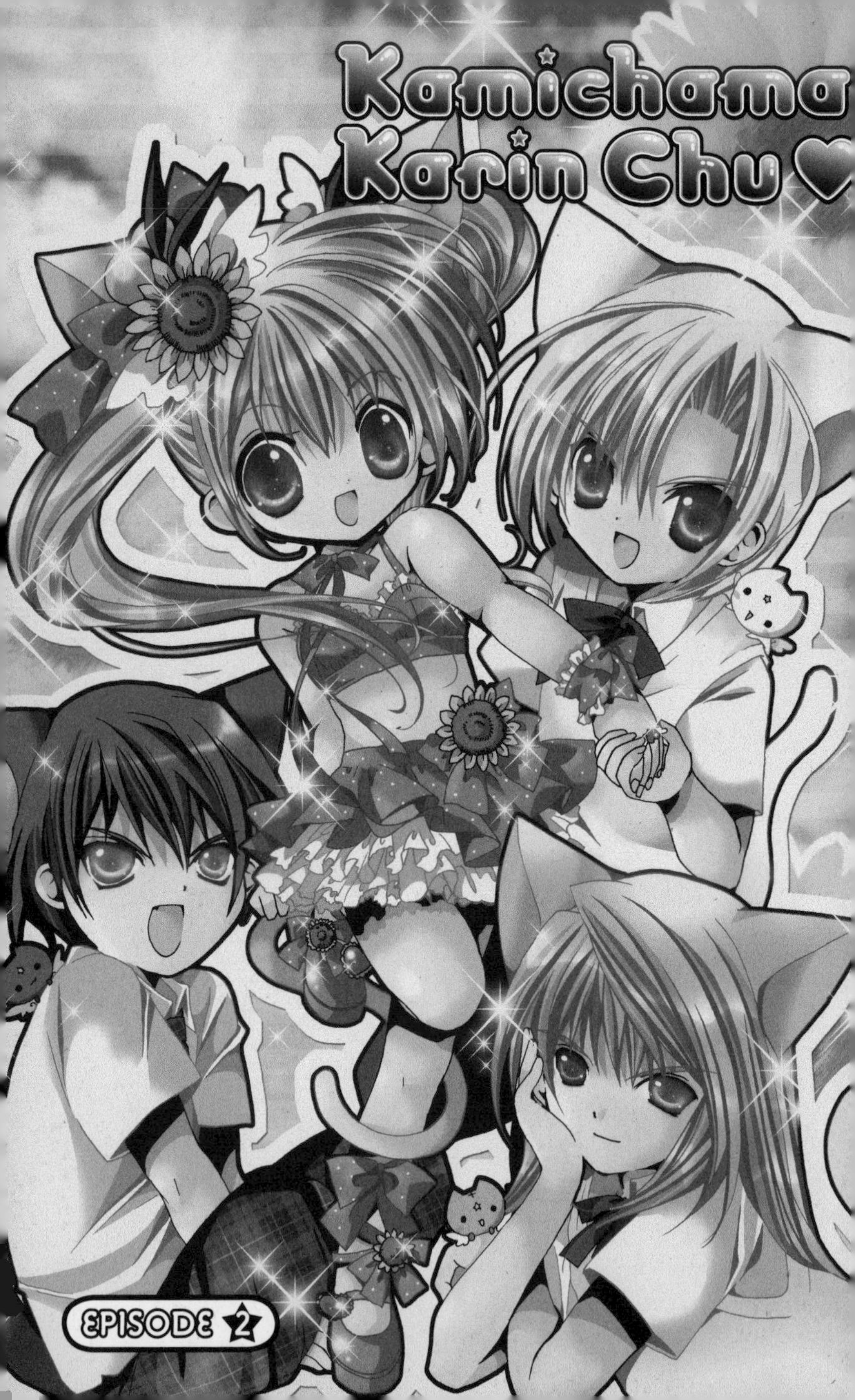
Kamichama Karin Chu♥
EPISODE 2

KARIN HANAZONO

BORN JULY 3, CANCER, AGE 14

BLOOD TYPE O

● MINI CHARACTER INTRODUCTION ●

THIS IS A TINY INTRODUCTION. FOR DETAILS, SEE THE DELUXE VERSION...

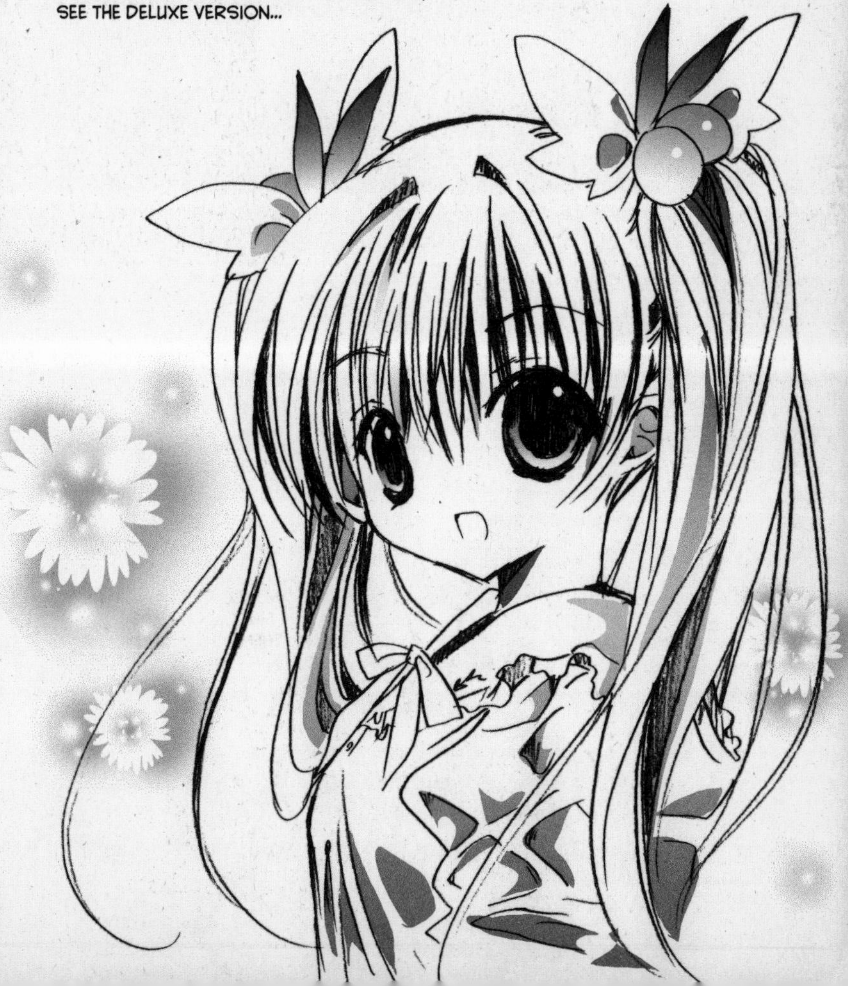

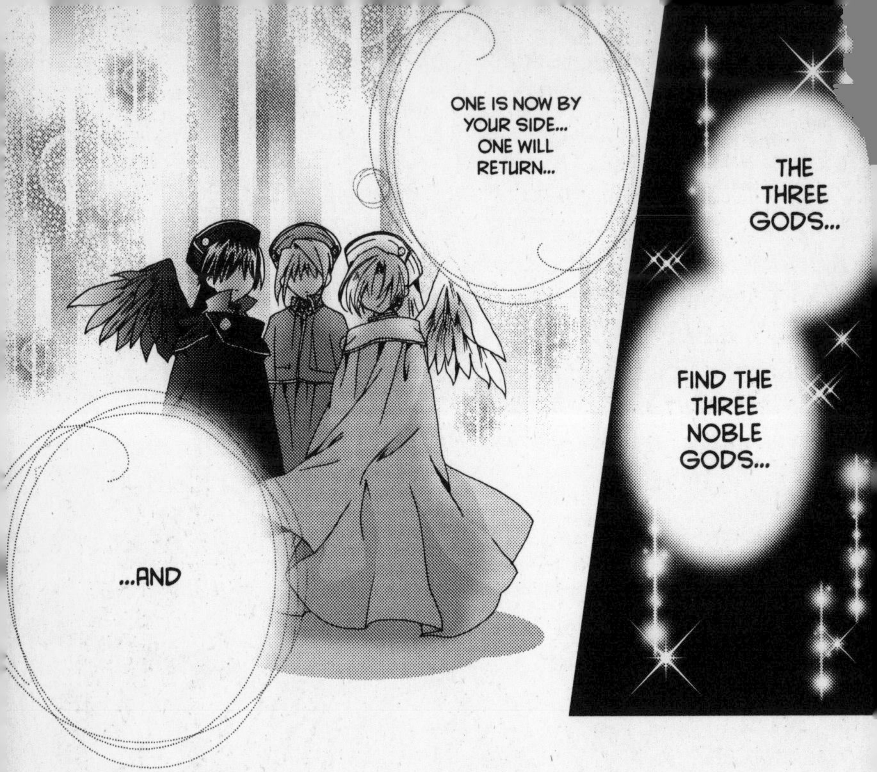
THE THREE GODS...
FIND THE THREE NOBLE GODS...
ONE IS NOW BY YOUR SIDE... ONE WILL RETURN...
...AND

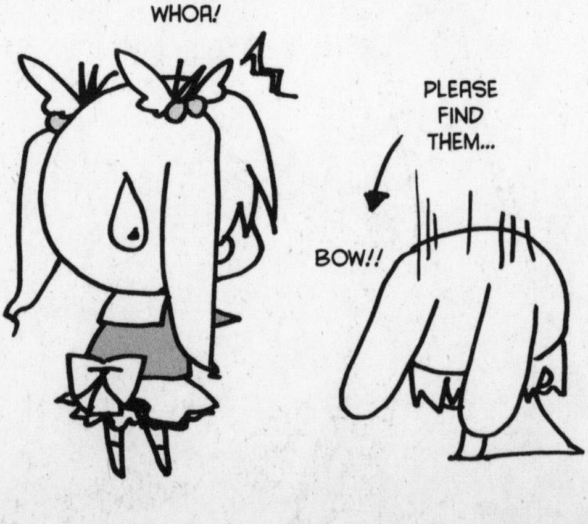
PLEASE FIND THEM...
BOW!!
WHOA!

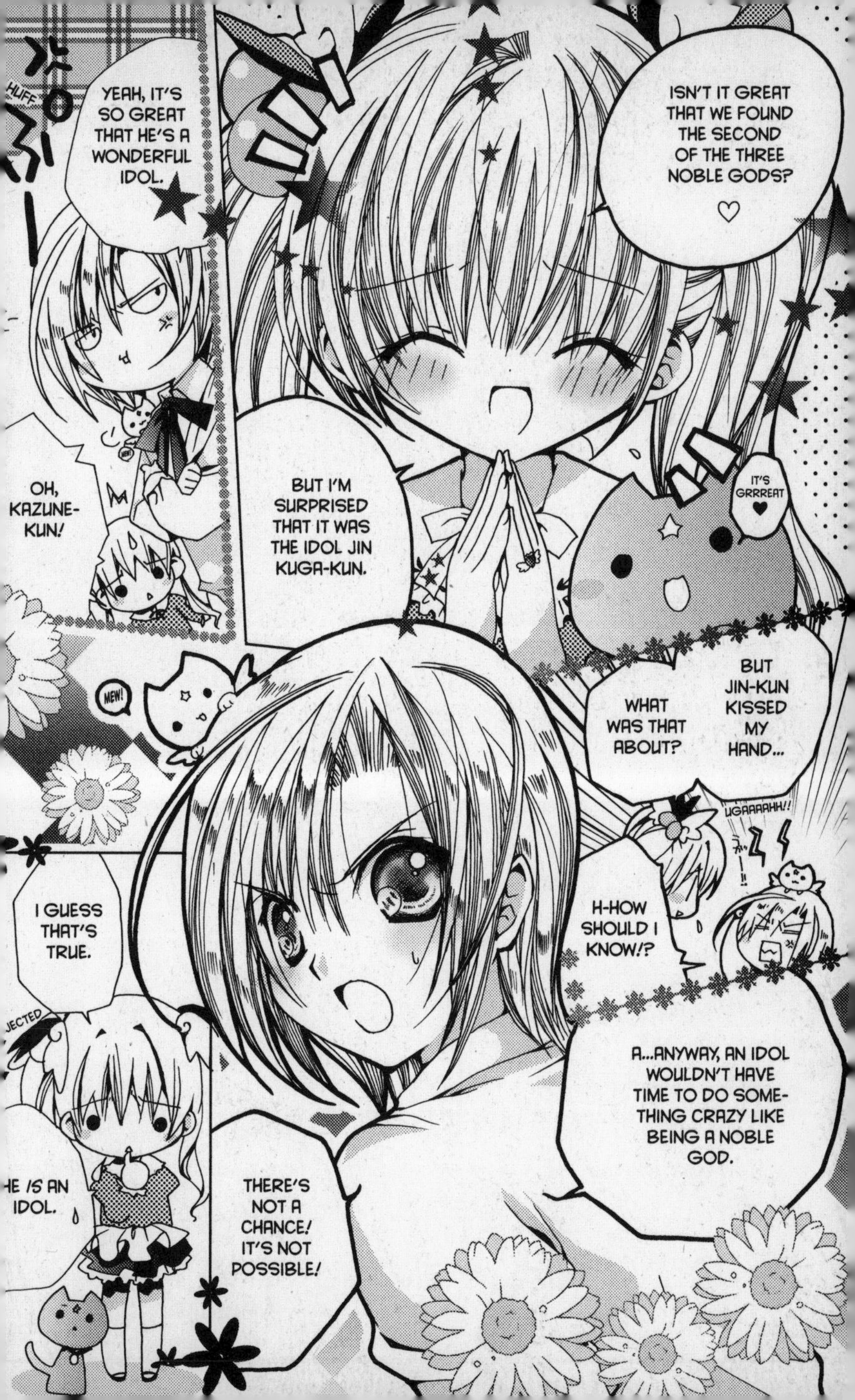

ISN'T IT GREAT THAT WE FOUND THE SECOND OF THE THREE NOBLE GODS? ♡
IT'S GRRREAT ♥
BUT I'M SURPRISED THAT IT WAS THE IDOL JIN KUGA-KUN.
YEAH, IT'S SO GREAT THAT HE'S A WONDERFUL IDOL.
HUFF
OH, KAZUNE-KUN!
MEW!
BUT JIN-KUN KISSED MY HAND...
WHAT WAS THAT ABOUT?
UGAAAAHH!!
H-HOW SHOULD I KNOW!?
A...ANYWAY, AN IDOL WOULDN'T HAVE TIME TO DO SOMETHING CRAZY LIKE BEING A NOBLE GOD.
THERE'S NOT A CHANCE! IT'S NOT POSSIBLE!
I GUESS THAT'S TRUE.
HE IS AN IDOL.

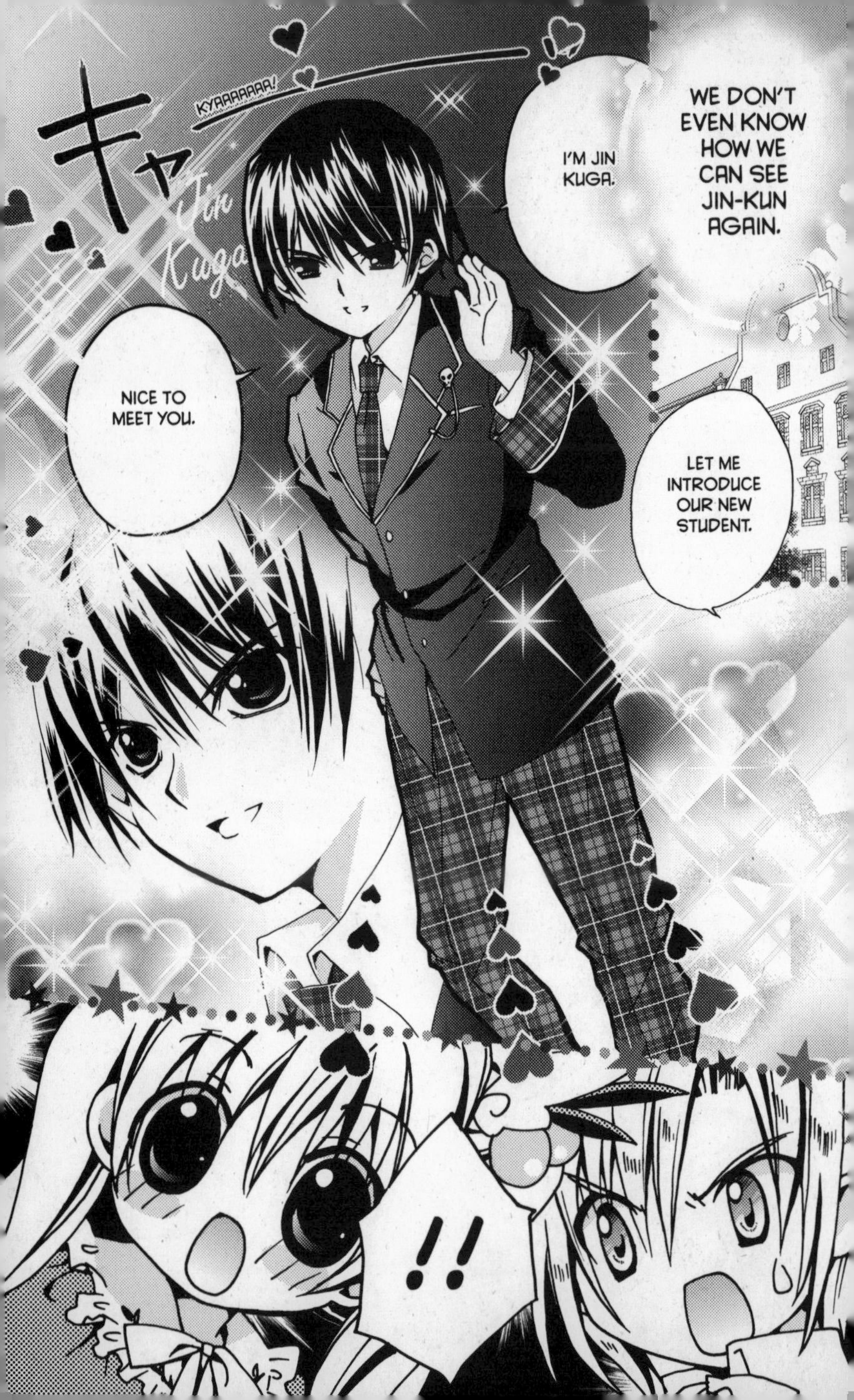
WE DON'T EVEN KNOW HOW WE CAN SEE JIN-KUN AGAIN.
I'M JIN KUGA.
KYAAAAAAA!
キャ
Jin Kuga
LET ME INTRODUCE OUR NEW STUDENT.
NICE TO MEET YOU.
!!

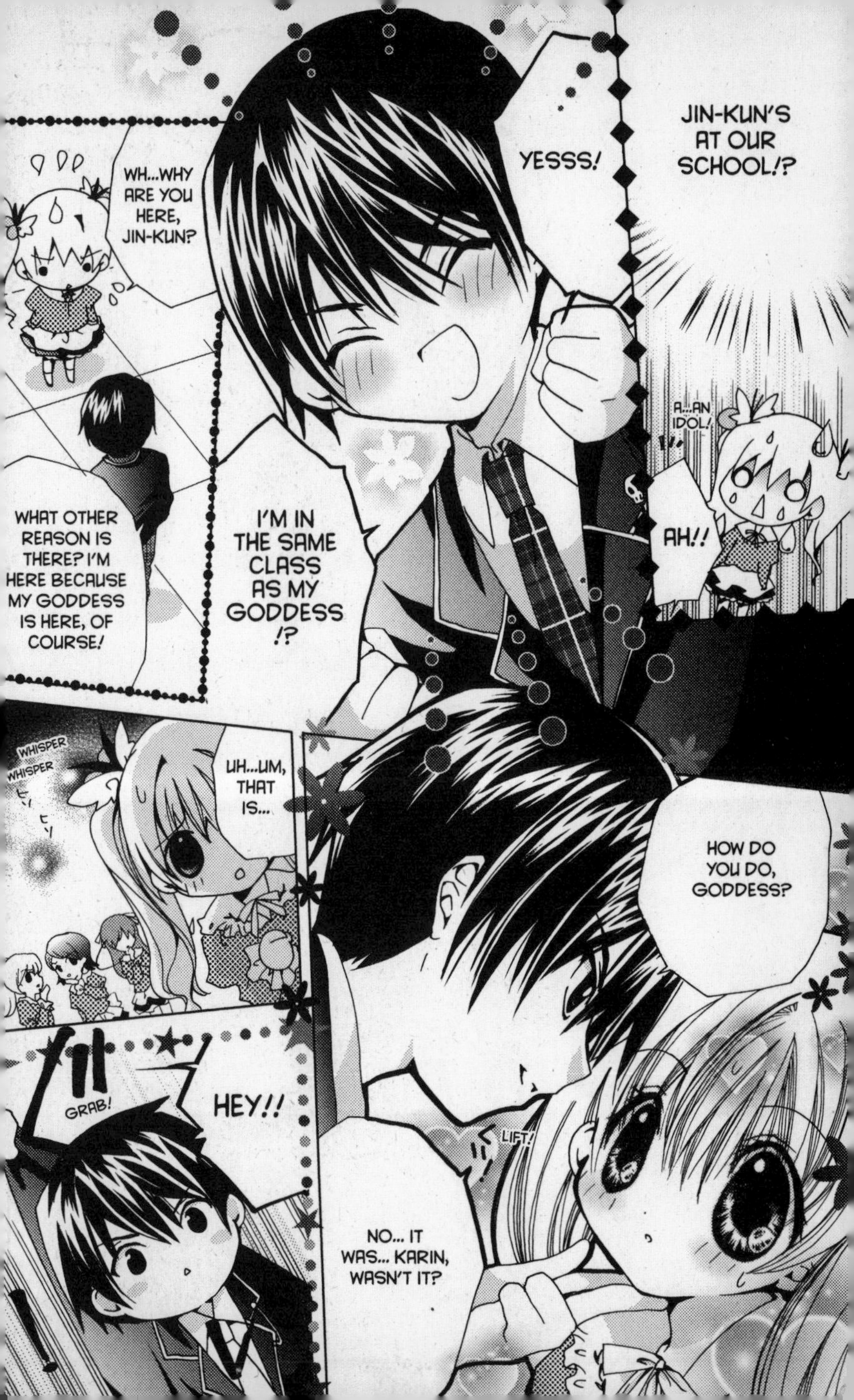

JIN-KUN'S AT OUR SCHOOL!?
A...AN IDOL!
AH!!
YESSS!
I'M IN THE SAME CLASS AS MY GODDESS!?
WH...WHY ARE YOU HERE, JIN-KUN?
WHAT OTHER REASON IS THERE? I'M HERE BECAUSE MY GODDESS IS HERE, OF COURSE!
HOW DO YOU DO, GODDESS?
LIFT!
NO... IT WAS... KARIN, WASN'T IT?
UH...UM, THAT IS...
WHISPER
WHISPER
HEY!!
GRAB!

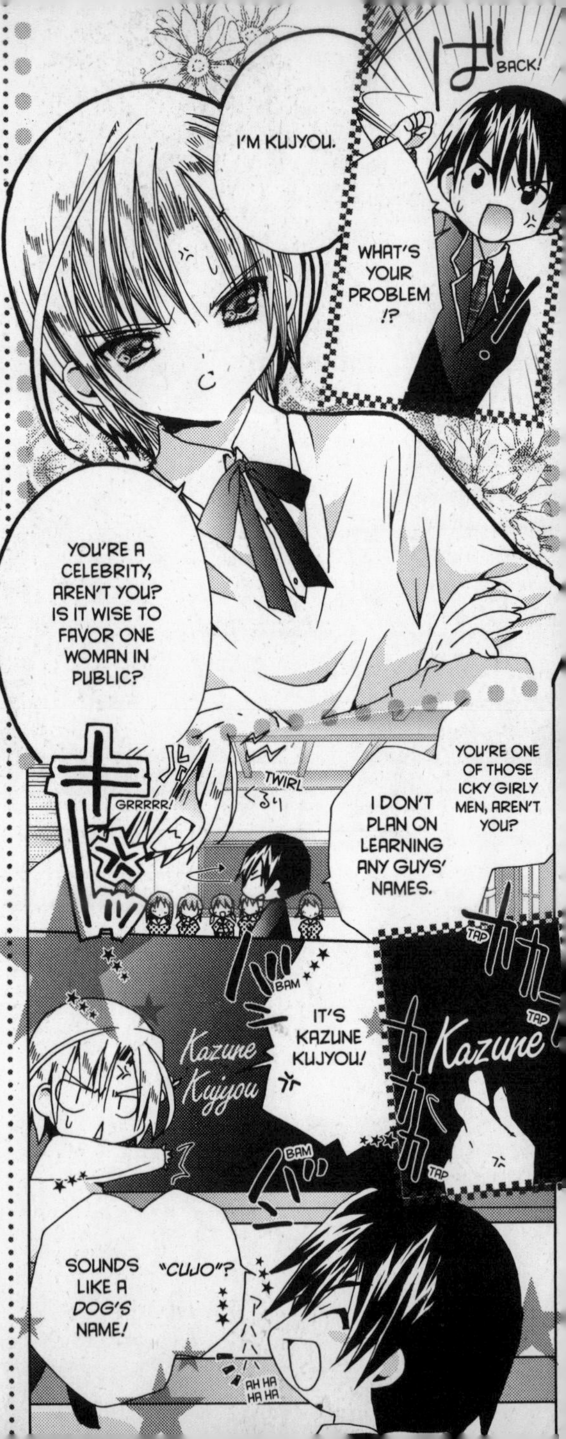
BACK!
WHAT'S YOUR PROBLEM !?
I'M KUJYOU.
YOU'RE A CELEBRITY, AREN'T YOU? IS IT WISE TO FAVOR ONE WOMAN IN PUBLIC?
YOU'RE ONE OF THOSE ICKY GIRLY MEN, AREN'T YOU?
I DON'T PLAN ON LEARNING ANY GUYS' NAMES.
TWIRL
GRRRRR!
TAP
Kazune
TAP
TAP
BAM
IT'S KAZUNE KUJYOU!
Kazune Kujyou
BAM
"CUJO"?
SOUNDS LIKE A DOG'S NAME!
AH HA HA HA

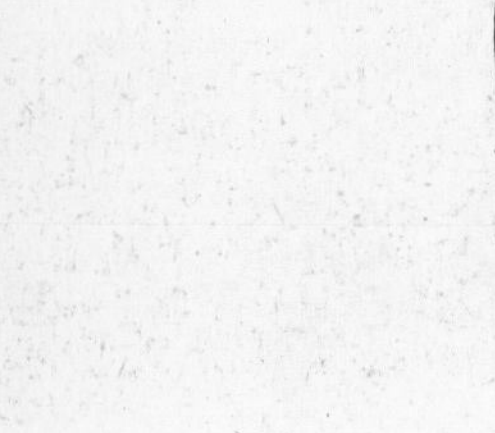
YOU'RE A CELEBRITY, AREN'T YOU?
HOW DID YOU GET INTO OUR SCHOOL?
YOU'RE SO RUDE.

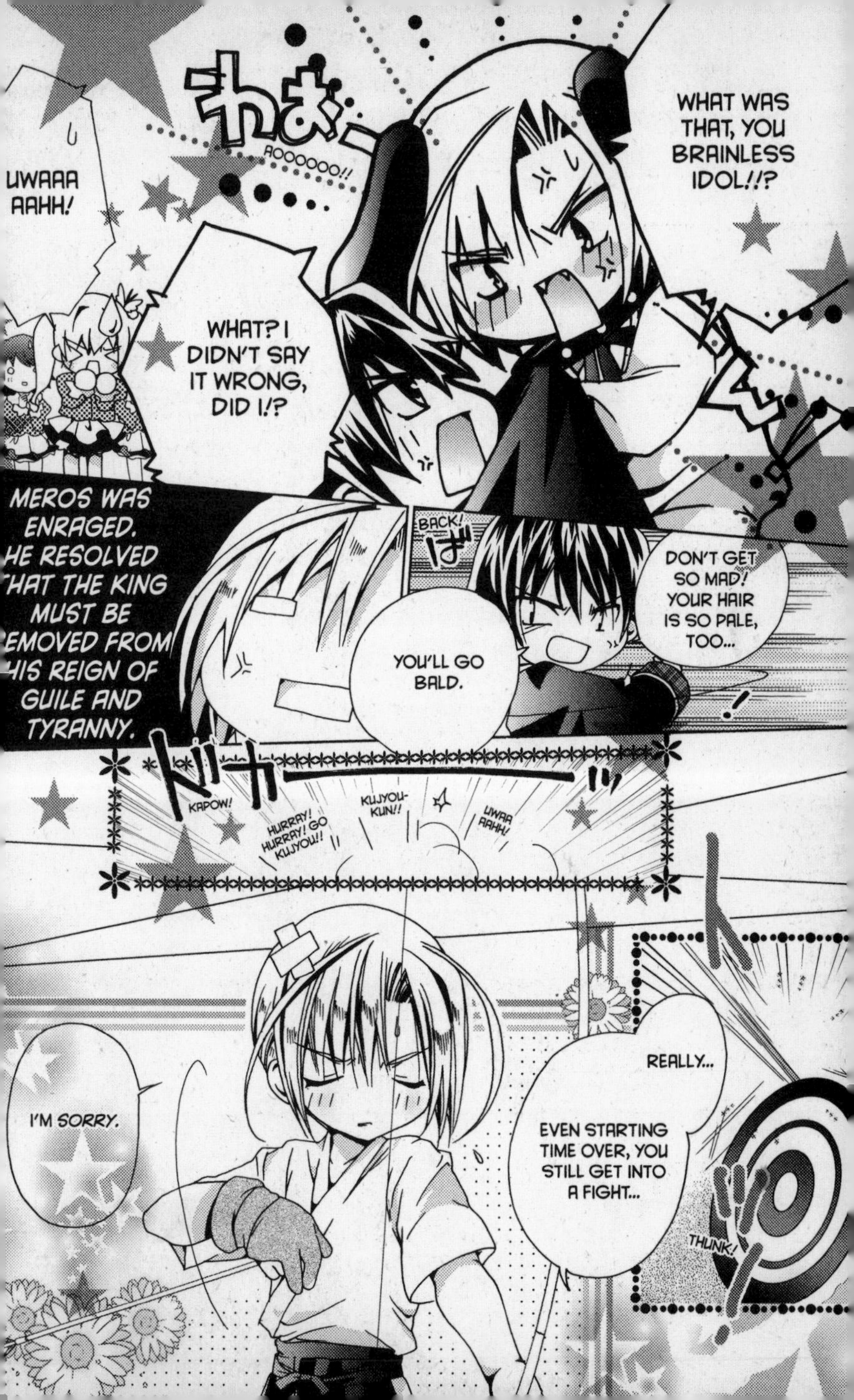
WHAT WAS THAT, YOU BRAINLESS IDOL!!?
AOOOOOOO!!
WHAT? I DIDN'T SAY IT WRONG, DID I!?
UWAAA AAHH!
BACK!
DON'T GET SO MAD! YOUR HAIR IS SO PALE, TOO...
YOU'LL GO BALD.
MEROS WAS ENRAGED. HE RESOLVED 'HAT THE KING MUST BE EMOVED FROM HIS REIGN OF GUILE AND TYRANNY.
KAPOW!
HURRAY! HURRAY! GO KUJYOU!!
KUJYOU-KUN!!
UWAA AAHH!
THUNK!
REALLY...
EVEN STARTING TIME OVER, YOU STILL GET INTO A FIGHT...
I'M SORRY.

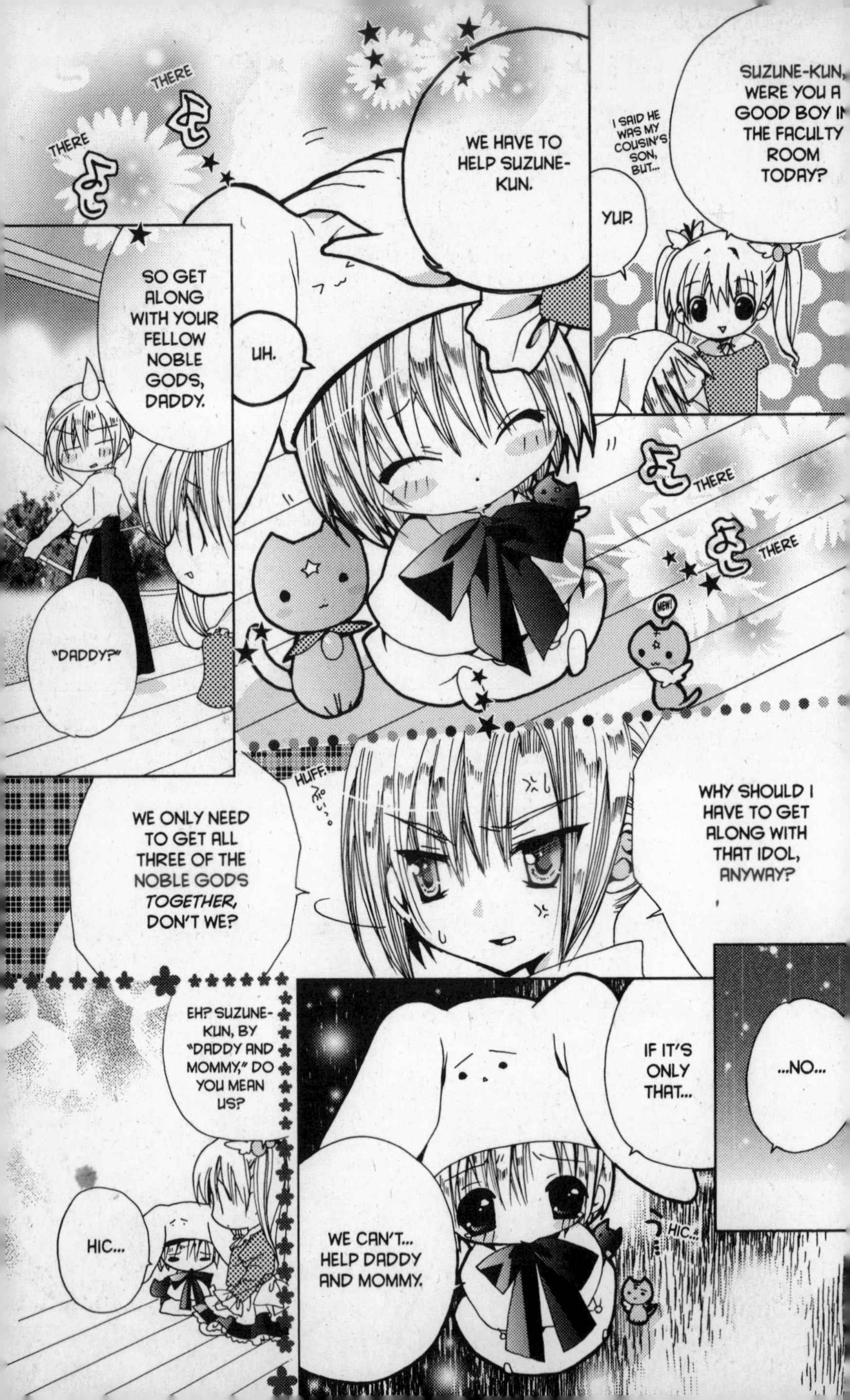
SUZUNE-KUN, WERE YOU A GOOD BOY IN THE FACULTY ROOM TODAY?
I SAID HE WAS MY COUSIN'S SON, BUT...
YUP.
THERE
THERE
MEW!
WE HAVE TO HELP SUZUNE-KUN.
THERE
THERE
SO GET ALONG WITH YOUR FELLOW NOBLE GODS, DADDY.
UH.
"DADDY?"
WHY SHOULD I HAVE TO GET ALONG WITH THAT IDOL, ANYWAY?
HUFF.
WE ONLY NEED TO GET ALL THREE OF THE NOBLE GODS *TOGETHER*, DON'T WE?
...NO...
IF IT'S ONLY THAT...
HIC...
WE CAN'T... HELP DADDY AND MOMMY.
EH? SUZUNE-KUN, BY "DADDY AND MOMMY," DO YOU MEAN US?
HIC...

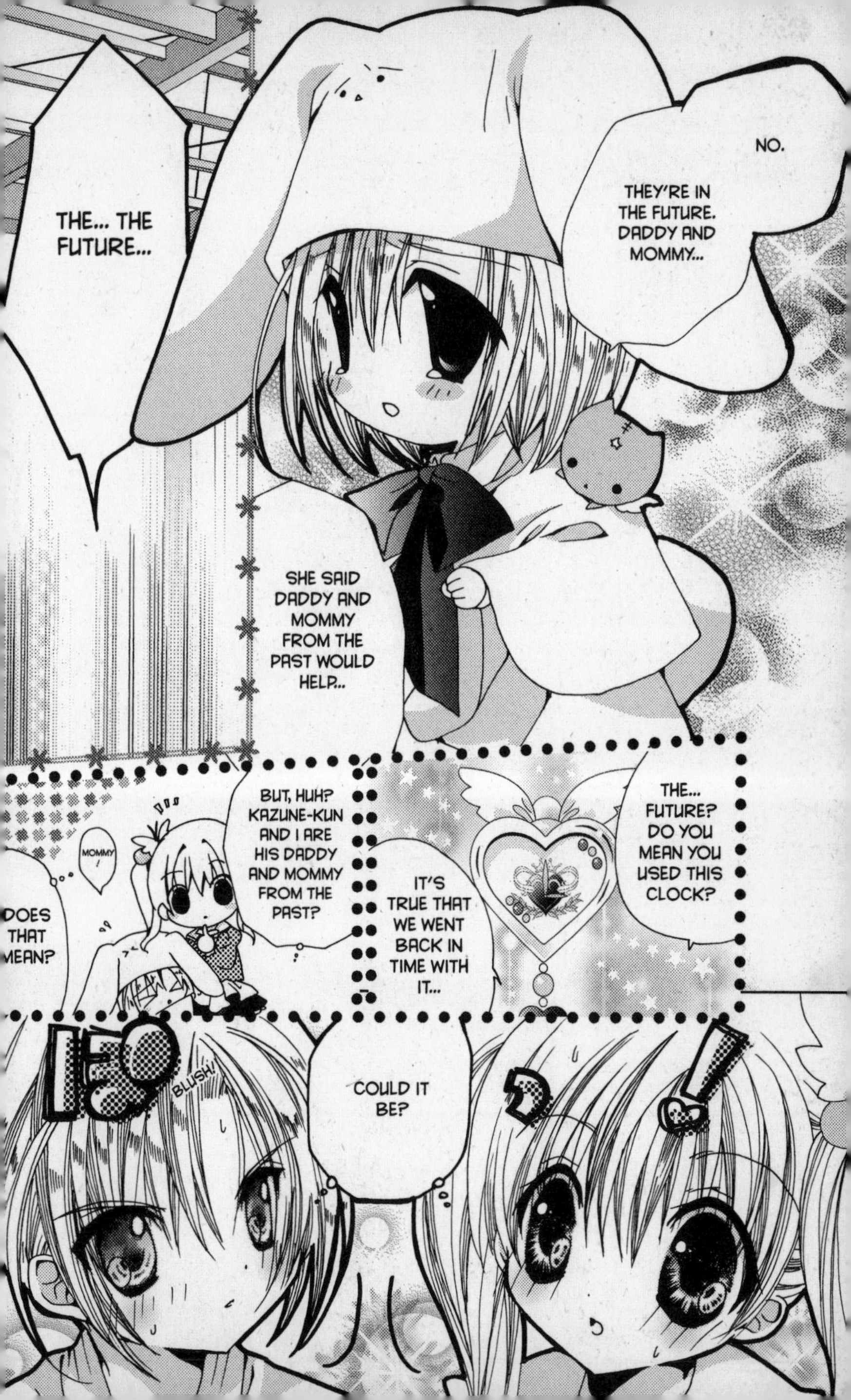

NO.
THEY'RE IN THE FUTURE. DADDY AND MOMMY...
SHE SAID DADDY AND MOMMY FROM THE PAST WOULD HELP...
THE... THE FUTURE...
THE... FUTURE? DO YOU MEAN YOU USED THIS CLOCK?
IT'S TRUE THAT WE WENT BACK IN TIME WITH IT...
BUT, HUH? KAZUNE-KUN AND I ARE HIS DADDY AND MOMMY FROM THE PAST?
MOMMY!
DOES THAT MEAN?
COULD IT BE?
BLUSH!

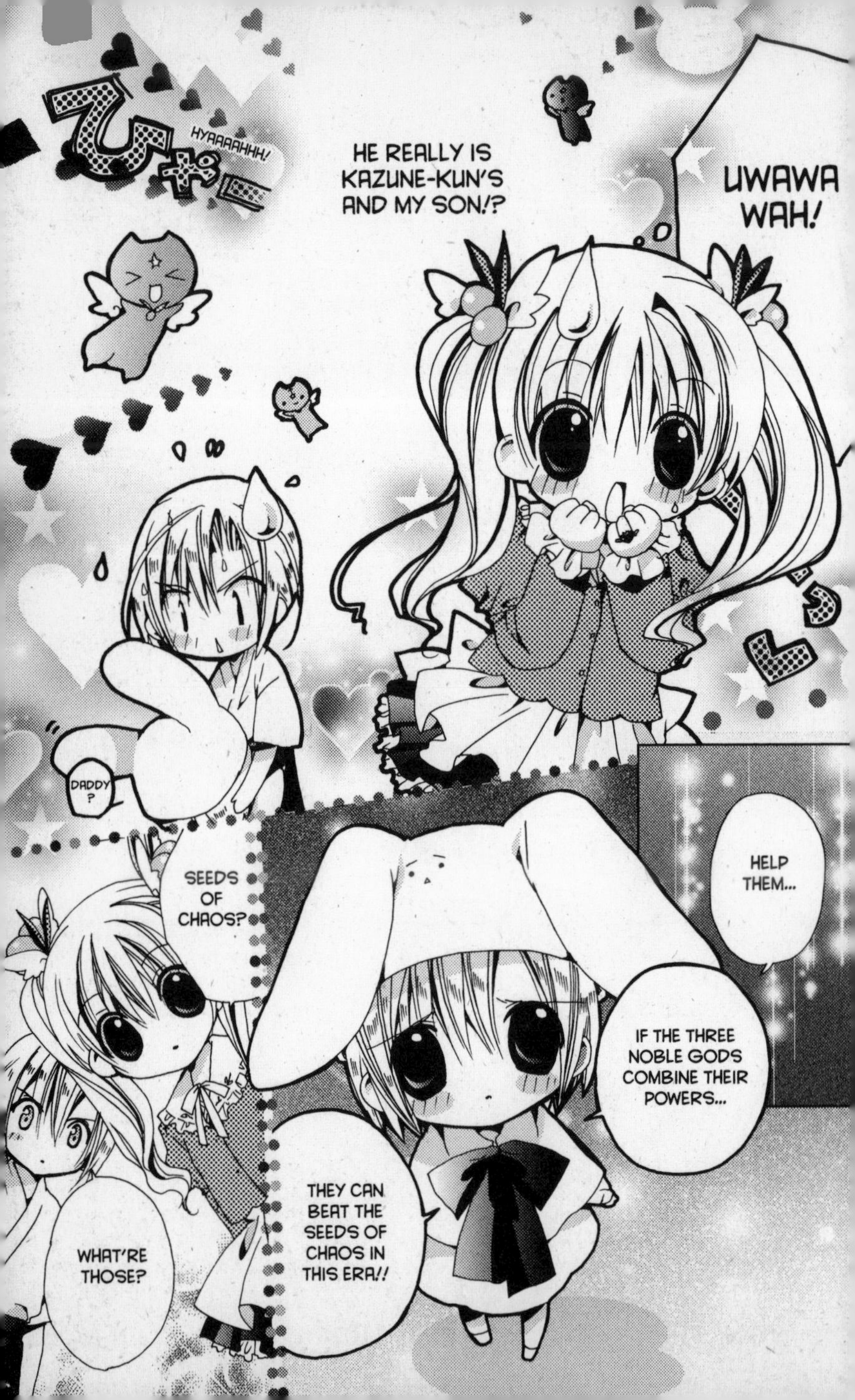
UWAWA WAH!
HE REALLY IS KAZUNE-KUN'S AND MY SON!?
HYAAAAHHH!
DADDY?
HELP THEM...
IF THE THREE NOBLE GODS COMBINE THEIR POWERS...
THEY CAN BEAT THE SEEDS OF CHAOS IN THIS ERA!!
SEEDS OF CHAOS?
WHAT'RE THOSE?

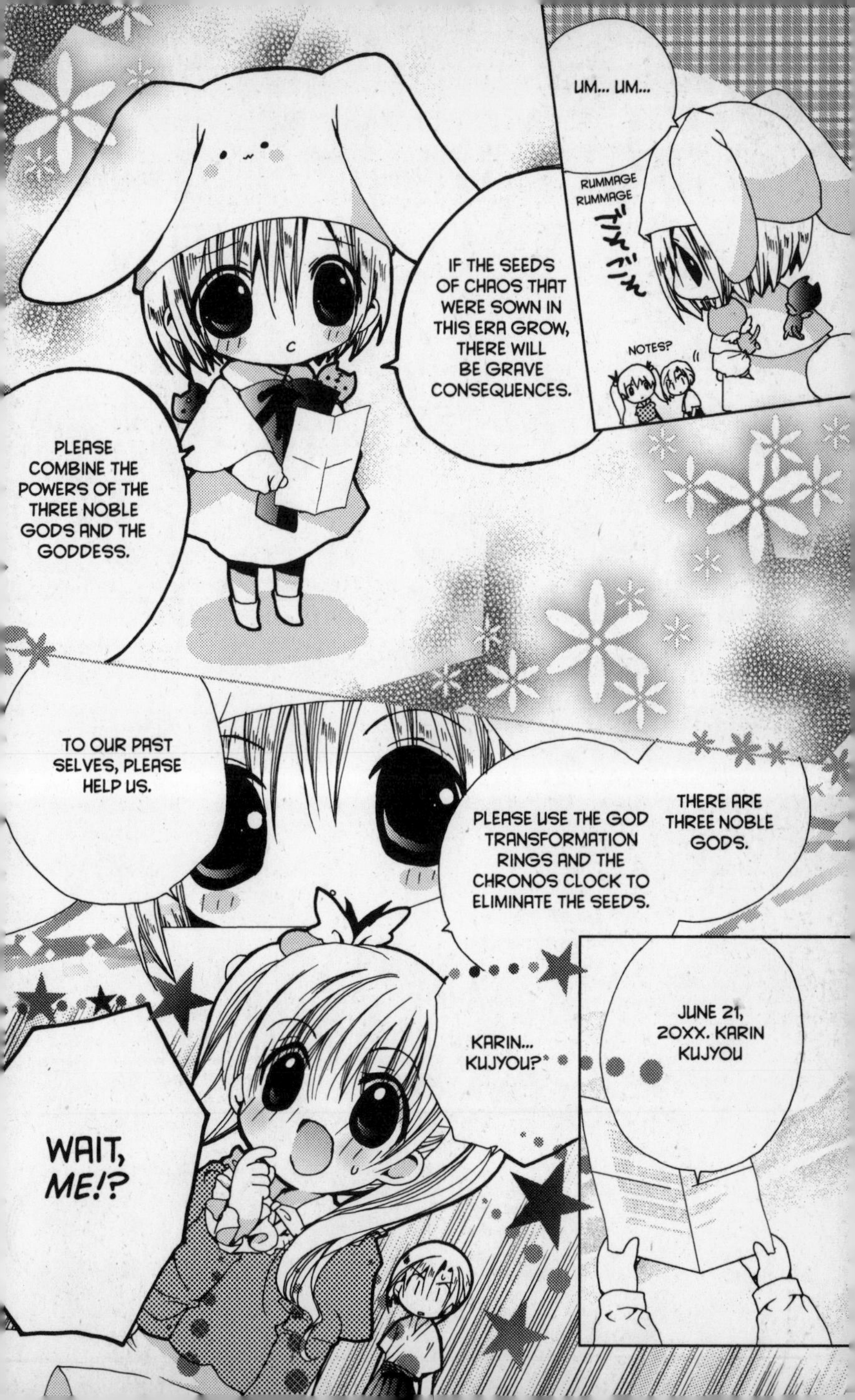
UM... UM...
RUMMAGE RUMMAGE
NOTES?
IF THE SEEDS OF CHAOS THAT WERE SOWN IN THIS ERA GROW, THERE WILL BE GRAVE CONSEQUENCES.
PLEASE COMBINE THE POWERS OF THE THREE NOBLE GODS AND THE GODDESS.
THERE ARE THREE NOBLE GODS.
PLEASE USE THE GOD TRANSFORMATION RINGS AND THE CHRONOS CLOCK TO ELIMINATE THE SEEDS.
TO OUR PAST SELVES, PLEASE HELP US.
JUNE 21, 20XX. KARIN KUJYOU
KARIN... KUJYOU?*
WAIT, ME!?

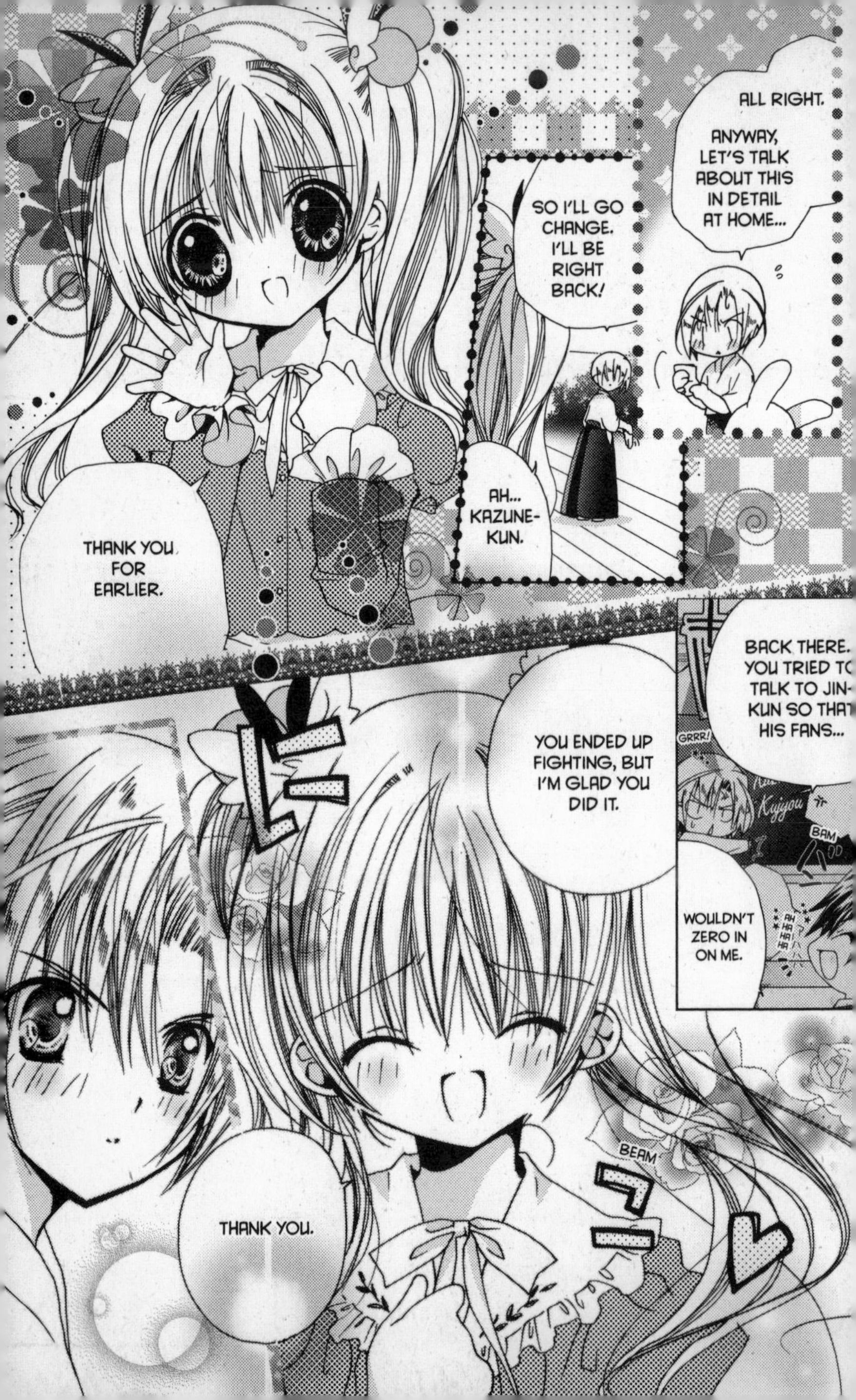
ALL RIGHT.
ANYWAY, LET'S TALK ABOUT THIS IN DETAIL AT HOME...
SO I'LL GO CHANGE. I'LL BE RIGHT BACK!
AH... KAZUNE-KUN.
THANK YOU FOR EARLIER.
BACK THERE. YOU TRIED TO TALK TO JIN-KUN SO THAT HIS FANS...
GRRR!
BAM
AH HA HA HA
WOULDN'T ZERO IN ON ME.
YOU ENDED UP FIGHTING, BUT I'M GLAD YOU DID IT.
BEAM
THANK YOU.

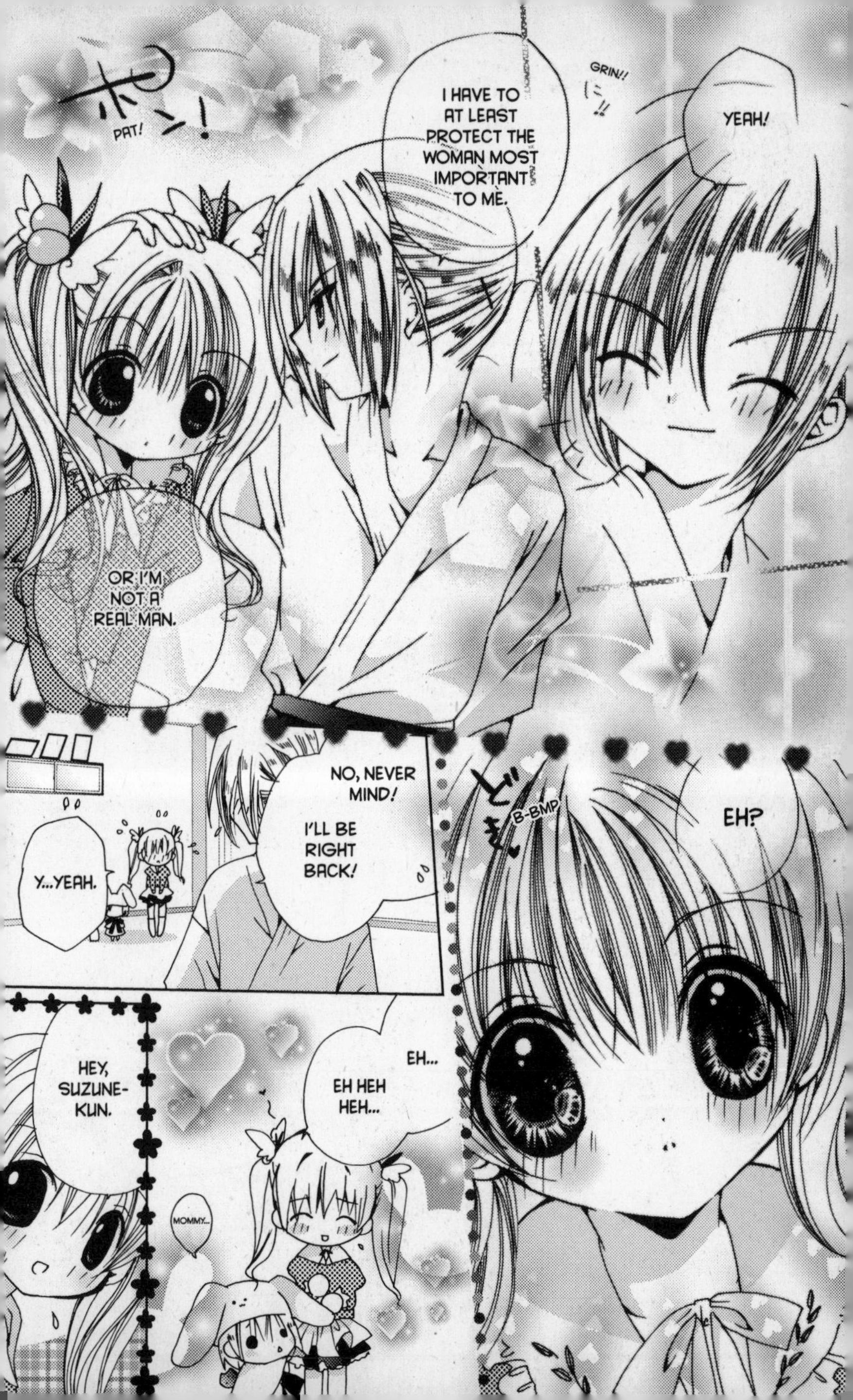
GRIN!!
YEAH!
I HAVE TO AT LEAST PROTECT THE WOMAN MOST IMPORTANT TO ME.
PAT!
OR I'M NOT A REAL MAN.
B-BMP
EH?
NO, NEVER MIND!
I'LL BE RIGHT BACK!
Y...YEAH.
EH...
EH HEH HEH...
MOMMY...
HEY, SUZUNE-KUN.

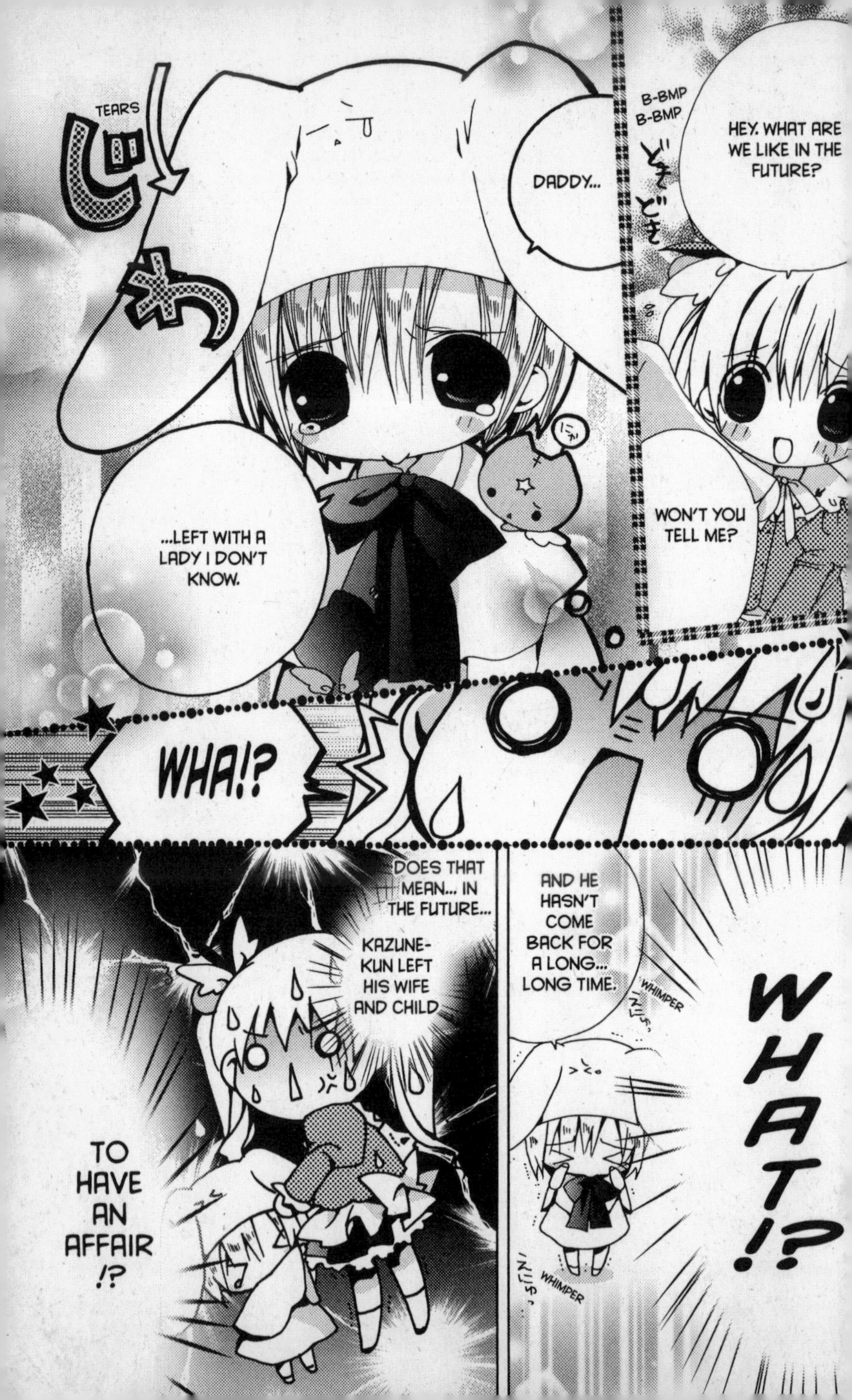
B-BMP
B-BMP
HEY. WHAT ARE WE LIKE IN THE FUTURE?
WON'T YOU TELL ME?
DADDY...
TEARS
...LEFT WITH A LADY I DON'T KNOW.
WHA!?
AND HE HASN'T COME BACK FOR A LONG... LONG TIME.
WHIMPER
WHIMPER
WHAT!?
DOES THAT MEAN... IN THE FUTURE...
KAZUNE-KUN LEFT HIS WIFE AND CHILD
TO HAVE AN AFFAIR!?

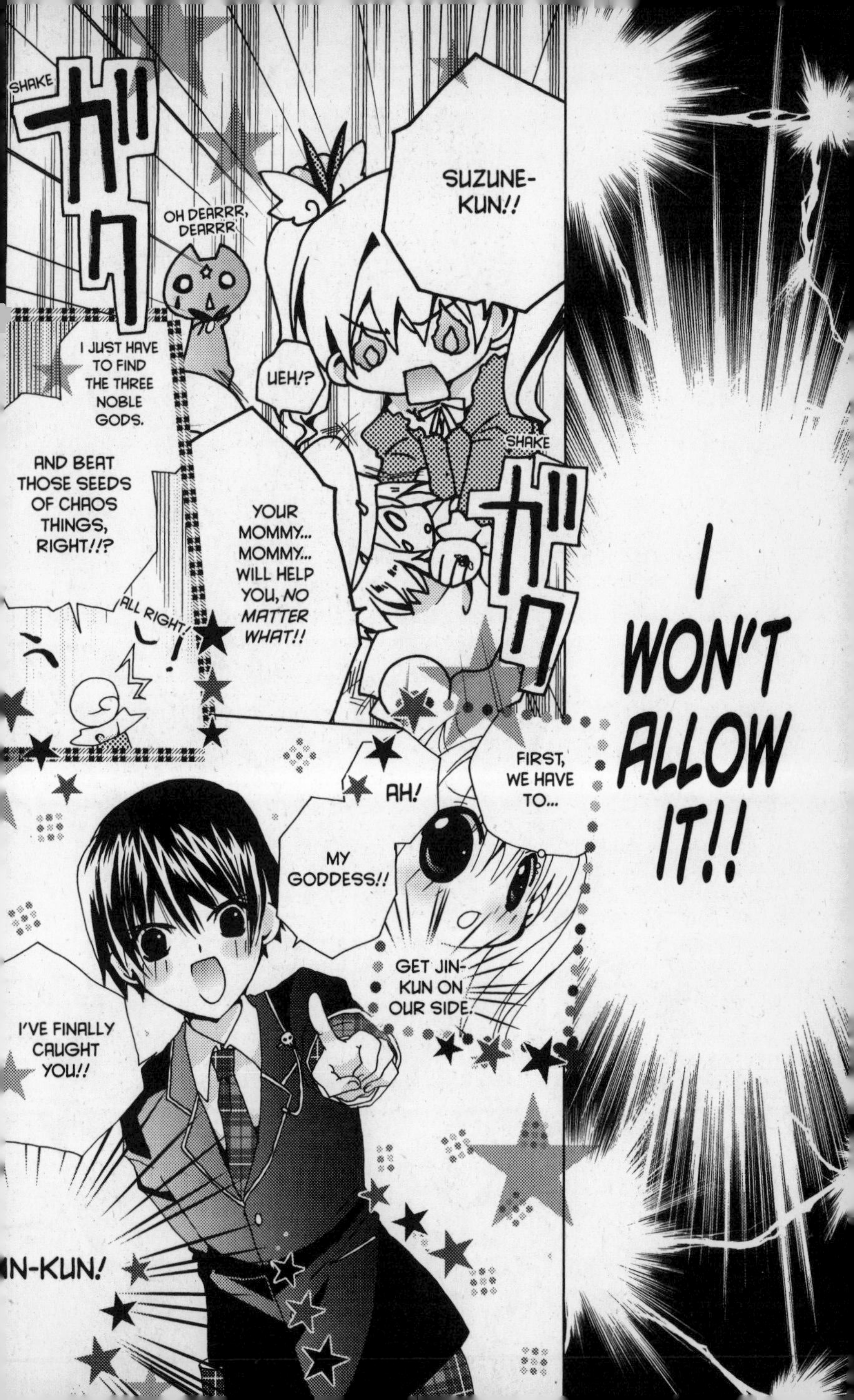
I WON'T ALLOW IT!!
SUZUNE-KUN!!
SHAKE
ガク
UEH!?
SHAKE
ガリ
OH DEARRR, DEARRR
I JUST HAVE TO FIND THE THREE NOBLE GODS.
YOUR MOMMY... MOMMY... WILL HELP YOU, NO MATTER WHAT!!
AND BEAT THOSE SEEDS OF CHAOS THINGS, RIGHT!!?
ALL RIGHT!
FIRST, WE HAVE TO...
GET JIN-KUN ON OUR SIDE.
AH!
MY GODDESS!!
I'VE FINALLY CAUGHT YOU!!
N-KUN!

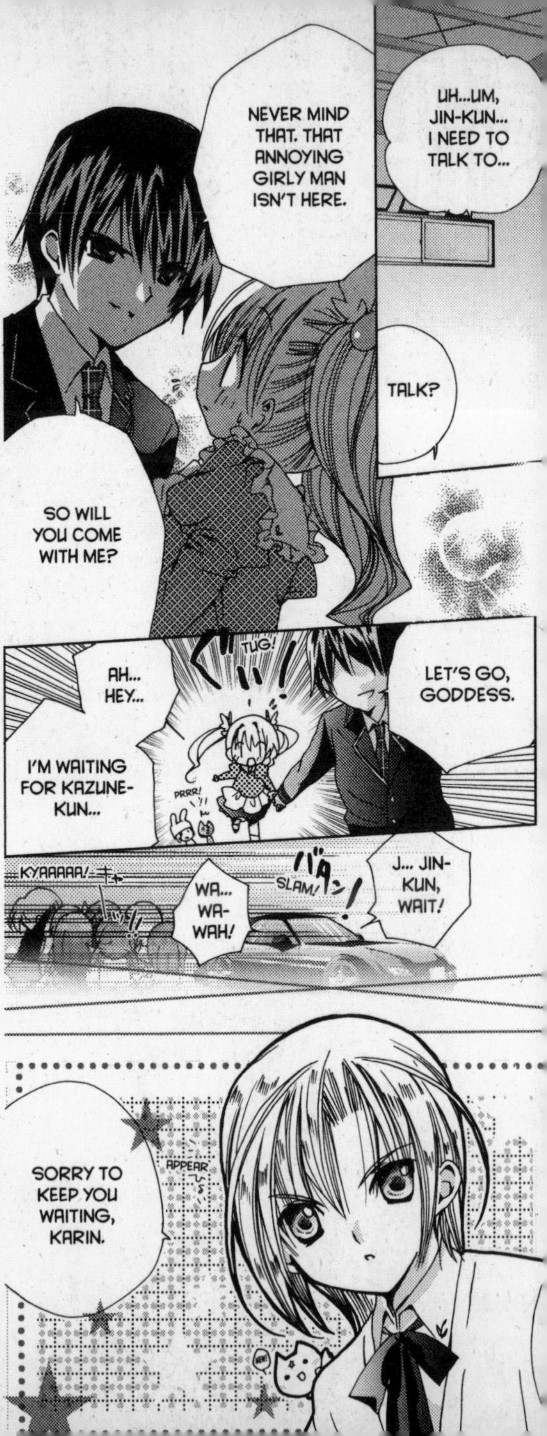
UH...UM, JIN-KUN... I NEED TO TALK TO...
NEVER MIND THAT. THAT ANNOYING GIRLY MAN ISN'T HERE.
TALK?
SO WILL YOU COME WITH ME?
LET'S GO, GODDESS.
TUG!
AH... HEY...
I'M WAITING FOR KAZUNE-KUN...
PRRR!
J... JIN-KUN, WAIT!
SLAM!
WA... WA-WAH!
KYAAAAA!
APPEAR
SORRY TO KEEP YOU WAITING, KARIN.
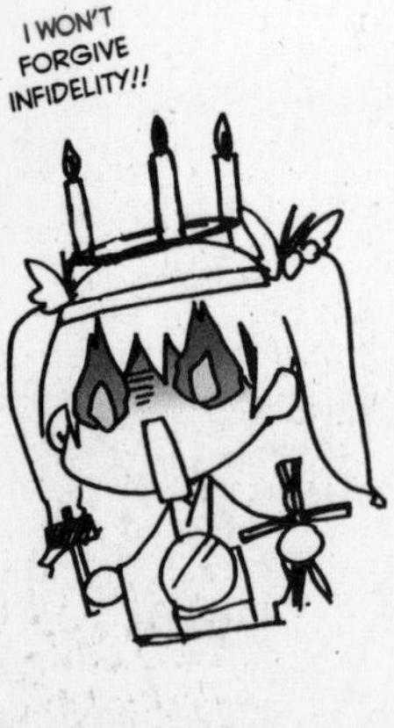
I WON'T FORGIVE INFIDELITY!!

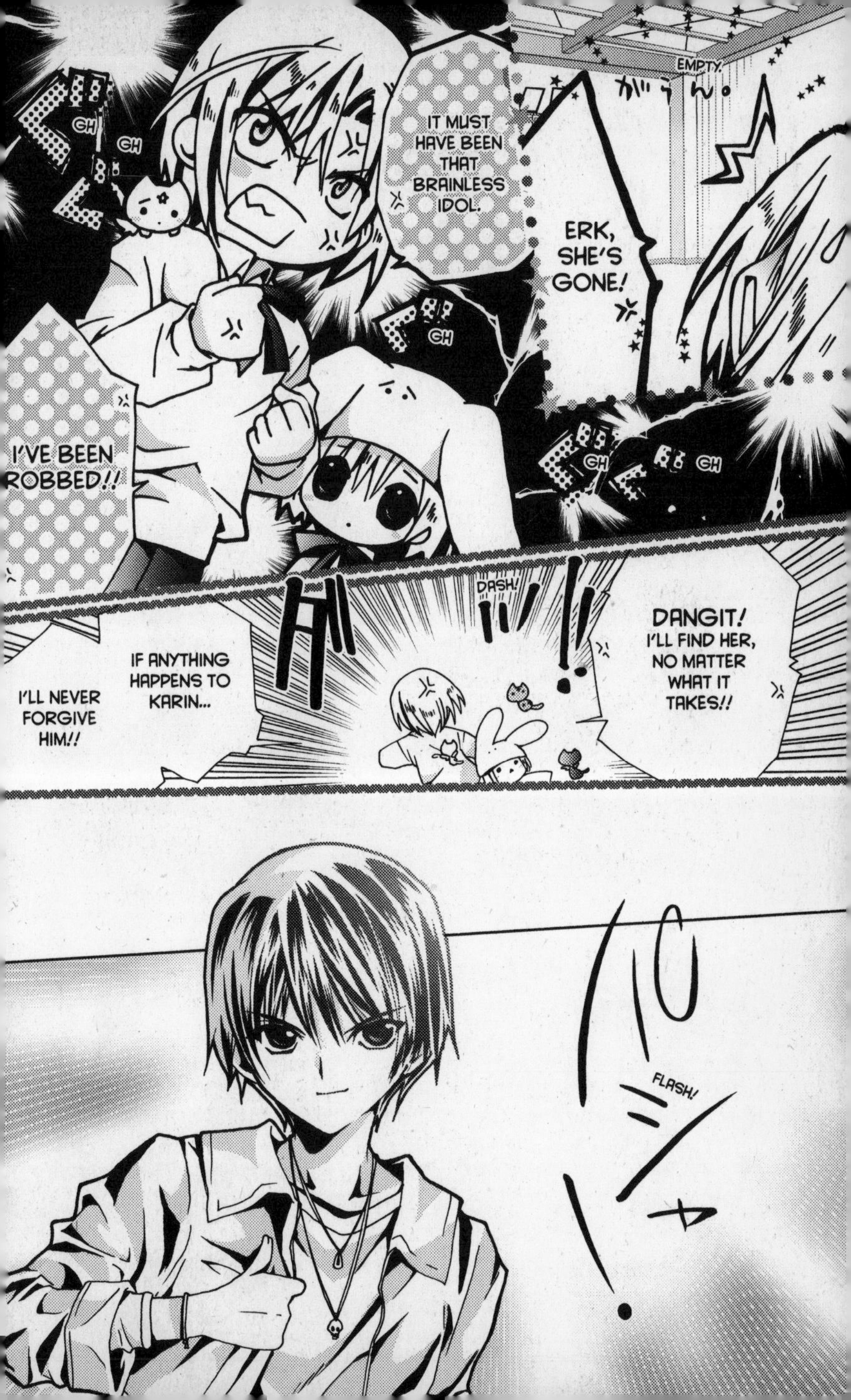
EMPTY.
がらん。
ERK, SHE'S GONE!
IT MUST HAVE BEEN THAT BRAINLESS IDOL.
GH
GH
GH
GH
GH
I'VE BEEN ROBBED!!
DANGIT! I'LL FIND HER, NO MATTER WHAT IT TAKES!!
DASH!
IF ANYTHING HAPPENS TO KARIN...
I'LL NEVER FORGIVE HIM!!
FLASH!

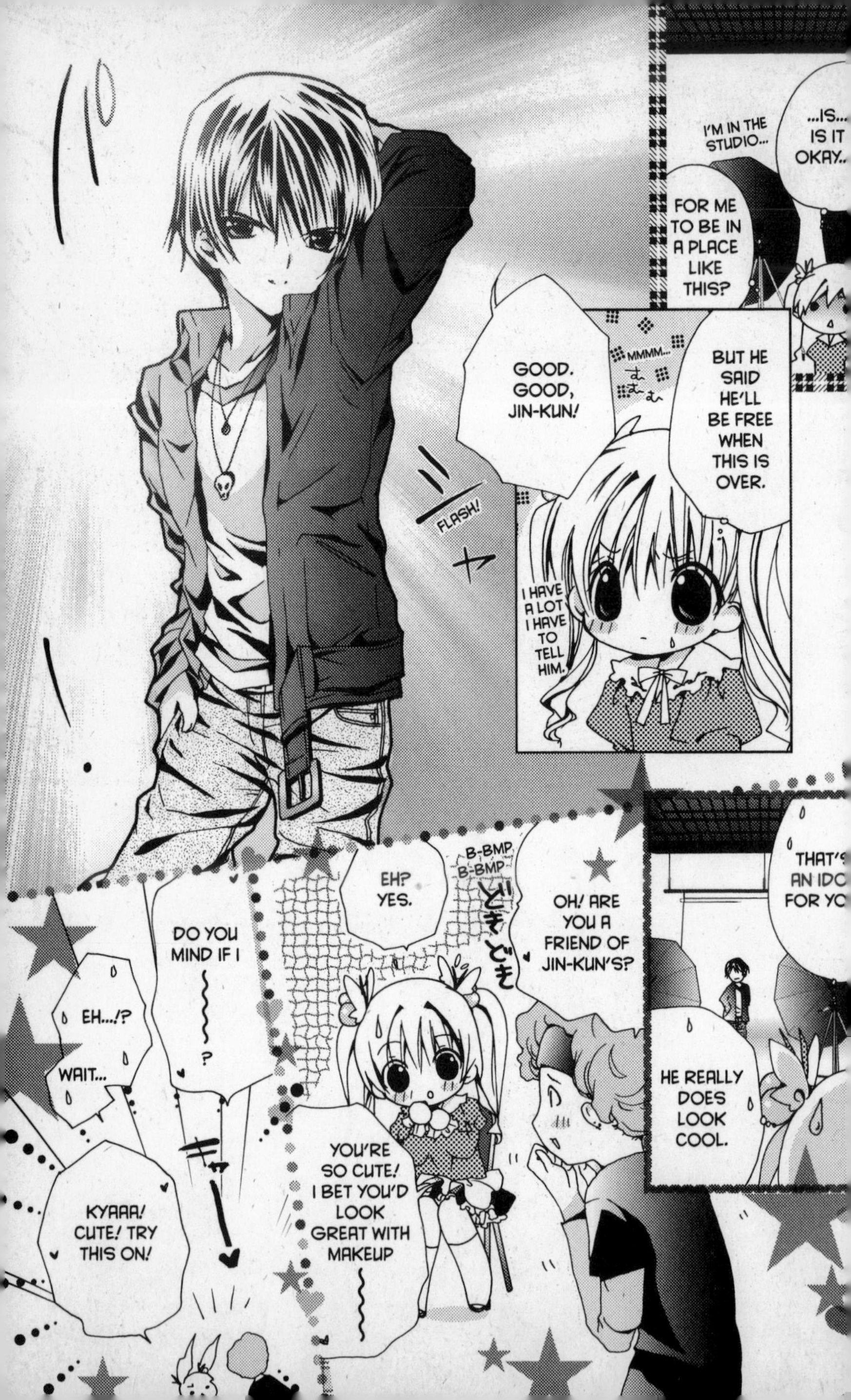

...IS... IS IT OKAY..
I'M IN THE STUDIO...
FOR ME TO BE IN A PLACE LIKE THIS?
BUT HE SAID HE'LL BE FREE WHEN THIS IS OVER.
MMMM...
I HAVE A LOT I HAVE TO TELL HIM.
GOOD. GOOD, JIN-KUN!
FLASH!
THAT'S AN IDO FOR YO
HE REALLY DOES LOOK COOL.
OH! ARE YOU A FRIEND OF JIN-KUN'S?
B-BMP B-BMP
EH? YES.
DO YOU MIND IF I ~~~?
YOU'RE SO CUTE! I BET YOU'D LOOK GREAT WITH MAKEUP
EH...!? WAIT...
KYAAA! CUTE! TRY THIS ON!

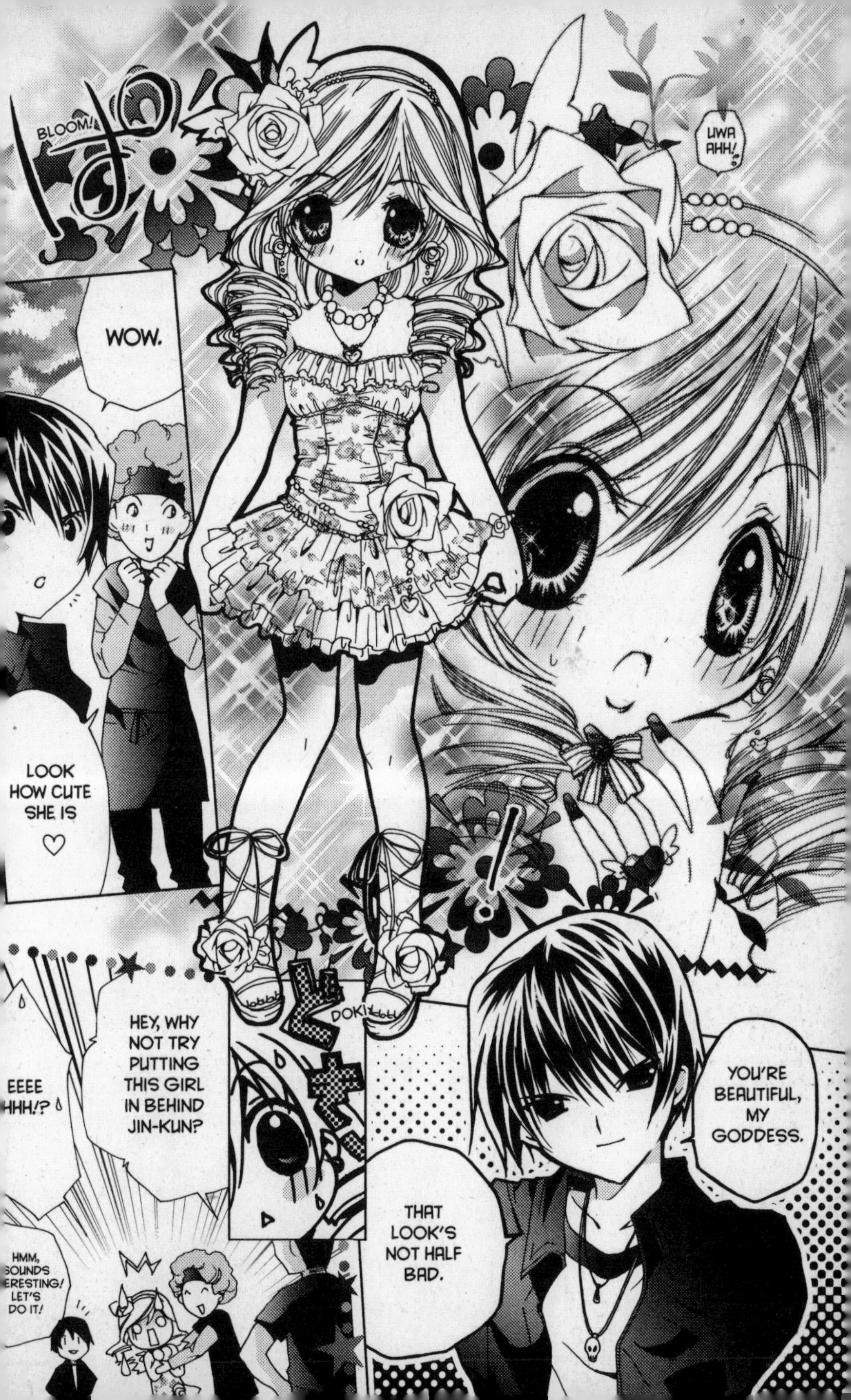
UWA AHH!
BLOOM!
WOW.
LOOK HOW CUTE SHE IS ♡
YOU'RE BEAUTIFUL, MY GODDESS.
THAT LOOK'S NOT HALF BAD.
DOKI
HEY, WHY NOT TRY PUTTING THIS GIRL IN BEHIND JIN-KUN?
EEEE HHH!?
HMM, SOUNDS ERESTING! LET'S DO IT!

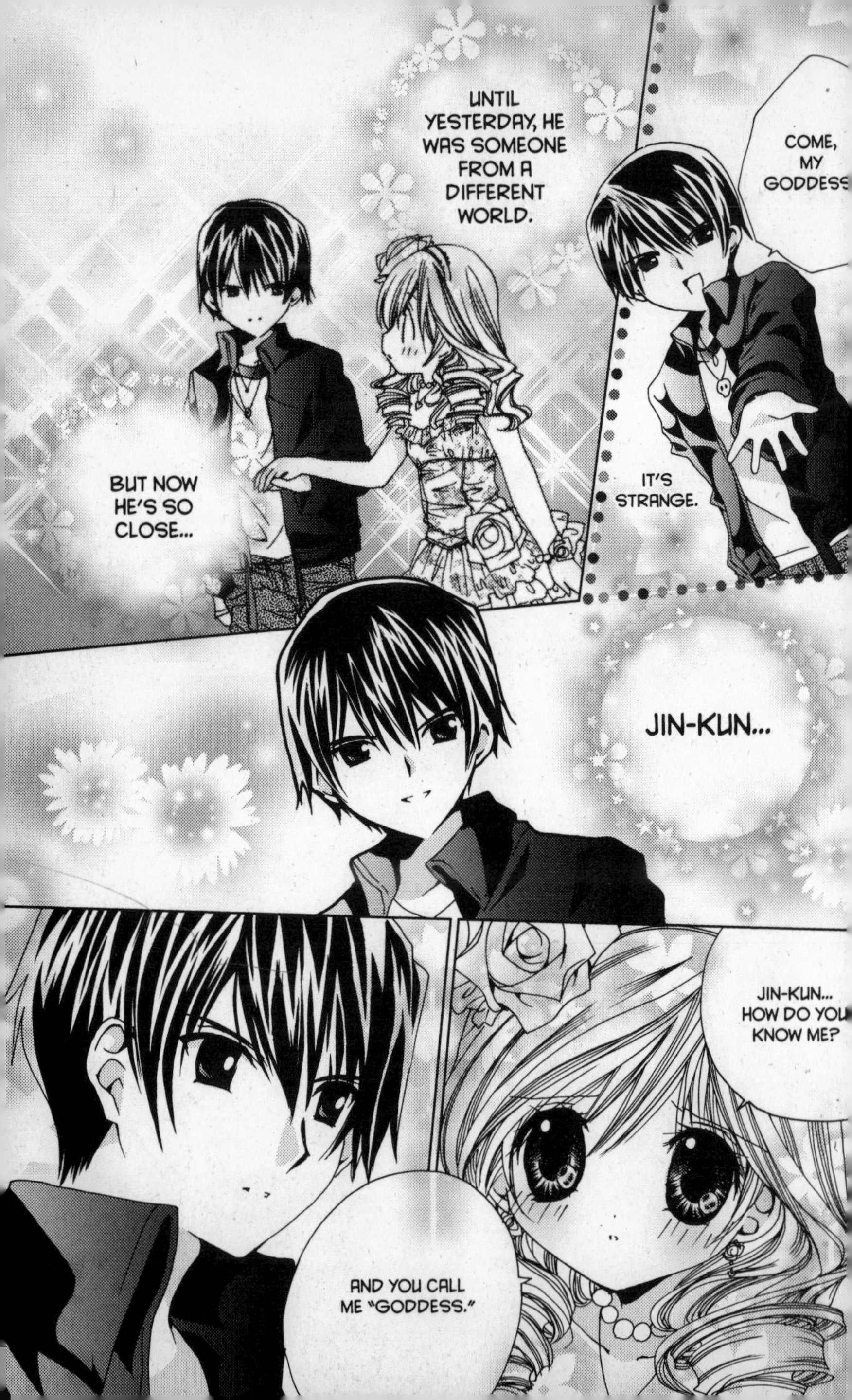
COME, MY GODDESS
IT'S STRANGE.
UNTIL YESTERDAY, HE WAS SOMEONE FROM A DIFFERENT WORLD.
BUT NOW HE'S SO CLOSE...
JIN-KUN...
JIN-KUN... HOW DO YOU KNOW ME?
AND YOU CALL ME "GODDESS."

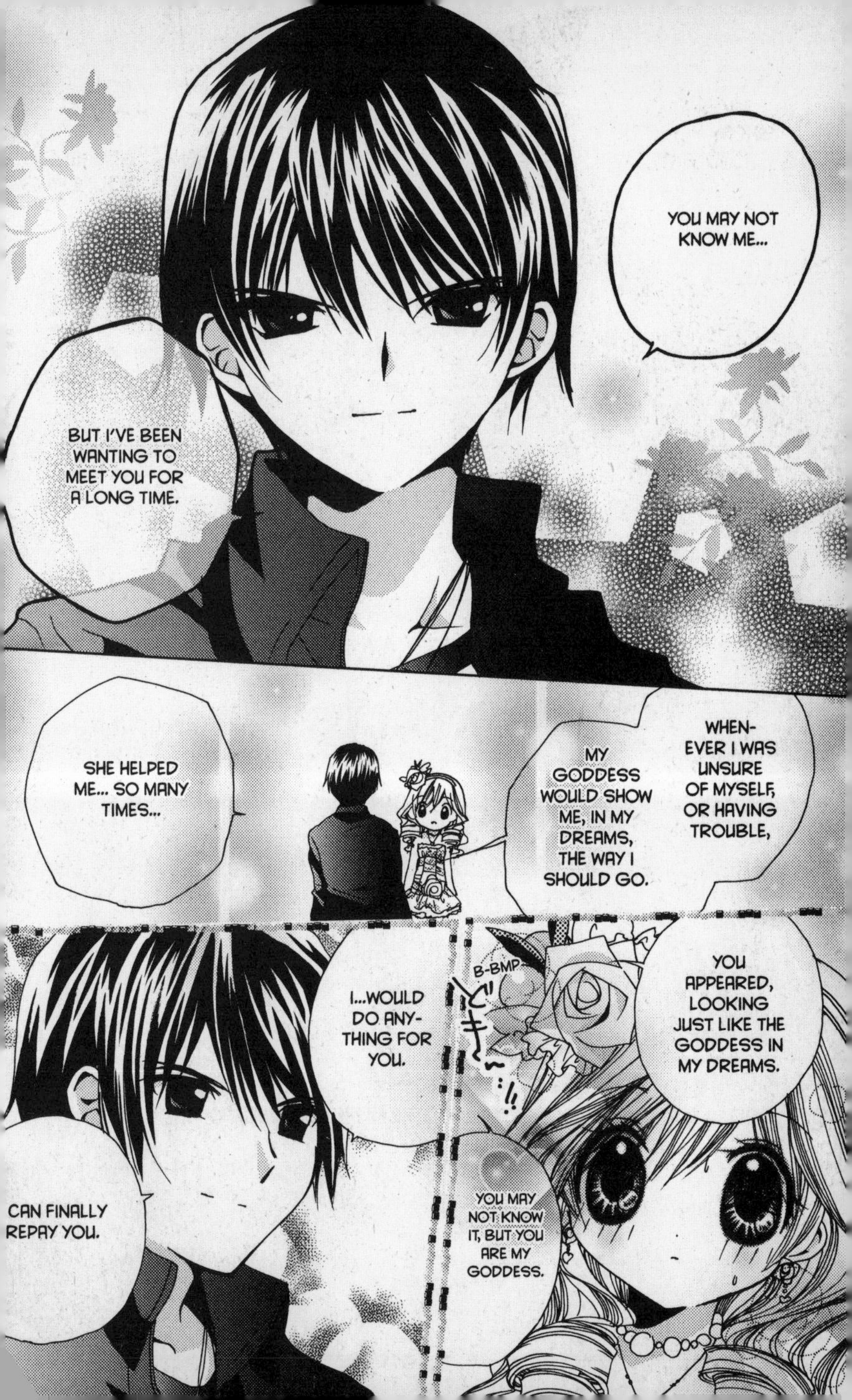
YOU MAY NOT KNOW ME...
BUT I'VE BEEN WANTING TO MEET YOU FOR A LONG TIME.
WHEN-EVER I WAS UNSURE OF MYSELF, OR HAVING TROUBLE,
MY GODDESS WOULD SHOW ME, IN MY DREAMS, THE WAY I SHOULD GO.
SHE HELPED ME... SO MANY TIMES...
YOU APPEARED, LOOKING JUST LIKE THE GODDESS IN MY DREAMS.
B-BMP
YOU MAY NOT KNOW IT, BUT YOU ARE MY GODDESS.
I...WOULD DO ANY-THING FOR YOU.
CAN FINALLY REPAY YOU.

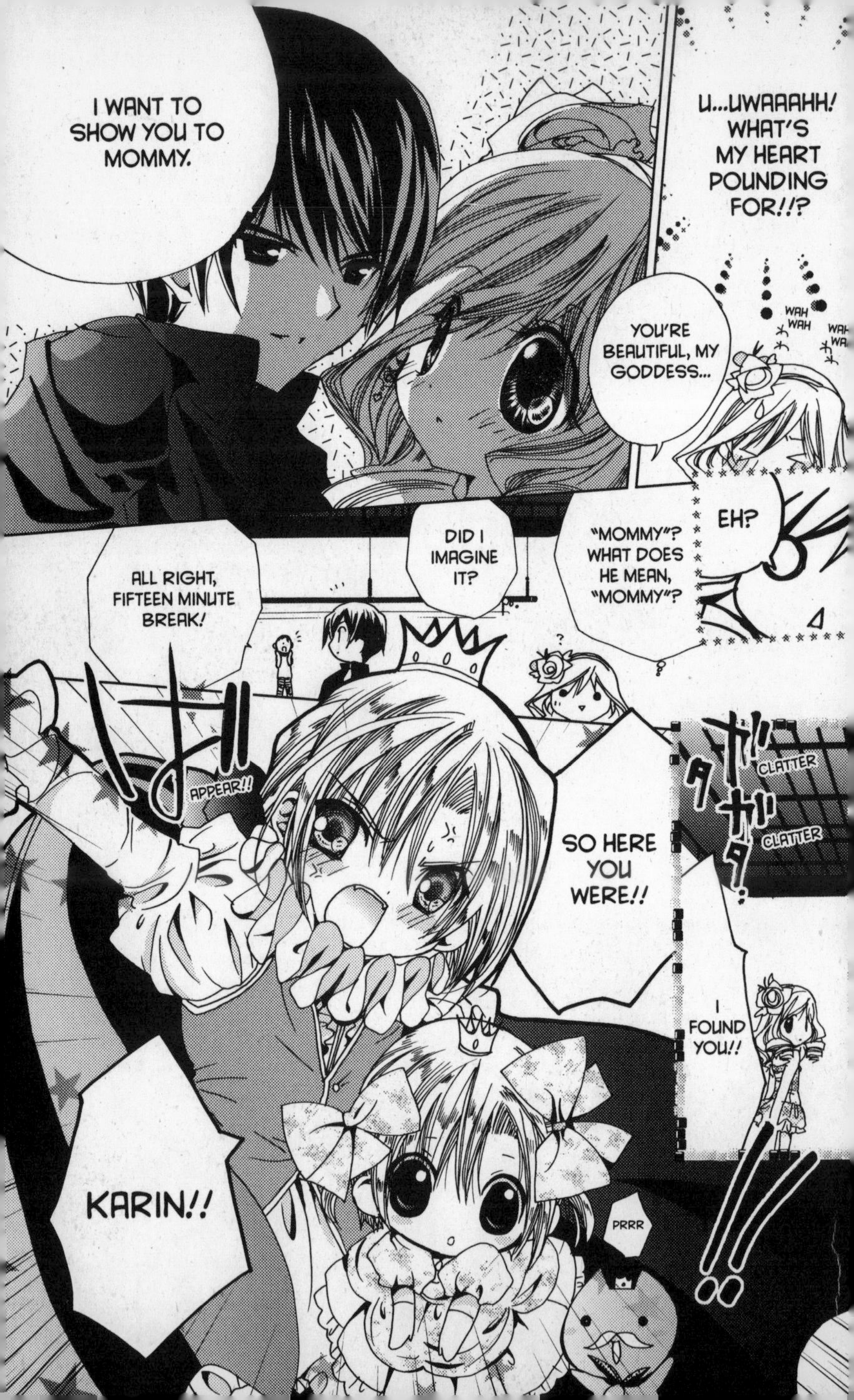
U...UWAAAAH! WHAT'S MY HEART POUNDING FOR!!?
WAH WAH
WAH WAH
YOU'RE BEAUTIFUL, MY GODDESS...
I WANT TO SHOW YOU TO MOMMY.
EH?
"MOMMY"? WHAT DOES HE MEAN, "MOMMY"?
DID I IMAGINE IT?
ALL RIGHT, FIFTEEN MINUTE BREAK!
CLATTER
CLATTER
I FOUND YOU!!
SO HERE YOU WERE!!
APPEAR!!
KARIN!!
PRRR

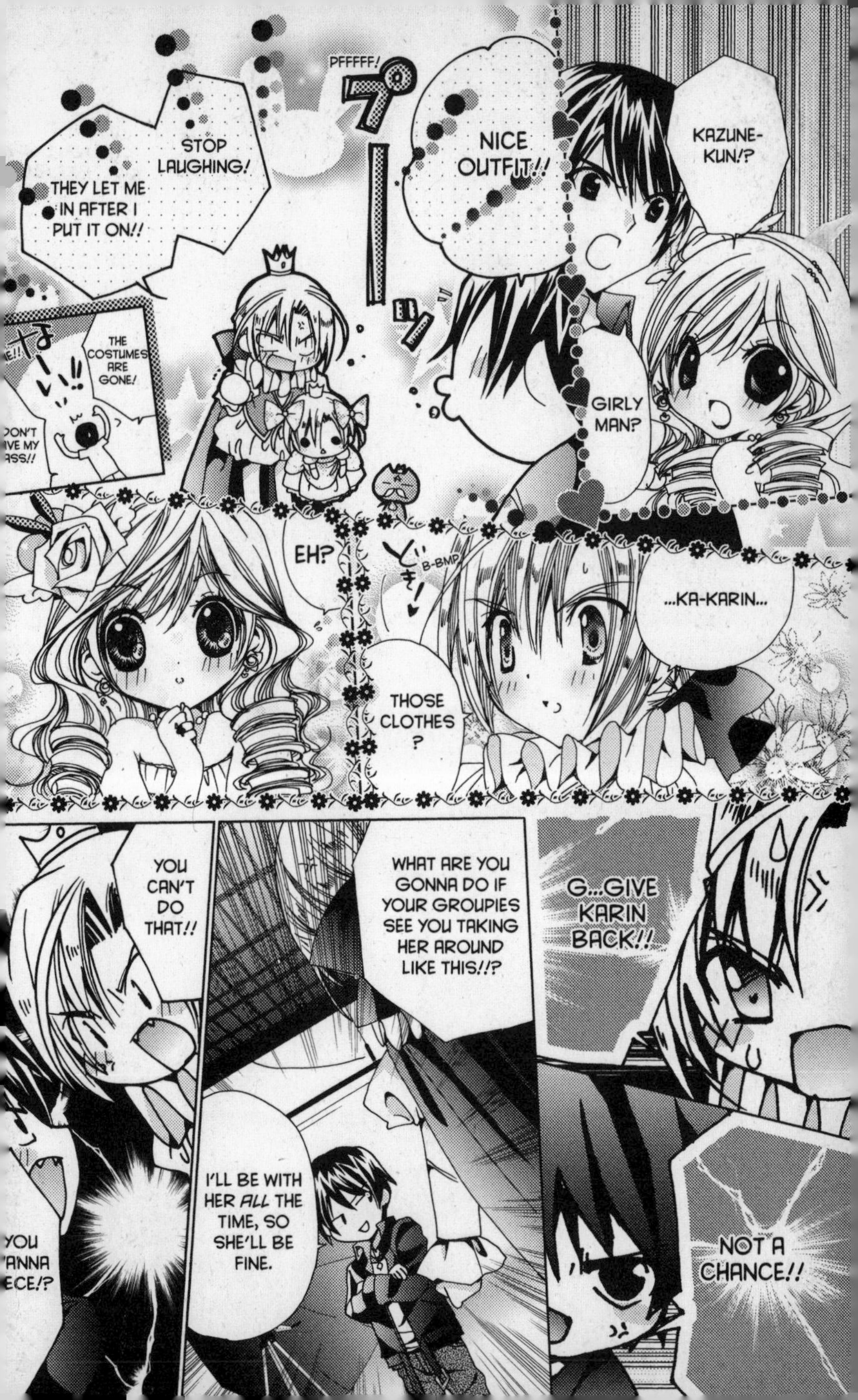
KAZUNE-KUN!?
GIRLY MAN?
PFFFFF!
NICE OUTFIT!!
STOP LAUGHING!
THEY LET ME IN AFTER I PUT IT ON!!
THE COSTUMES ARE GONE!
...KA-KARIN...
B-BMP
THOSE CLOTHES ?
EH?
G...GIVE KARIN BACK!!
NOT A CHANCE!!
WHAT ARE YOU GONNA DO IF YOUR GROUPIES SEE YOU TAKING HER AROUND LIKE THIS!!?
I'LL BE WITH HER *ALL* THE TIME, SO SHE'LL BE FINE.
YOU CAN'T DO THAT!!

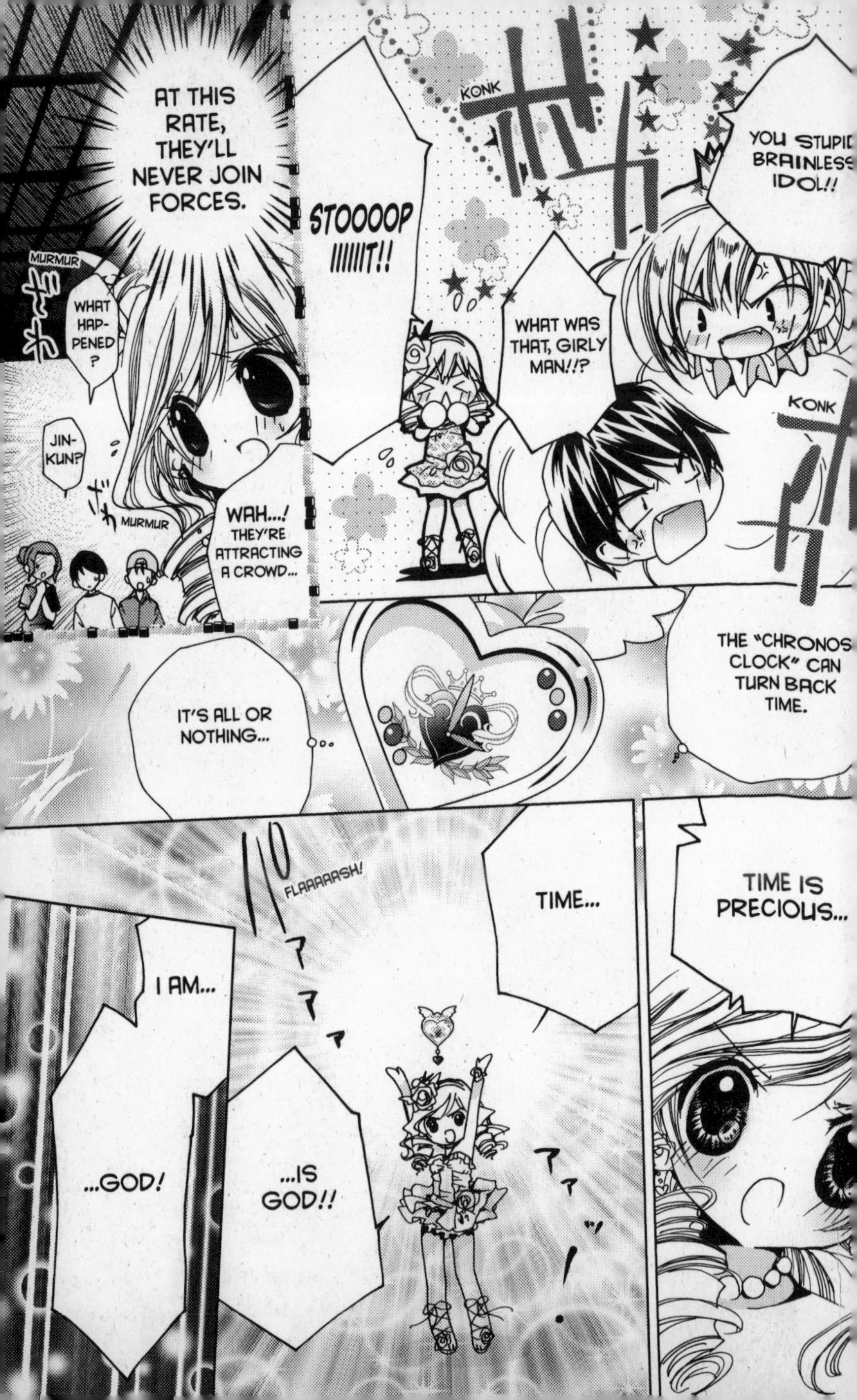
KONK
YOU STUPID BRAINLESS IDOL!!
WHAT WAS THAT, GIRLY MAN!!?
KONK
STOOOOP IIIIIIT!!
AT THIS RATE, THEY'LL NEVER JOIN FORCES.
MURMUR
WHAT HAP-PENED?
JIN-KUN?
MURMUR
WAH...! THEY'RE ATTRACTING A CROWD...
THE "CHRONOS CLOCK" CAN TURN BACK TIME.
IT'S ALL OR NOTHING...
TIME IS PRECIOUS...
TIME...
FLAAAAASH!
...IS GOD!!
I AM...
...GOD!

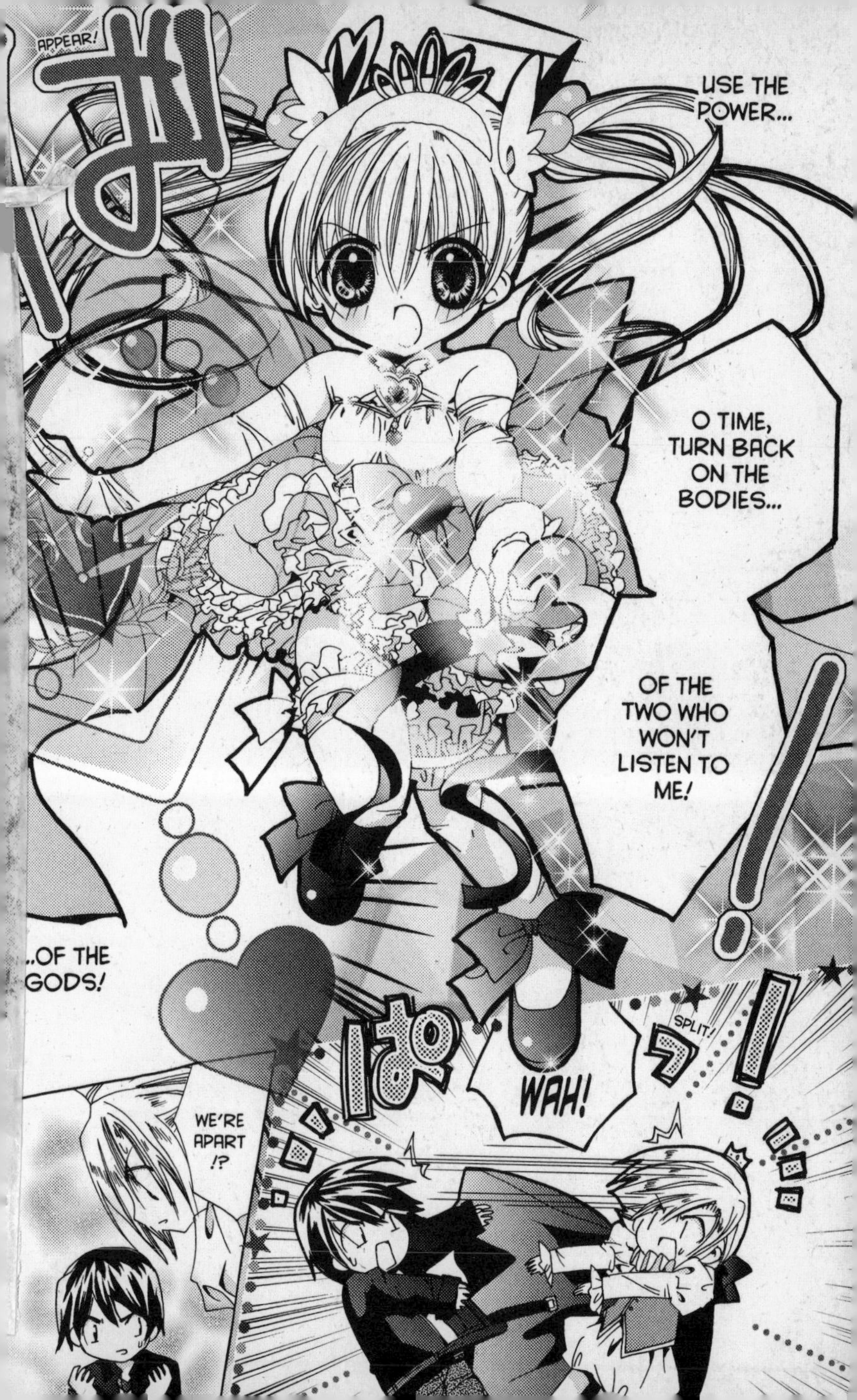
APPEAR!
USE THE POWER...
O TIME, TURN BACK ON THE BODIES...
OF THE TWO WHO WON'T LISTEN TO ME!
..OF THE GODS!
SPLIT!
WAH!
WE'RE APART !?

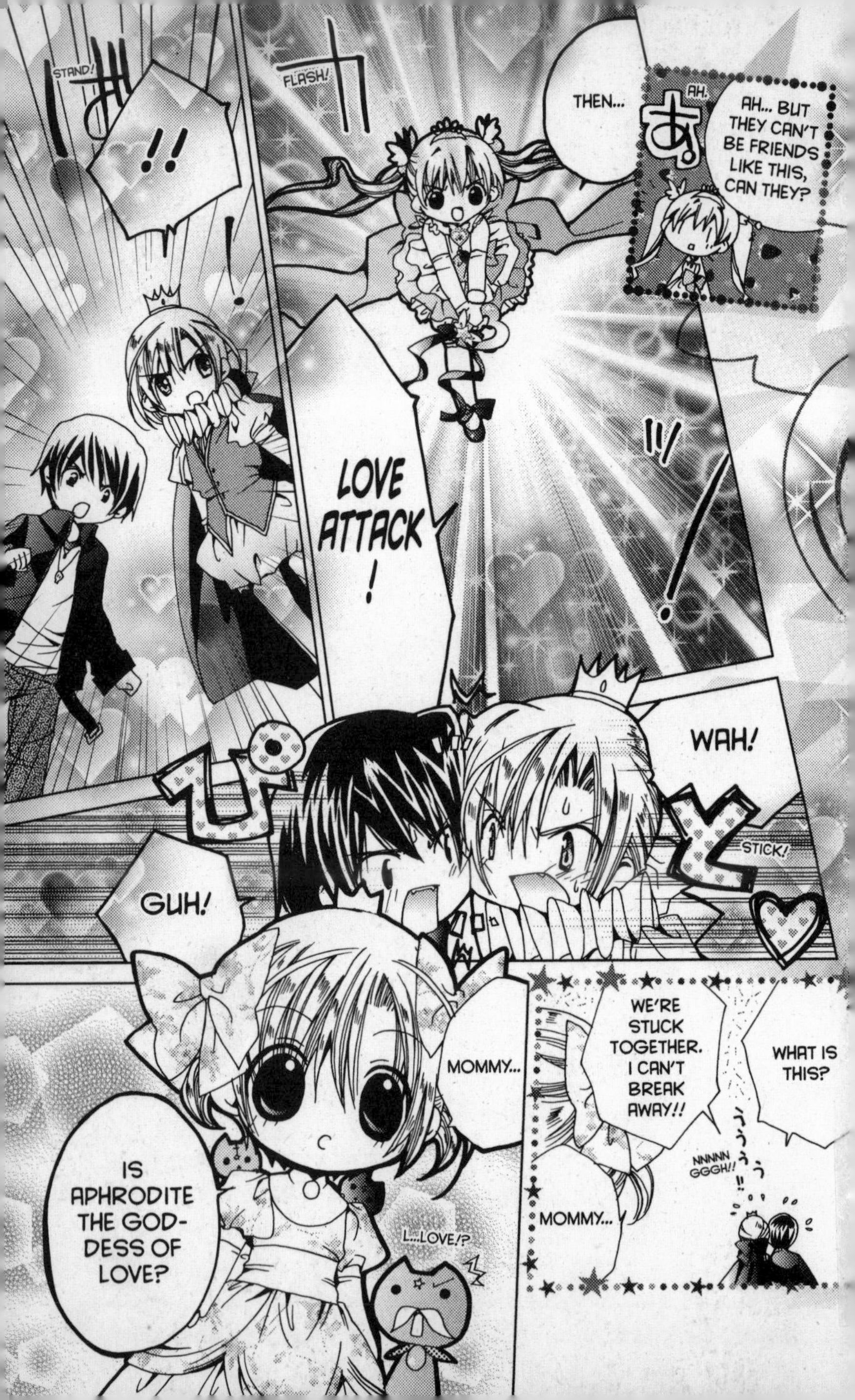
THEN...
AH.
AH... BUT THEY CAN'T BE FRIENDS LIKE THIS, CAN THEY?
FLASH!
LOVE ATTACK!
!!
STAND!
!!
WAH!
STICK!
GUH!
WHAT IS THIS?
WE'RE STUCK TOGETHER. I CAN'T BREAK AWAY!!
NNNNN GGGH!!
MOMMY...
MOMMY...
IS APHRODITE THE GOD-DESS OF LOVE?
L...LOVE!?

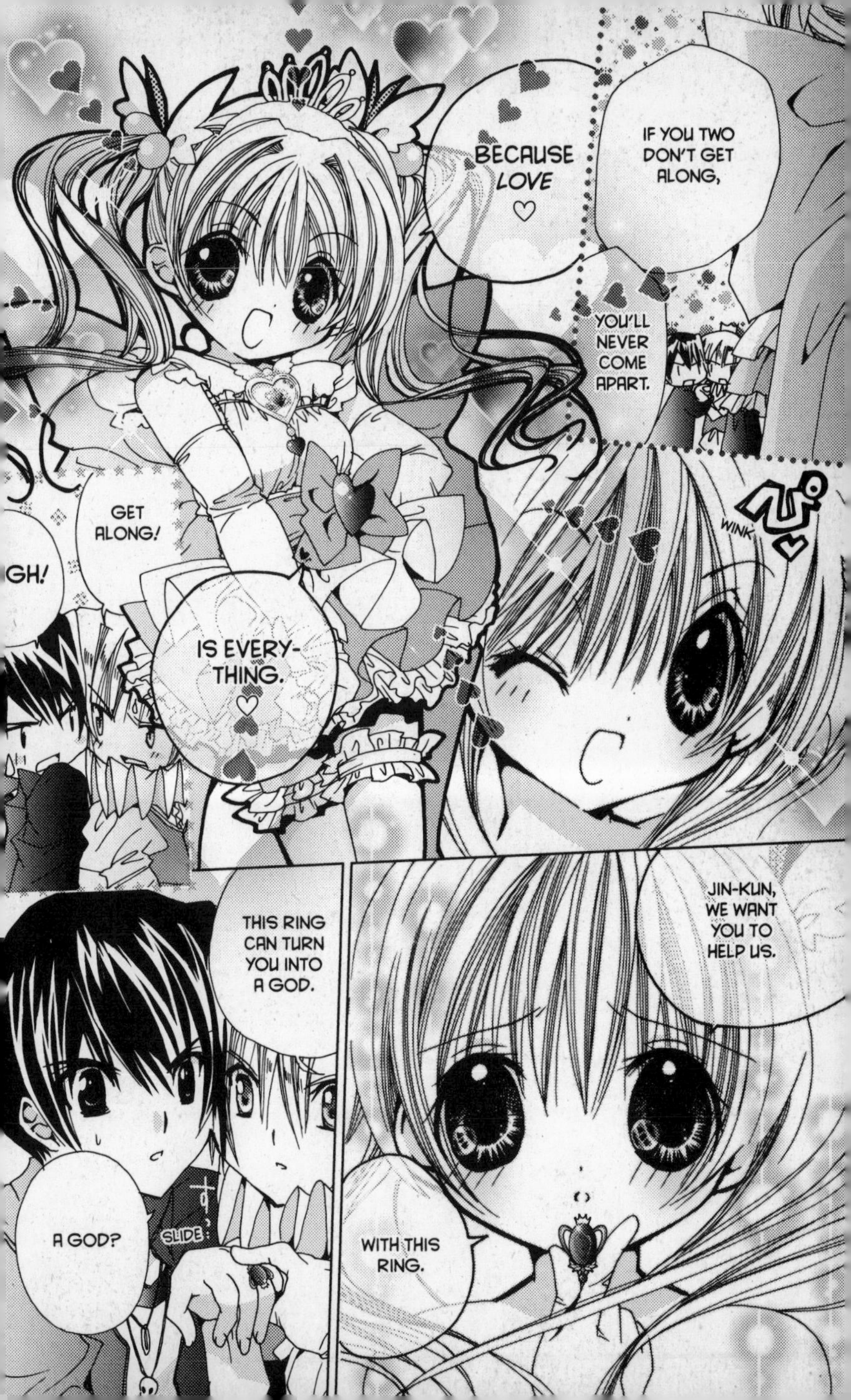
IF YOU TWO DON'T GET ALONG,
YOU'LL NEVER COME APART.
WINK
BECAUSE LOVE ♡
IS EVERY-THING. ♡
GET ALONG!
GH!
JIN-KUN, WE WANT YOU TO HELP US.
WITH THIS RING.
THIS RING CAN TURN YOU INTO A GOD.
SLIDE
A GOD?

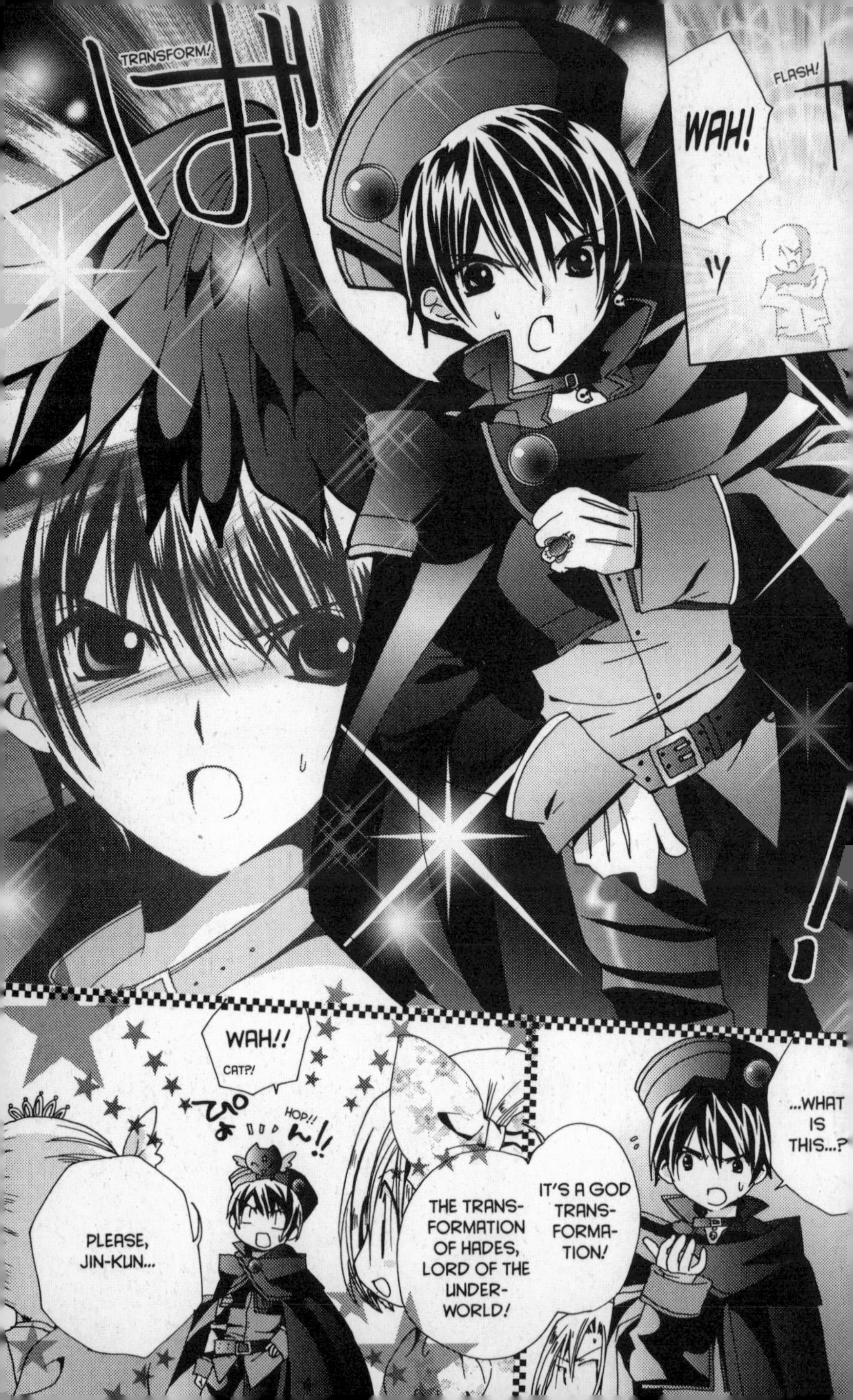

FLASH!
WAH!
TRANSFORM!
...WHAT IS THIS...?
IT'S A GOD TRANS-FORMA-TION!
THE TRANS-FORMATION OF HADES, LORD OF THE UNDER-WORLD!
WAH!! CAT?!
HOP!!
PLEASE, JIN-KUN...

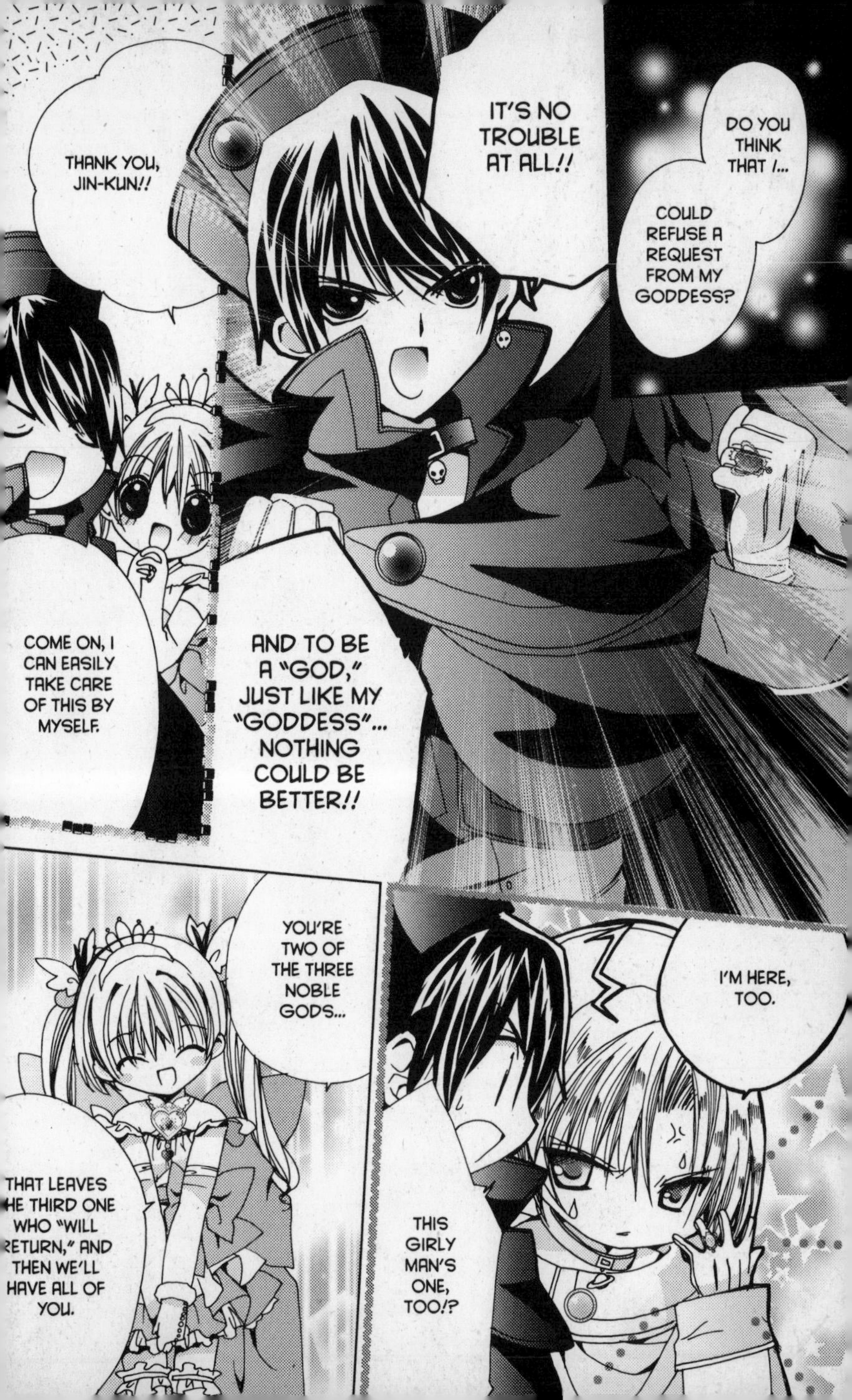
DO YOU THINK THAT I...
COULD REFUSE A REQUEST FROM MY GODDESS?
IT'S NO TROUBLE AT ALL!!
AND TO BE A "GOD," JUST LIKE MY "GODDESS"... NOTHING COULD BE BETTER!!
THANK YOU, JIN-KUN!!
COME ON, I CAN EASILY TAKE CARE OF THIS BY MYSELF.
I'M HERE, TOO.
THIS GIRLY MAN'S ONE, TOO!?
YOU'RE TWO OF THE THREE NOBLE GODS...
THAT LEAVES HE THIRD ONE WHO "WILL ETURN," AND THEN WE'LL HAVE ALL OF YOU.

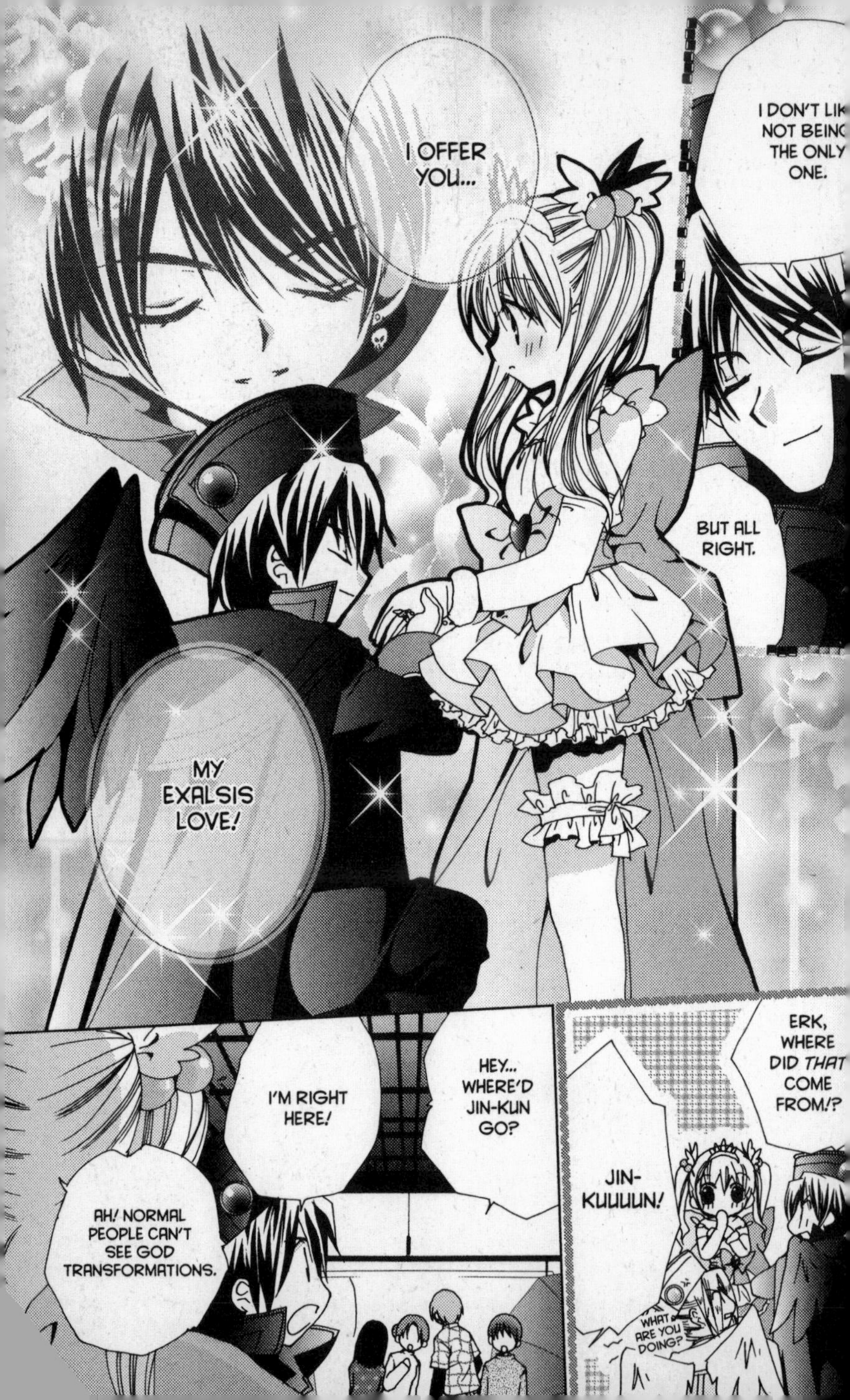

I DON'T LIK NOT BEING THE ONLY ONE.
BUT ALL RIGHT.
I OFFER YOU...
MY EXALSIS LOVE!
ERK, WHERE DID *THAT* COME FROM!?
JIN-KUUUUN!
WHAT ARE YOU DOING?
HEY... WHERE'D JIN-KUN GO?
I'M RIGHT HERE!
AH! NORMAL PEOPLE CAN'T SEE GOD TRANSFORMATIONS.

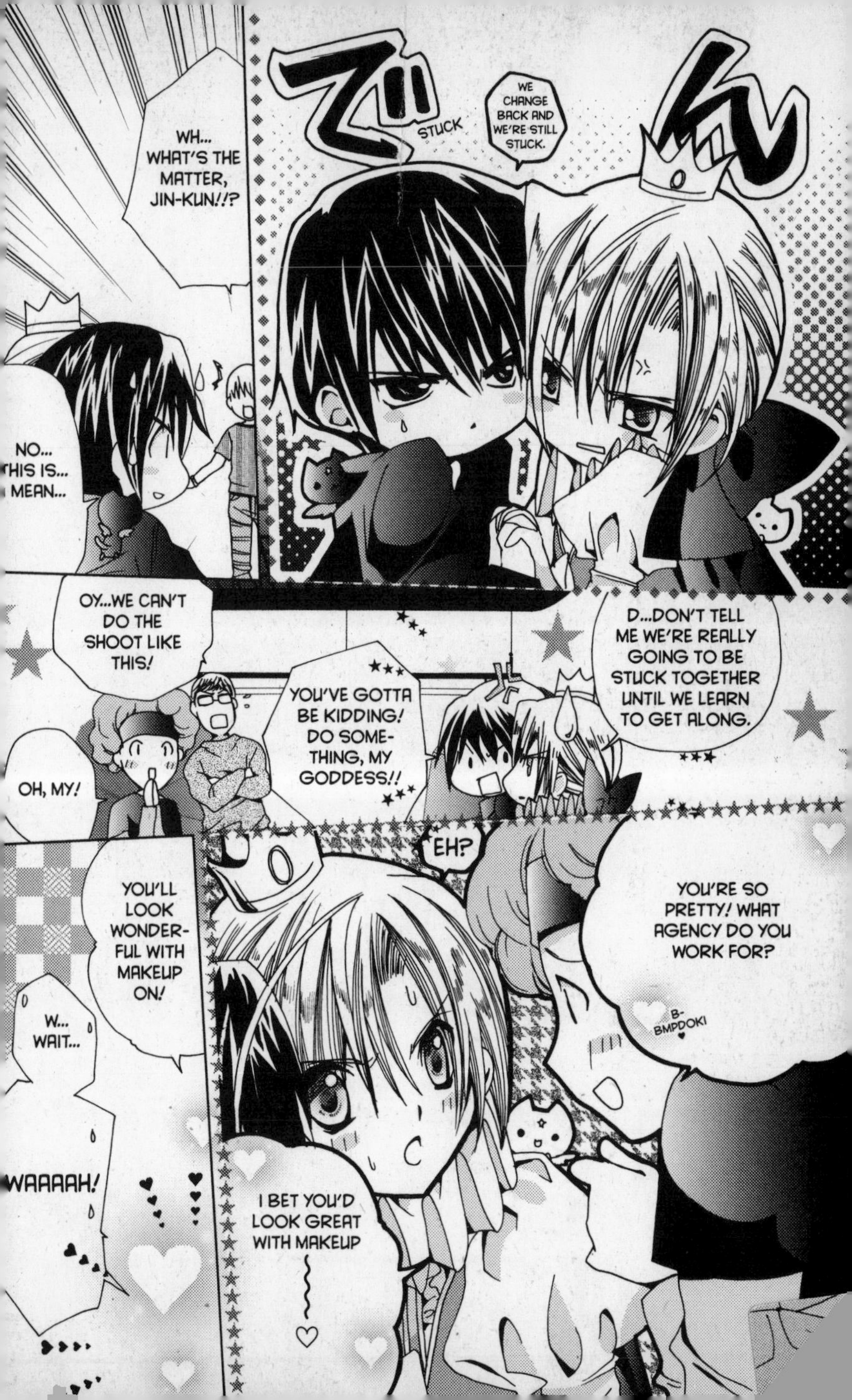
STUCK
WE CHANGE BACK AND WE'RE STILL STUCK.
WH... WHAT'S THE MATTER, JIN-KUN!!?
NO... THIS IS... MEAN...
D...DON'T TELL ME WE'RE REALLY GOING TO BE STUCK TOGETHER UNTIL WE LEARN TO GET ALONG.
YOU'VE GOTTA BE KIDDING! DO SOME-THING, MY GODDESS!!
OY...WE CAN'T DO THE SHOOT LIKE THIS!
OH, MY!
YOU'RE SO PRETTY! WHAT AGENCY DO YOU WORK FOR?
B-BMPDOKI
EH?
I BET YOU'D LOOK GREAT WITH MAKEUP
YOU'LL LOOK WONDER-FUL WITH MAKEUP ON!
W... WAIT...
WAAAAH!

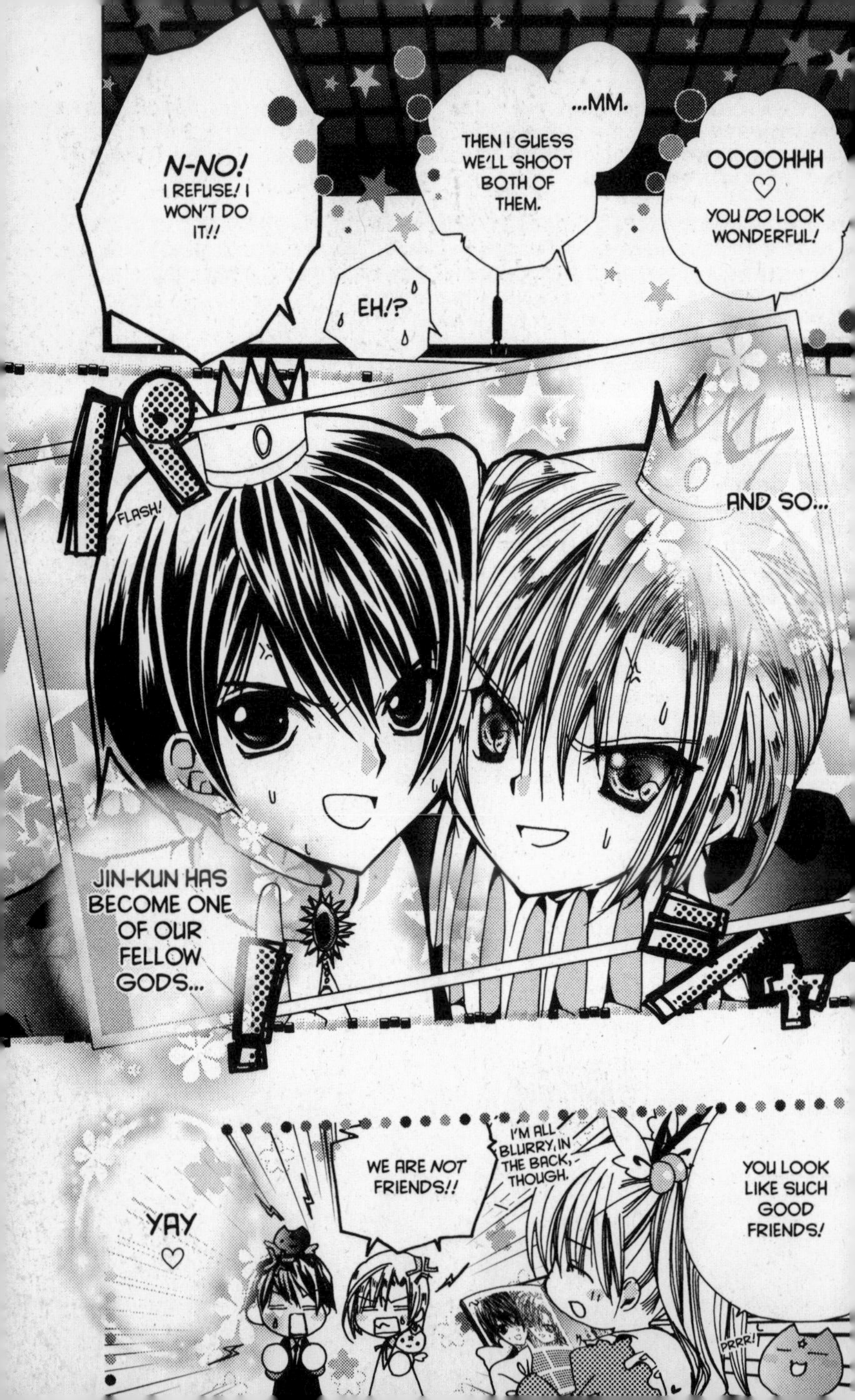
OOOOHHH ♡ YOU DO LOOK WONDERFUL!
...MM.
THEN I GUESS WE'LL SHOOT BOTH OF THEM.
EH!?
N-NO! I REFUSE! I WON'T DO IT!!
AND SO...
FLASH!
JIN-KUN HAS BECOME ONE OF OUR FELLOW GODS...
YOU LOOK LIKE SUCH GOOD FRIENDS!
PRRR!
I'M ALL BLURRY IN THE BACK, THOUGH.
WE ARE NOT FRIENDS!!
YAY ♡

LLO! TO THOSE I HAVEN'T MET BEFORE, NICE TO MEET YOU!! I'M KOGE-DONBO. THANK YOU VERY JCH FOR PICKING UP *KAMICHAMA KARIN CHU.*

TER SEVEN VOLUMES OF *KAMICHAMA KARIN,* THE NEW SERIES, *KAMICHAMA KARIN CHU,* HAS FI-ALLY BEGUN! WELL-KNOWN CHARACTERS LIKE KARIN-CHAN, KAZUNE-KUN, AND MICCHI WILL APPEAR GAIN! AND WITH THE NEW CHARACTERS JIN-KUN AND SUZUNE-KUN, I THINK WE'LL HAVE EVEN MORE IN AND EXCITEMENT THAN BEFORE!

HEN STARTING THE NEW SERIES, I WAS PRETTY WORRIED ABOUT HOW MUCH I SHOULD TAKE FROM E FIRST SERIES AND HOW I SHOULD ADD NEW ELEMENTS...THINKING ABOUT THINGS LIKE HOW JCH I SHOULD MIX SERIOUSNESS AND COMEDY, AND HOW I COULD MAKE IT ENJOYABLE FOR PEO-E WHO READ THE OLD SERIES AS WELL AS PEOPLE WHO OULD START WITH THE NEW SERIES. IT WAS A WHOLE N MONTHS BETWEEN THE LAST CHAPTER OF THE OLD RIES AND THE FIRST CHAPTER OF THE NEW SERIES, D I SPENT ALMOST THAT WHOLE TIME FINE-TUNING E BALANCE. BUT I HAVE CONFIDENCE THAT FOR ALL MY ORK, I'VE MADE SOMETHING YOU CAN ALL ENJOY!

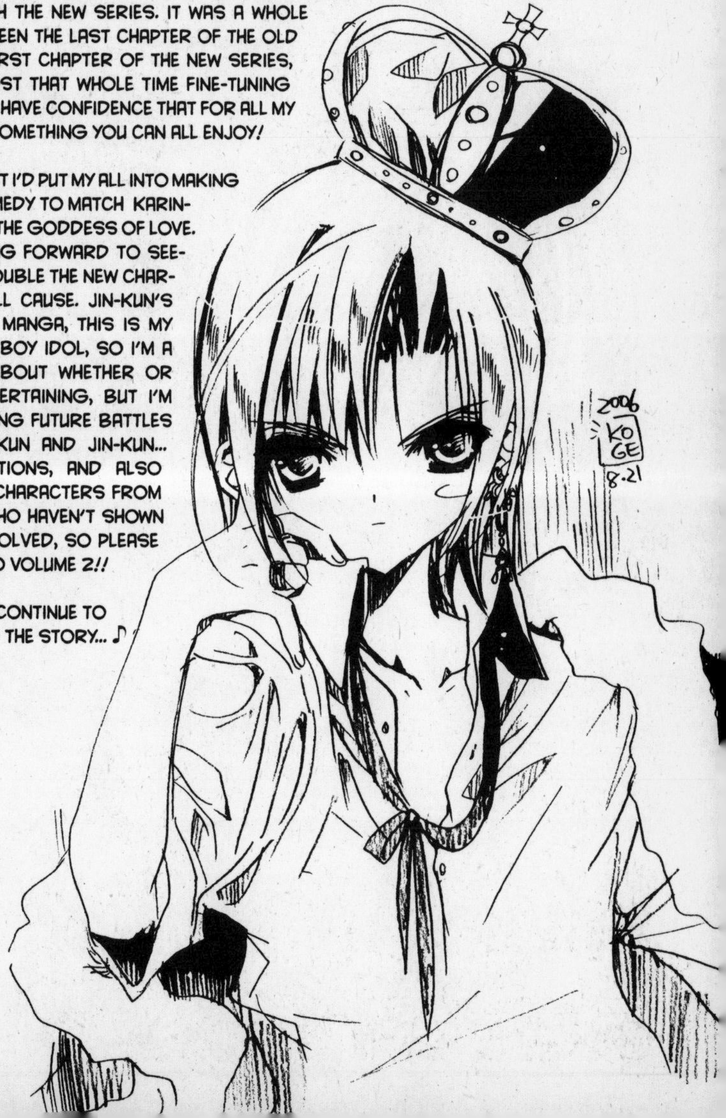
2006
KOGE
8.21

IIS TIME, I THOUGHT I'D PUT MY ALL INTO MAKING A ROMANTIC COMEDY TO MATCH KARIN-IAN'S NEW GOD, THE GODDESS OF LOVE. TOO, AM LOOKING FORWARD TO SEE-G HOW MUCH TROUBLE THE NEW CHAR-TER JIN-KUN WILL CAUSE. JIN-KUN'S I *IDOL!!* EVEN IN MANGA, THIS IS MY RST TIME WITH A BOY IDOL, SO I'M A TTLE NERVOUS ABOUT WHETHER OR OT HE'LL BE ENTERTAINING, BUT I'M IRRENTLY PLANNING FUTURE BATTLES TWEEN KAZUNE-KUN AND JIN-KUN... ID MICCHI'S ACTIONS, AND ALSO IINGS LIKE HOW CHARACTERS FROM E OLD SERIES WHO HAVEN'T SHOWN ' YET WILL BE INVOLVED, SO PLEASE OOK FORWARD TO VOLUME 2!!

OW THEN, PLEASE CONTINUE TO JOY THE REST OF THE STORY... ♪

IGUST 2006
OGE-DONBO

ECIAL THANKS!
E-SAN.
ANK YOU...
OW BEFORE YOU...

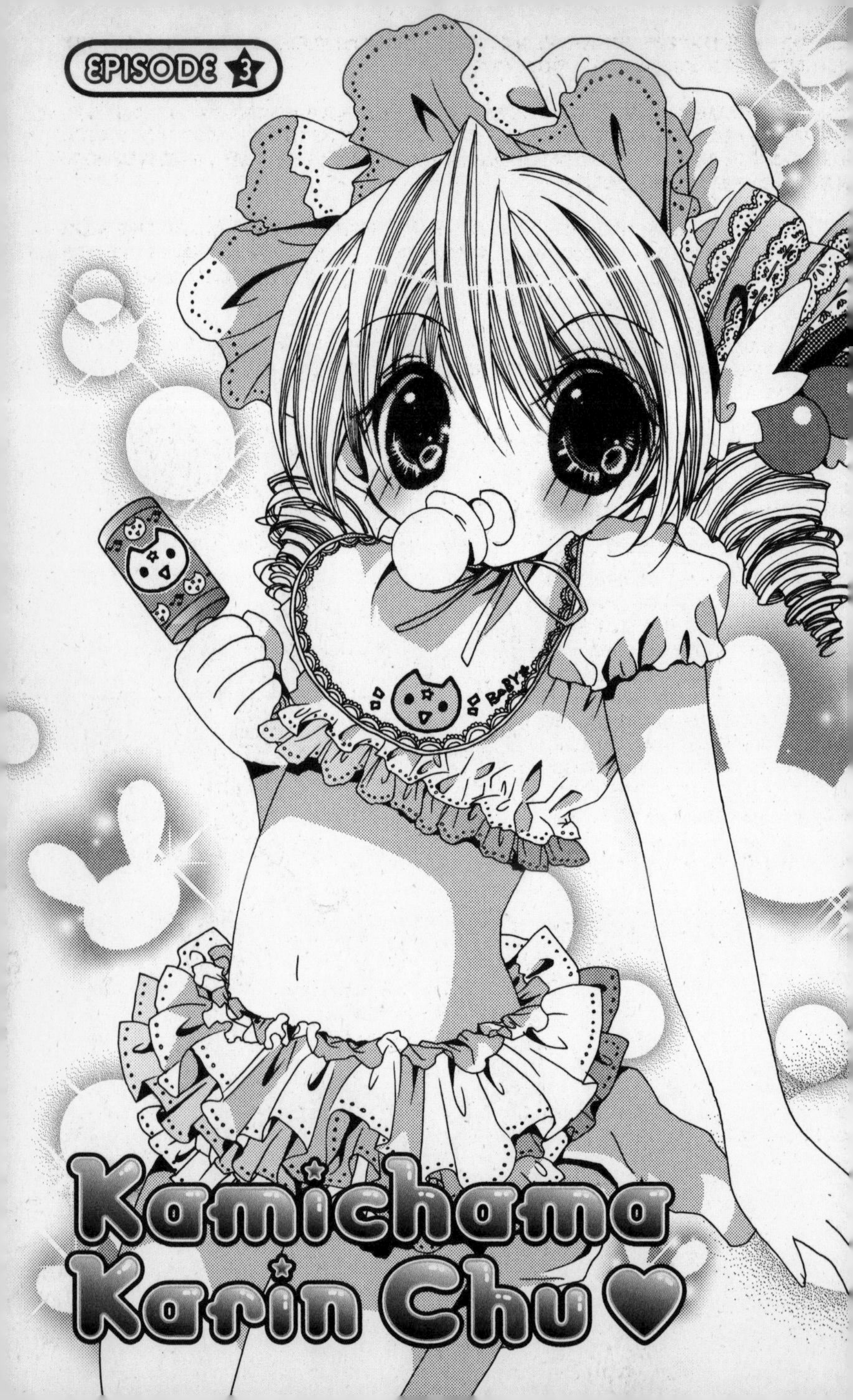
EPISODE 3
BABY
Kamichama Karin Chu♥

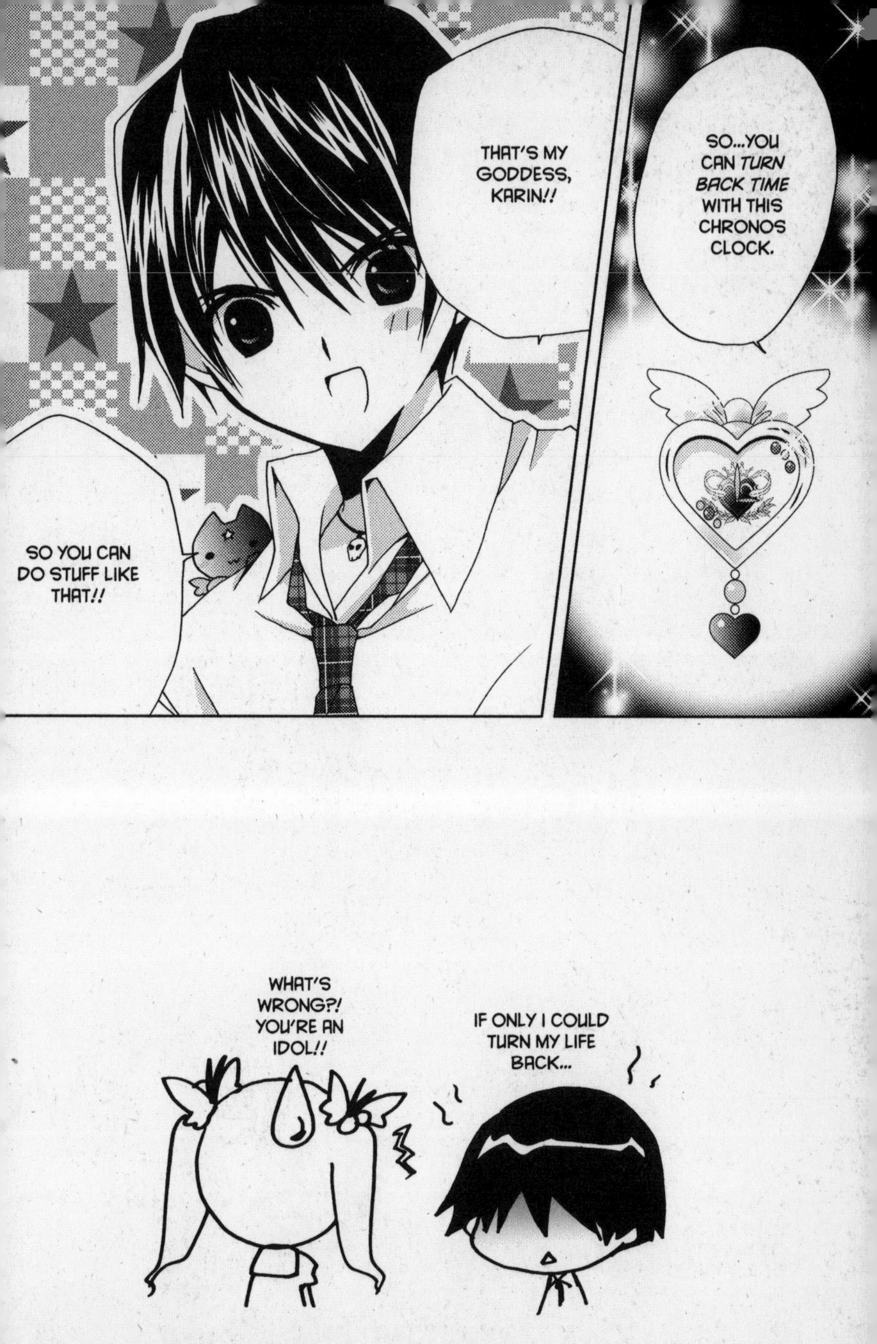
SO...YOU CAN *TURN BACK TIME* WITH THIS CHRONOS CLOCK.
THAT'S MY GODDESS, KARIN!!
SO YOU CAN DO STUFF LIKE THAT!!
IF ONLY I COULD TURN MY LIFE BACK...
WHAT'S WRONG?! YOU'RE AN IDOL!!

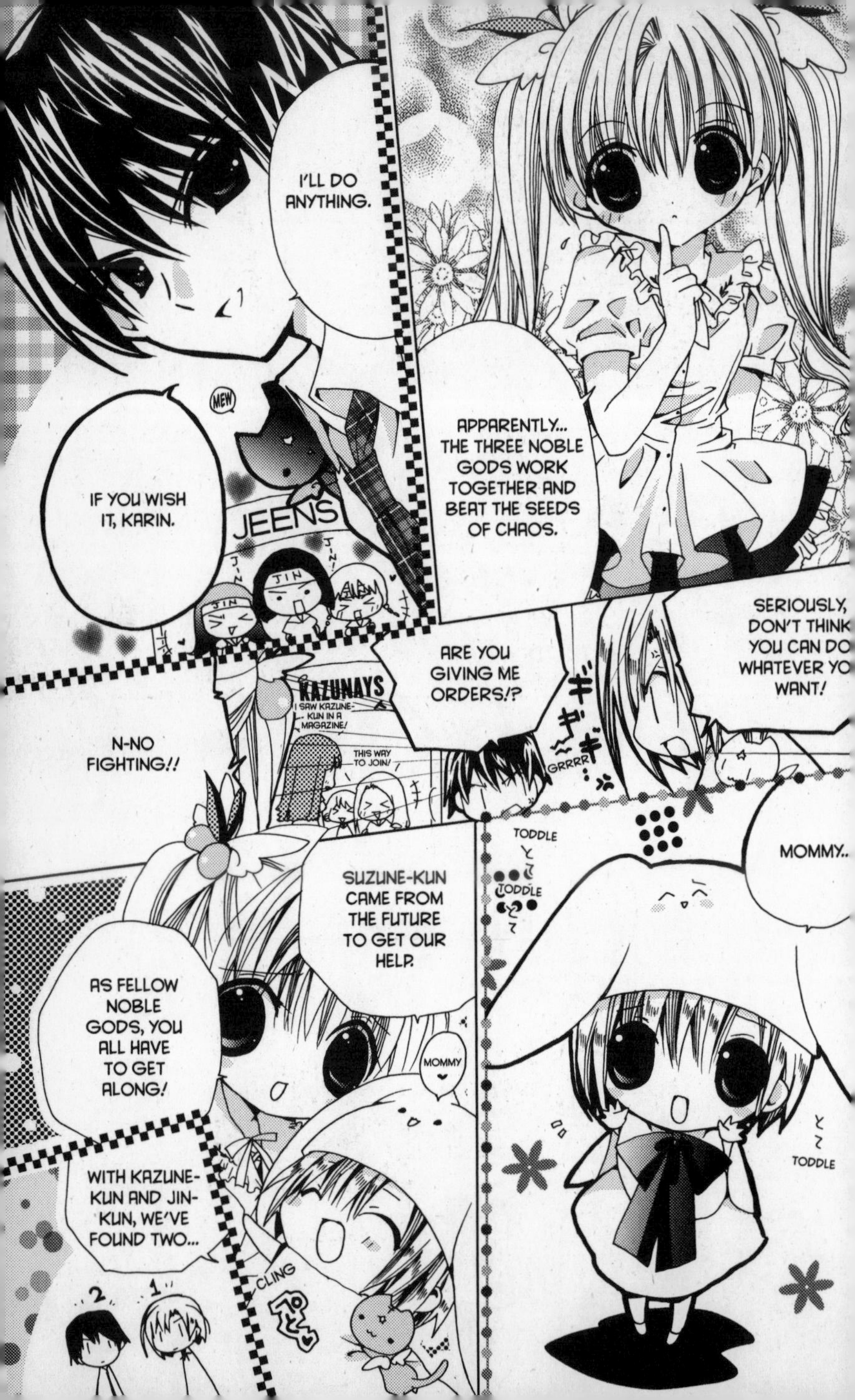
APPARENTLY... THE THREE NOBLE GODS WORK TOGETHER AND BEAT THE SEEDS OF CHAOS.
I'LL DO ANYTHING.
MEW
IF YOU WISH IT, KARIN.
JEENS
JIN
J-I-N!
SERIOUSLY, DON'T THINK YOU CAN DO WHATEVER YO WANT!
ARE YOU GIVING ME ORDERS!?
GRRRR
N-NO FIGHTING!!
KAZUNAYS
I SAW KAZUNE-KUN IN A MAGAZINE!
THIS WAY TO JOIN!
TODDLE
TODDLE
MOMMY..
TODDLE
SUZUNE-KUN CAME FROM THE FUTURE TO GET OUR HELP.
AS FELLOW NOBLE GODS, YOU ALL HAVE TO GET ALONG!
MOMMY
WITH KAZUNE-KUN AND JIN-KUN, WE'VE FOUND TWO...
CLING
2
1

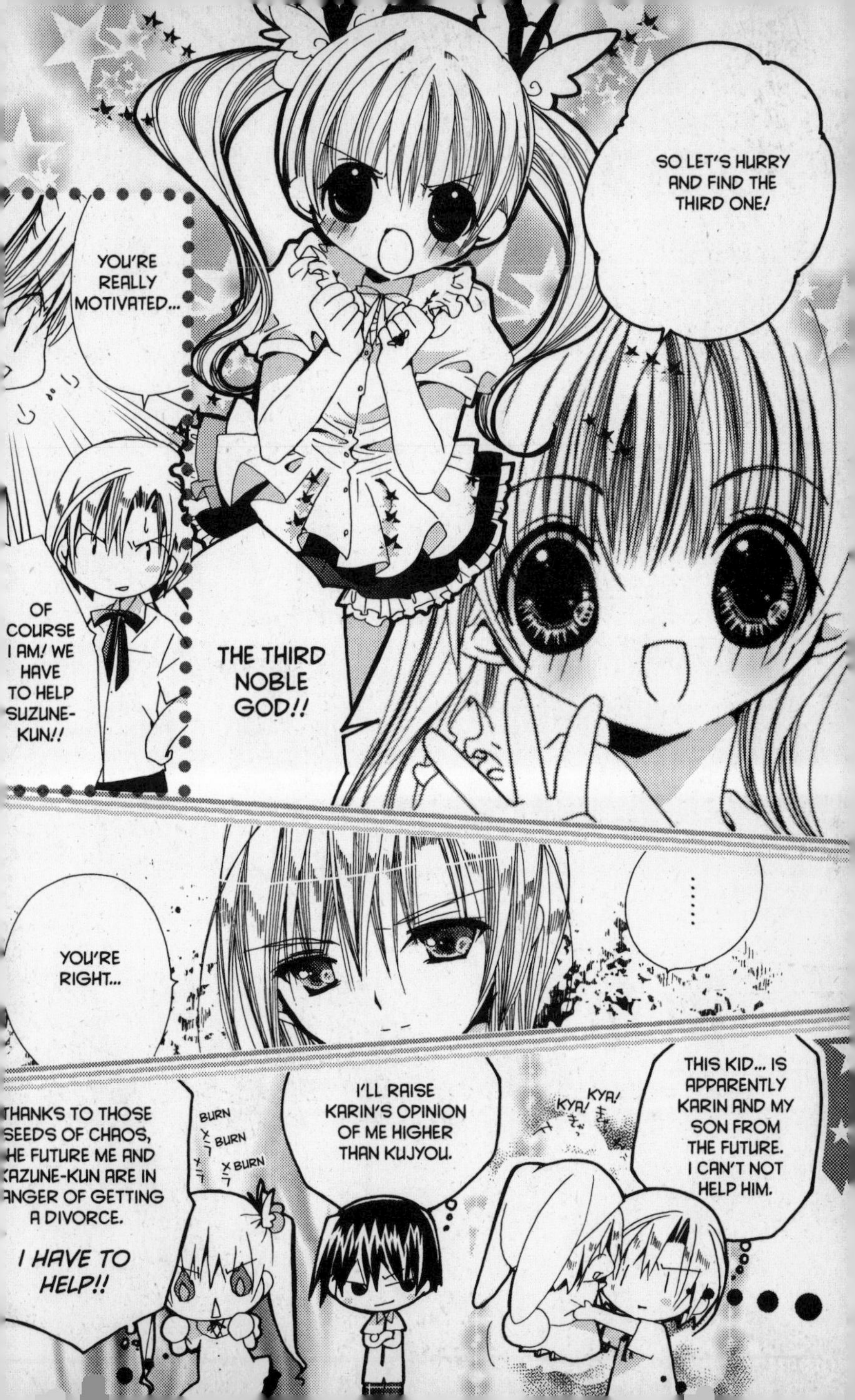
SO LET'S HURRY AND FIND THE THIRD ONE!
THE THIRD NOBLE GOD!!
YOU'RE REALLY MOTIVATED...
OF COURSE I AM! WE HAVE TO HELP SUZUNE-KUN!!
......
YOU'RE RIGHT...
THIS KID... IS APPARENTLY KARIN AND MY SON FROM THE FUTURE. I CAN'T NOT HELP HIM.
KYA! KYA!
I'LL RAISE KARIN'S OPINION OF ME HIGHER THAN KUJYOU.
BURN BURN BURN
THANKS TO THOSE SEEDS OF CHAOS, HE FUTURE ME AND KAZUNE-KUN ARE IN ANGER OF GETTING A DIVORCE.
I HAVE TO HELP!!

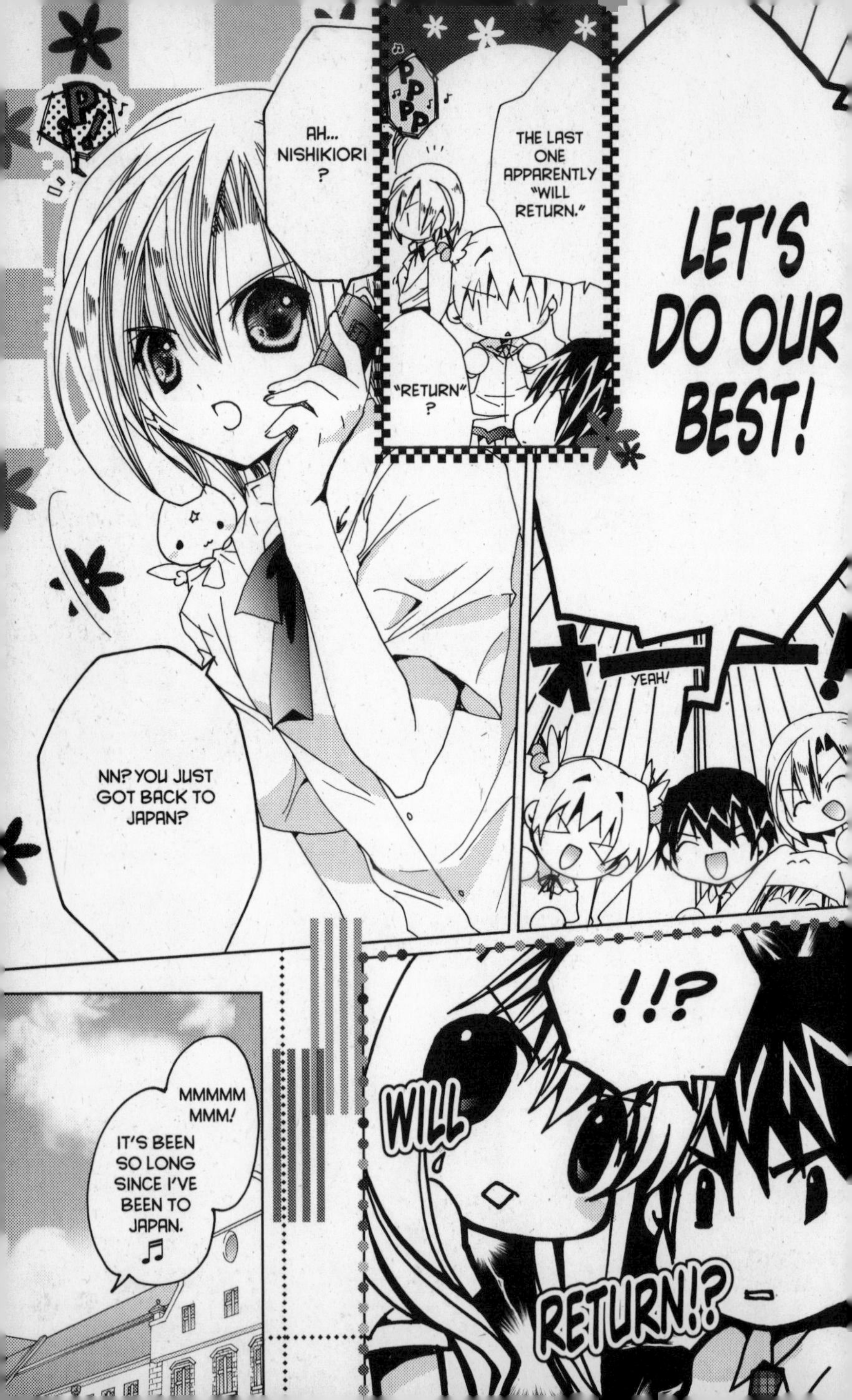
LET'S DO OUR BEST!
YEAH!
THE LAST ONE APPARENTLY "WILL RETURN."
PPPP
"RETURN" ?
PI!
AH... NISHIKIORI ?
NN? YOU JUST GOT BACK TO JAPAN?
!!?
WILL RETURN!?
MMMMM MMM! IT'S BEEN SO LONG SINCE I'VE BEEN TO JAPAN. ♫

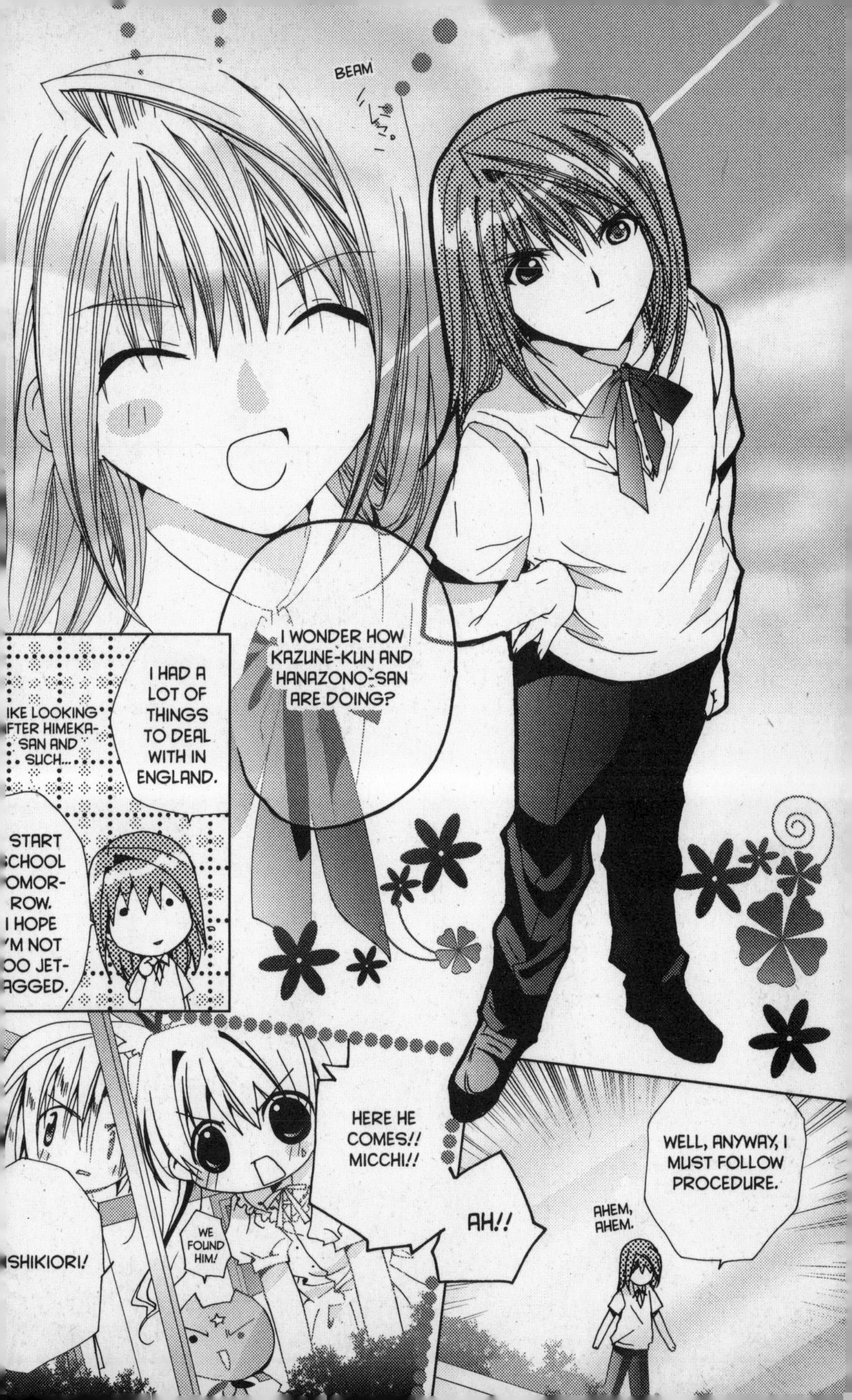
BEAM
I WONDER HOW KAZUNE-KUN AND HANAZONO-SAN ARE DOING?
I HAD A LOT OF THINGS TO DEAL WITH IN ENGLAND.
IKE LOOKING FTER HIMEKA-SAN AND SUCH...
START SCHOOL OMOR-ROW. I HOPE 'M NOT OO JET-AGGED.
WELL, ANYWAY, I MUST FOLLOW PROCEDURE.
AHEM, AHEM.
AH!!
HERE HE COMES!! MICCHI!!
WE FOUND HIM!
SHIKIORI!

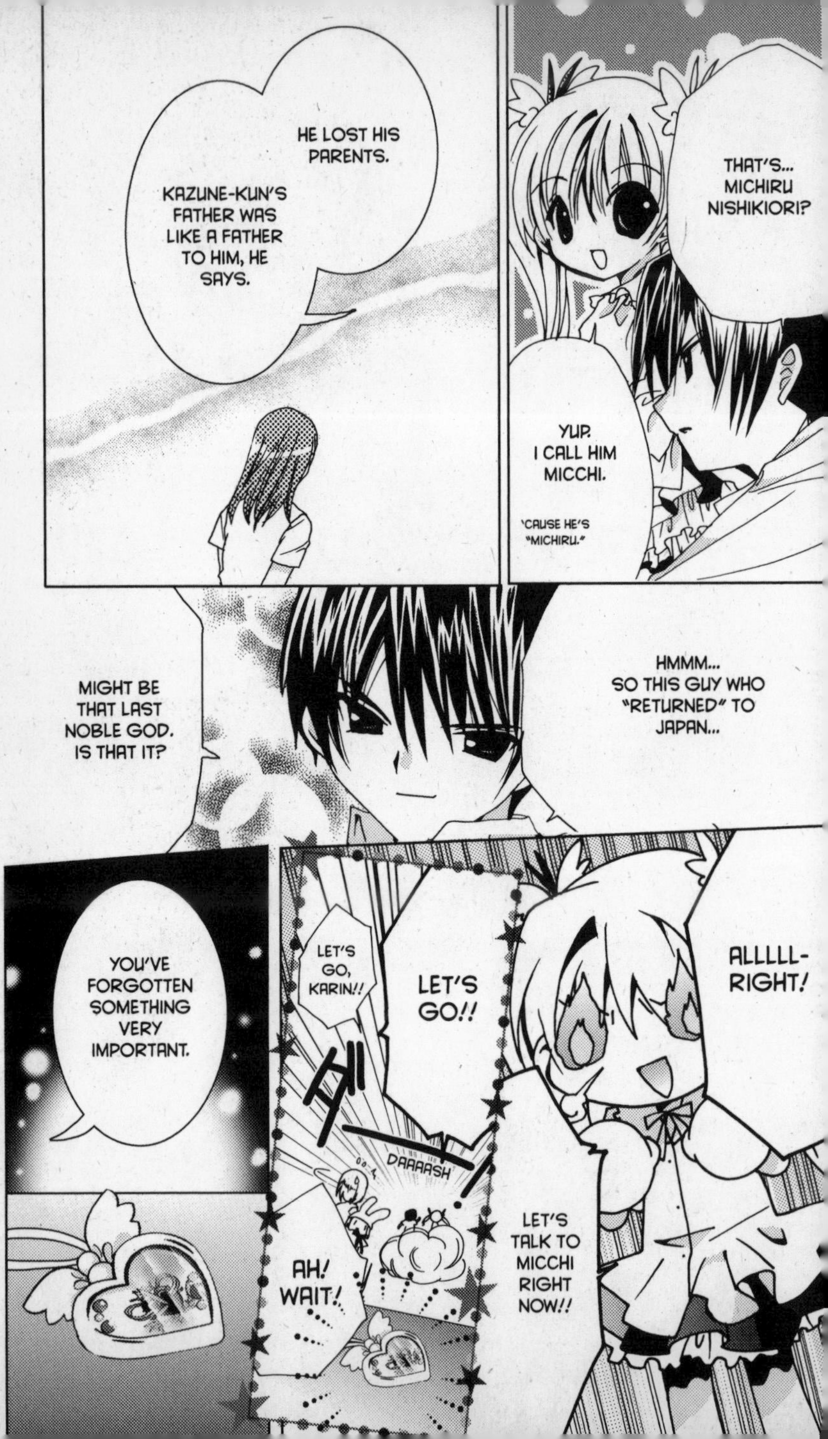
THAT'S... MICHIRU NISHIKIORI?
YUP. I CALL HIM MICCHI.
'CAUSE HE'S "MICHIRU."
HE LOST HIS PARENTS.
KAZUNE-KUN'S FATHER WAS LIKE A FATHER TO HIM, HE SAYS.
HMMM... SO THIS GUY WHO "RETURNED" TO JAPAN...
MIGHT BE THAT LAST NOBLE GOD. IS THAT IT?
ALLLLL-RIGHT!
LET'S TALK TO MICCHI RIGHT NOW!!
LET'S GO!!
LET'S GO, KARIN!!
DAAAASH
AH! WAIT!
YOU'VE FORGOTTEN SOMETHING VERY IMPORTANT.

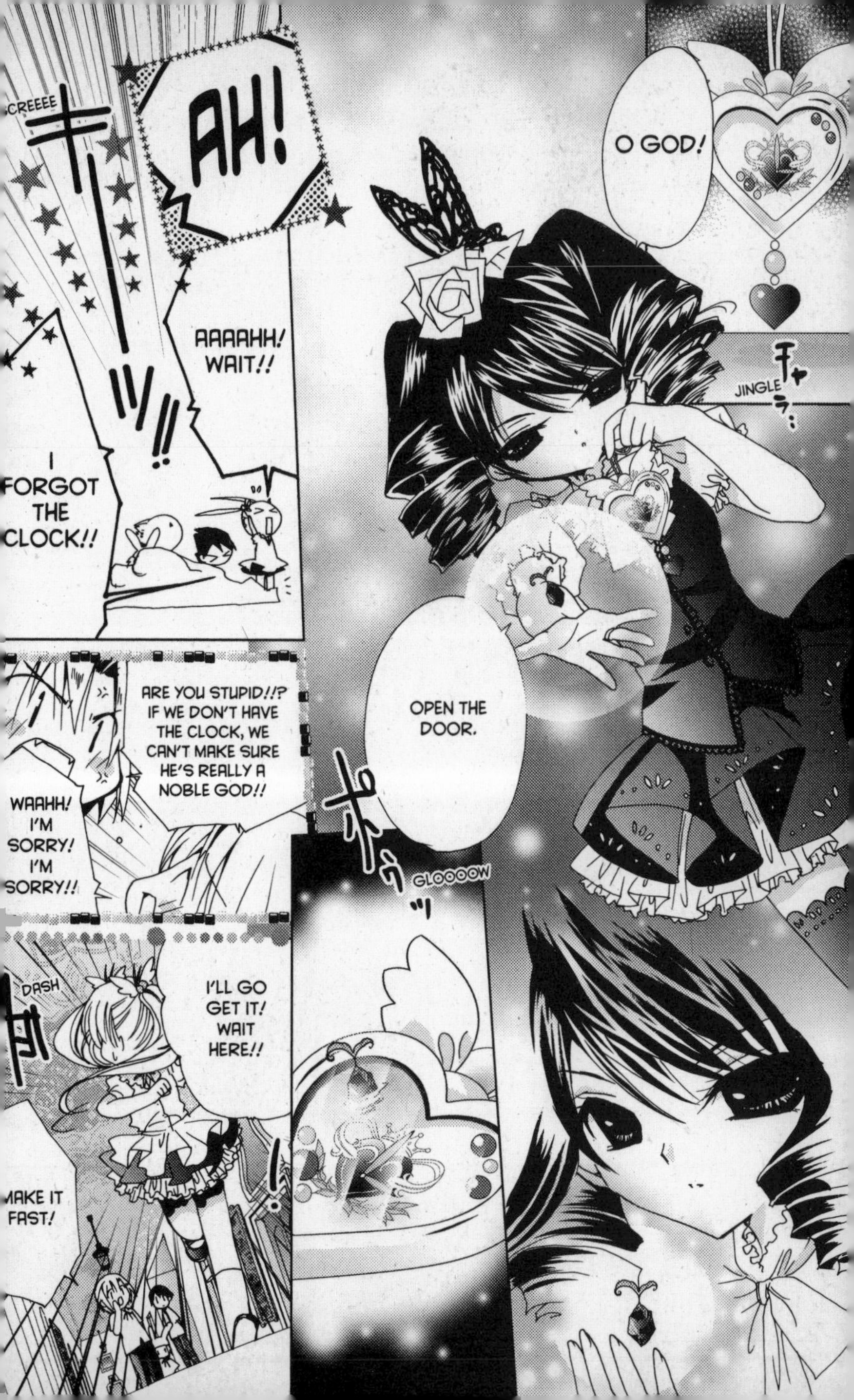
O GOD!
JINGLE
OPEN THE DOOR.
GLOOOOW
AH!
AAAAHH! WAIT!!
CREEEE
I FORGOT THE CLOCK!!
ARE YOU STUPID!!? IF WE DON'T HAVE THE CLOCK, WE CAN'T MAKE SURE HE'S REALLY A NOBLE GOD!!
WAAHH! I'M SORRY! I'M SORRY!!
DASH
I'LL GO GET IT! WAIT HERE!!
MAKE IT FAST!

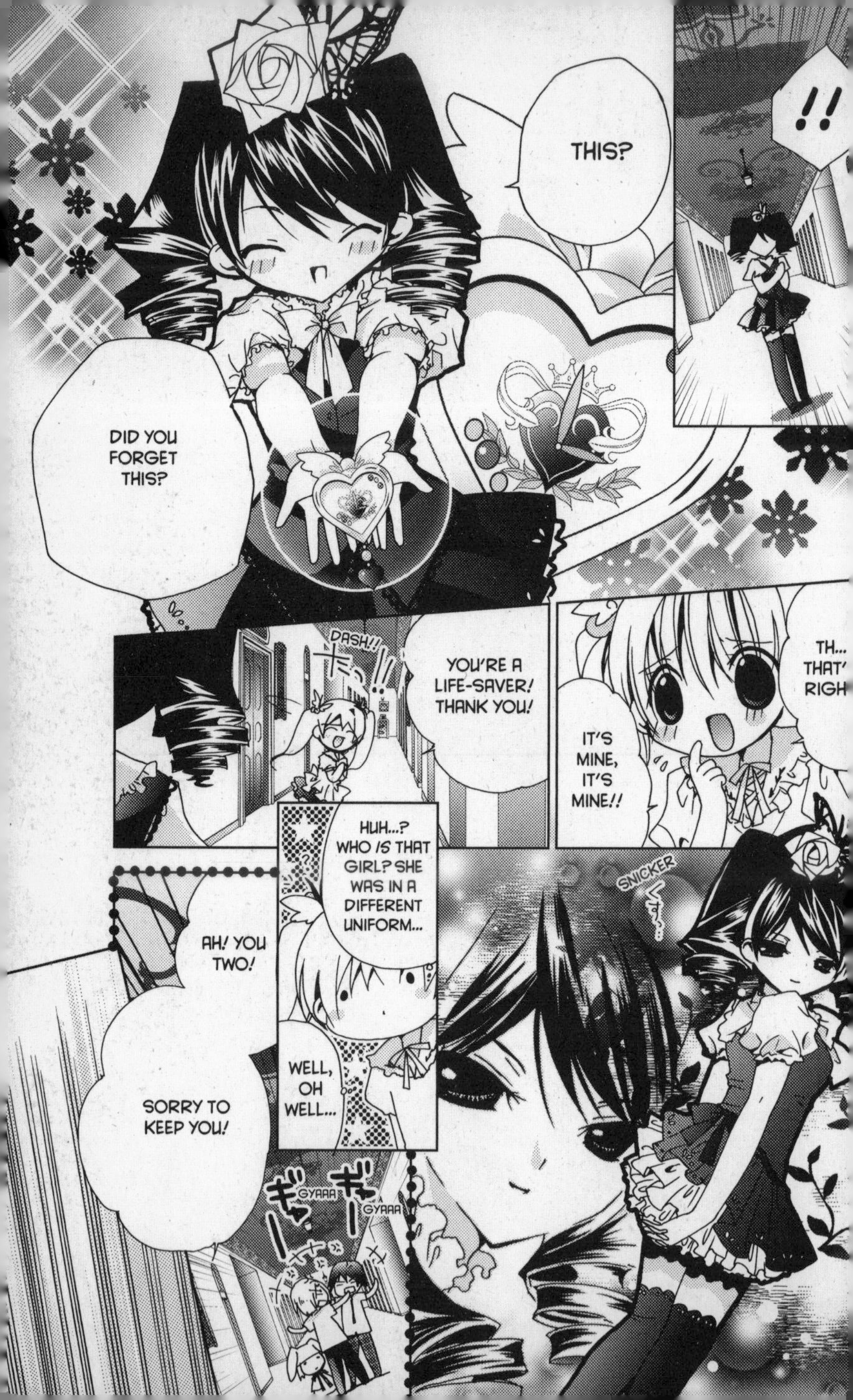
!!
THIS?
DID YOU FORGET THIS?
TH... THAT' RIGH
IT'S MINE, IT'S MINE!!
DASH!!
YOU'RE A LIFE-SAVER! THANK YOU!
SNICKER
HUH...? WHO *IS* THAT GIRL? SHE WAS IN A DIFFERENT UNIFORM...
WELL, OH WELL...
AH! YOU TWO!
SORRY TO KEEP YOU!
GYAAA
GYAAA

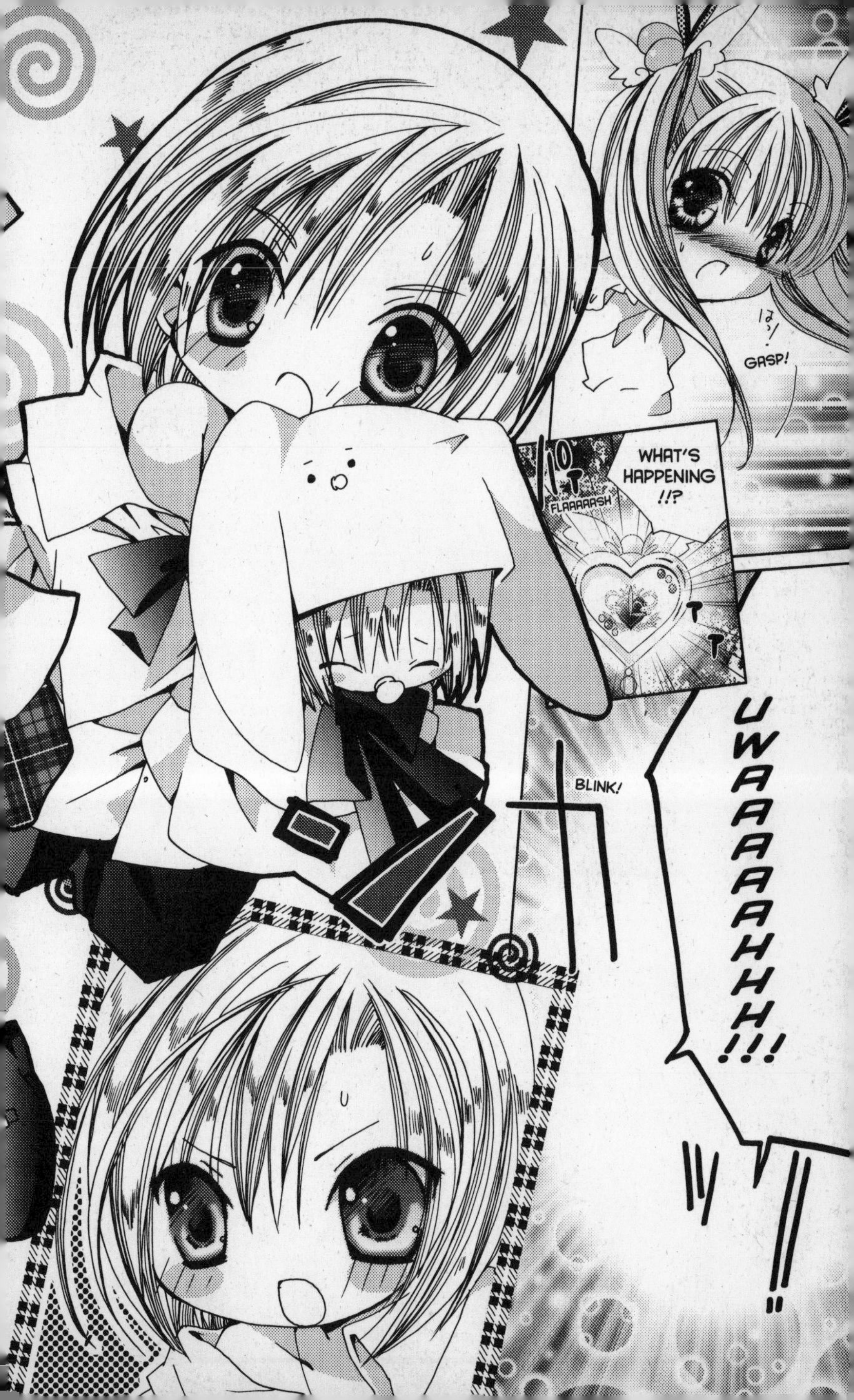
はっ!
GASP!
WHAT'S HAPPENING !!?
FLAAAAASH
UWAAAAAHHH!!!
BLINK!

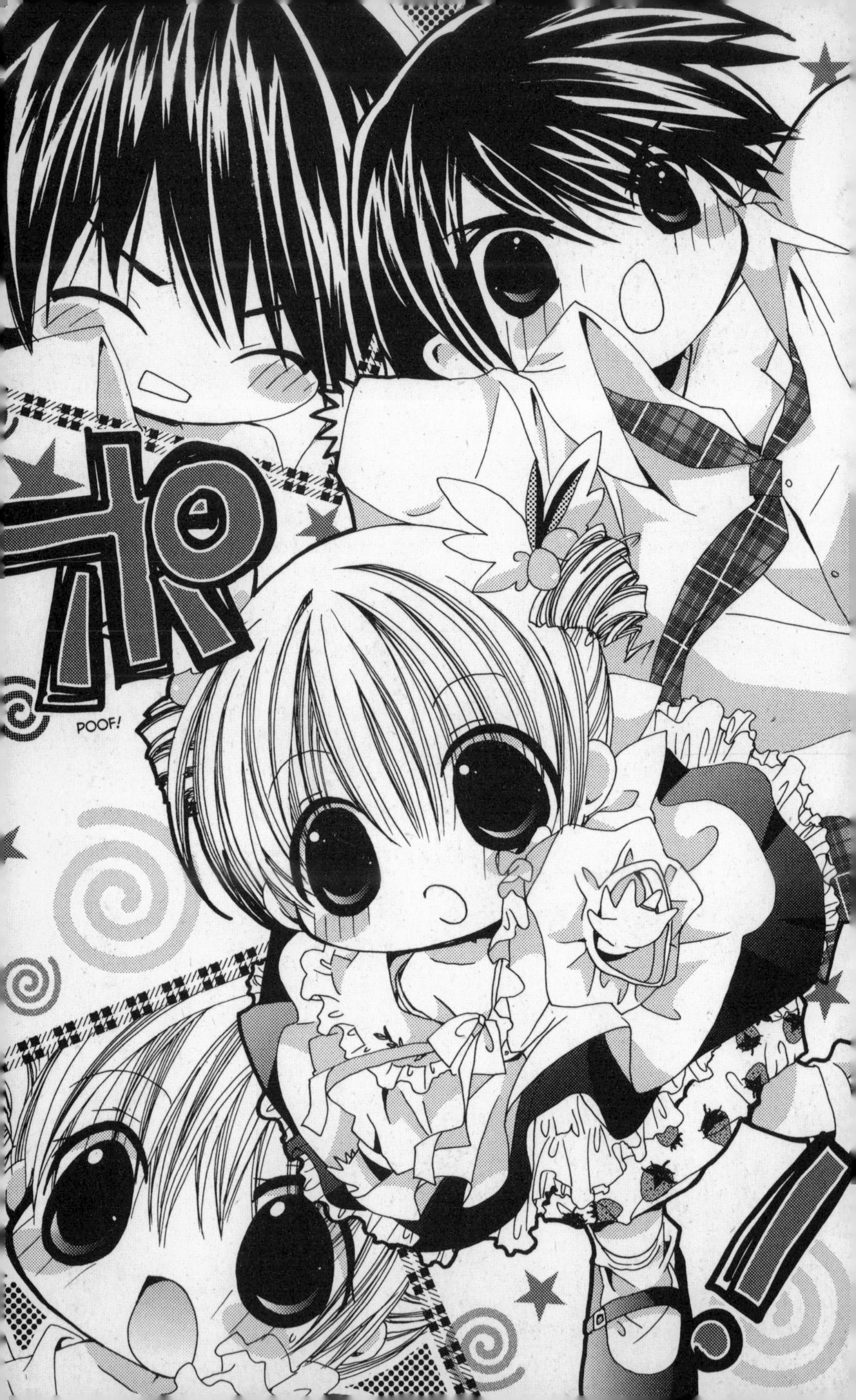
POOF!

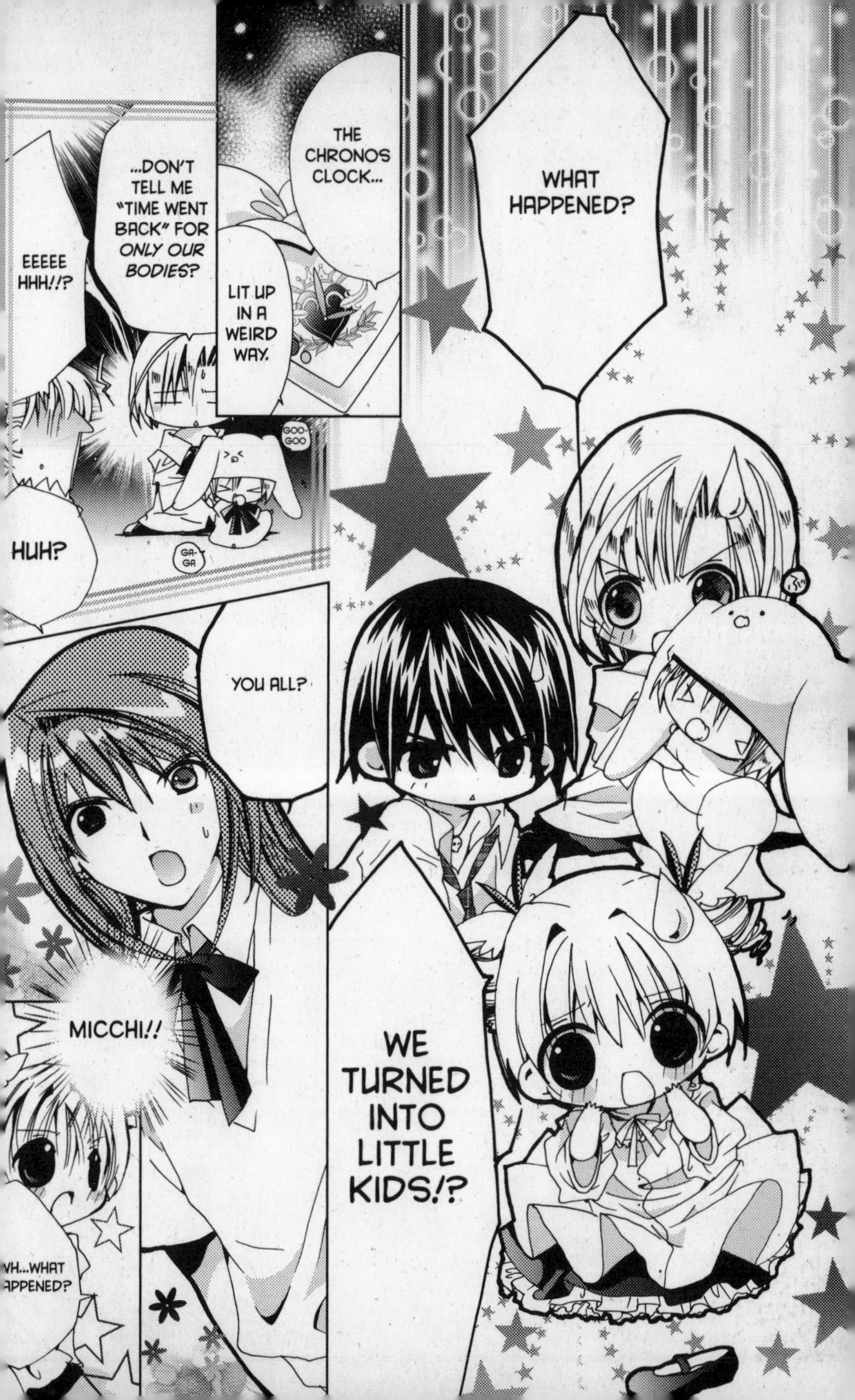
WHAT HAPPENED?
WE TURNED INTO LITTLE KIDS!?
THE CHRONOS CLOCK...
LIT UP IN A WEIRD WAY.
...DON'T TELL ME "TIME WENT BACK" FOR *ONLY OUR BODIES?*
EEEEE HHH!!?
GOO-GOO
HUH?
GA-GA
YOU ALL?
MICCHI!!
WH...WHAT APPENED?

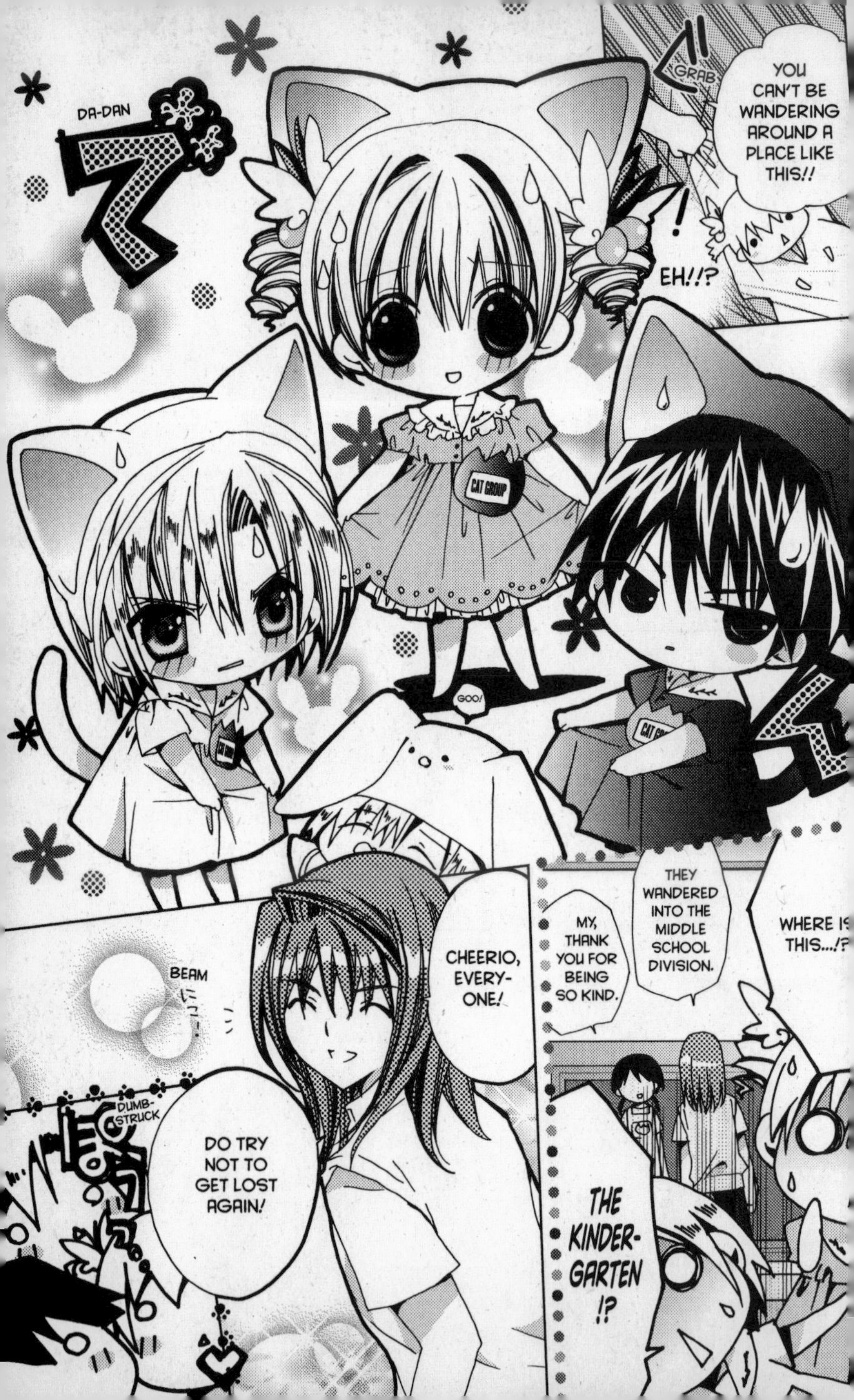
GRAB
YOU CAN'T BE WANDERING AROUND A PLACE LIKE THIS!!
EH!!?
DA-DAN
CAT GROUP
GOO!
WHERE IS THIS...!?
THEY WANDERED INTO THE MIDDLE SCHOOL DIVISION.
MY, THANK YOU FOR BEING SO KIND.
THE KINDER-GARTEN!?
CHEERIO, EVERY-ONE!
BEAM
DO TRY NOT TO GET LOST AGAIN!
DUMB-STRUCK

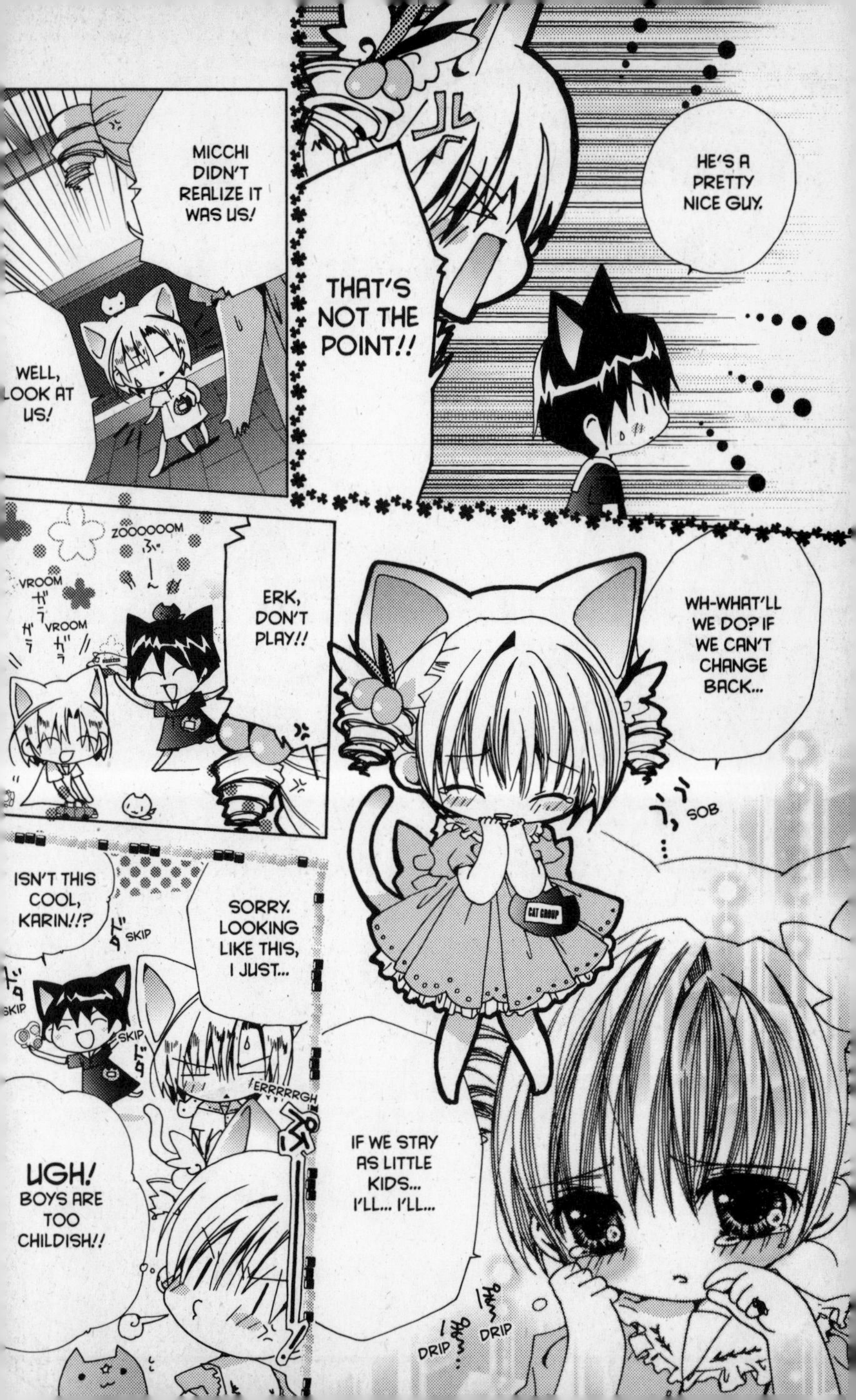
HE'S A PRETTY NICE GUY.
THAT'S NOT THE POINT!!
MICCHI DIDN'T REALIZE IT WAS US!
WELL, LOOK AT US!
WH-WHAT'LL WE DO? IF WE CAN'T CHANGE BACK...
SOB
IF WE STAY AS LITTLE KIDS... I'LL... I'LL...
DRIP
DRIP
ERK, DON'T PLAY!!
ZOOOOOOM
VROOM
VROOM
SORRY. LOOKING LIKE THIS, I JUST...
ISN'T THIS COOL, KARIN!!?
SKIP
SKIP
SKIP
ERRRRRGH
UGH! BOYS ARE TOO CHILDISH!!

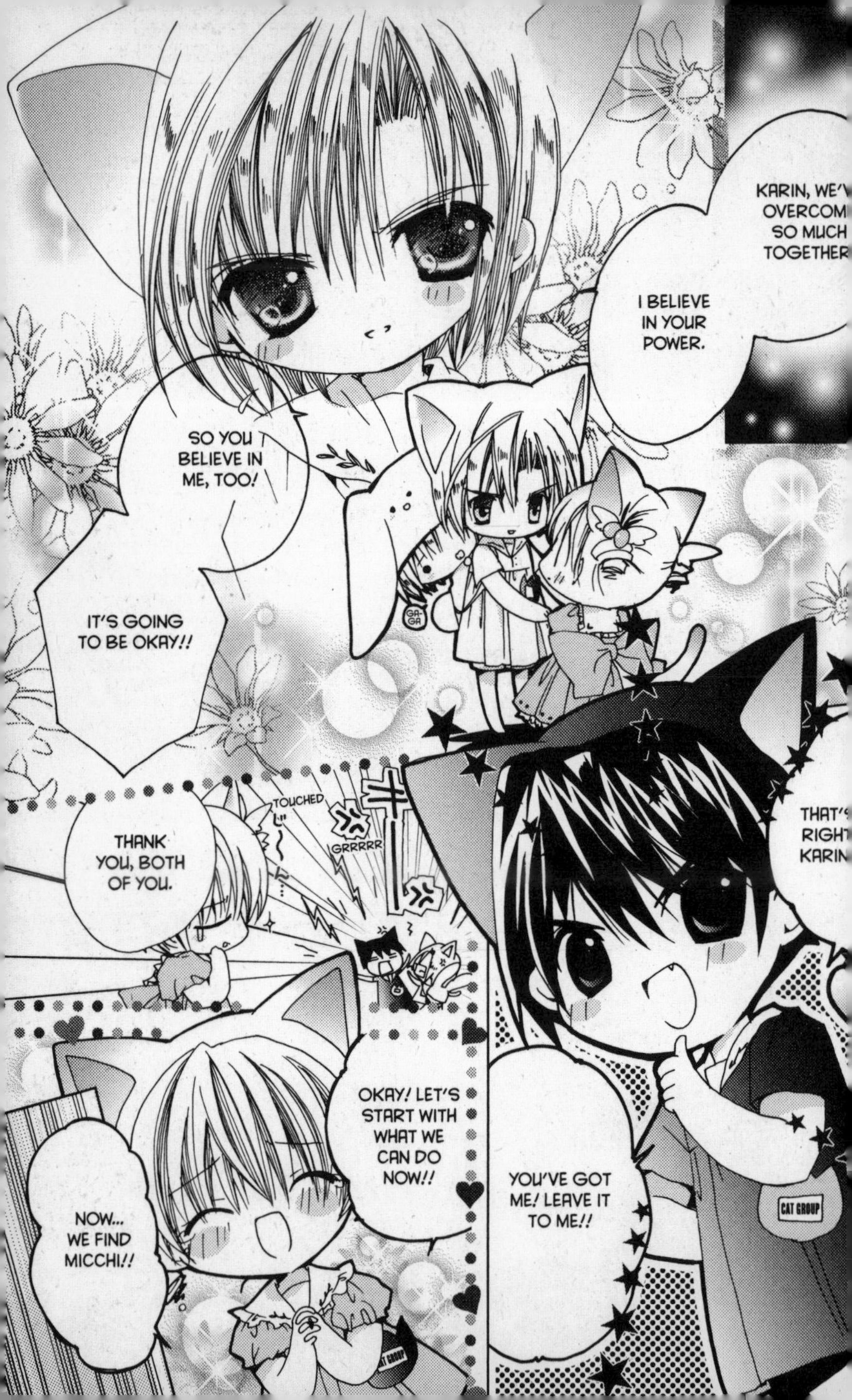
KARIN, WE'V OVERCOM SO MUCH TOGETHER
I BELIEVE IN YOUR POWER.
SO YOU BELIEVE IN ME, TOO!
IT'S GOING TO BE OKAY!!
GA-GA
THAT'S RIGHT KARIN
YOU'VE GOT ME! LEAVE IT TO ME!!
CAT GROUP
THANK YOU, BOTH OF YOU.
TOUCHED
GRRRRR
OKAY! LET'S START WITH WHAT WE CAN DO NOW!!
NOW... WE FIND MICCHI!!
CAT GROUP

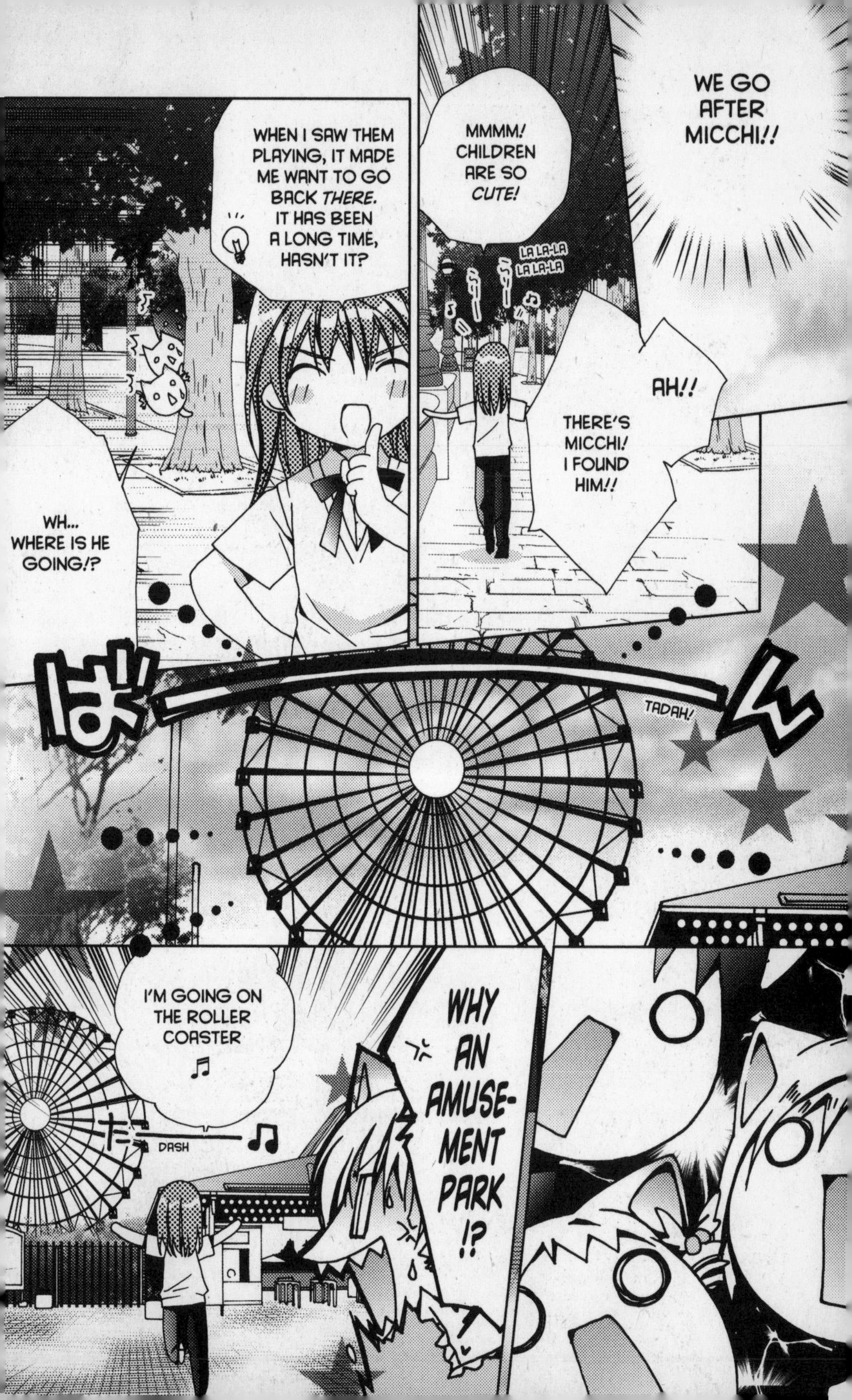
WE GO AFTER MICCHI!!
MMMM! CHILDREN ARE SO CUTE!
LA LA-LA LA LA-LA
AH!!
THERE'S MICCHI! I FOUND HIM!!
WHEN I SAW THEM PLAYING, IT MADE ME WANT TO GO BACK THERE. IT HAS BEEN A LONG TIME, HASN'T IT?
WH... WHERE IS HE GOING!?
ばーーん
TADAH!
WHY AN AMUSEMENT PARK!?
I'M GOING ON THE ROLLER COASTER ♪
たーー DASH ♪

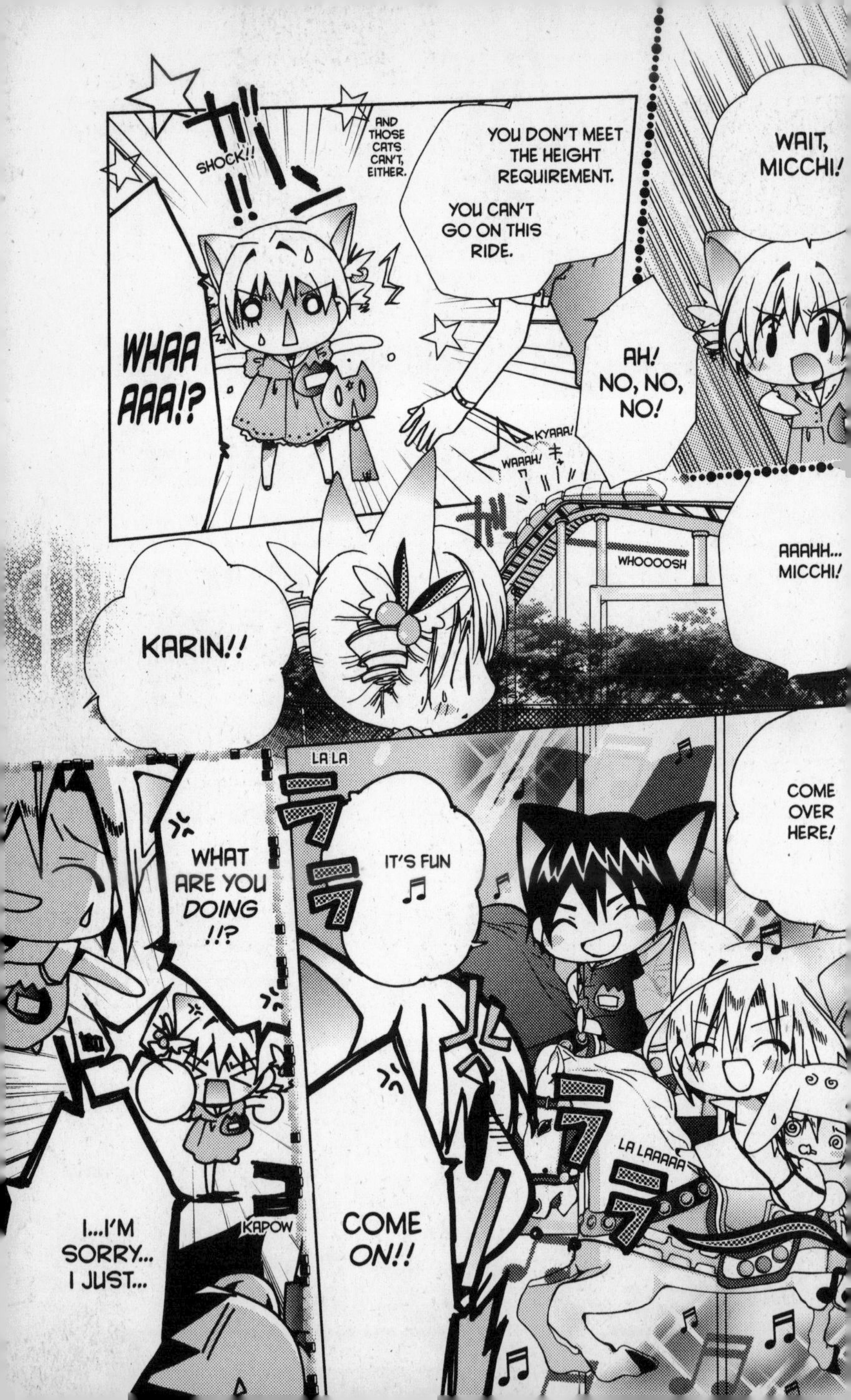
WAIT, MICCHI!
AH! NO, NO, NO!
YOU DON'T MEET THE HEIGHT REQUIREMENT.
YOU CAN'T GO ON THIS RIDE.
AND THOSE CATS CAN'T, EITHER.
SHOCK!!
WHAA AAA!?
KYAAA!
WAAAH!
AAAHH... MICCHI!
WHOOOOSH
KARIN!!
COME OVER HERE!
LA LA
IT'S FUN ♫
LA LAAAAA
COME ON!!
WHAT ARE YOU DOING !!?
KAPOW
I...I'M SORRY... I JUST...

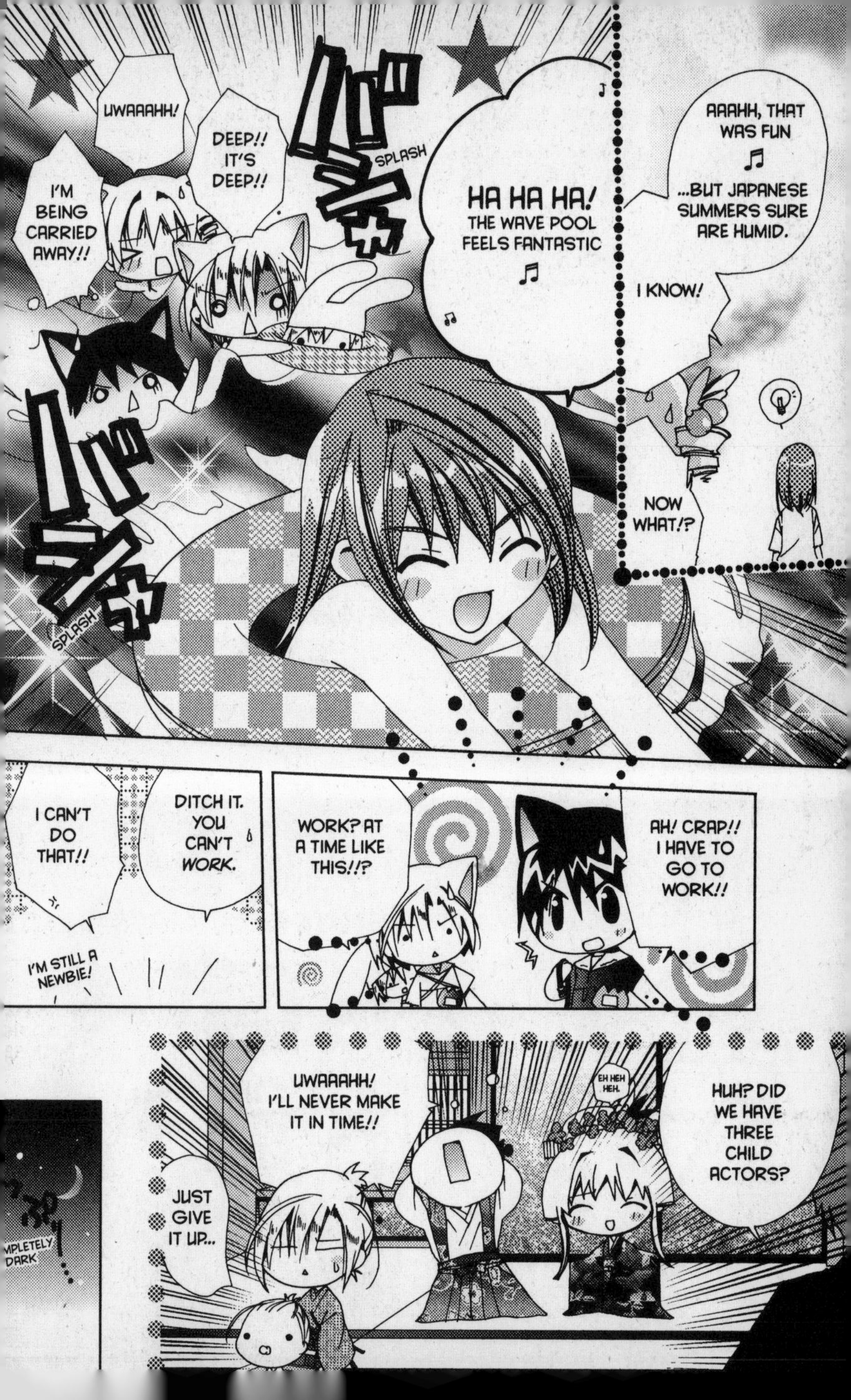
AAAHH, THAT WAS FUN ♫ ...BUT JAPANESE SUMMERS SURE ARE HUMID.
I KNOW!
NOW WHAT!?
HA HA HA! THE WAVE POOL FEELS FANTASTIC ♫
SPLASH
DEEP!! IT'S DEEP!!
UWAAAHH!
I'M BEING CARRIED AWAY!!
SPLASH
AH! CRAP!! I HAVE TO GO TO WORK!!
WORK? AT A TIME LIKE THIS!!?
DITCH IT. YOU CAN'T WORK.
I CAN'T DO THAT!!
I'M STILL A NEWBIE!
HUH? DID WE HAVE THREE CHILD ACTORS?
EH HEH HEH.
UWAAAHH! I'LL NEVER MAKE IT IN TIME!!
JUST GIVE IT UP...
MPLETELY DARK

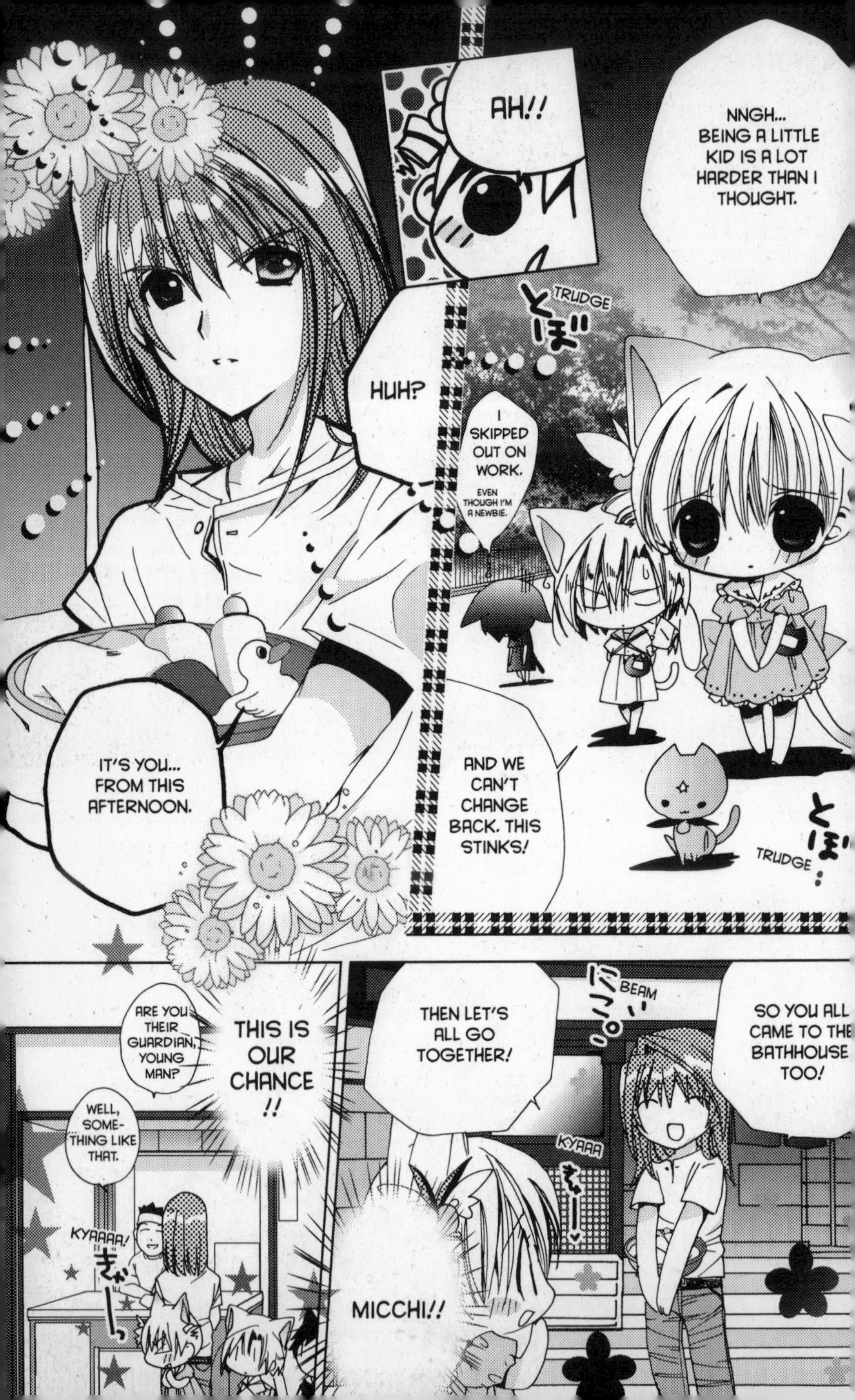
NNGH... BEING A LITTLE KID IS A LOT HARDER THAN I THOUGHT.
とぼ TRUDGE
I SKIPPED OUT ON WORK.
EVEN THOUGH I'M A NEWBIE.
AND WE CAN'T CHANGE BACK. THIS STINKS!
とぼ TRUDGE
AH!!
HUH?
IT'S YOU... FROM THIS AFTERNOON.
SO YOU ALL CAME TO THE BATHHOUSE TOO!
にこっ BEAM
THEN LET'S ALL GO TOGETHER!
きゃー KYAAA
MICCHI!!
THIS IS OUR CHANCE!!
ARE YOU THEIR GUARDIAN, YOUNG MAN?
WELL, SOME-THING LIKE THAT.
KYAAAA!

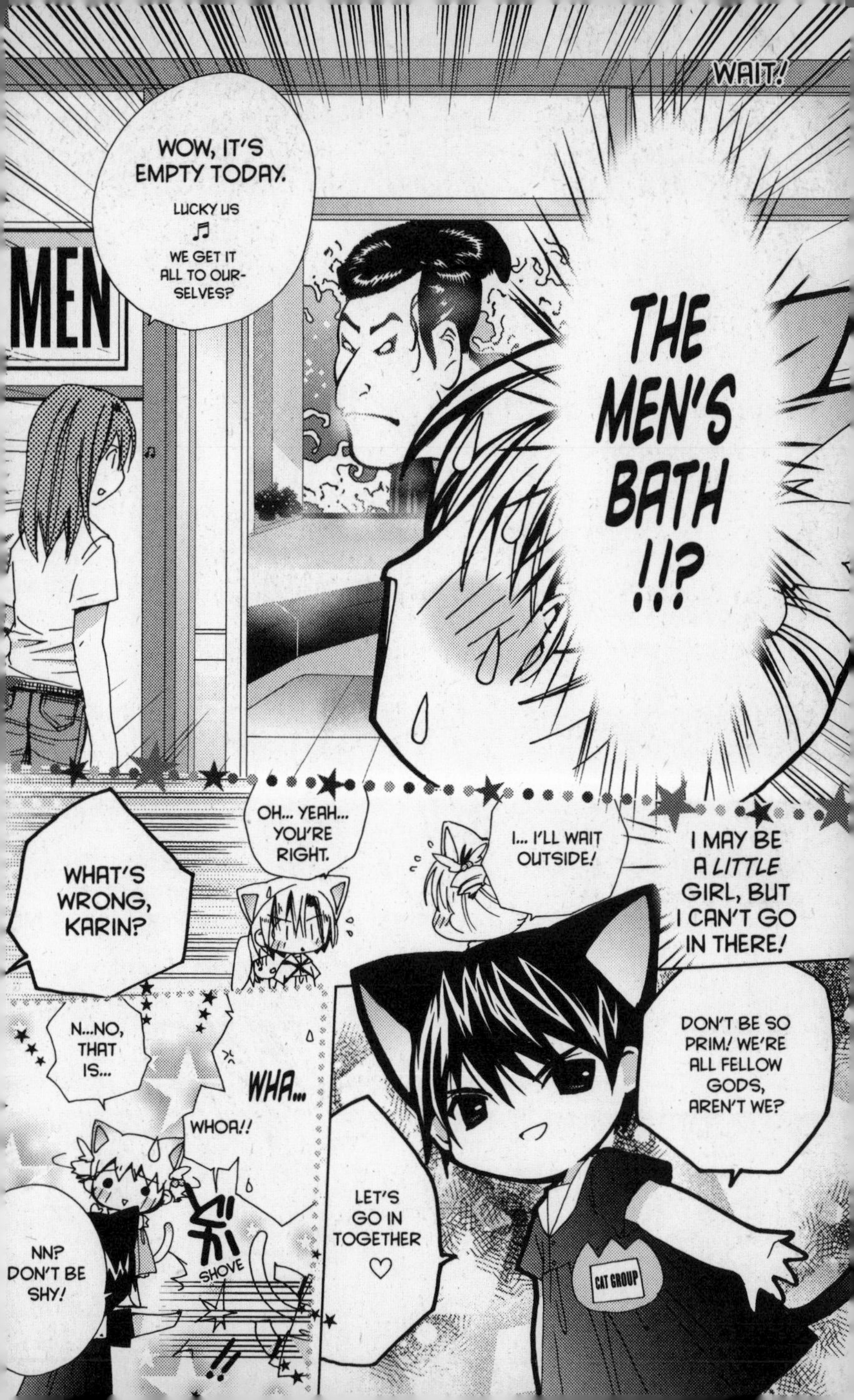
WAIT!
THE MEN'S BATH !!?
WOW, IT'S EMPTY TODAY.
LUCKY US ♫
WE GET IT ALL TO OUR-SELVES?
MEN
I MAY BE A *LITTLE* GIRL, BUT I CAN'T GO IN THERE!
I... I'LL WAIT OUTSIDE!
OH... YEAH... YOU'RE RIGHT.
WHAT'S WRONG, KARIN?
DON'T BE SO PRIM! WE'RE ALL FELLOW GODS, AREN'T WE?
CAT GROUP
LET'S GO IN TOGETHER ♡
N...NO, THAT IS...
WHA...
WHOA!!
SHOVE
NN? DON'T BE SHY!
!!

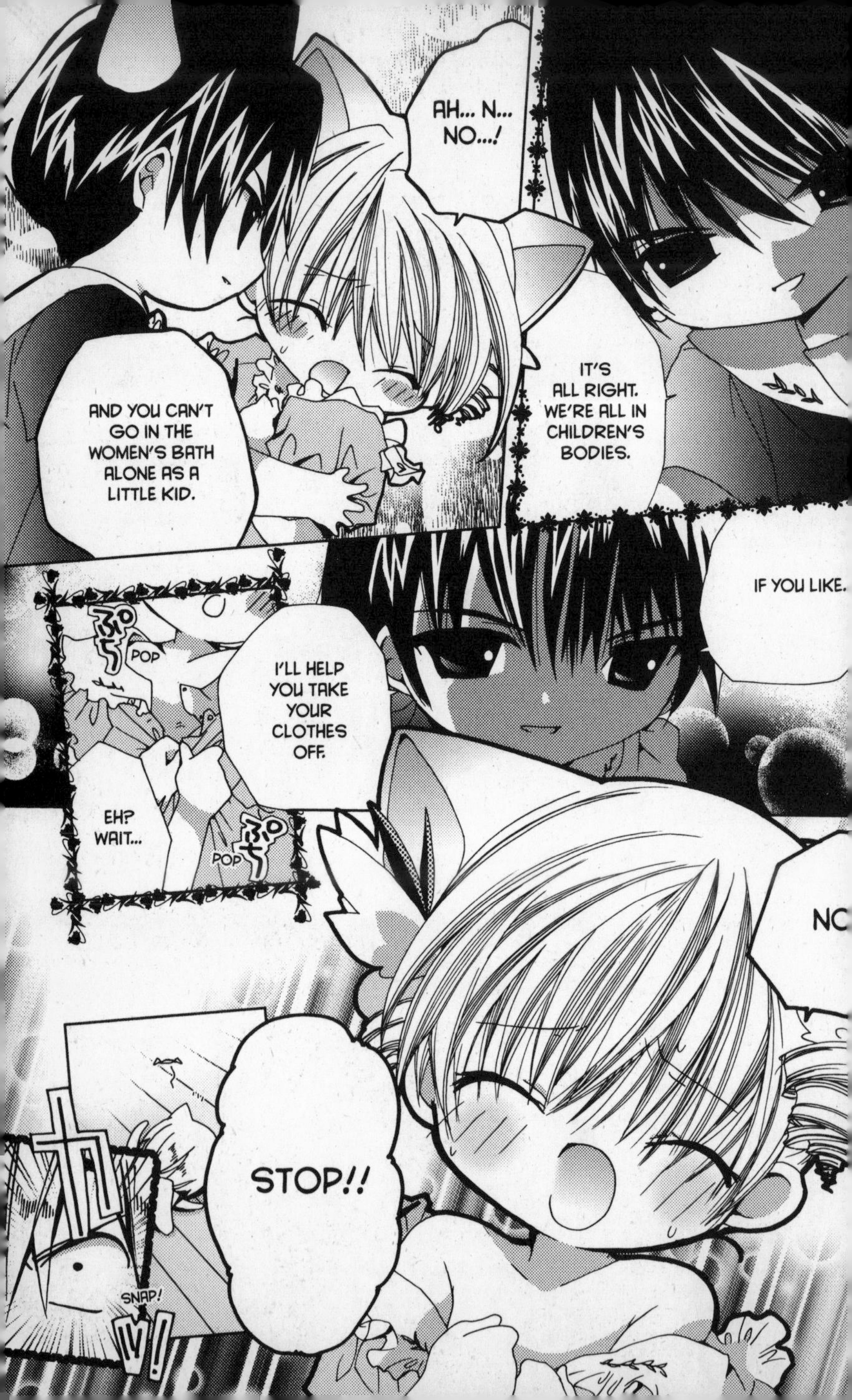

AH... N... NO...!
IT'S ALL RIGHT. WE'RE ALL IN CHILDREN'S BODIES.
AND YOU CAN'T GO IN THE WOMEN'S BATH ALONE AS A LITTLE KID.
IF YOU LIKE.
I'LL HELP YOU TAKE YOUR CLOTHES OFF.
ぷち POP
EH? WAIT...
ぷち POP
NO
STOP!!
SNAP!

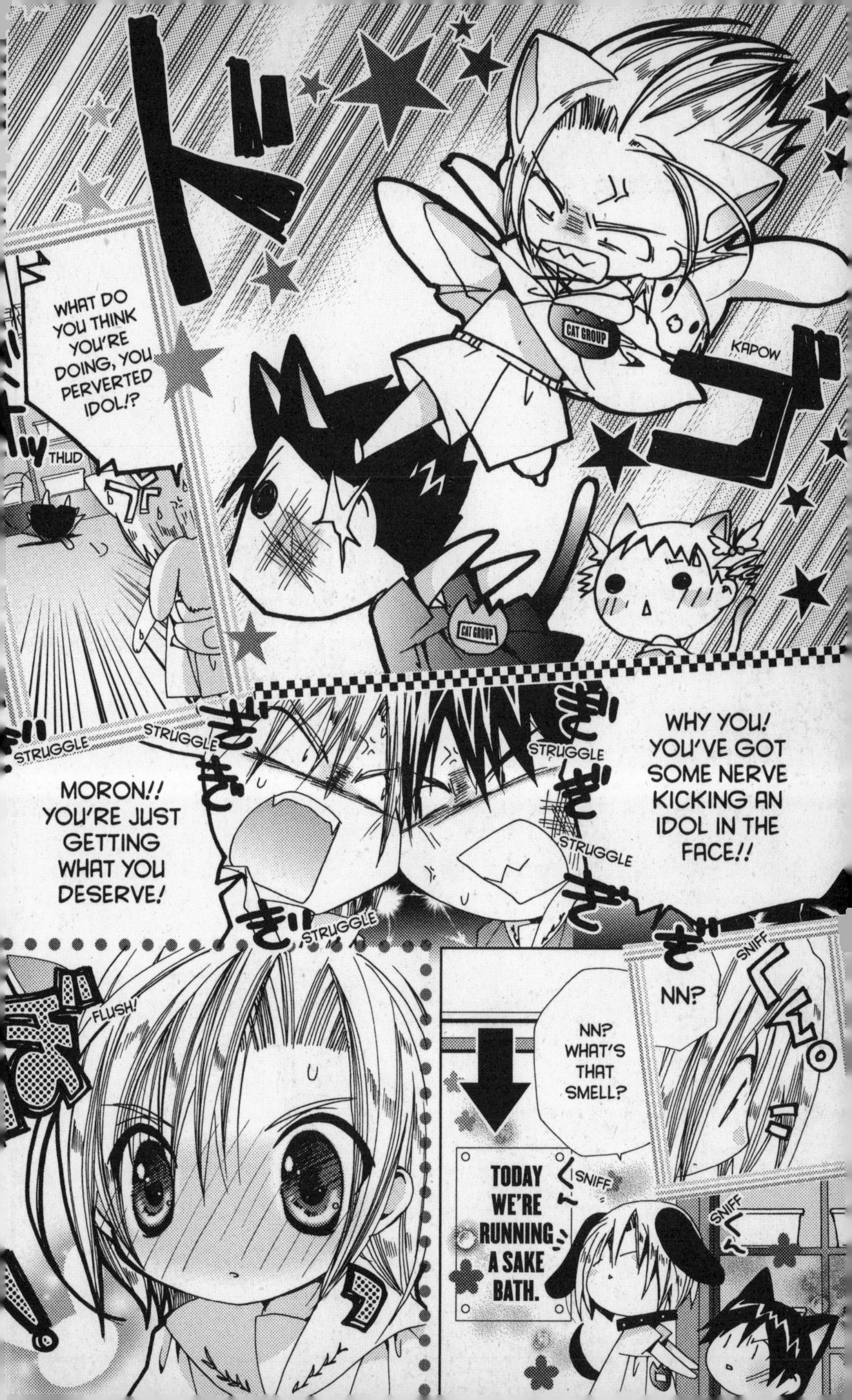
KAPOW
WHAT DO YOU THINK YOU'RE DOING, YOU PERVERTED IDOL!?
THUD
WHY YOU! YOU'VE GOT SOME NERVE KICKING AN IDOL IN THE FACE!!
STRUGGLE
STRUGGLE
STRUGGLE
STRUGGLE
STRUGGLE
MORON!! YOU'RE JUST GETTING WHAT YOU DESERVE!
SNIFF
NN?
NN? WHAT'S THAT SMELL?
TODAY WE'RE RUNNING A SAKE BATH.
SNIFF
SNIFF
FLUSH!

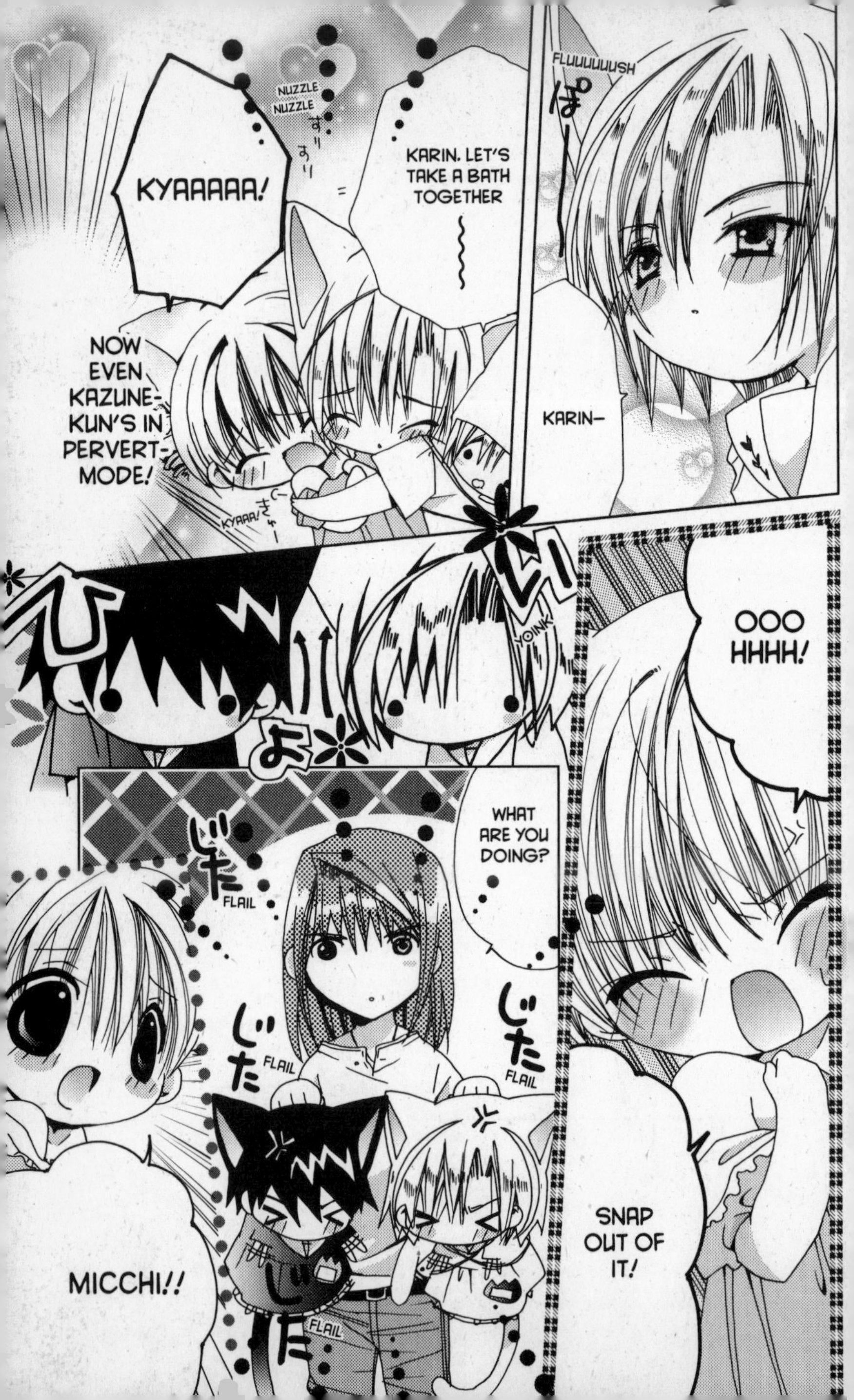

FLUUUUUUSH
ぽー
KARIN—
NUZZLE NUZZLE
すりすり
KARIN. LET'S TAKE A BATH TOGETHER ~~~
KYAAAAA!
NOW EVEN KAZUNE-KUN'S IN PERVERT-MODE!
KYAAA!
きゃー
OOO HHHH!
SNAP OUT OF IT!
ひょい
YOINK
ひょい
WHAT ARE YOU DOING?
じたじた
FLAIL
じたじた
FLAIL
じたじた
FLAIL
じたじた
FLAIL
MICCHI!!

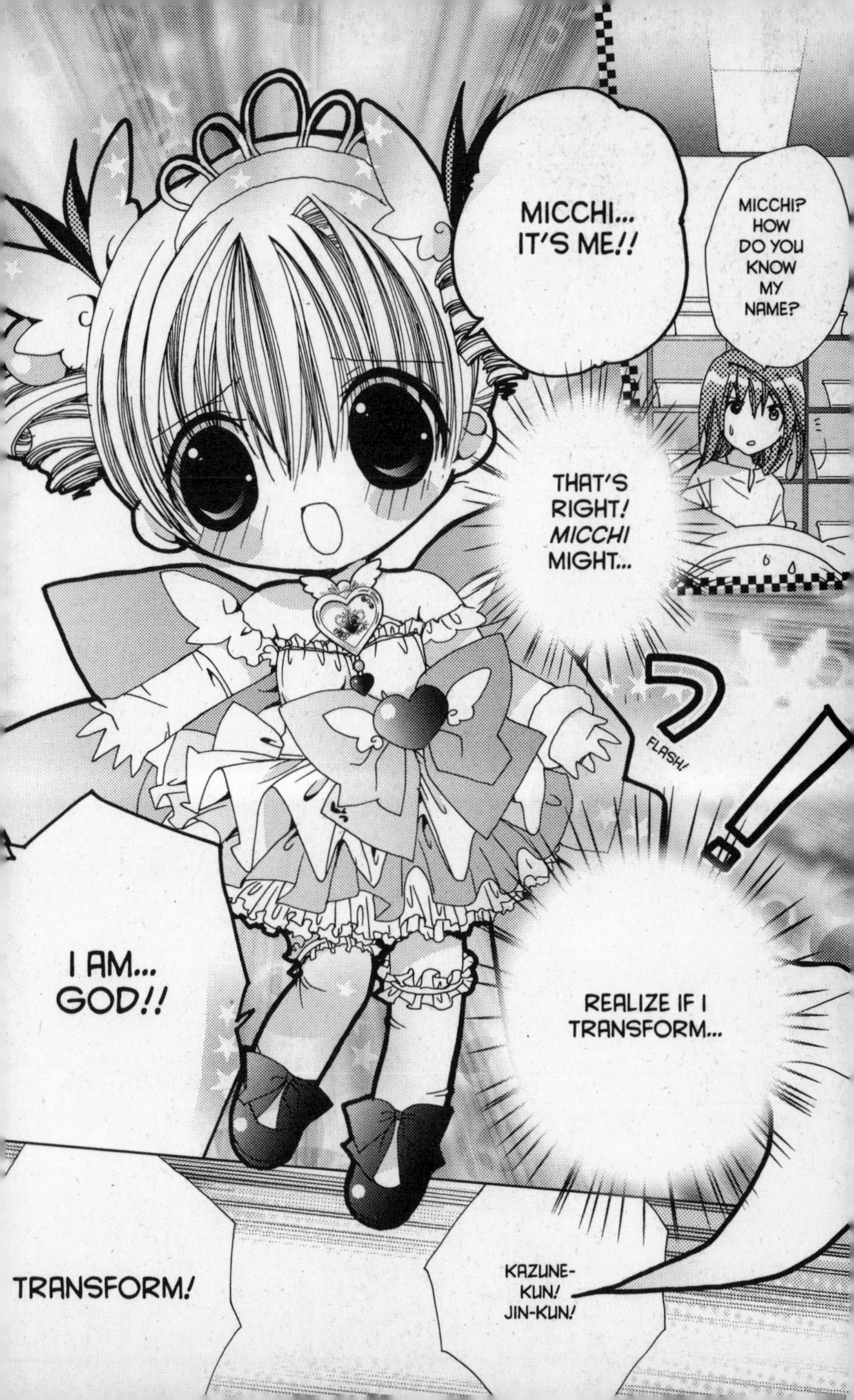
MICCHI? HOW DO YOU KNOW MY NAME?
MICCHI... IT'S ME!!
THAT'S RIGHT! MICCHI MIGHT...
REALIZE IF I TRANSFORM...
FLASH!
I AM... GOD!!
KAZUNE-KUN! JIN-KUN!
TRANSFORM!

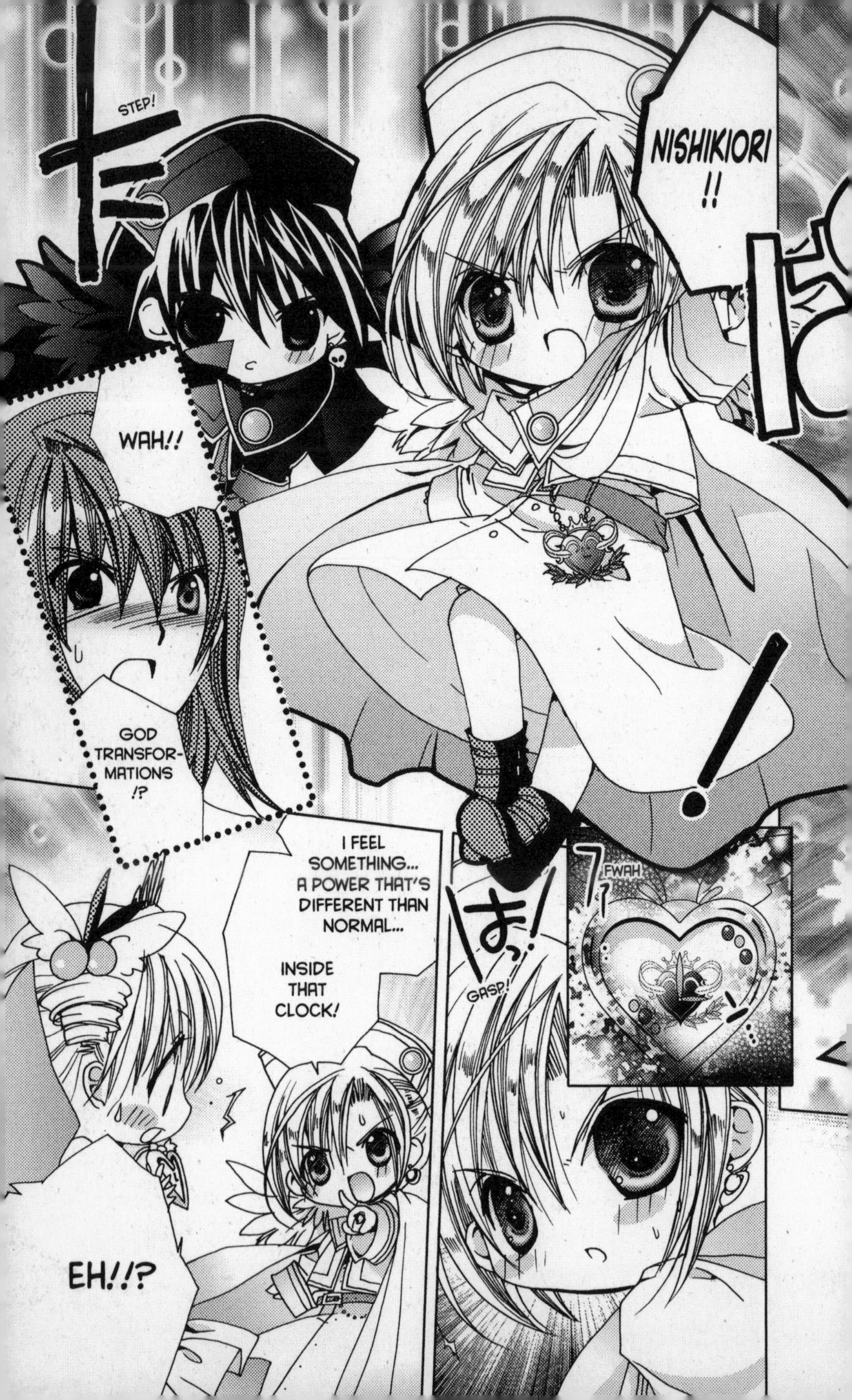
NISHIKIORI !!
STEP!
WAH!!
GOD TRANSFOR-MATIONS !?
FWAH
GASP!
I FEEL SOMETHING... A POWER THAT'S DIFFERENT THAN NORMAL...
INSIDE THAT CLOCK!
EH!!?

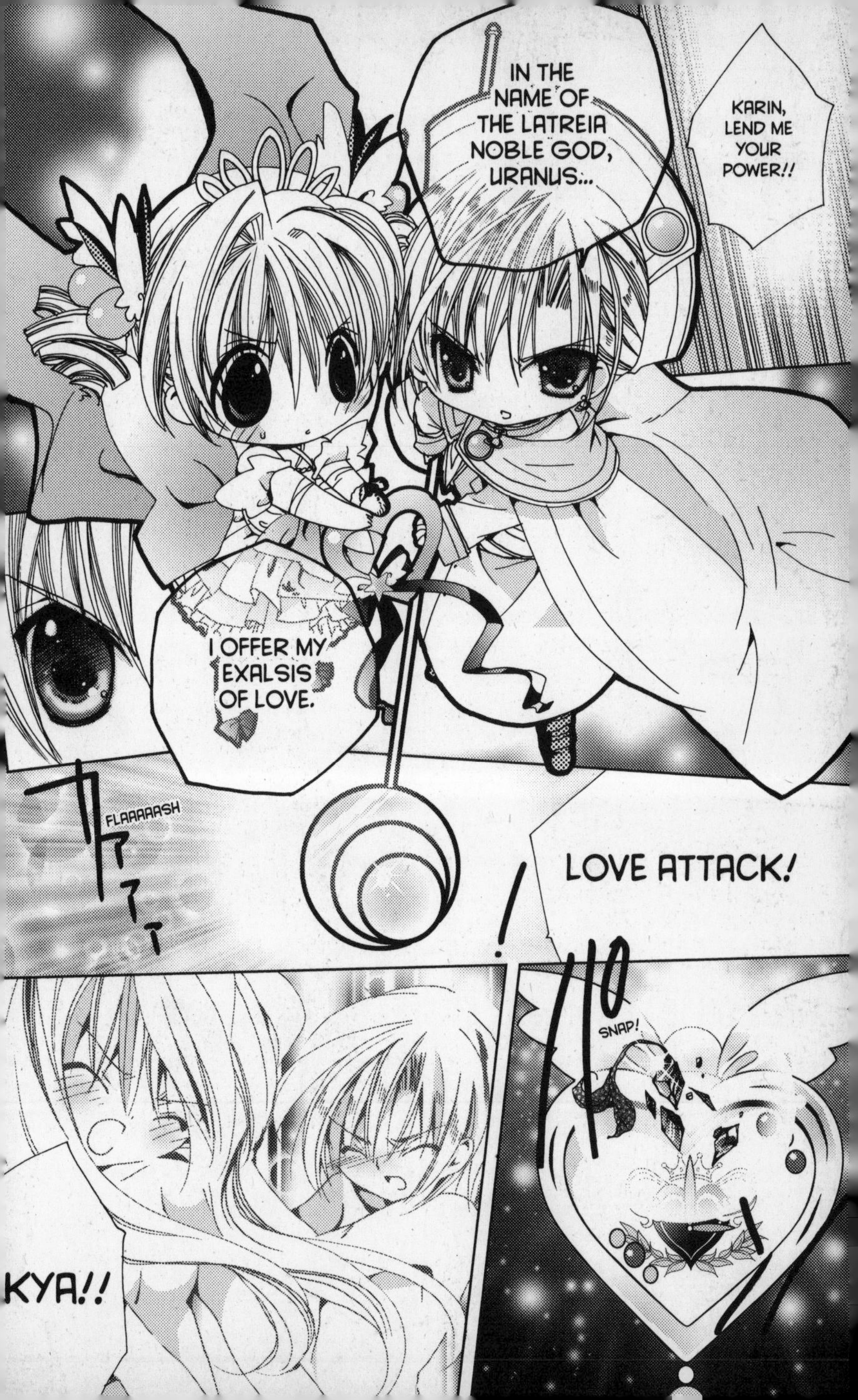
KARIN, LEND ME YOUR POWER!!
IN THE NAME OF THE LATREIA NOBLE GOD, URANUS...
I OFFER MY EXALSIS OF LOVE.
LOVE ATTACK!
FLAAAAASH
SNAP!
KYA!!

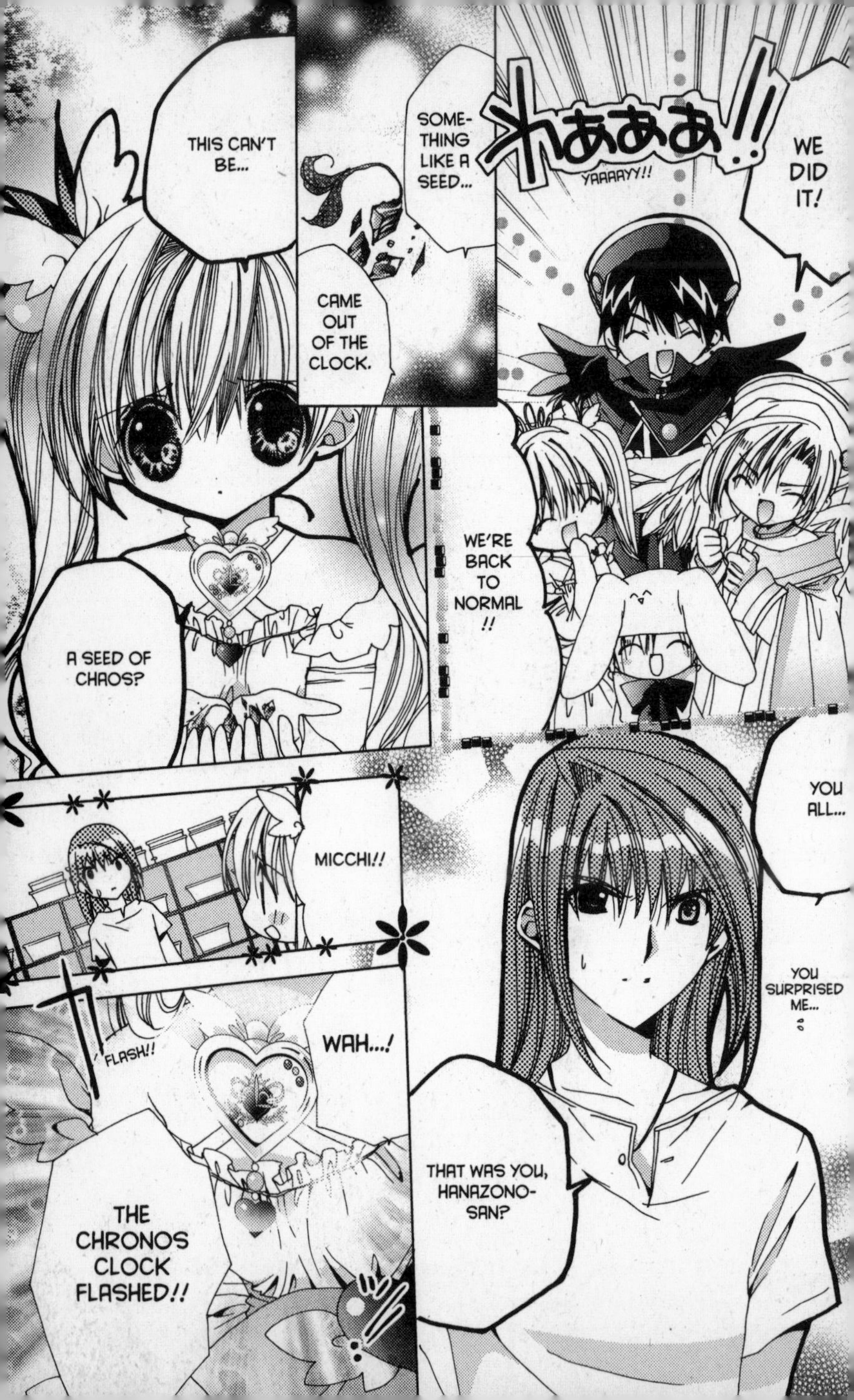
WE DID IT!
わあああ!!
YAAAAYY!!
WE'RE BACK TO NORMAL!!
SOME-THING LIKE A SEED...
CAME OUT OF THE CLOCK.
THIS CAN'T BE...
A SEED OF CHAOS?
YOU ALL...
YOU SURPRISED ME...
THAT WAS YOU, HANAZONO-SAN?
MICCHI!!
FLASH!!
WAH...!
THE CHRONOS CLOCK FLASHED!!

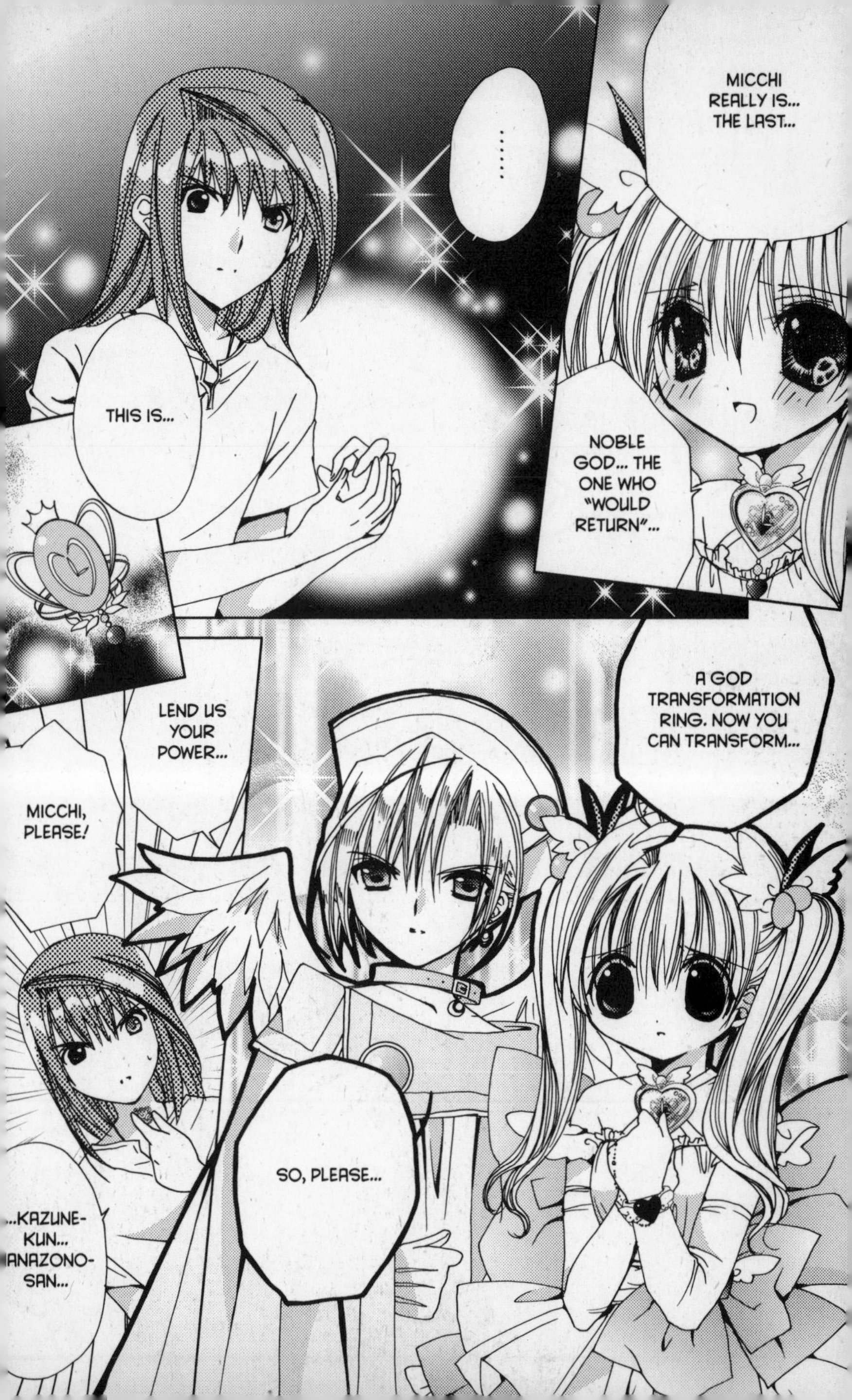
MICCHI REALLY IS... THE LAST...
NOBLE GOD... THE ONE WHO "WOULD RETURN"...
......
THIS IS...
A GOD TRANSFORMATION RING. NOW YOU CAN TRANSFORM...
LEND US YOUR POWER...
MICCHI, PLEASE!
SO, PLEASE...
...KAZUNE-KUN... ANAZONO-SAN...

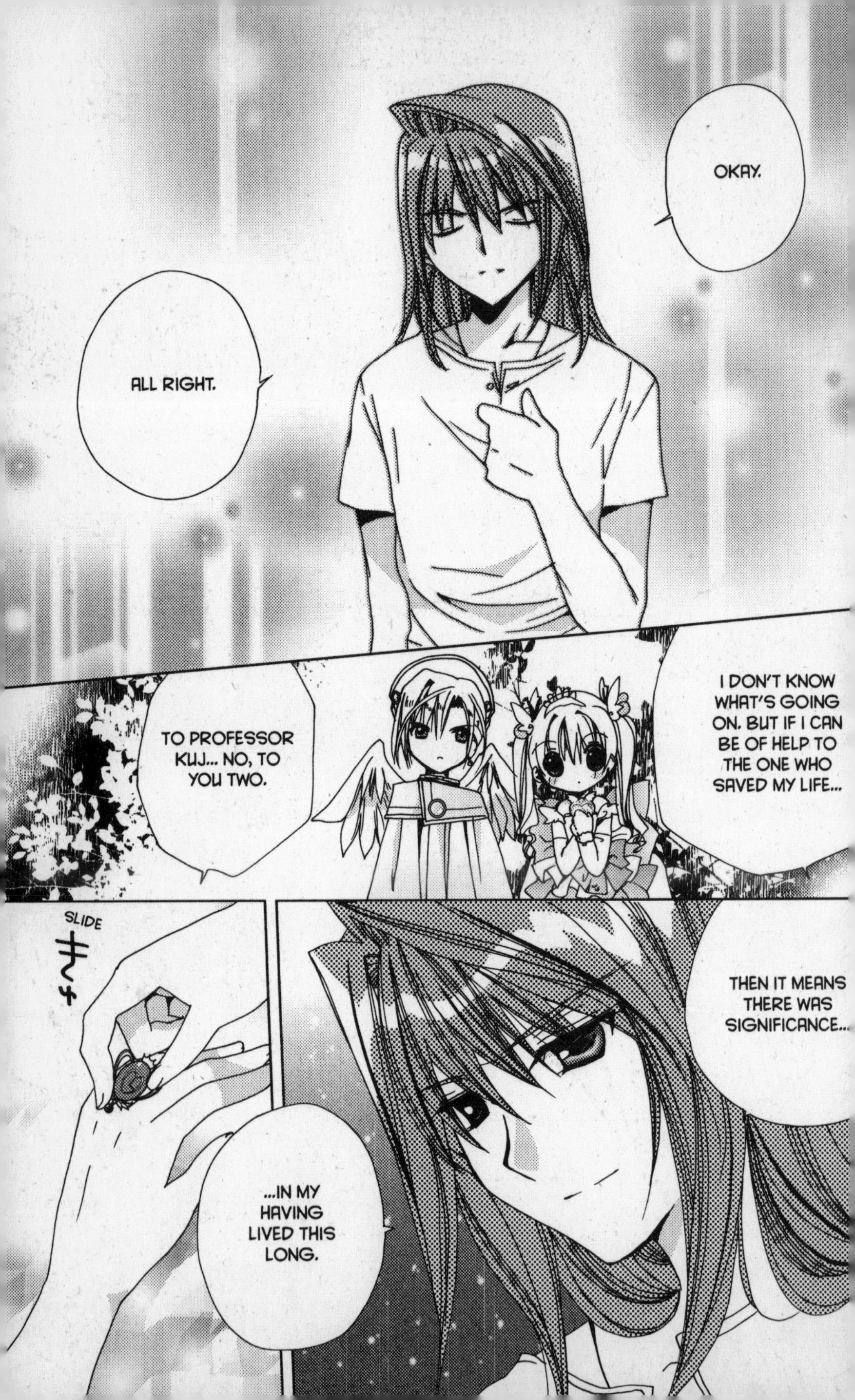
OKAY.
ALL RIGHT.
I DON'T KNOW WHAT'S GOING ON. BUT IF I CAN BE OF HELP TO THE ONE WHO SAVED MY LIFE...
TO PROFESSOR KUJ... NO, TO YOU TWO.
THEN IT MEANS THERE WAS SIGNIFICANCE...
...IN MY HAVING LIVED THIS LONG.
SLIDE

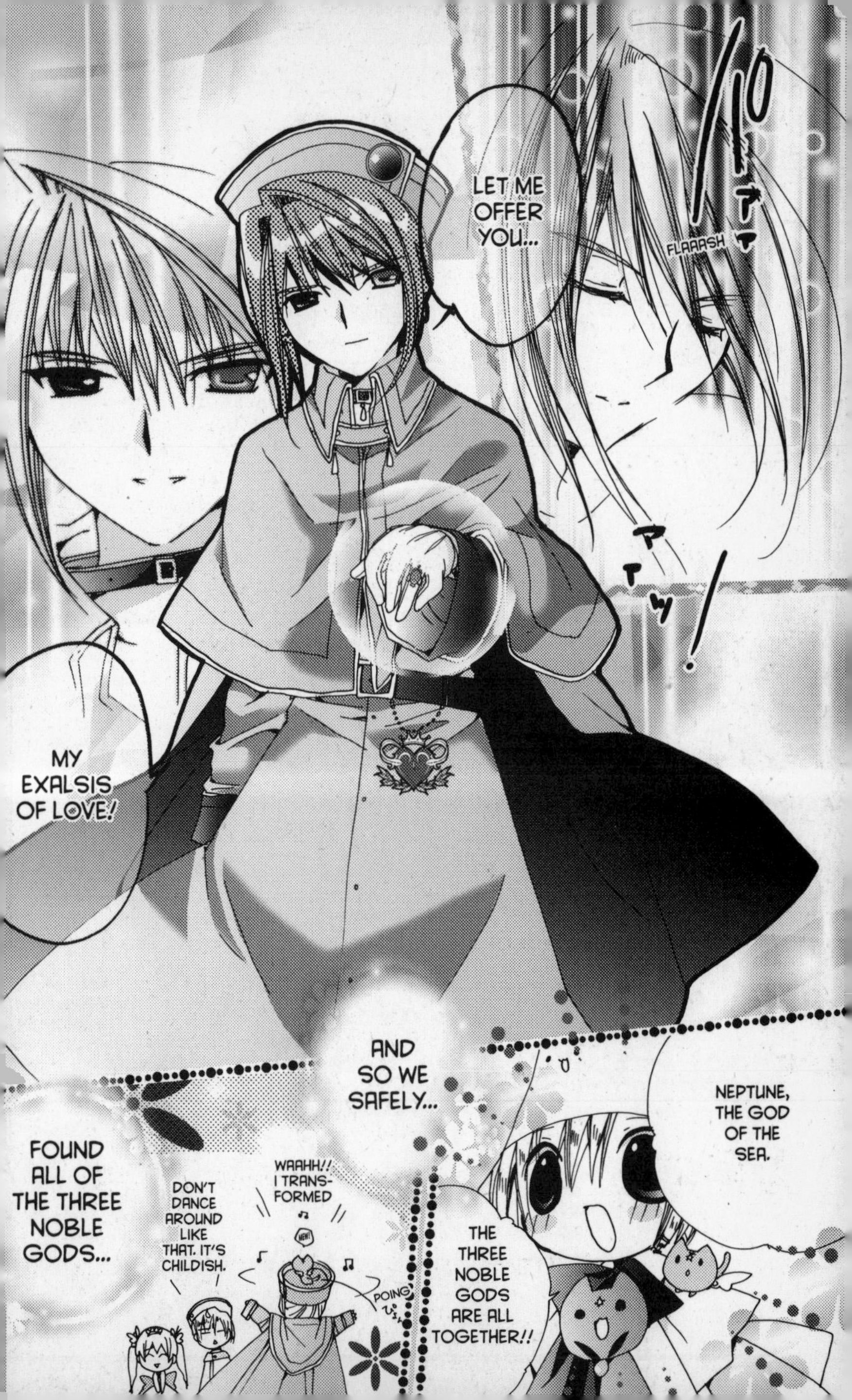
FLAAASH
LET ME OFFER YOU...
MY EXALSIS OF LOVE!
NEPTUNE, THE GOD OF THE SEA.
THE THREE NOBLE GODS ARE ALL TOGETHER!!
AND SO WE SAFELY...
WAAHH!! I TRANSFORMED
MEW!
POING
DON'T DANCE AROUND LIKE THAT. IT'S CHILDISH.
FOUND ALL OF THE THREE NOBLE GODS...

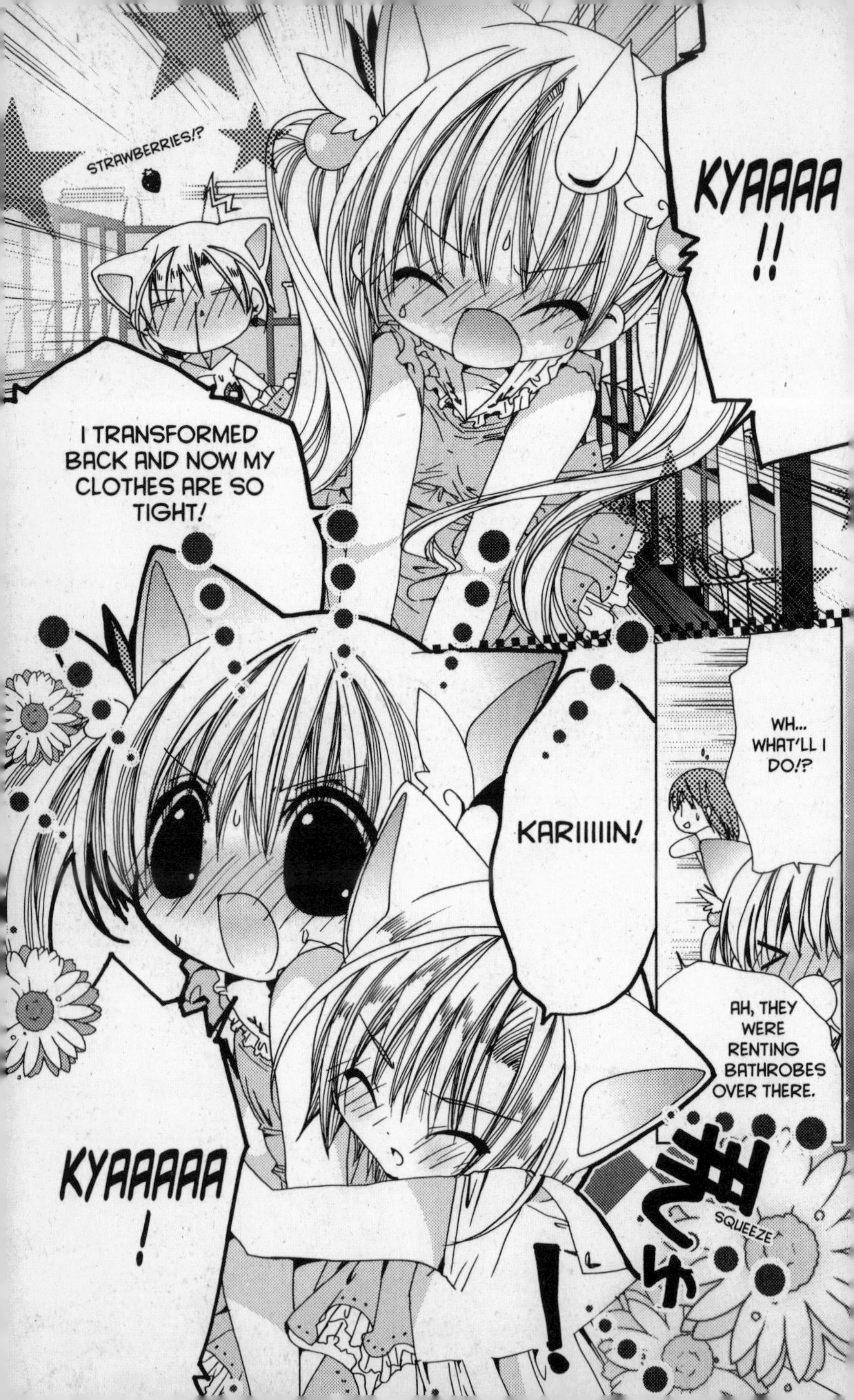

KYAAAA!!
STRAWBERRIES!?
I TRANSFORMED BACK AND NOW MY CLOTHES ARE SO TIGHT!
WH... WHAT'LL I DO!?
AH, THEY WERE RENTING BATHROBES OVER THERE.
KARIIIIIN!
SQUEEZE
KYAAAAAA!

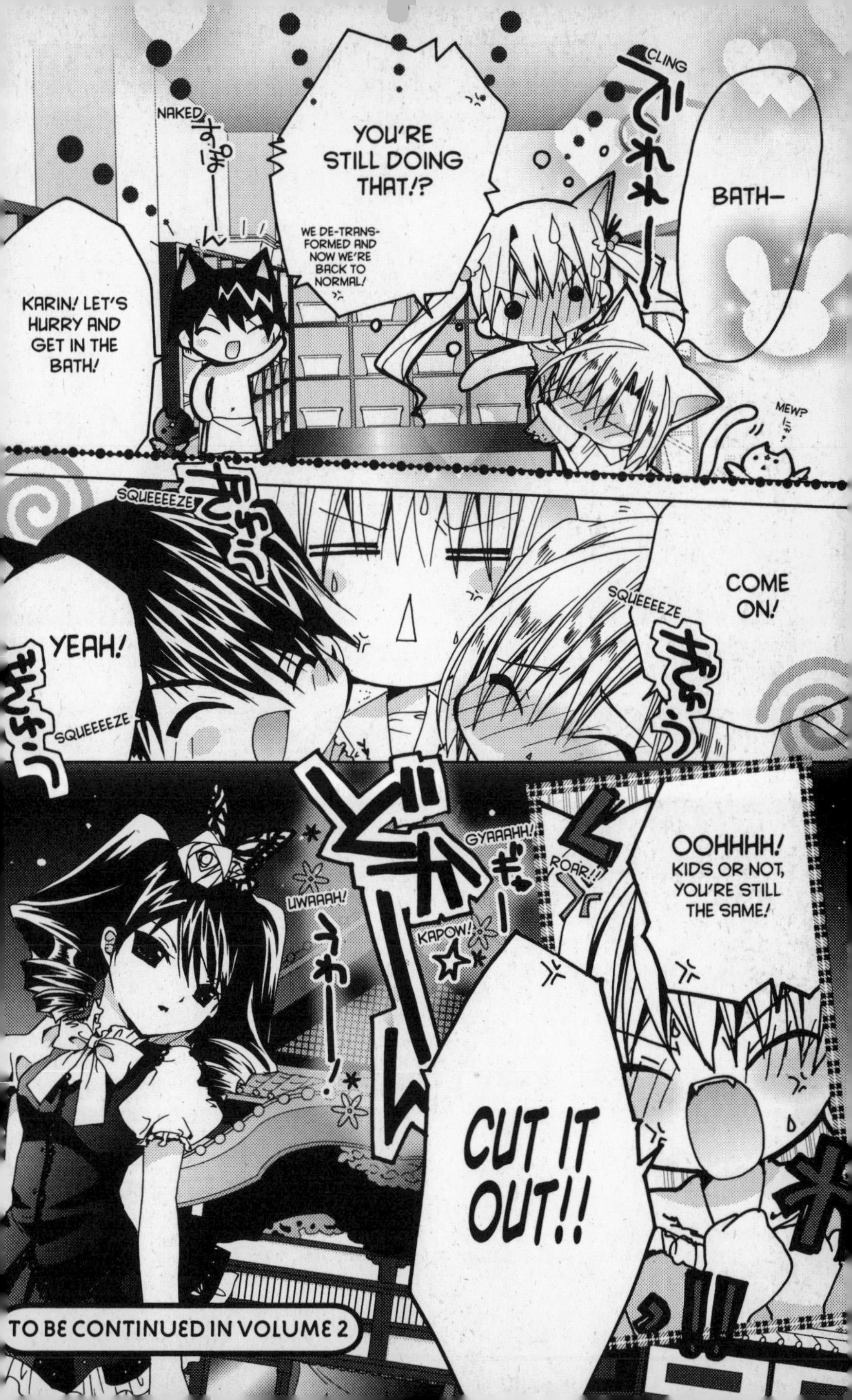
CLING
BATH—
YOU'RE STILL DOING THAT!?
WE DE-TRANSFORMED AND NOW WE'RE BACK TO NORMAL!
NAKED
KARIN! LET'S HURRY AND GET IN THE BATH!
MEW?
COME ON!
SQUEEEEZE
SQUEEEEZE
YEAH!
SQUEEEEZE
OOHHHH! KIDS OR NOT, YOU'RE STILL THE SAME!
ROAR!!
GYAAAHH!
KAPOW!!
UWAAAH!
CUT IT OUT!!
TO BE CONTINUED IN VOLUME 2

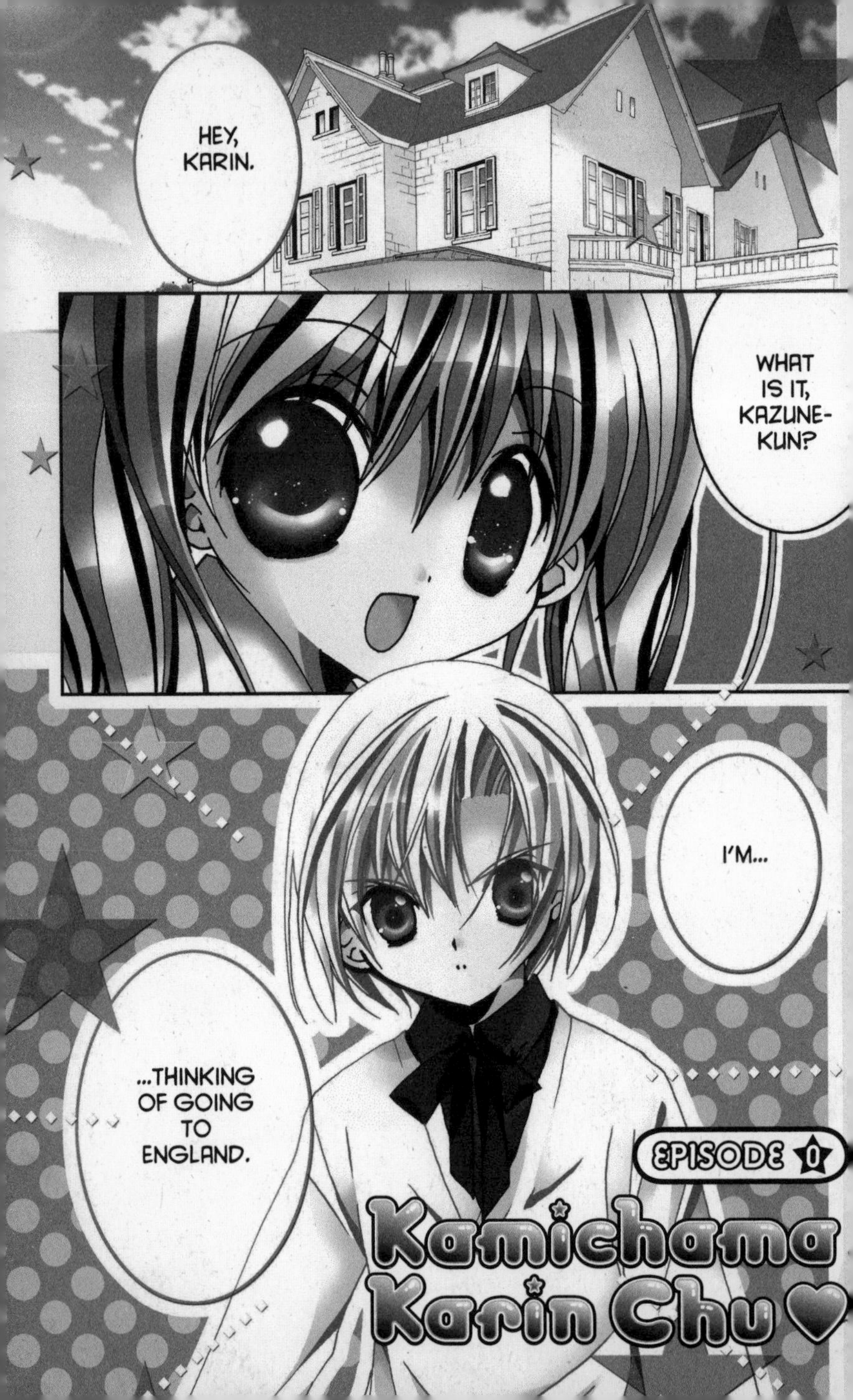
HEY, KARIN.
WHAT IS IT, KAZUNE-KUN?
I'M...
...THINKING OF GOING TO ENGLAND.
EPISODE 0
Kamichama Karin Chu♥

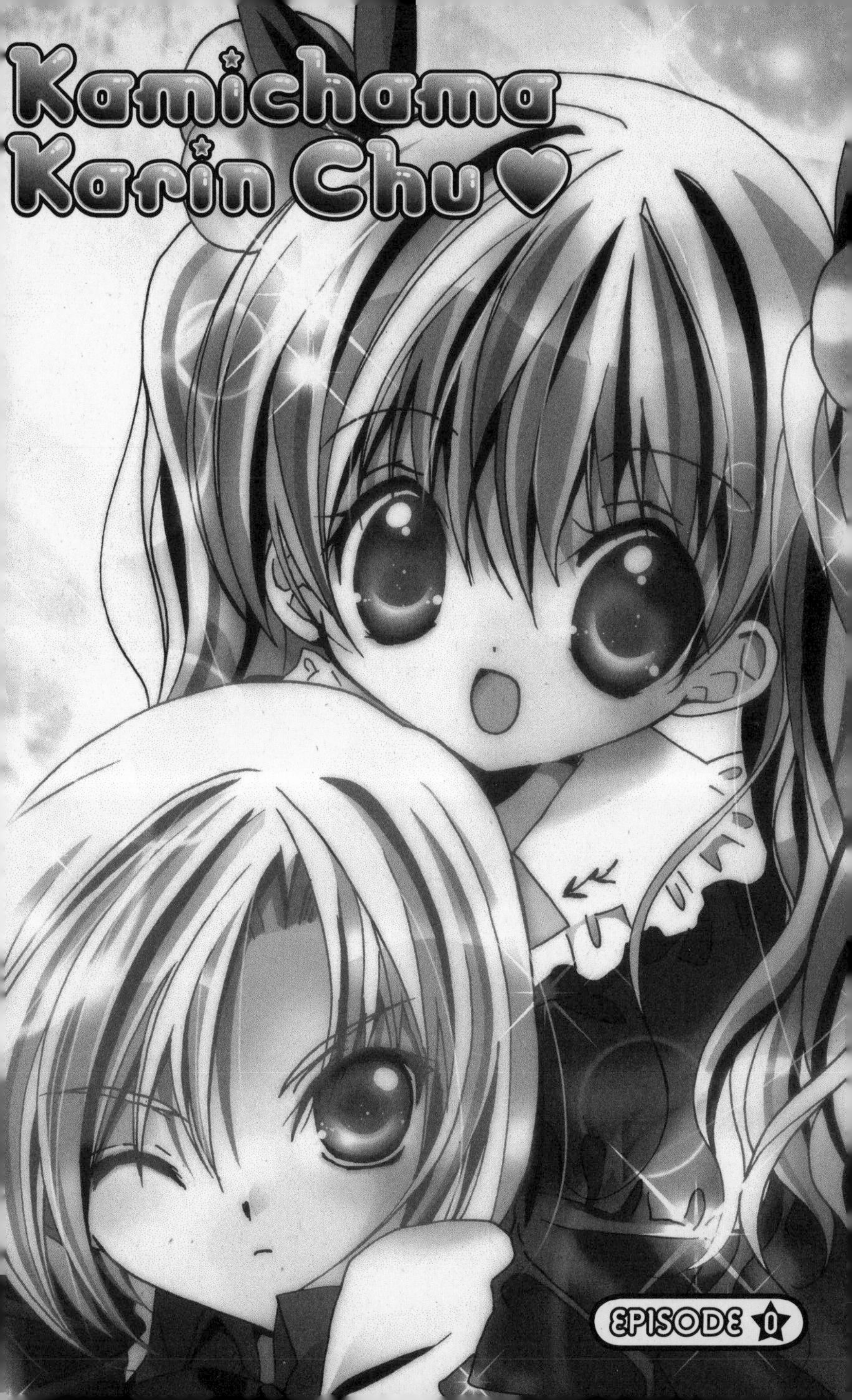
Kamichama Karin Chu♥
EPISODE 0

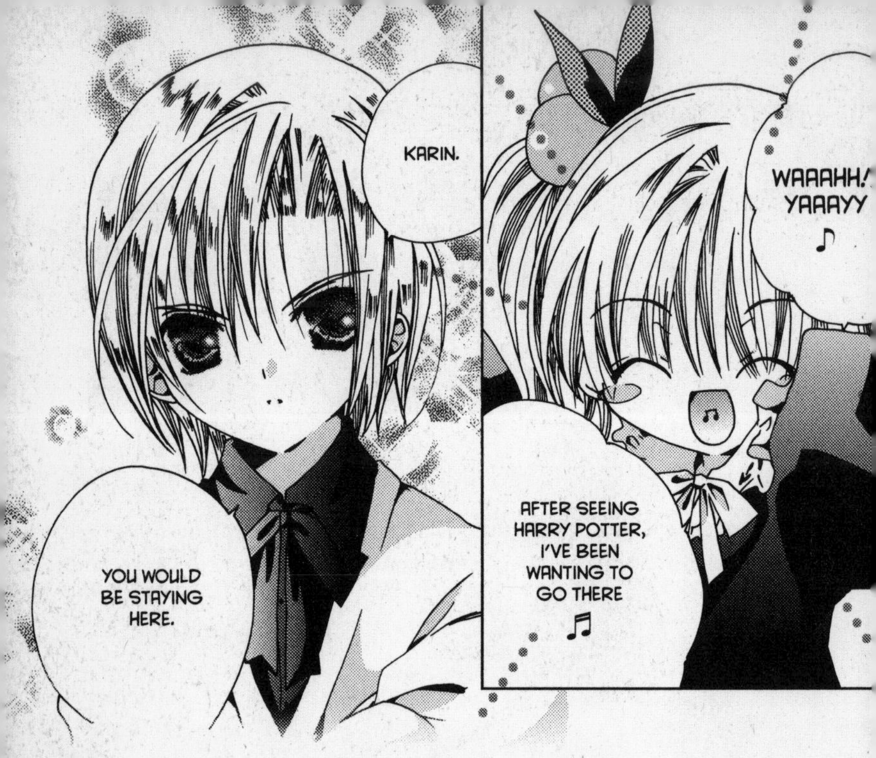
WAAAHH! YAAAYY ♪
AFTER SEEING HARRY POTTER, I'VE BEEN WANTING TO GO THERE ♫
KARIN.
YOU WOULD BE STAYING HERE.

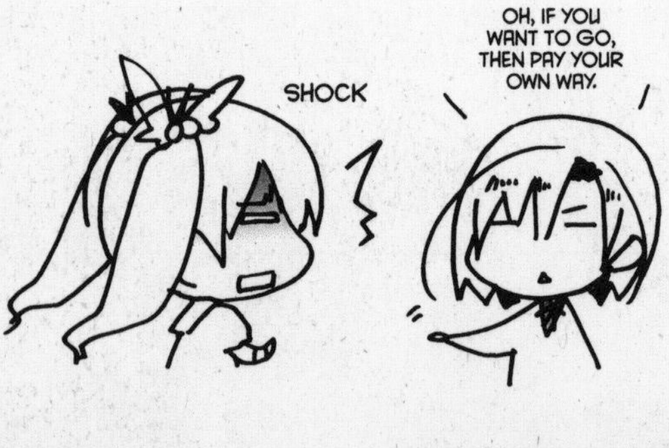
OH, IF YOU WANT TO GO, THEN PAY YOUR OWN WAY.
SHOCK

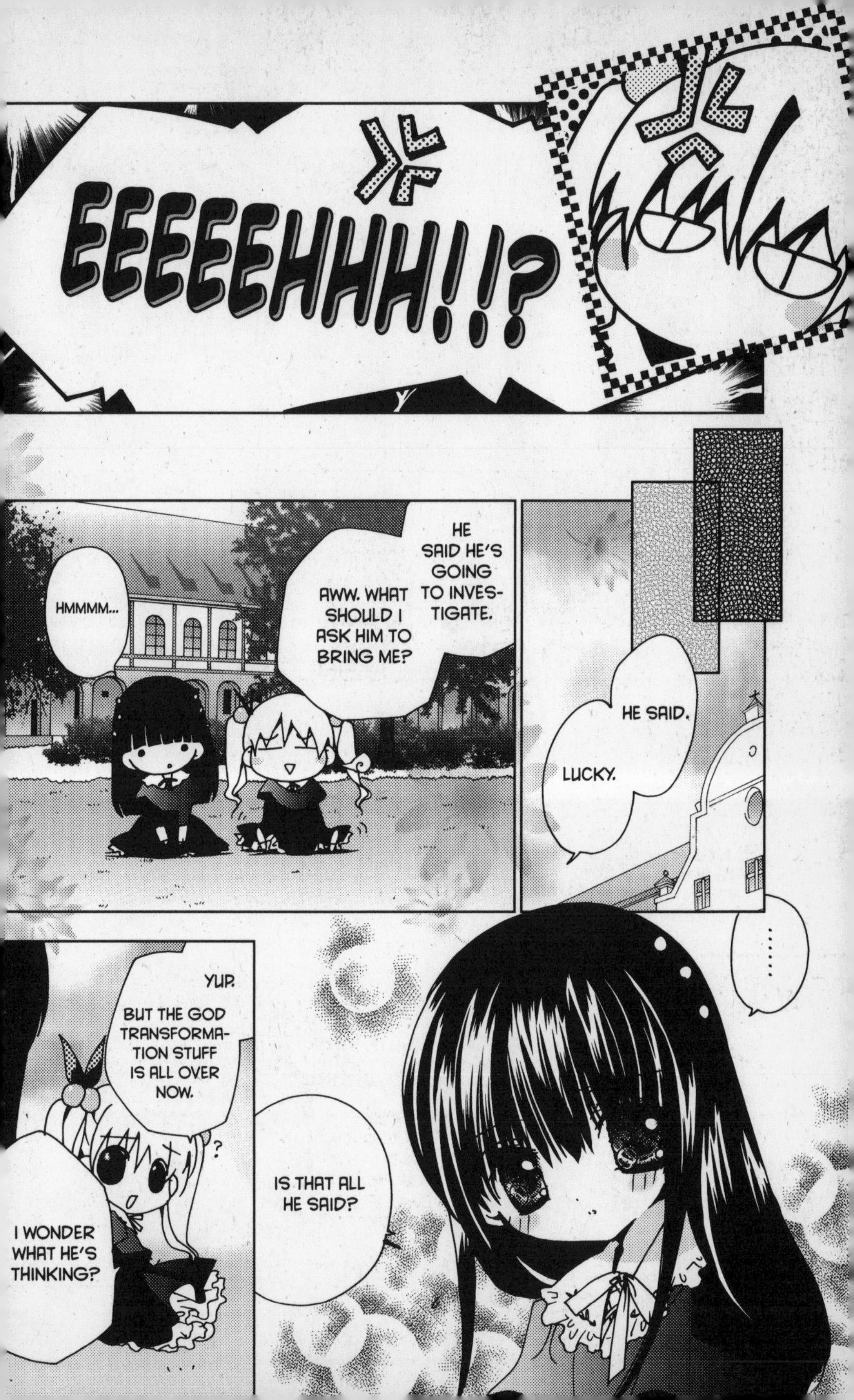
EEEEEHHH!!?
HE SAID.
LUCKY.
HE SAID HE'S GOING TO INVES-TIGATE.
AWW. WHAT SHOULD I ASK HIM TO BRING ME?
HMMMM...
......
IS THAT ALL HE SAID?
YUP.
BUT THE GOD TRANSFORMA-TION STUFF IS ALL OVER NOW.
?
I WONDER WHAT HE'S THINKING?

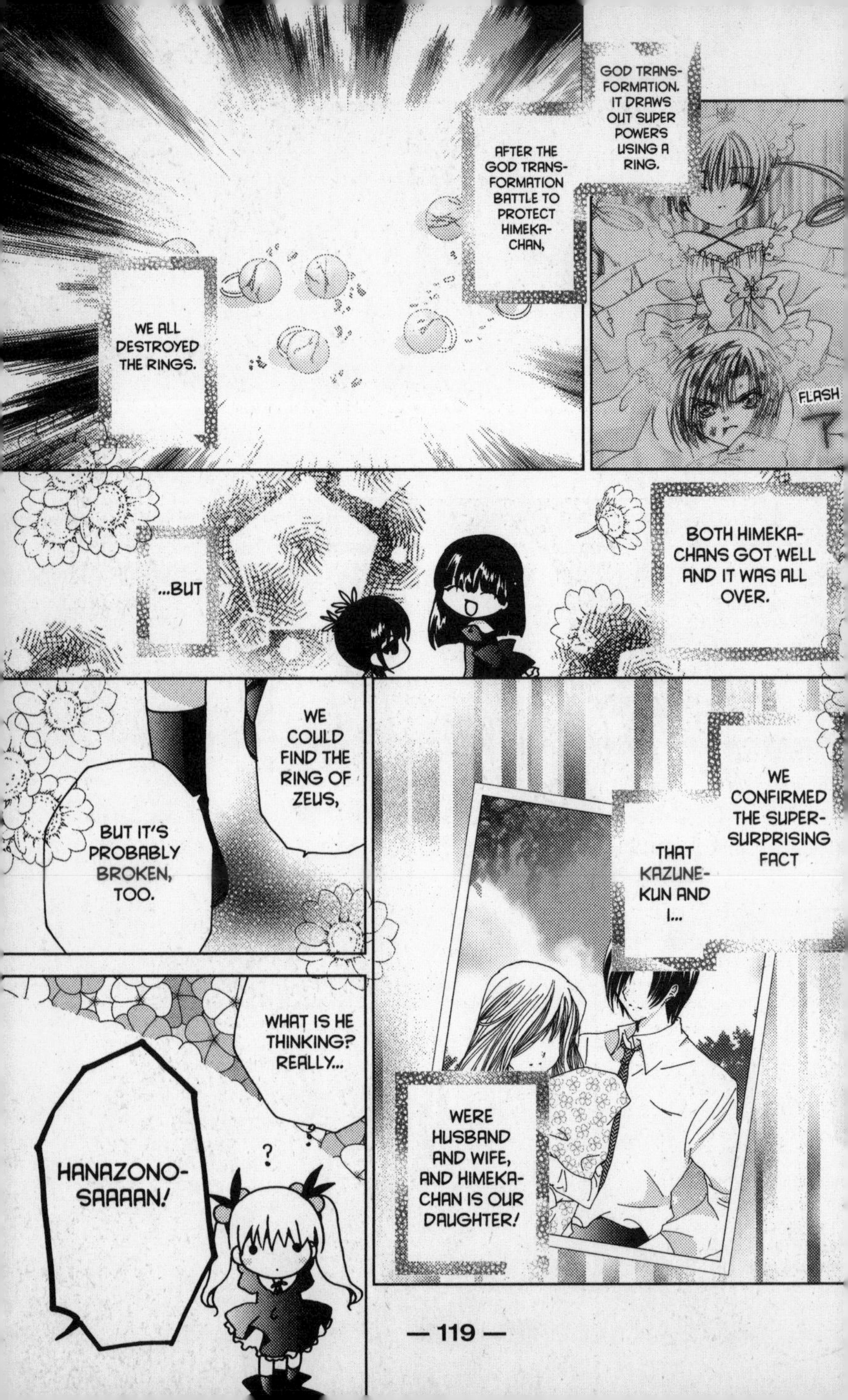
GOD TRANSFORMATION. IT DRAWS OUT SUPER POWERS USING A RING.
AFTER THE GOD TRANSFORMATION BATTLE TO PROTECT HIMEKA-CHAN,
FLASH
WE ALL DESTROYED THE RINGS.
BOTH HIMEKA-CHANS GOT WELL AND IT WAS ALL OVER.
...BUT
WE CONFIRMED THE SUPER-SURPRISING FACT
THAT KAZUNE-KUN AND I...
WERE HUSBAND AND WIFE, AND HIMEKA-CHAN IS OUR DAUGHTER!
WE COULD FIND THE RING OF ZEUS,
BUT IT'S PROBABLY BROKEN, TOO.
WHAT IS HE THINKING? REALLY...
?
HANAZONO-SAAAAN!

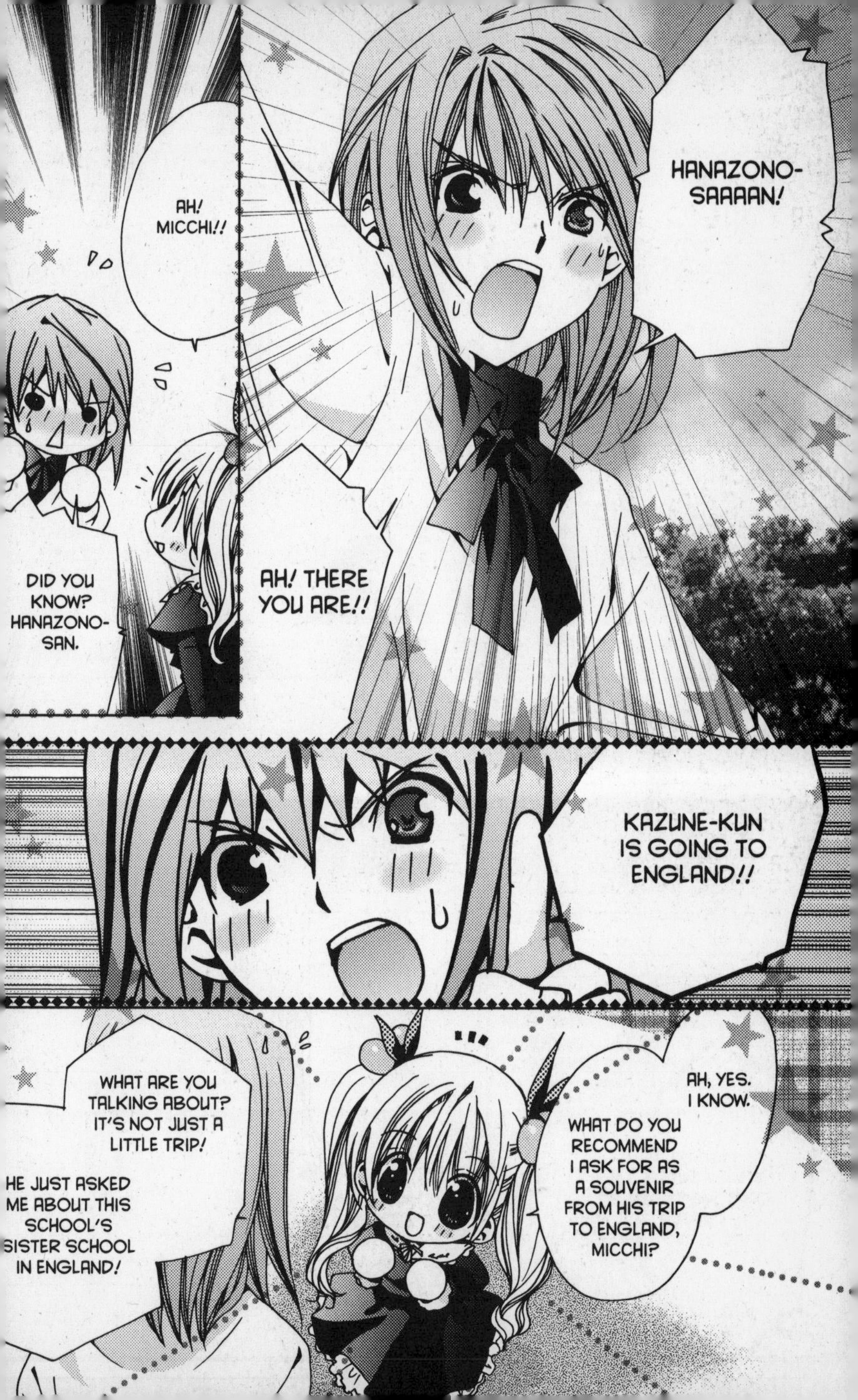
HANAZONO-SAAAAN!
AH! THERE YOU ARE!!
AH! MICCHI!!
DID YOU KNOW? HANAZONO-SAN.
KAZUNE-KUN IS GOING TO ENGLAND!!
AH, YES. I KNOW.
WHAT DO YOU RECOMMEND I ASK FOR AS A SOUVENIR FROM HIS TRIP TO ENGLAND, MICCHI?
WHAT ARE YOU TALKING ABOUT? IT'S NOT JUST A LITTLE TRIP!
HE JUST ASKED ME ABOUT THIS SCHOOL'S SISTER SCHOOL IN ENGLAND!

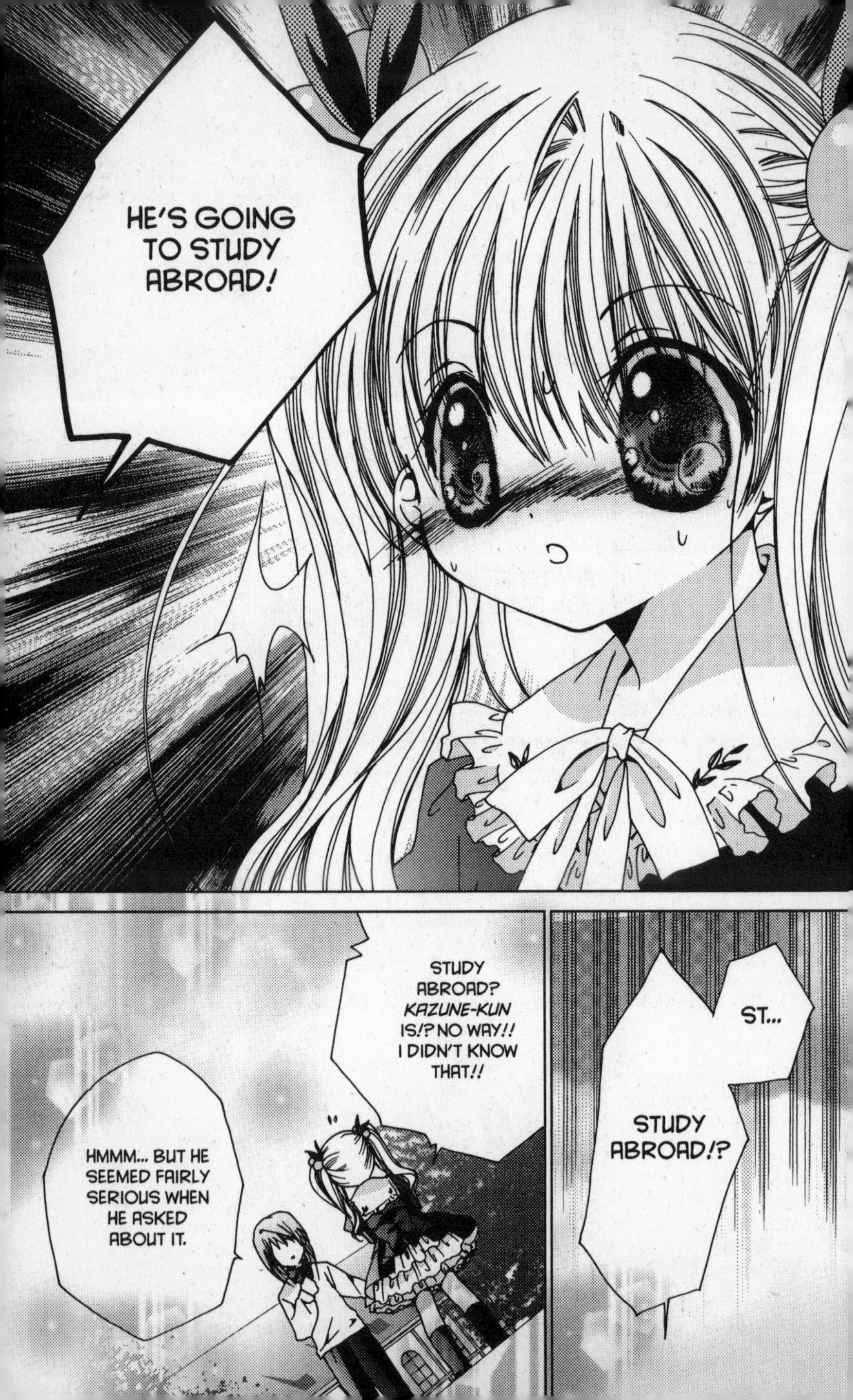
HE'S GOING TO STUDY ABROAD!
ST...
STUDY ABROAD!?
STUDY ABROAD? *KAZUNE-KUN* IS!? NO WAY!! I DIDN'T KNOW THAT!!
HMMM... BUT HE SEEMED FAIRLY SERIOUS WHEN HE ASKED ABOUT IT.

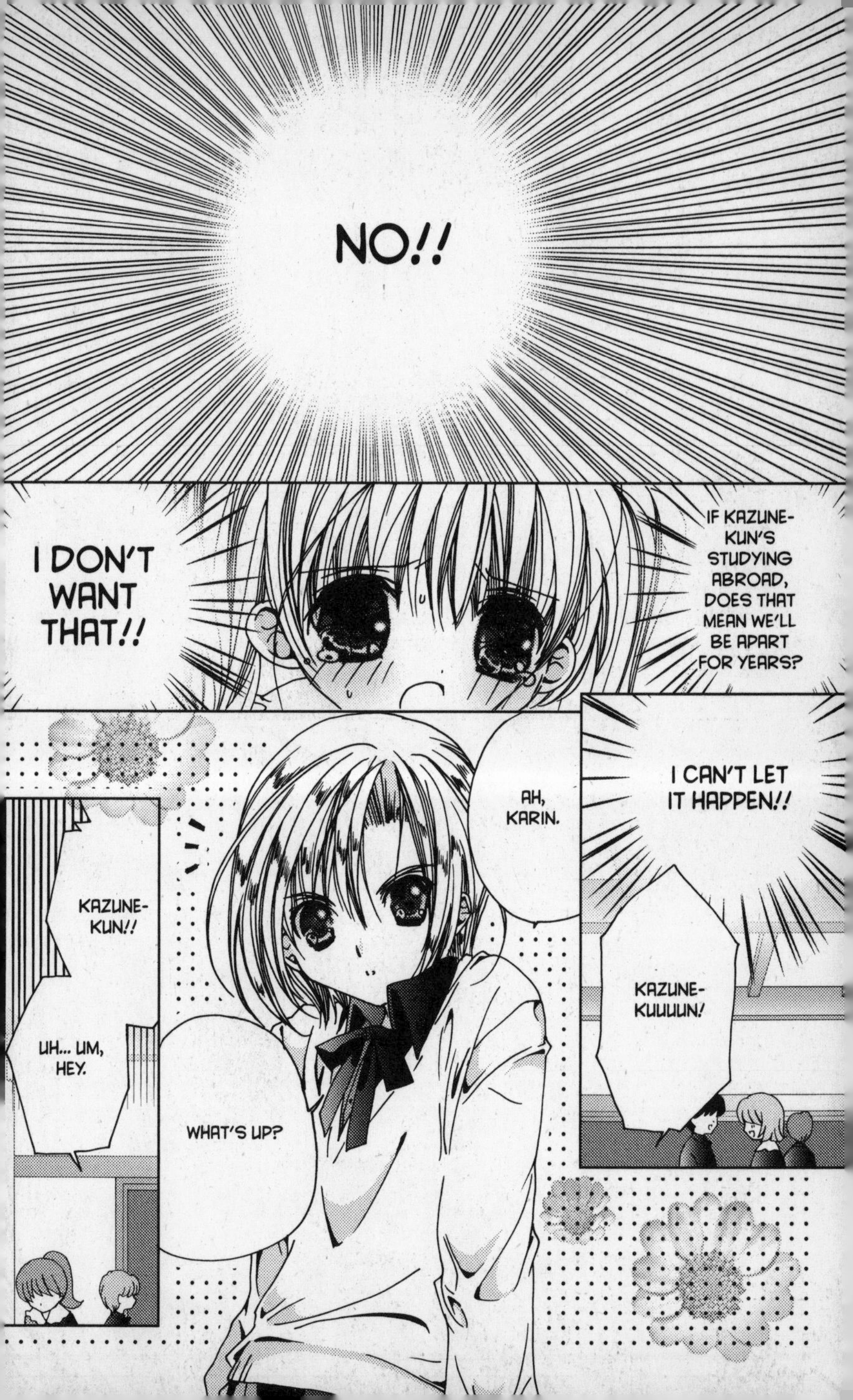
NO!!
IF KAZUNE-KUN'S STUDYING ABROAD, DOES THAT MEAN WE'LL BE APART FOR YEARS?
I DON'T WANT THAT!!
I CAN'T LET IT HAPPEN!!
KAZUNE-KUUUUN!
AH, KARIN.
WHAT'S UP?
KAZUNE-KUN!!
UH... UM, HEY.

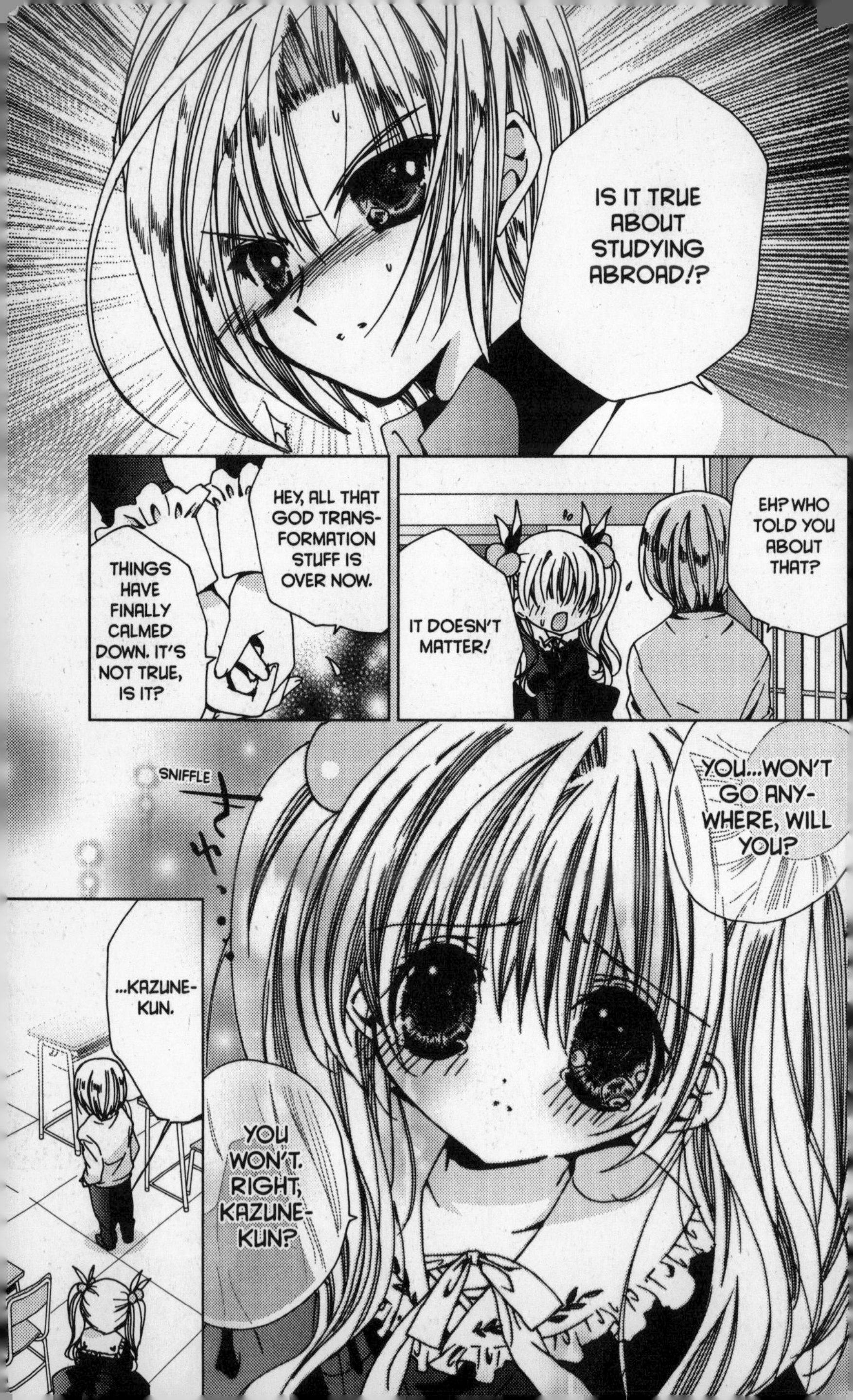
IS IT TRUE ABOUT STUDYING ABROAD!?
EH? WHO TOLD YOU ABOUT THAT?
IT DOESN'T MATTER!
HEY, ALL THAT GOD TRANS-FORMATION STUFF IS OVER NOW.
THINGS HAVE FINALLY CALMED DOWN. IT'S NOT TRUE, IS IT?
YOU...WON'T GO ANY-WHERE, WILL YOU?
SNIFFLE
YOU WON'T. RIGHT, KAZUNE-KUN?
...KAZUNE-KUN.

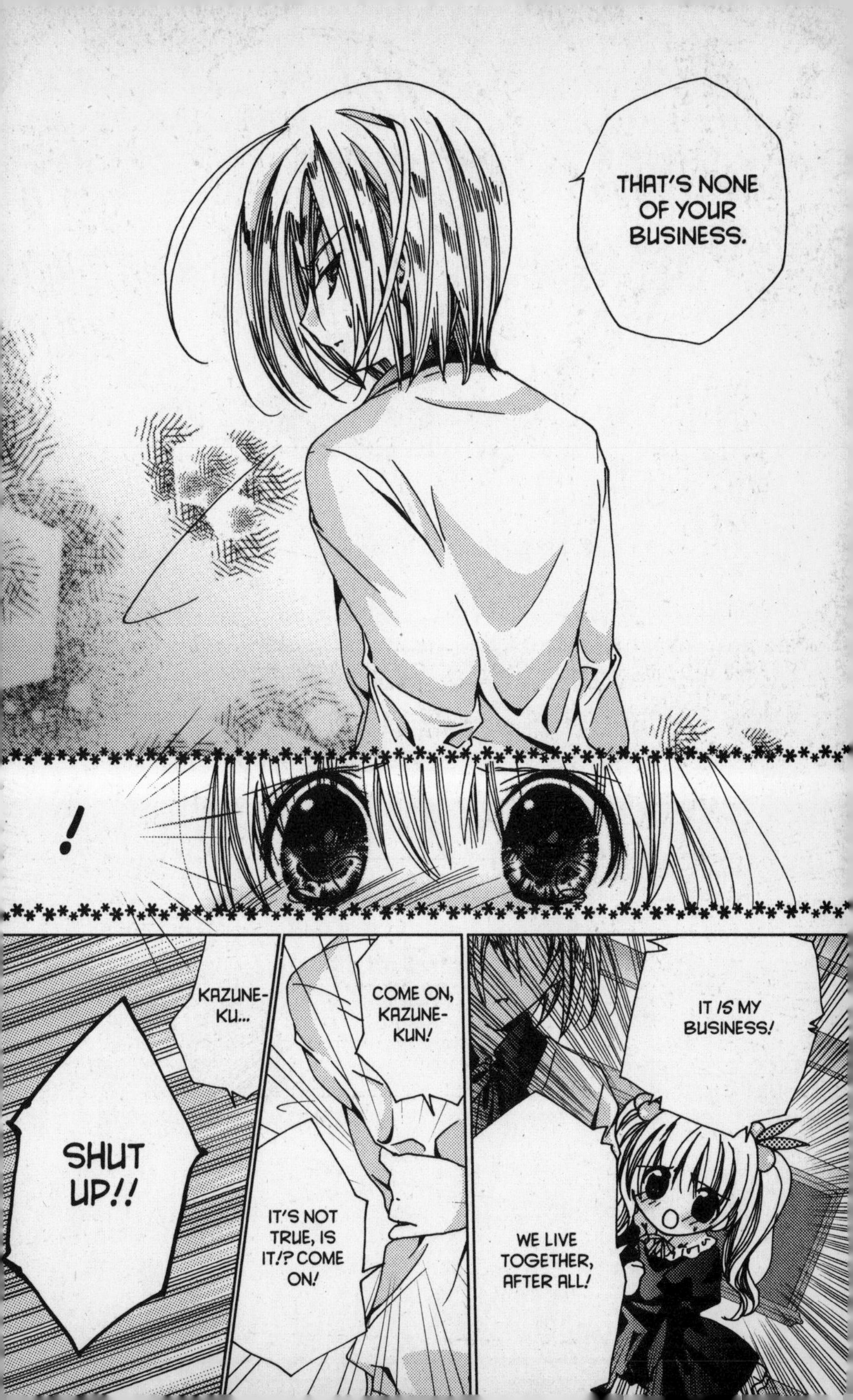
THAT'S NONE OF YOUR BUSINESS.
!
IT *IS* MY BUSINESS!
WE LIVE TOGETHER, AFTER ALL!
COME ON, KAZUNE-KUN!
IT'S NOT TRUE, IS IT!? COME ON!
KAZUNE-KU...
SHUT UP!!

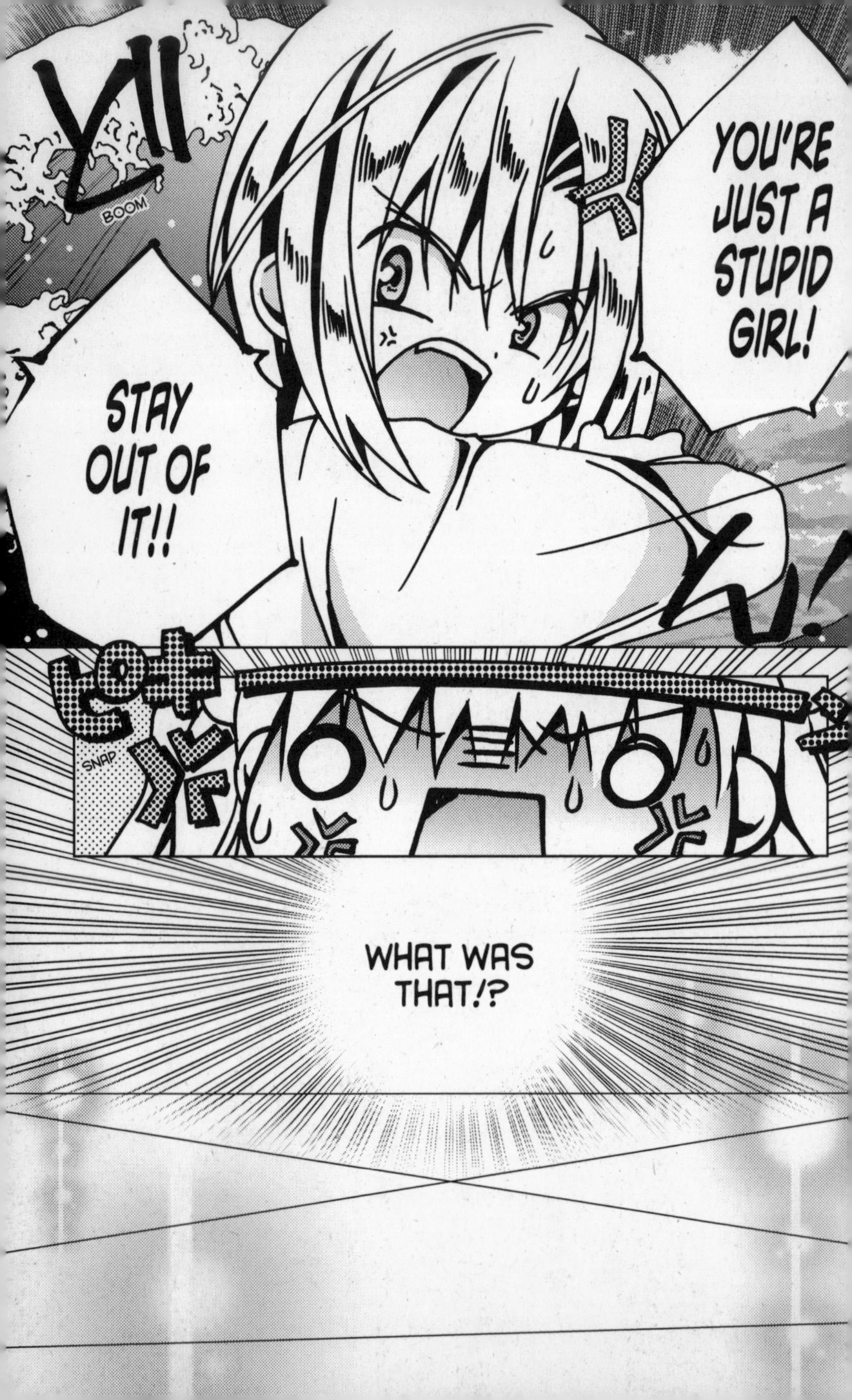
YOU'RE JUST A STUPID GIRL!
STAY OUT OF IT!!
BOOM
SNAP
WHAT WAS THAT!?

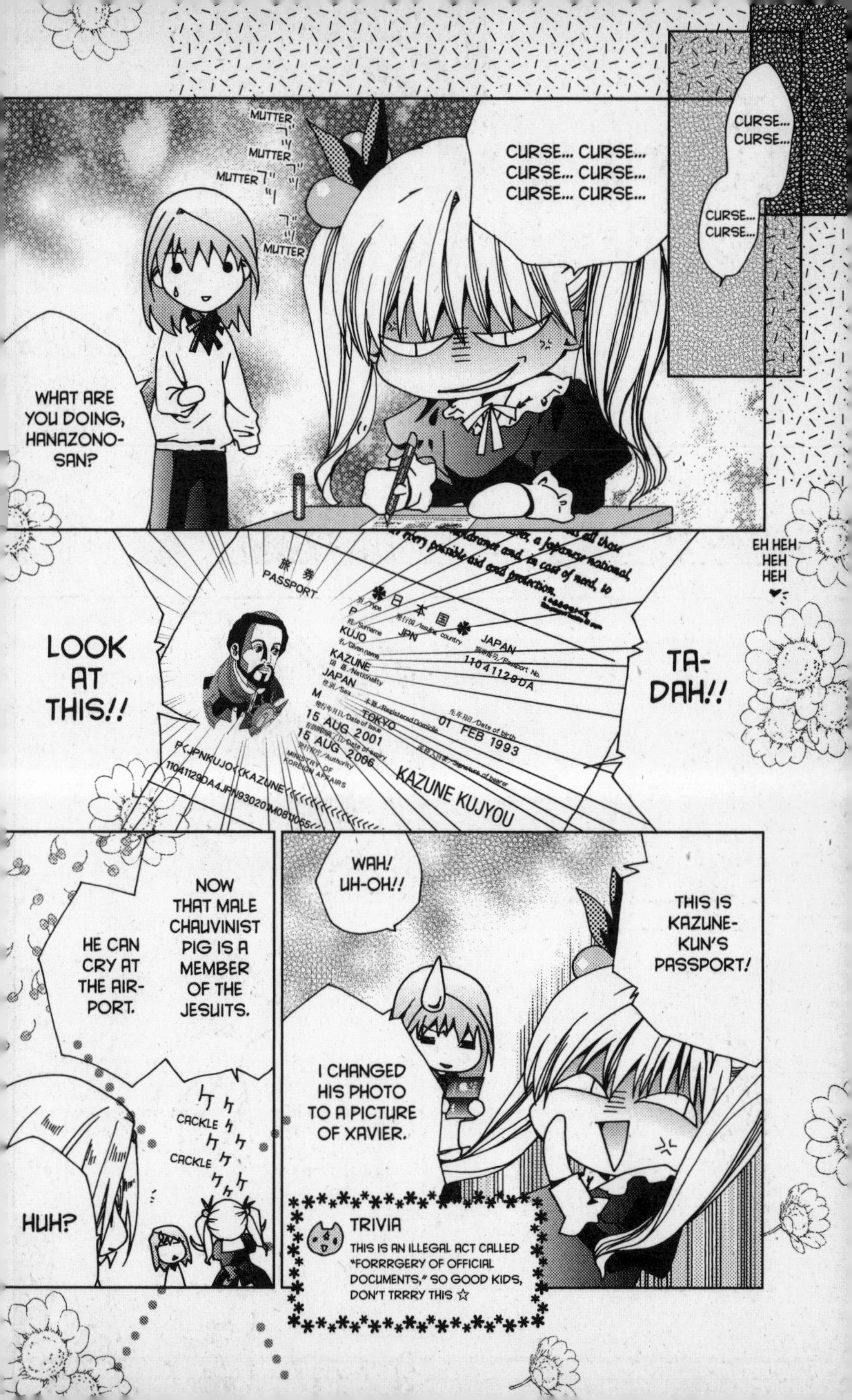
CURSE... CURSE...
CURSE... CURSE...
CURSE... CURSE... CURSE... CURSE... CURSE... CURSE...
MUTTER MUTTER MUTTER MUTTER
WHAT ARE YOU DOING, HANAZONO-SAN?
EH HEH HEH HEH
TA-DAH!!
PASSPORT
KUJO
KAZUNE
JAPAN
TOKYO
01 FEB 1993
15 AUG 2001
15 AUG 2006
KAZUNE KUJYOU
LOOK AT THIS!!
THIS IS KAZUNE-KUN'S PASSPORT!
WAH! UH-OH!!
I CHANGED HIS PHOTO TO A PICTURE OF XAVIER.
TRIVIA
THIS IS AN ILLEGAL ACT CALLED "FORRRGERY OF OFFICIAL DOCUMENTS," SO GOOD KIDS, DON'T TRRRY THIS ☆
NOW THAT MALE CHAUVINIST PIG IS A MEMBER OF THE JESUITS.
HE CAN CRY AT THE AIRPORT.
CACKLE CACKLE
HUH?

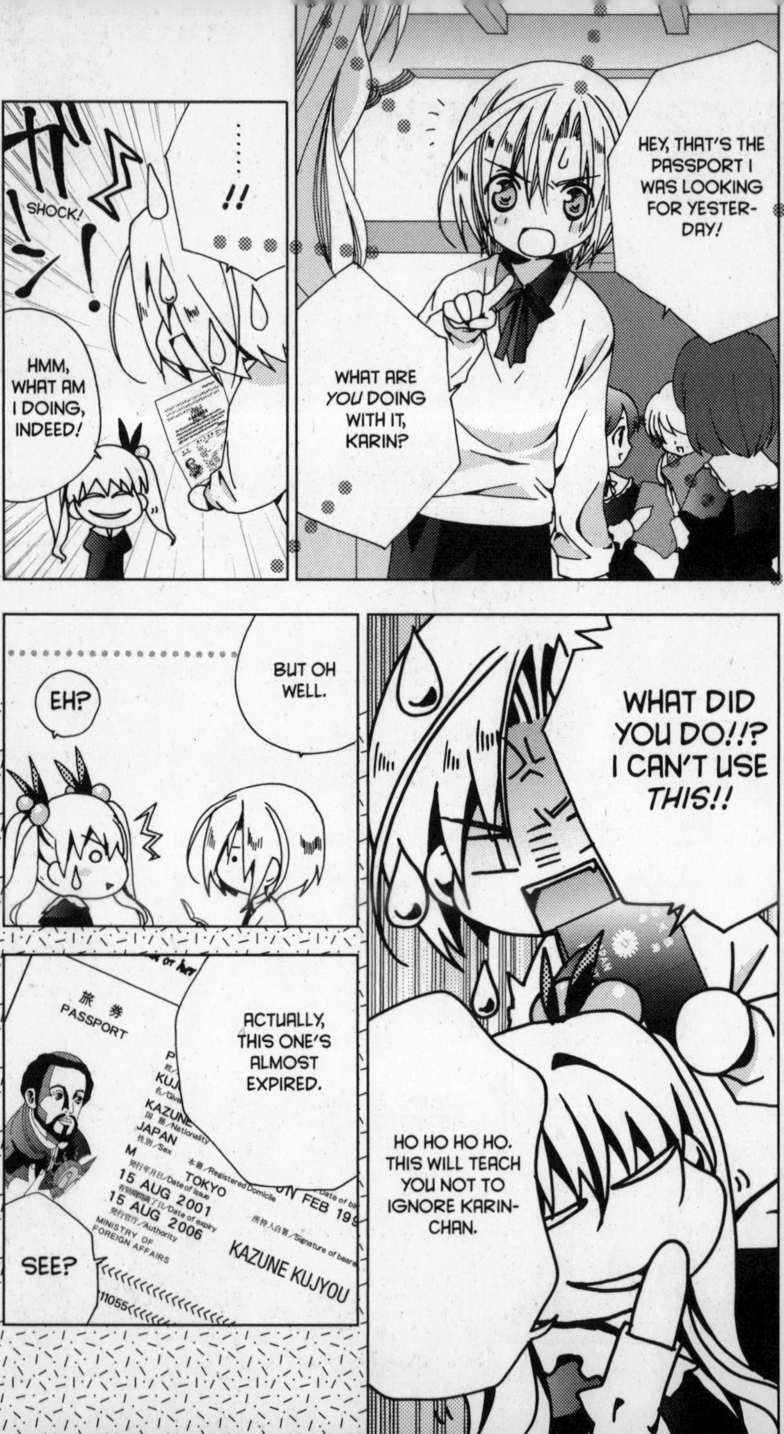
HEY, THAT'S THE PASSPORT I WAS LOOKING FOR YESTER-DAY!
WHAT ARE *YOU* DOING WITH IT, KARIN?
!!
SHOCK!
HMM, WHAT AM I DOING, INDEED!
WHAT DID YOU DO!!? I CAN'T USE *THIS!!*
HO HO HO HO. THIS WILL TEACH YOU NOT TO IGNORE KARIN-CHAN.
BUT OH WELL.
EH?
ACTUALLY, THIS ONE'S ALMOST EXPIRED.
旅券
PASSPORT
KAZUNE
JAPAN
M
TOKYO
15 AUG 2001
15 AUG 2006
MINISTRY OF FOREIGN AFFAIRS
KAZUNE KUJYOU
SEE?

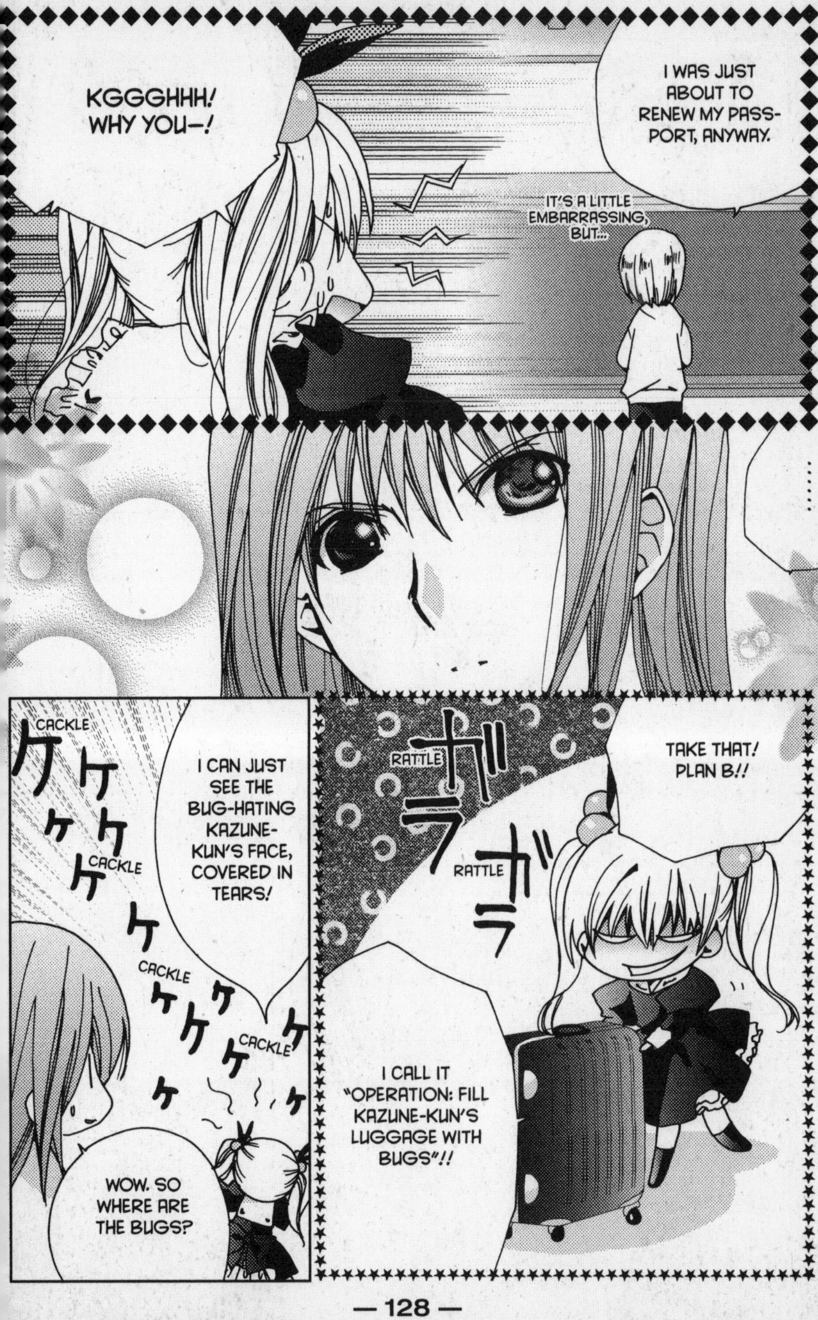
I WAS JUST ABOUT TO RENEW MY PASS-PORT, ANYWAY.
IT'S A LITTLE EMBARRASSING, BUT...
KGGGHHH! WHY YOU—!
......
TAKE THAT! PLAN B!!
RATTLE ガラ
RATTLE ガラ
I CALL IT "OPERATION: FILL KAZUNE-KUN'S LUGGAGE WITH BUGS"!!
CACKLE ケケケ
CACKLE ケケケ
I CAN JUST SEE THE BUG-HATING KAZUNE-KUN'S FACE, COVERED IN TEARS!
CACKLE ケケケ
CACKLE ケケケ
WOW. SO WHERE ARE THE BUGS?

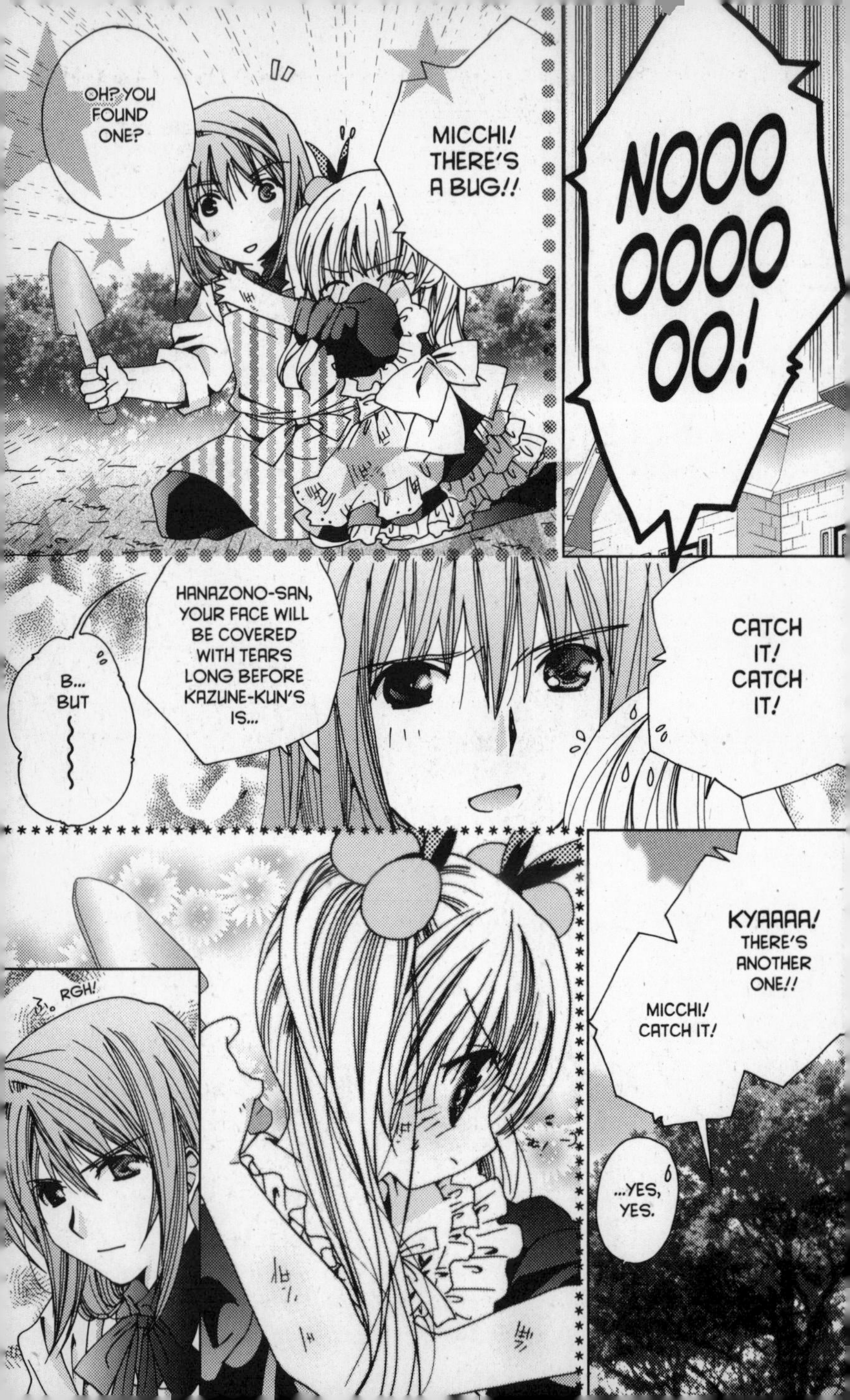
NOOOOOOOOOO!
MICCHI! THERE'S A BUG!!
OH? YOU FOUND ONE?
CATCH IT! CATCH IT!
HANAZONO-SAN, YOUR FACE WILL BE COVERED WITH TEARS LONG BEFORE KAZUNE-KUN'S IS...
B... BUT
KYAAAA! THERE'S ANOTHER ONE!!
MICCHI! CATCH IT!
...YES, YES.
RGH!

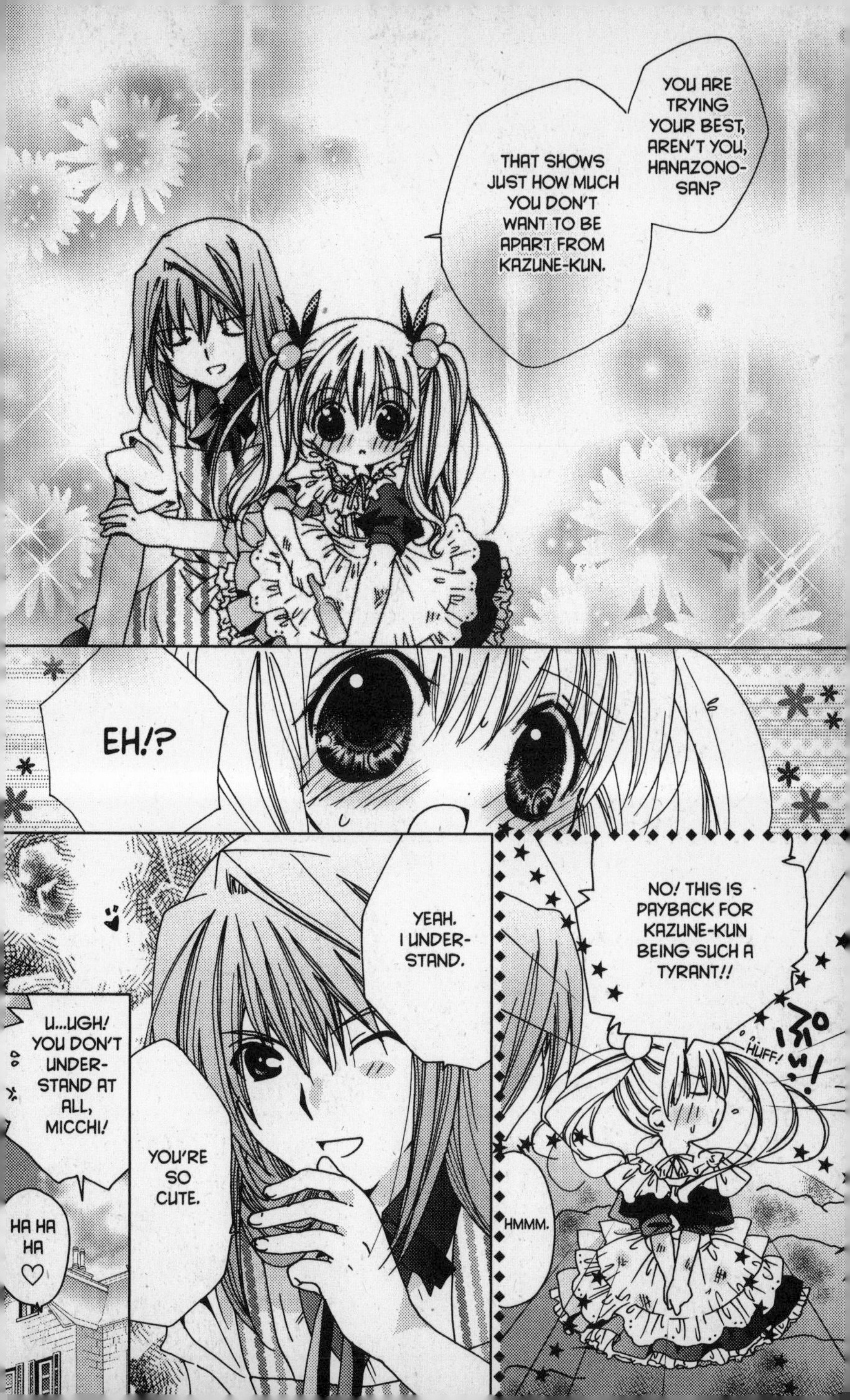
YOU ARE TRYING YOUR BEST, AREN'T YOU, HANAZONO-SAN?
THAT SHOWS JUST HOW MUCH YOU DON'T WANT TO BE APART FROM KAZUNE-KUN.
EH!?
NO! THIS IS PAYBACK FOR KAZUNE-KUN BEING SUCH A TYRANT!!
HUFF!
HMMM.
YEAH. I UNDER-STAND.
YOU'RE SO CUTE.
U...UGH! YOU DON'T UNDER-STAND AT ALL, MICCHI!
HA HA HA ♡

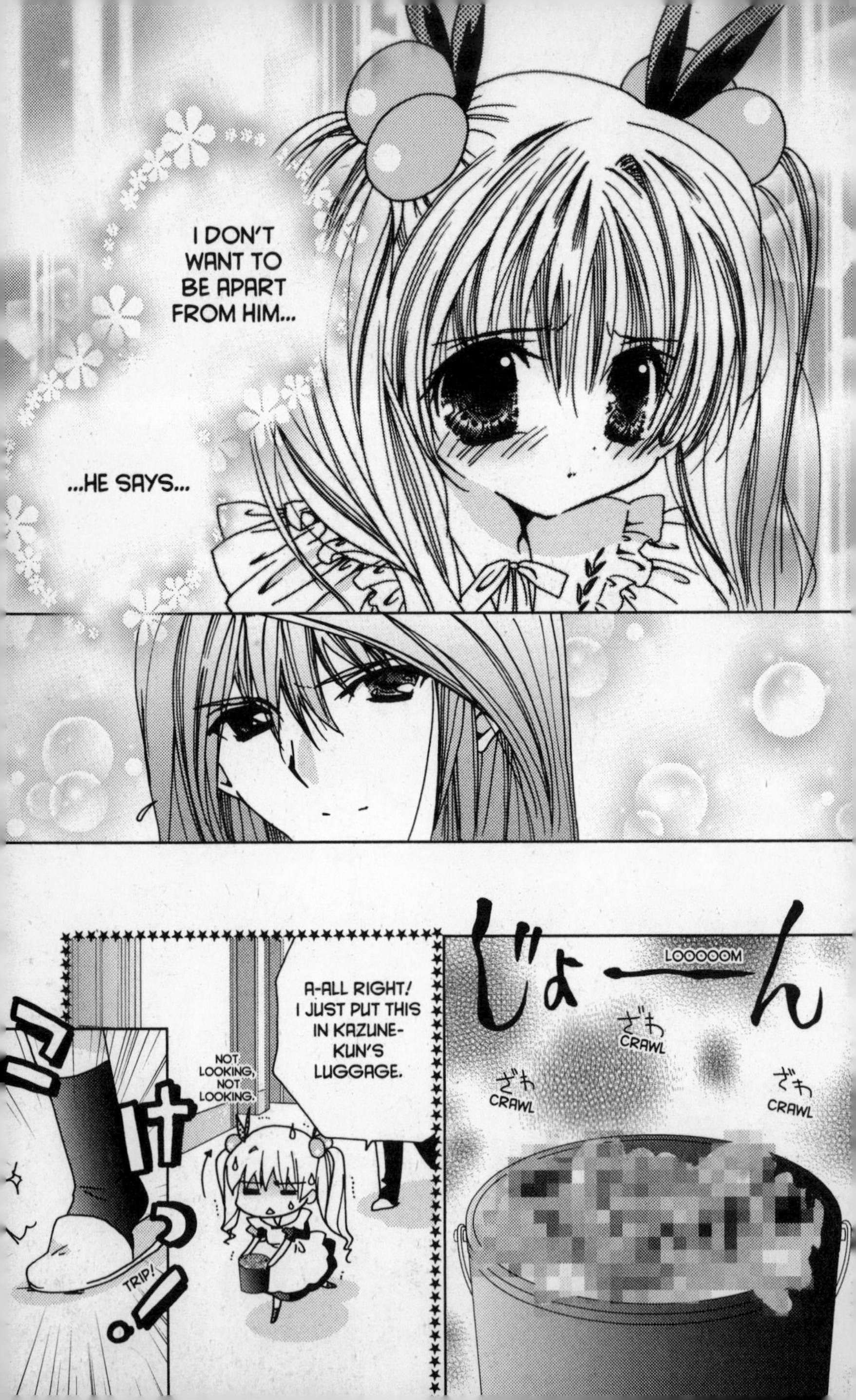

I DON'T WANT TO BE APART FROM HIM...
...HE SAYS...
じょーん
LOOOOOM
ざわ
CRAWL
ざわ
CRAWL
ざわ
CRAWL
A-ALL RIGHT! I JUST PUT THIS IN KAZUNE-KUN'S LUGGAGE.
NOT LOOKING, NOT LOOKING.
TRIP!

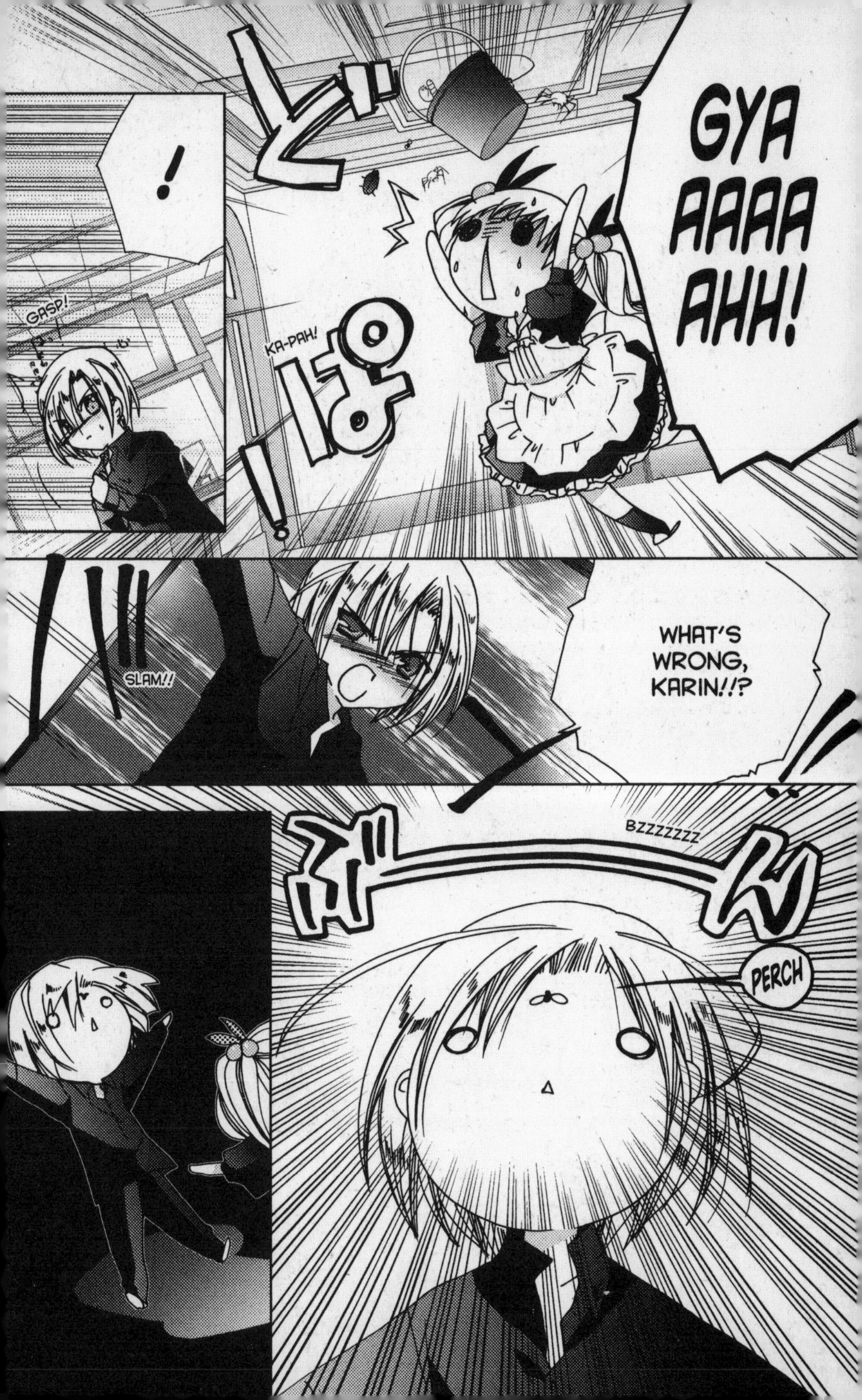
GYAAAAAAHH!
KA-PAH!
!
GASP!
WHAT'S WRONG, KARIN!!?
SLAM!!
BZZZZZZZ
PERCH

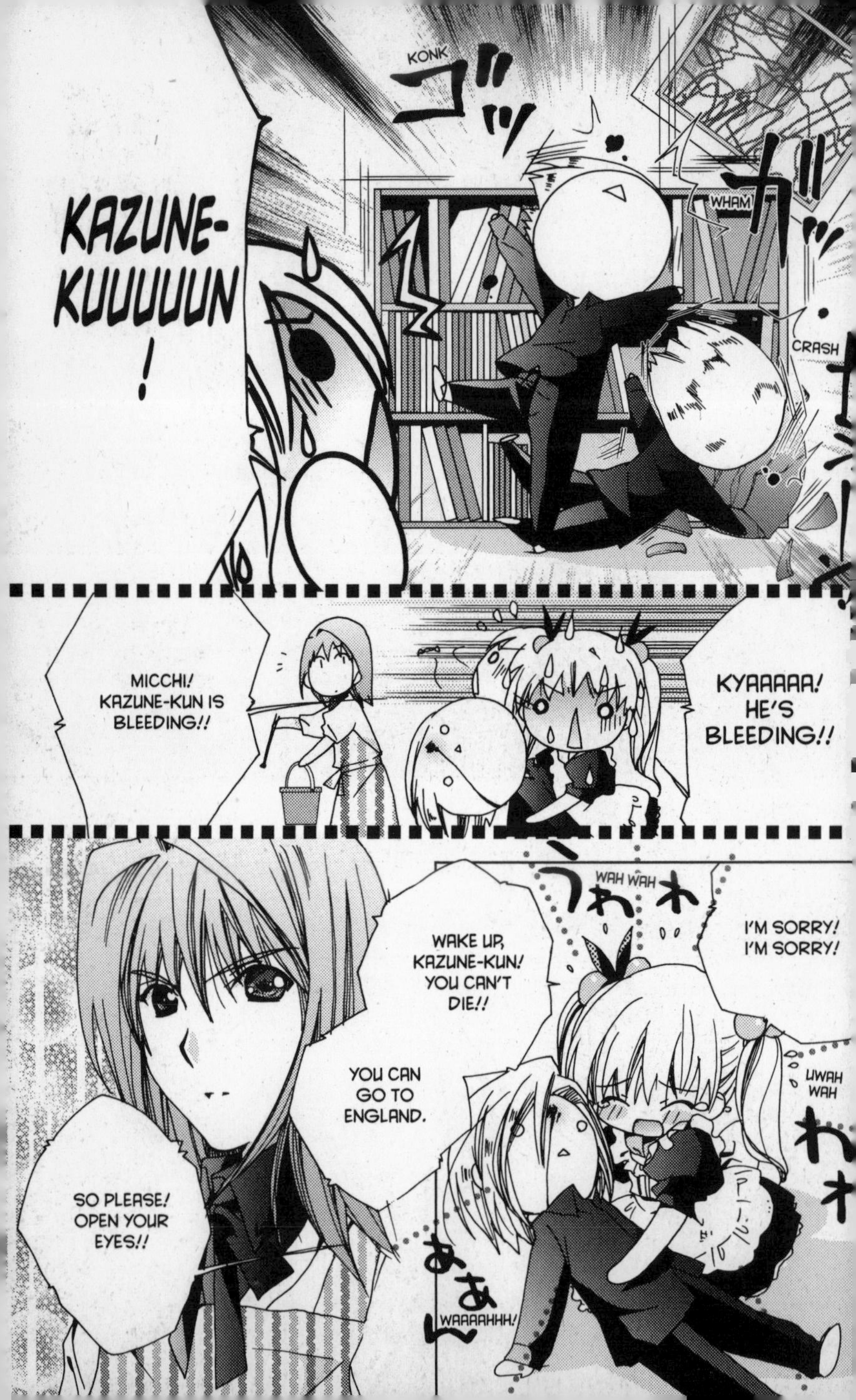
KONK
WHAM
CRASH
KAZUNE-KUUUUUN!
KYAAAAAA! HE'S BLEEDING!!
MICCHI! KAZUNE-KUN IS BLEEDING!!
I'M SORRY! I'M SORRY!
WAH WAH
WAKE UP, KAZUNE-KUN! YOU CAN'T DIE!!
UWAH WAH
YOU CAN GO TO ENGLAND.
WAAAAHHH!
SO PLEASE! OPEN YOUR EYES!!

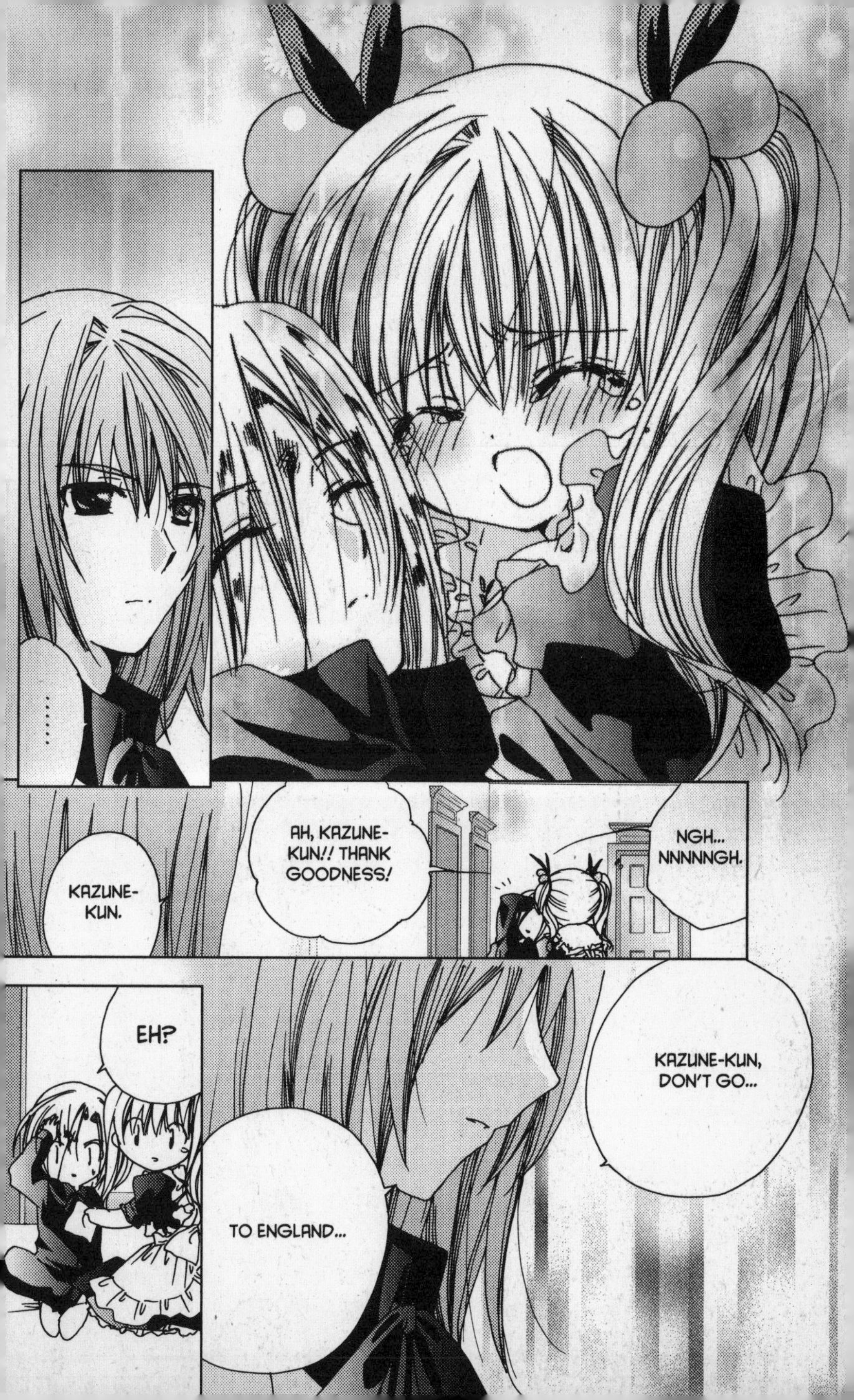
......
NGH... NNNNNGH.
AH, KAZUNE-KUN!! THANK GOODNESS!
KAZUNE-KUN.
KAZUNE-KUN, DON'T GO...
TO ENGLAND...
EH?

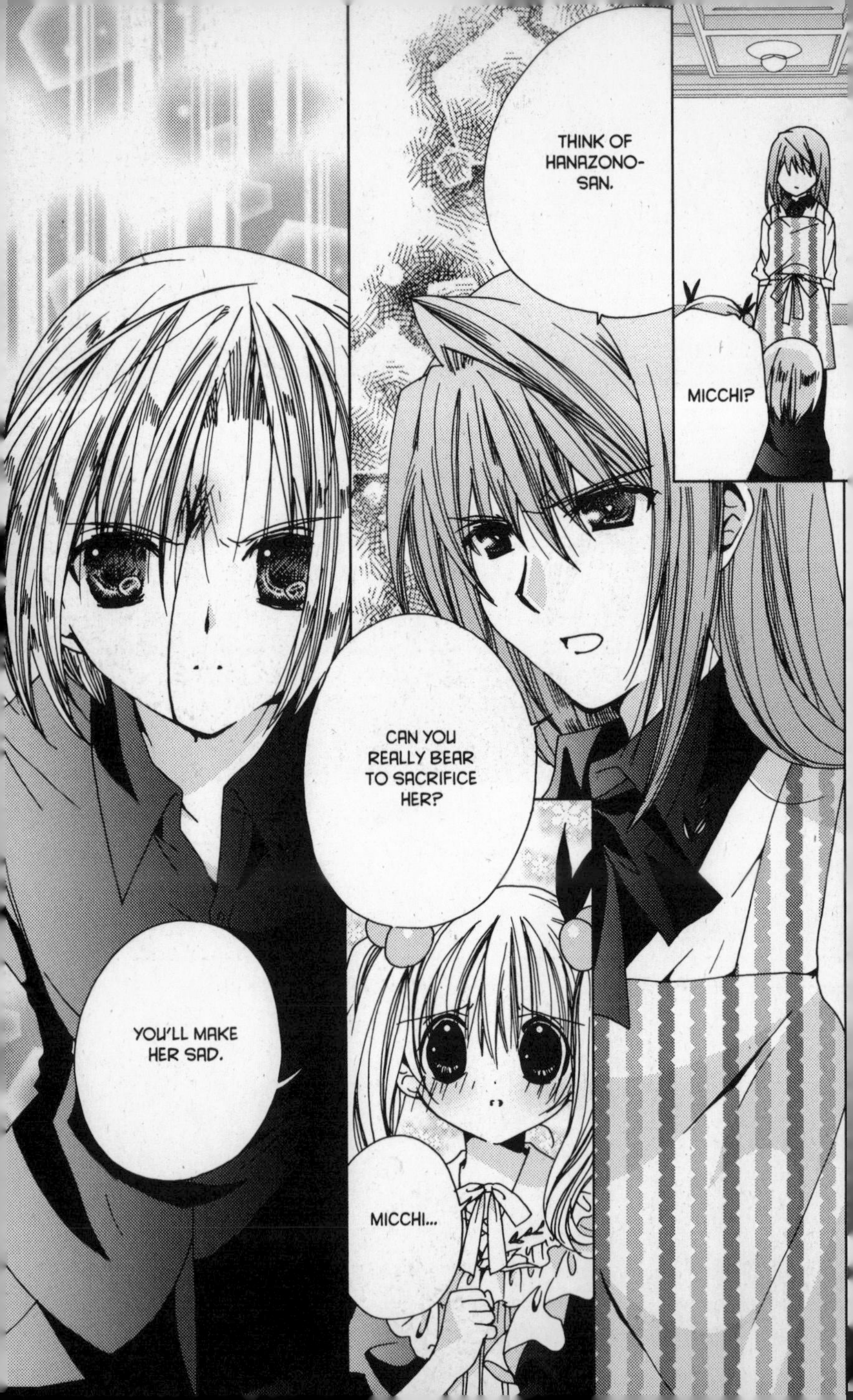
MICCHI?
THINK OF HANAZONO-SAN.
CAN YOU REALLY BEAR TO SACRIFICE HER?
MICCHI...
YOU'LL MAKE HER SAD.

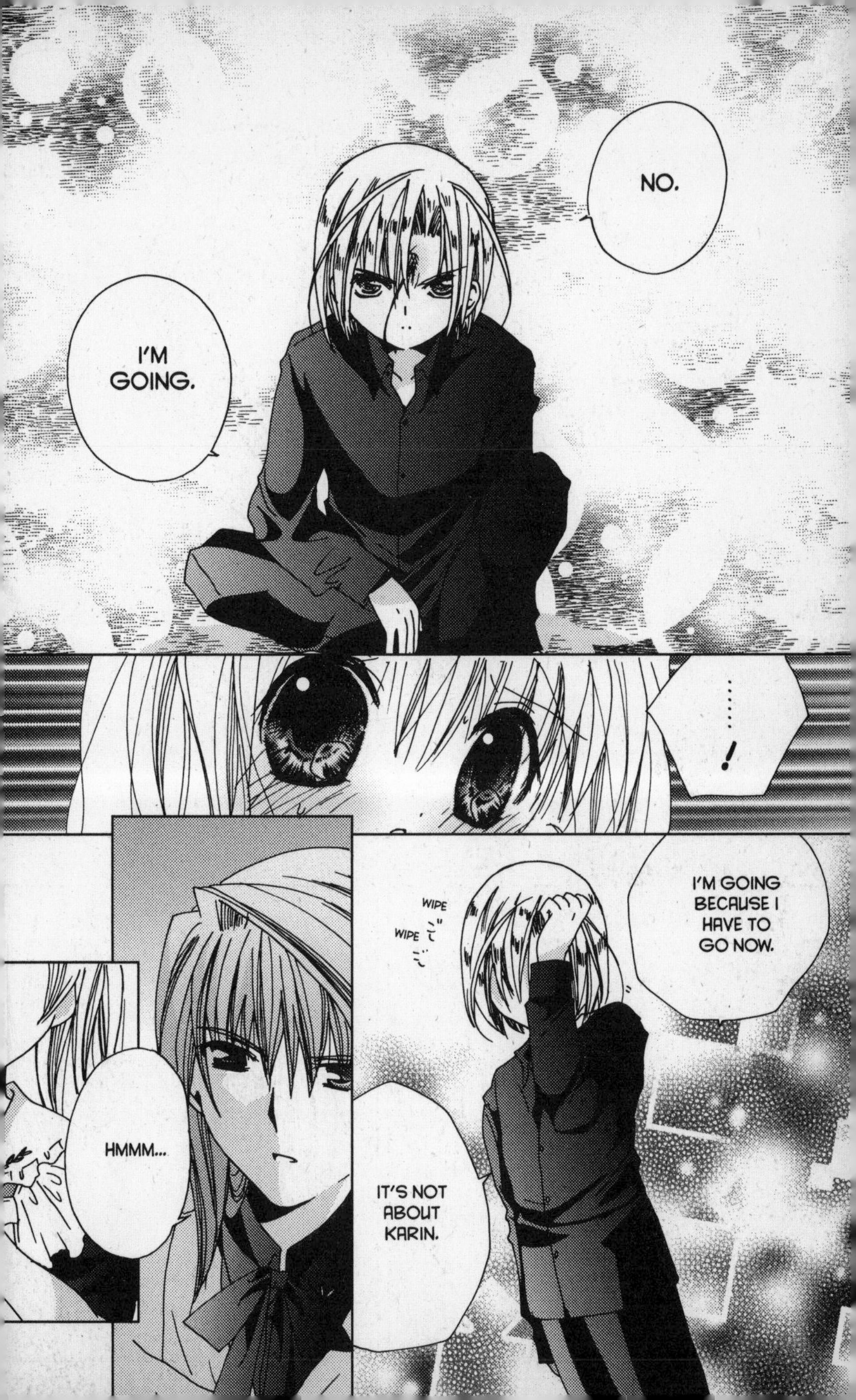
NO.
I'M GOING.
......!
I'M GOING BECAUSE I HAVE TO GO NOW.
WIPE WIPE
IT'S NOT ABOUT KARIN.
HMMM...

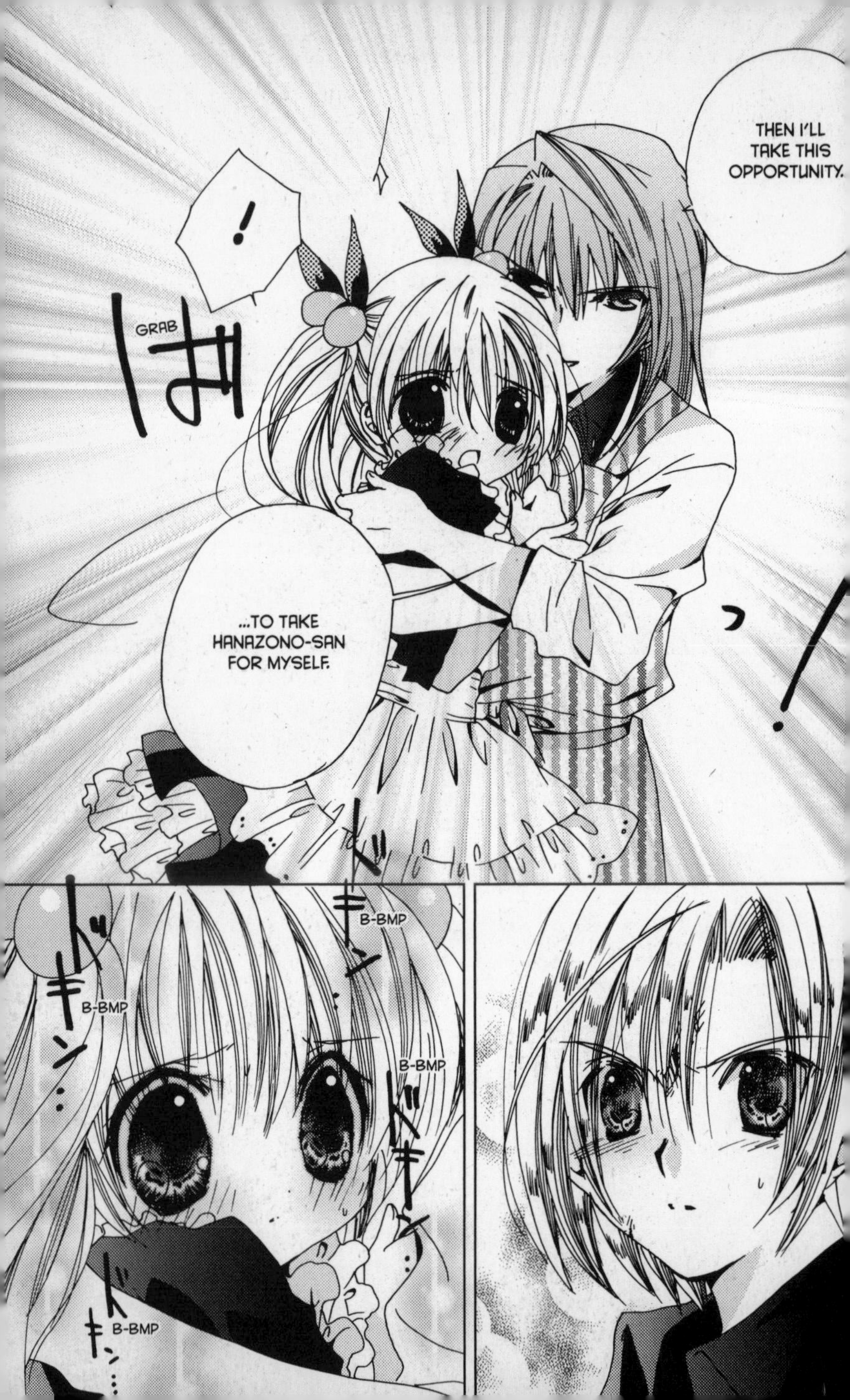
THEN I'LL TAKE THIS OPPORTUNITY.
!
GRAB
...TO TAKE HANAZONO-SAN FOR MYSELF.
B-BMP
B-BMP
B-BMP
B-BMP

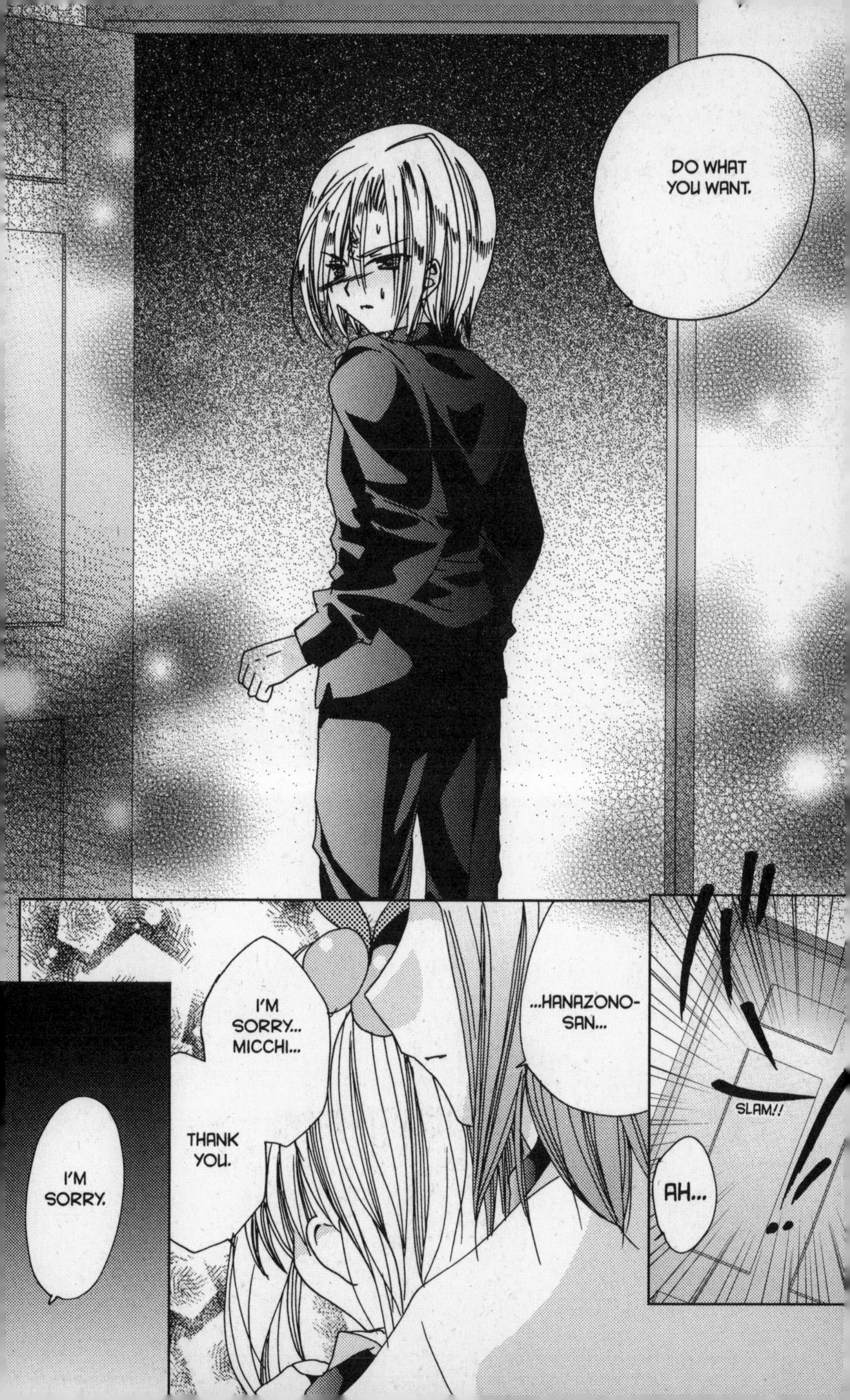
DO WHAT YOU WANT.
SLAM!!
AH...
...HANAZONO-SAN...
I'M SORRY... MICCHI...
THANK YOU.
I'M SORRY.

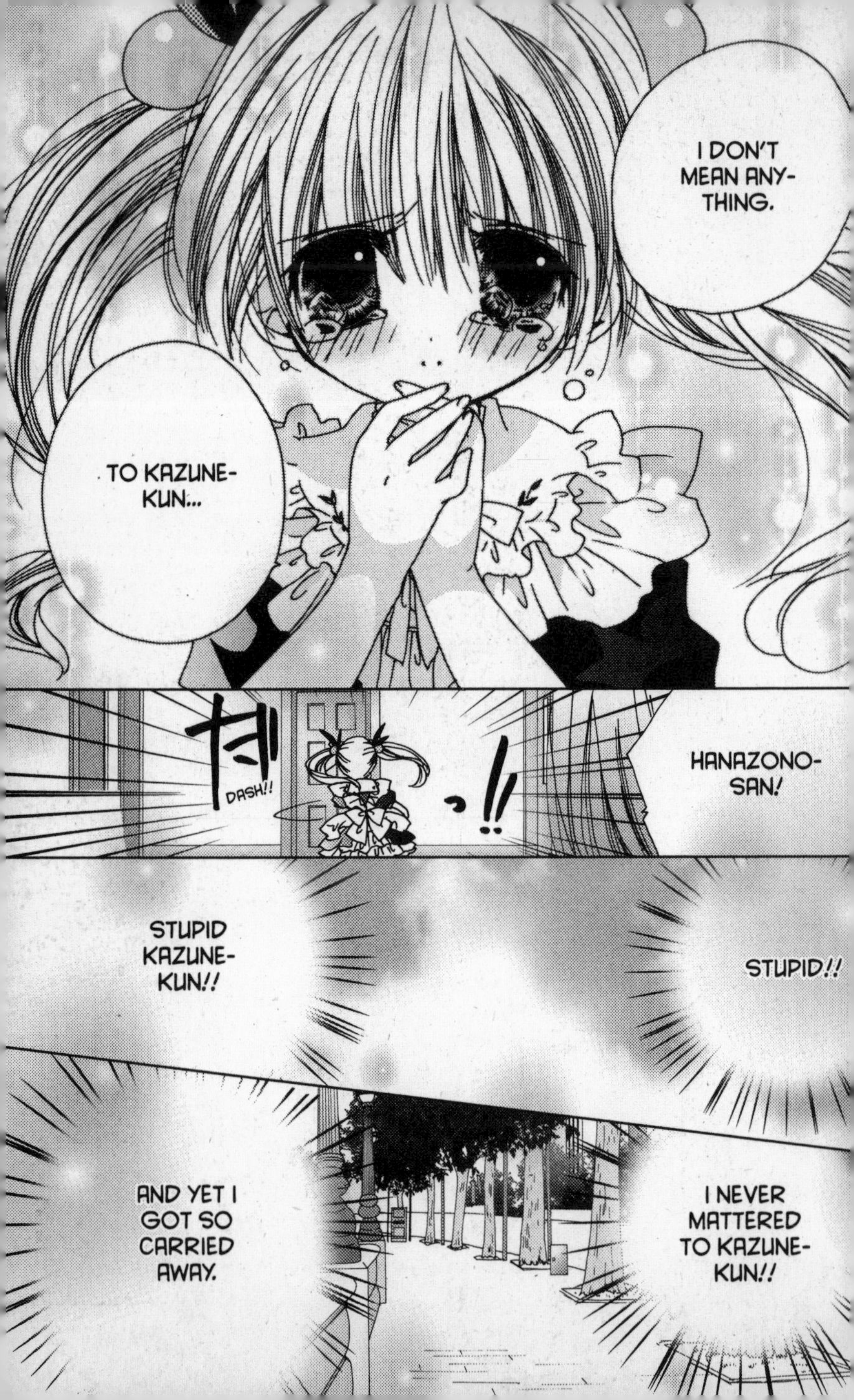
I DON'T MEAN ANY-THING.
TO KAZUNE-KUN...
HANAZONO-SAN!
DASH!!
STUPID!!
STUPID KAZUNE-KUN!!
I NEVER MATTERED TO KAZUNE-KUN!!
AND YET I GOT SO CARRIED AWAY.

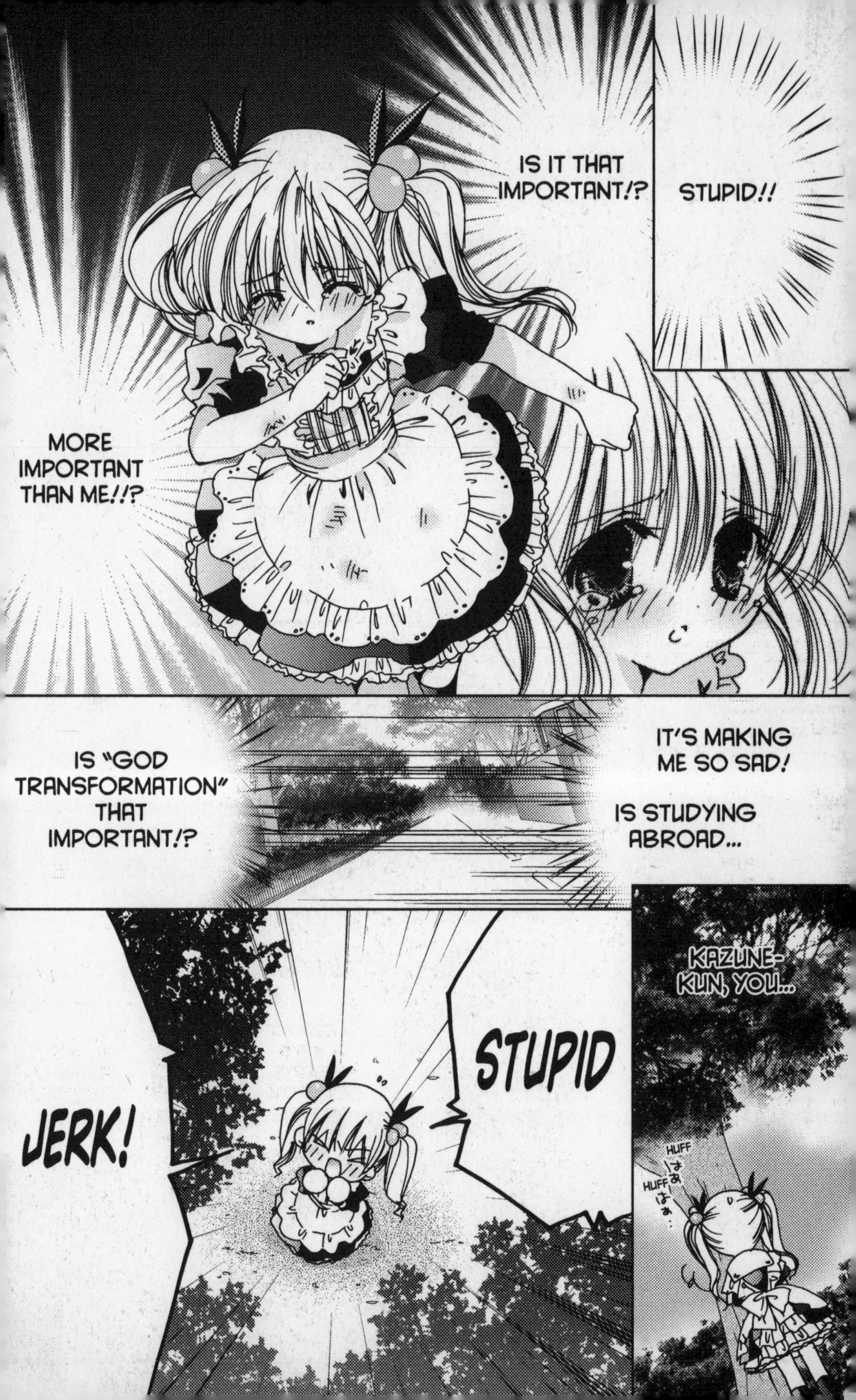
STUPID!!
IS IT THAT IMPORTANT!?
MORE IMPORTANT THAN ME!!?
IT'S MAKING ME SO SAD!
IS STUDYING ABROAD...
IS "GOD TRANSFORMATION" THAT IMPORTANT!?
KAZUNE-KUN, YOU...
HUFF
HUFF
STUPID
JERK!

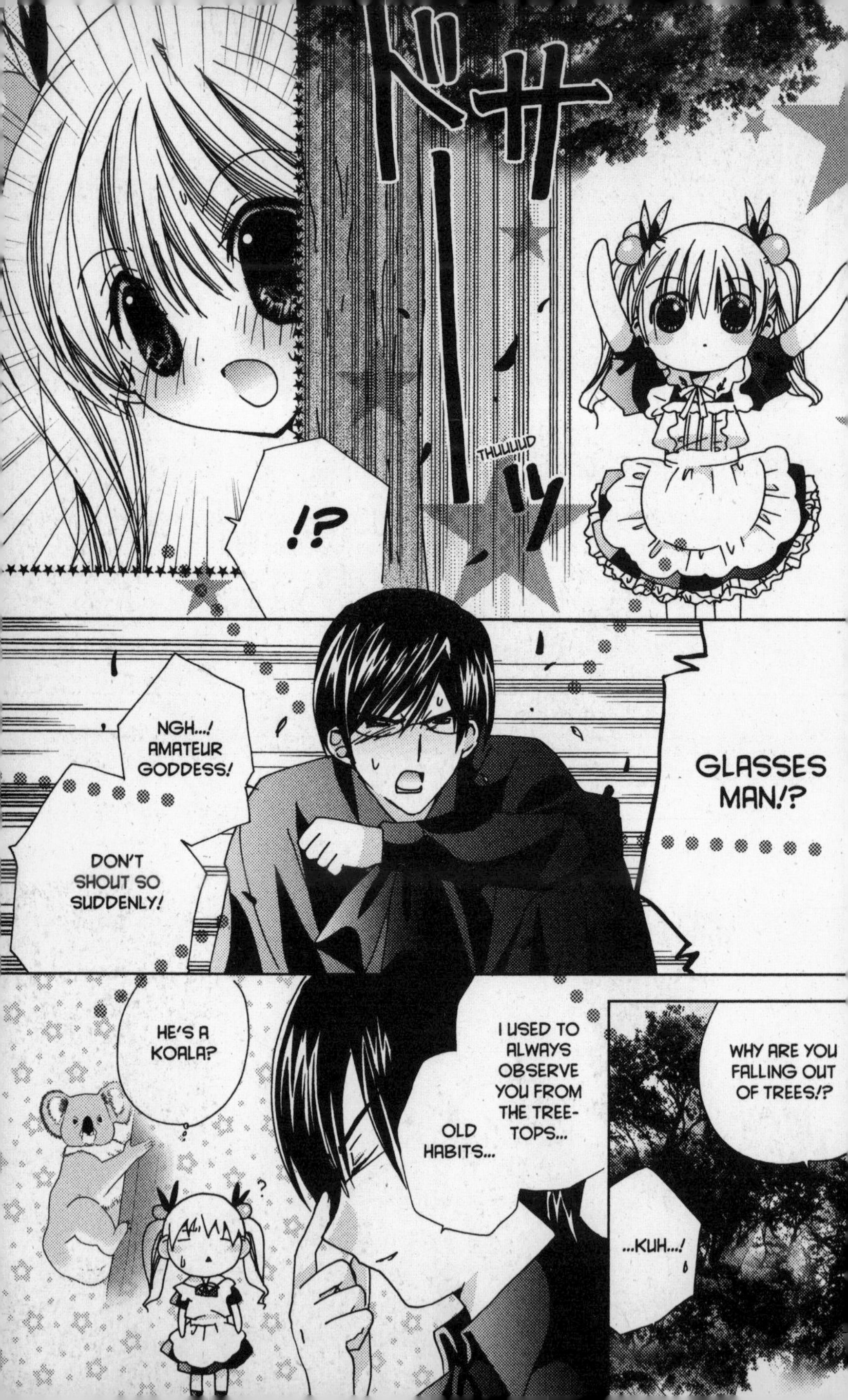

ドサ
THUUUUD
!?
GLASSES MAN!?
NGH...! AMATEUR GODDESS!
DON'T SHOUT SO SUDDENLY!
WHY ARE YOU FALLING OUT OF TREES!?
...KUH...!
I USED TO ALWAYS OBSERVE YOU FROM THE TREE-TOPS...
OLD HABITS...
HE'S A KOALA?

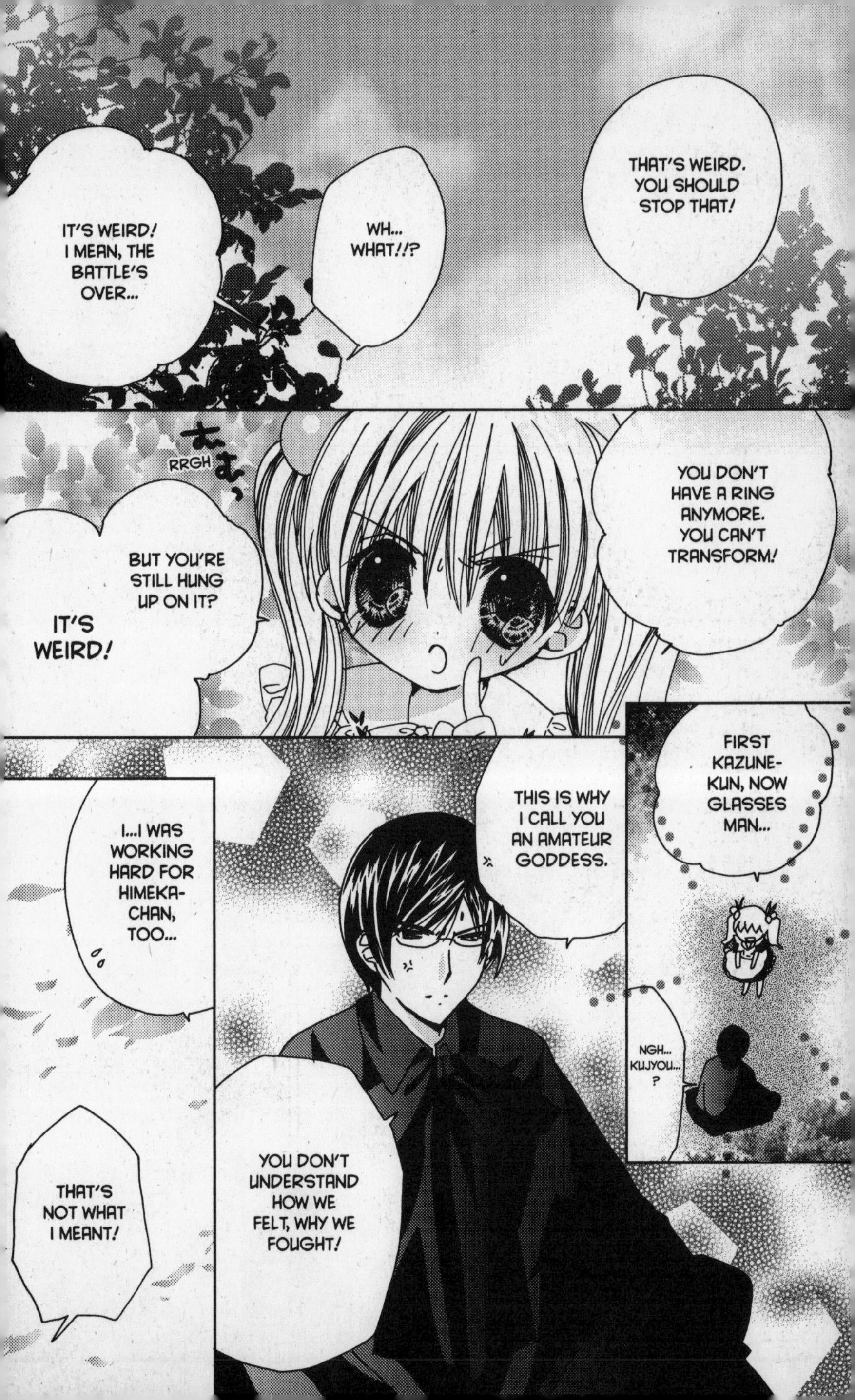
THAT'S WEIRD. YOU SHOULD STOP THAT!
WH... WHAT!!?
IT'S WEIRD! I MEAN, THE BATTLE'S OVER...
YOU DON'T HAVE A RING ANYMORE. YOU CAN'T TRANSFORM!
RRGH
BUT YOU'RE STILL HUNG UP ON IT?
IT'S WEIRD!
FIRST KAZUNE-KUN, NOW GLASSES MAN...
NGH... KUJYOU...?
THIS IS WHY I CALL YOU AN AMATEUR GODDESS.
I...I WAS WORKING HARD FOR HIMEKA-CHAN, TOO...
YOU DON'T UNDERSTAND HOW WE FELT, WHY WE FOUGHT!
THAT'S NOT WHAT I MEANT!

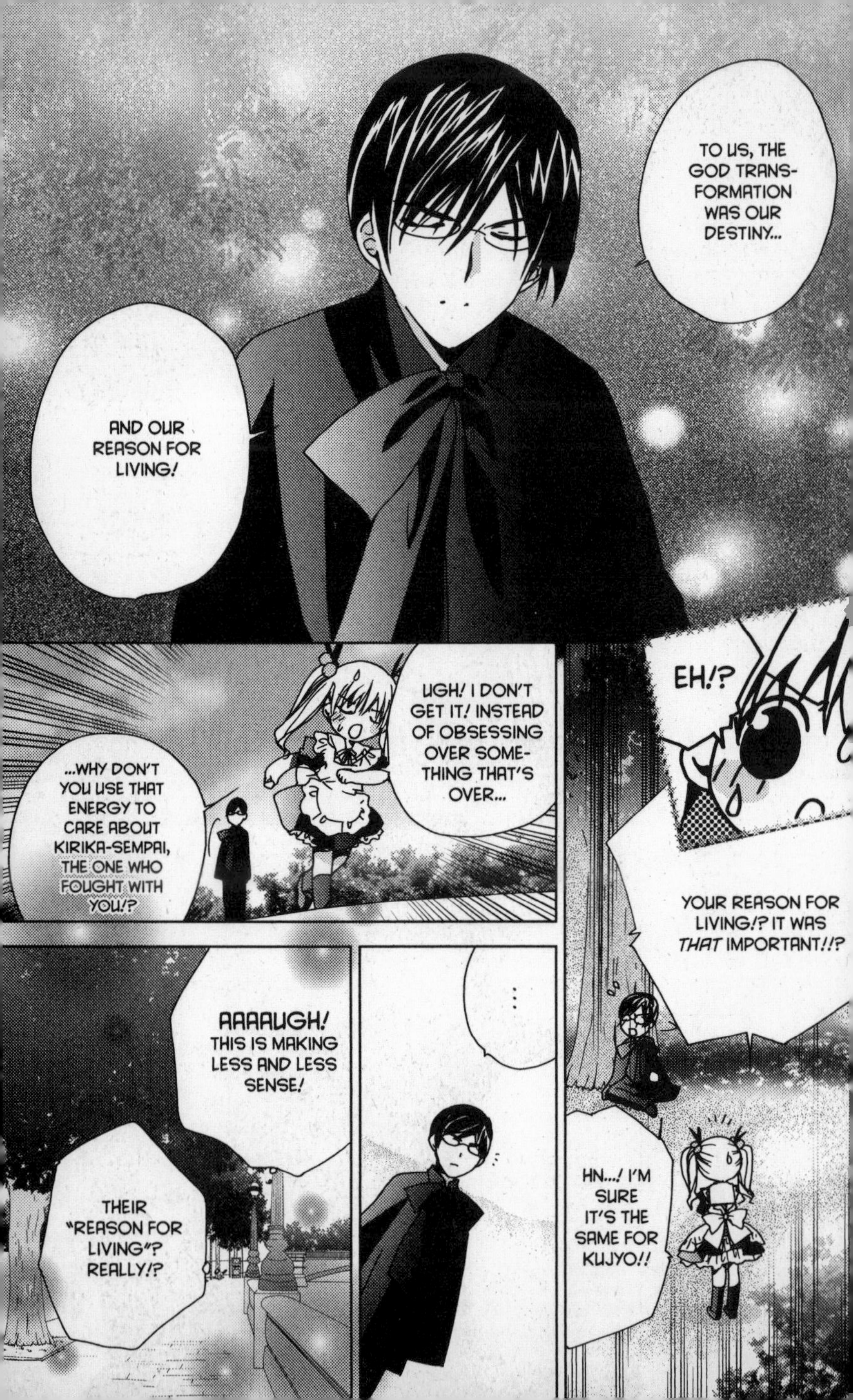
TO US, THE GOD TRANS-FORMATION WAS OUR DESTINY...
AND OUR REASON FOR LIVING!
EH!?
YOUR REASON FOR LIVING!? IT WAS *THAT* IMPORTANT!!?
HN...! I'M SURE IT'S THE SAME FOR KUJYO!!
UGH! I DON'T GET IT! INSTEAD OF OBSESSING OVER SOME-THING THAT'S OVER...
...WHY DON'T YOU USE THAT ENERGY TO CARE ABOUT KIRIKA-SEMPAI, THE ONE WHO FOUGHT WITH YOU!?
...
AAAAUGH! THIS IS MAKING LESS AND LESS SENSE!
THEIR "REASON FOR LIVING"? REALLY!?

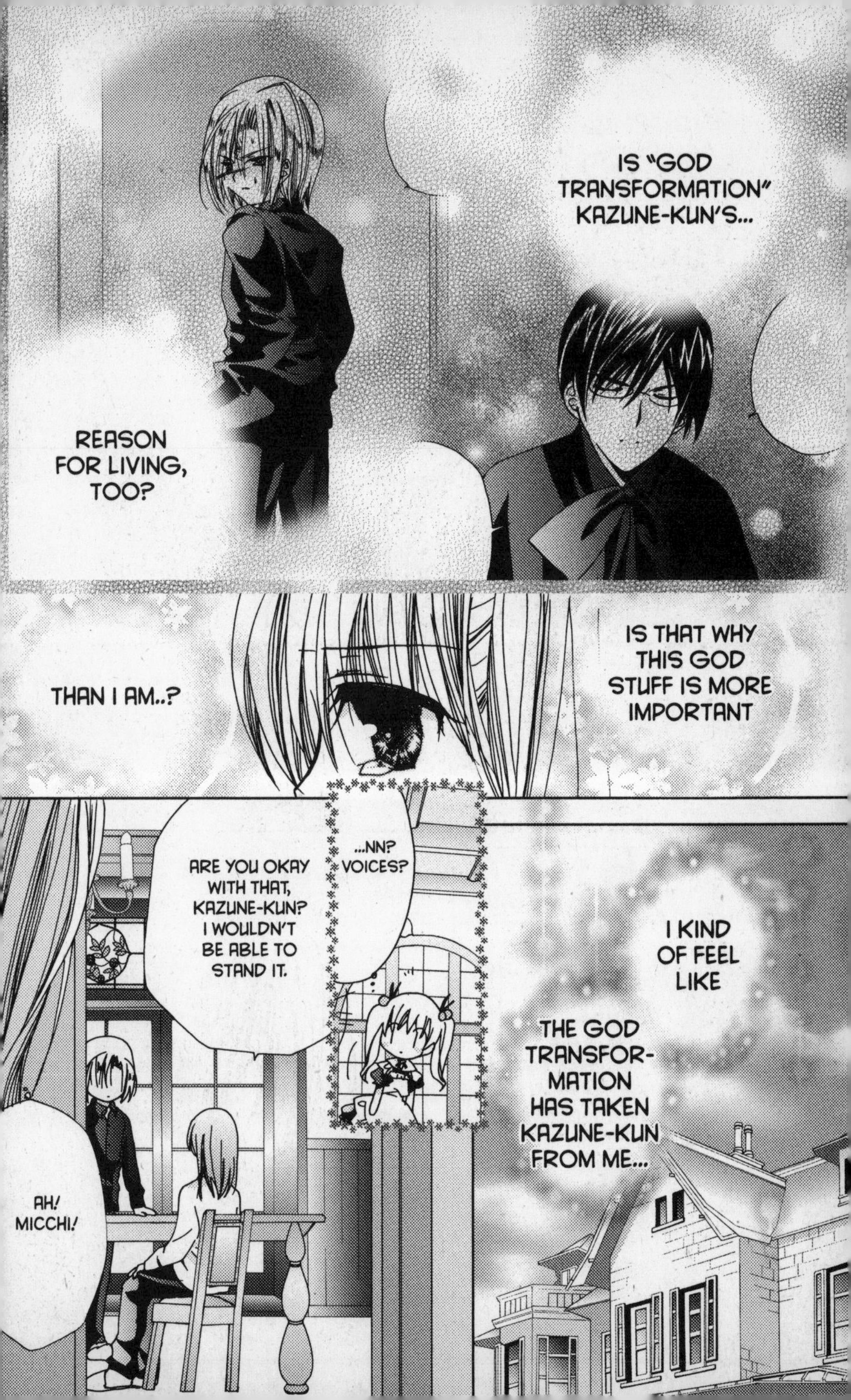
IS "GOD TRANSFORMATION" KAZUNE-KUN'S...
REASON FOR LIVING, TOO?
IS THAT WHY THIS GOD STUFF IS MORE IMPORTANT
THAN I AM..?
I KIND OF FEEL LIKE
THE GOD TRANSFOR-MATION HAS TAKEN KAZUNE-KUN FROM ME...
...NN? VOICES?
ARE YOU OKAY WITH THAT, KAZUNE-KUN? I WOULDN'T BE ABLE TO STAND IT.
AH! MICCHI!

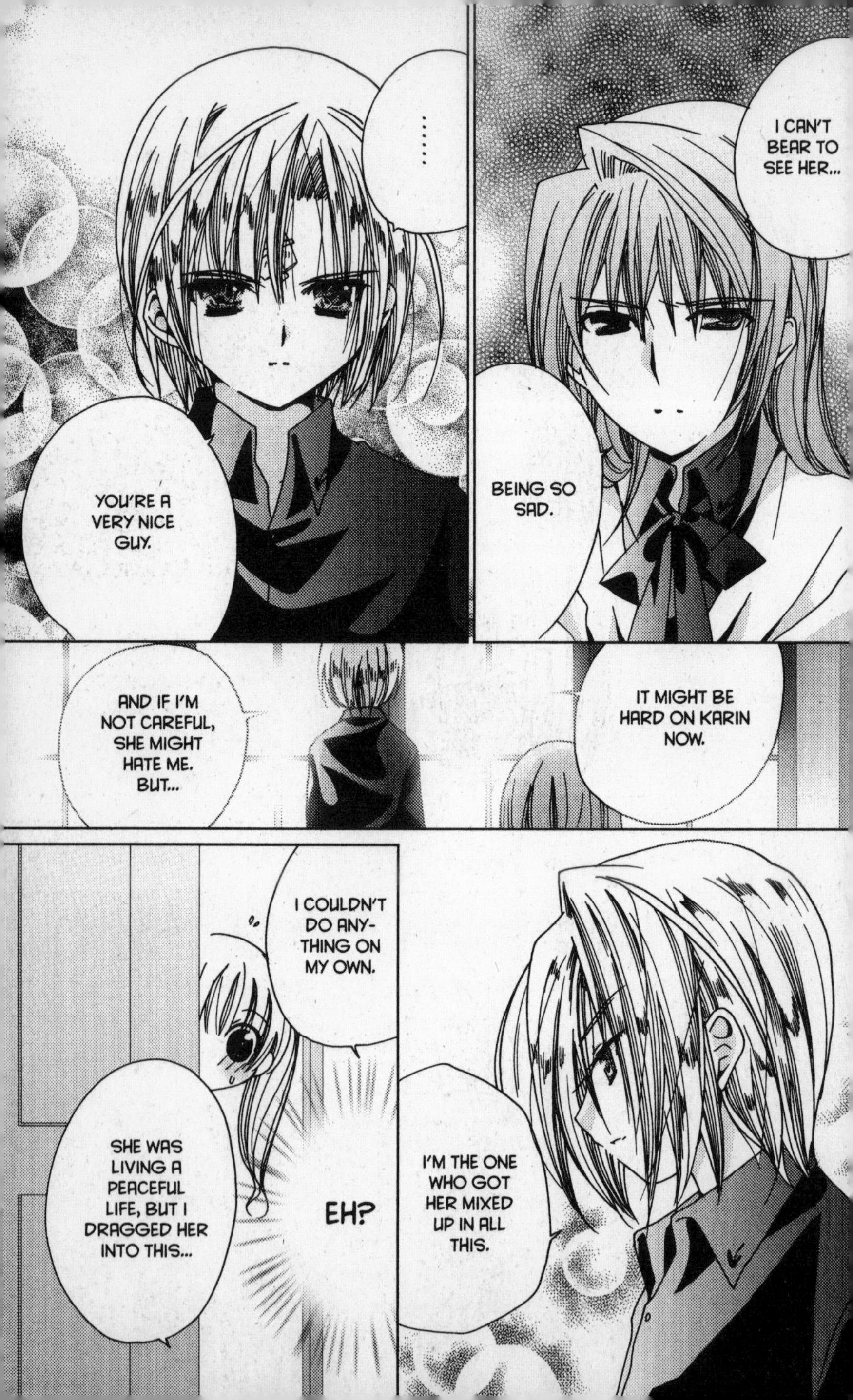
I CAN'T BEAR TO SEE HER...
BEING SO SAD.
......
YOU'RE A VERY NICE GUY.
IT MIGHT BE HARD ON KARIN NOW.
AND IF I'M NOT CAREFUL, SHE MIGHT HATE ME. BUT...
I'M THE ONE WHO GOT HER MIXED UP IN ALL THIS.
I COULDN'T DO ANY-THING ON MY OWN.
EH?
SHE WAS LIVING A PEACEFUL LIFE, BUT I DRAGGED HER INTO THIS...

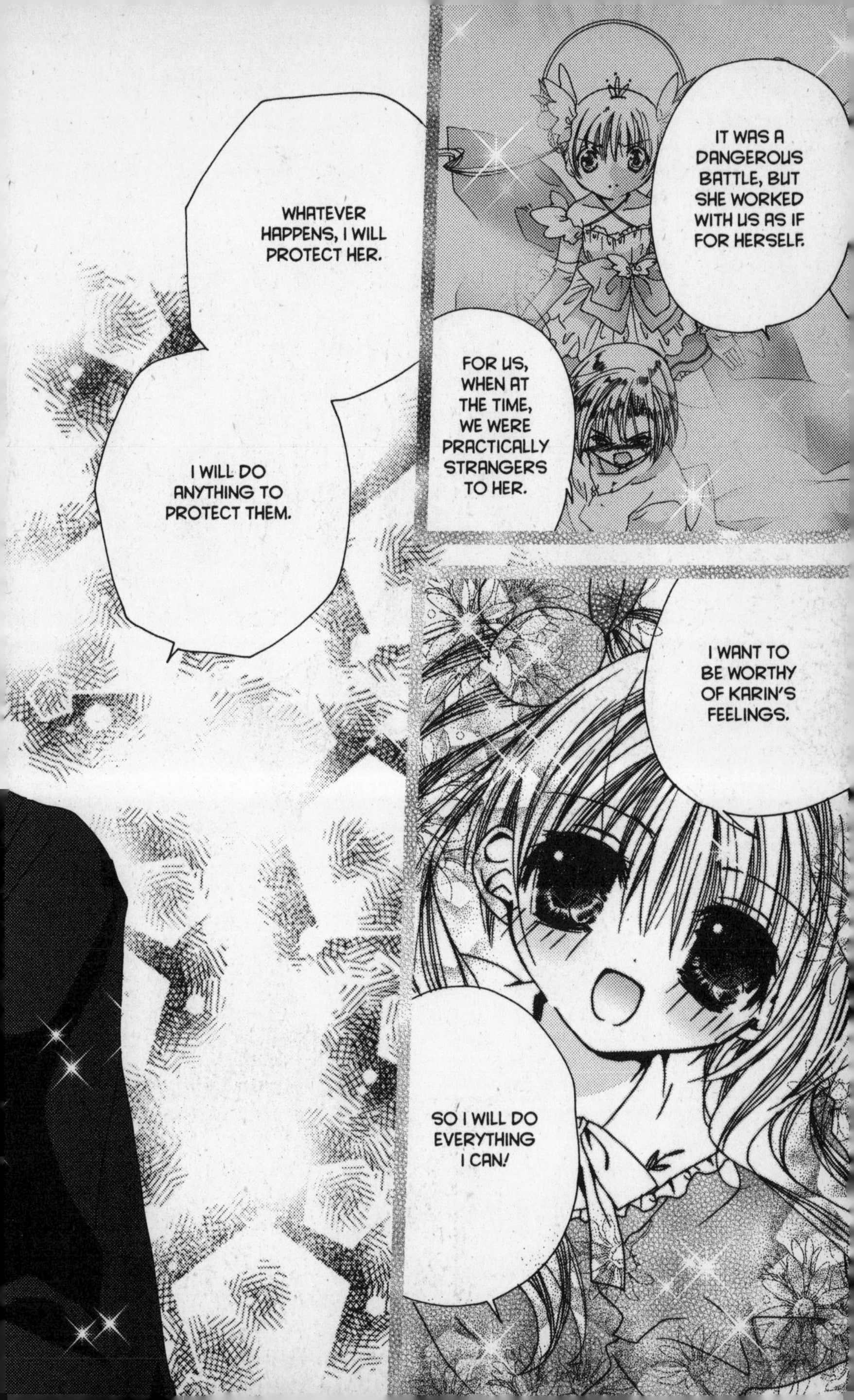
IT WAS A DANGEROUS BATTLE, BUT SHE WORKED WITH US AS IF FOR HERSELF.
FOR US, WHEN AT THE TIME, WE WERE PRACTICALLY STRANGERS TO HER.
I WANT TO BE WORTHY OF KARIN'S FEELINGS.
SO I WILL DO EVERYTHING I CAN!
WHATEVER HAPPENS, I WILL PROTECT HER.
I WILL DO ANYTHING TO PROTECT THEM.

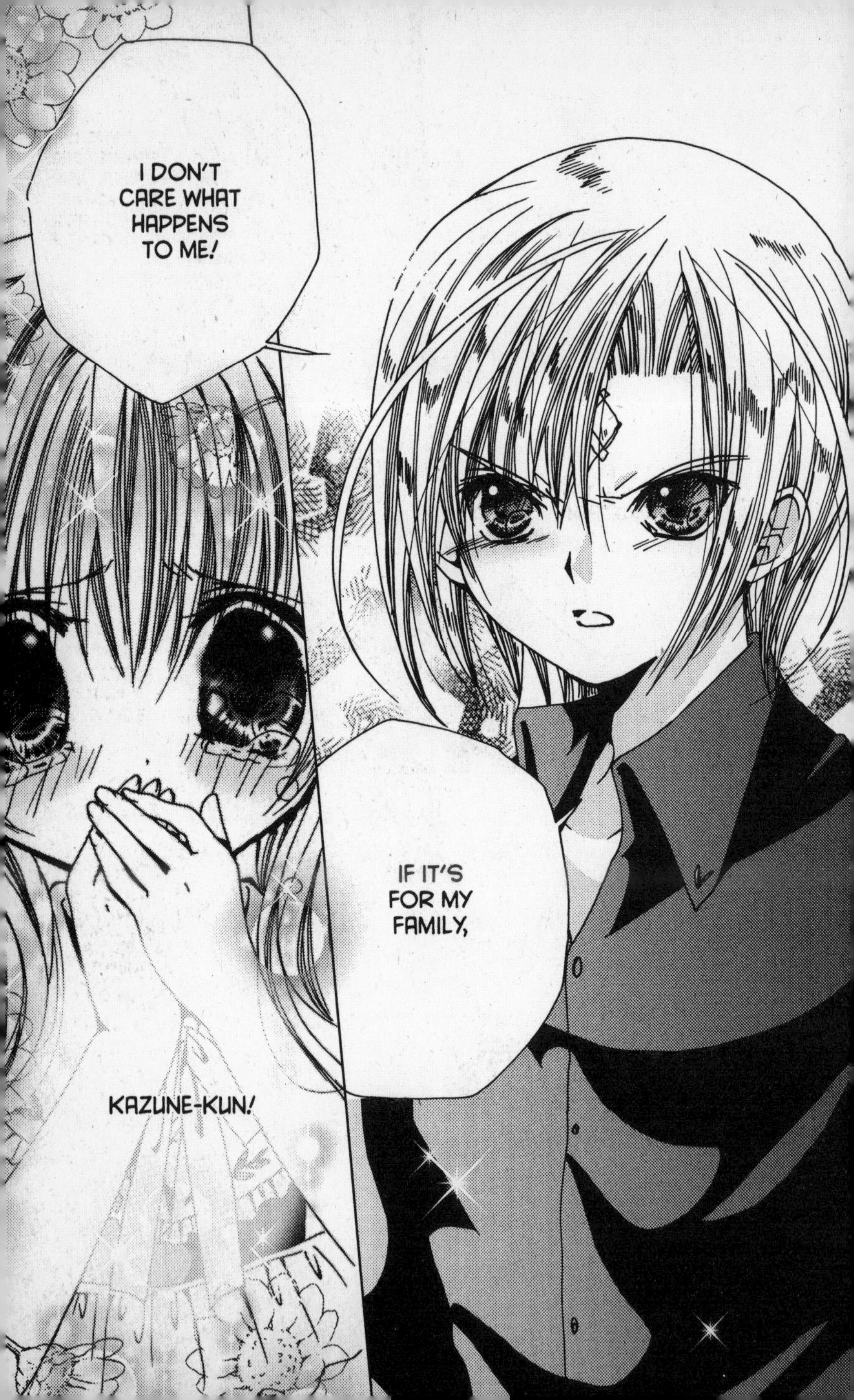
IF IT'S FOR MY FAMILY,
I DON'T CARE WHAT HAPPENS TO ME!
KAZUNE-KUN!

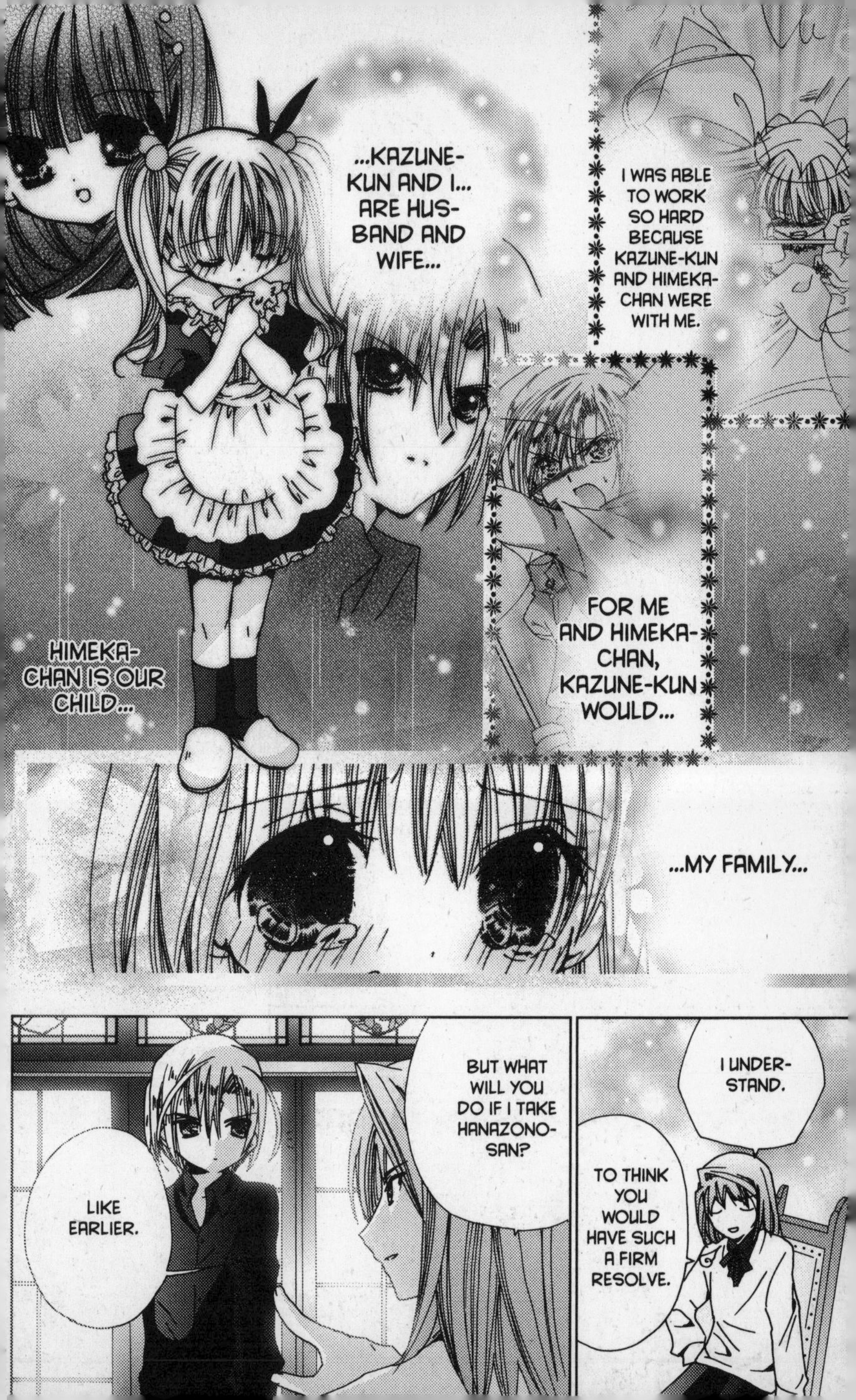
I WAS ABLE TO WORK SO HARD BECAUSE KAZUNE-KUN AND HIMEKA-CHAN WERE WITH ME.
FOR ME AND HIMEKA-CHAN, KAZUNE-KUN WOULD...
...KAZUNE-KUN AND I... ARE HUS-BAND AND WIFE...
HIMEKA-CHAN IS OUR CHILD...
...MY FAMILY...
I UNDER-STAND.
TO THINK YOU WOULD HAVE SUCH A FIRM RESOLVE.
BUT WHAT WILL YOU DO IF I TAKE HANAZONO-SAN?
LIKE EARLIER.

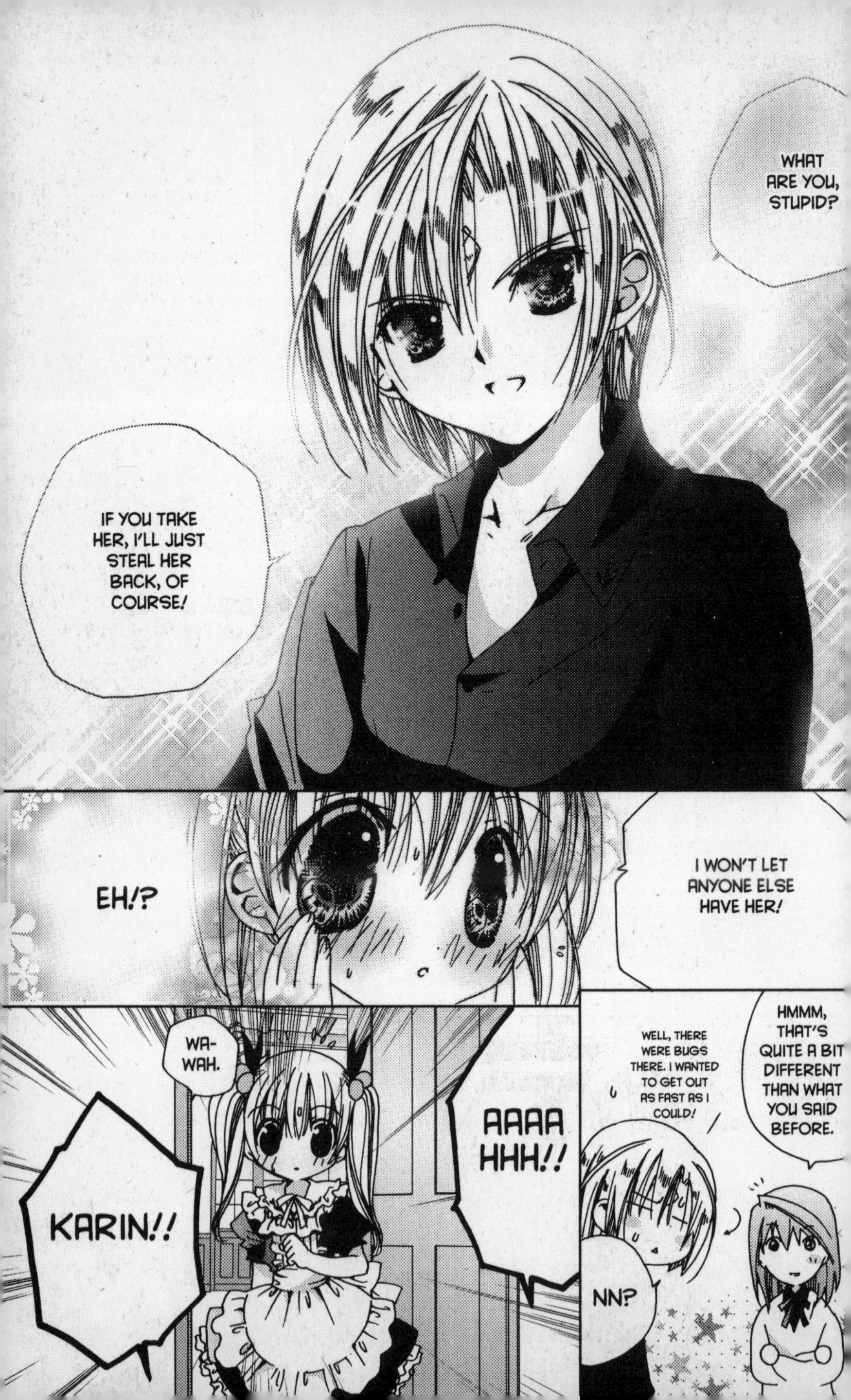
WHAT ARE YOU, STUPID?
IF YOU TAKE HER, I'LL JUST STEAL HER BACK, OF COURSE!
I WON'T LET ANYONE ELSE HAVE HER!
EH!?
HMMM, THAT'S QUITE A BIT DIFFERENT THAN WHAT YOU SAID BEFORE.
WELL, THERE WERE BUGS THERE. I WANTED TO GET OUT AS FAST AS I COULD!
NN?
AAAA HHH!!
WA-WAH.
KARIN!!

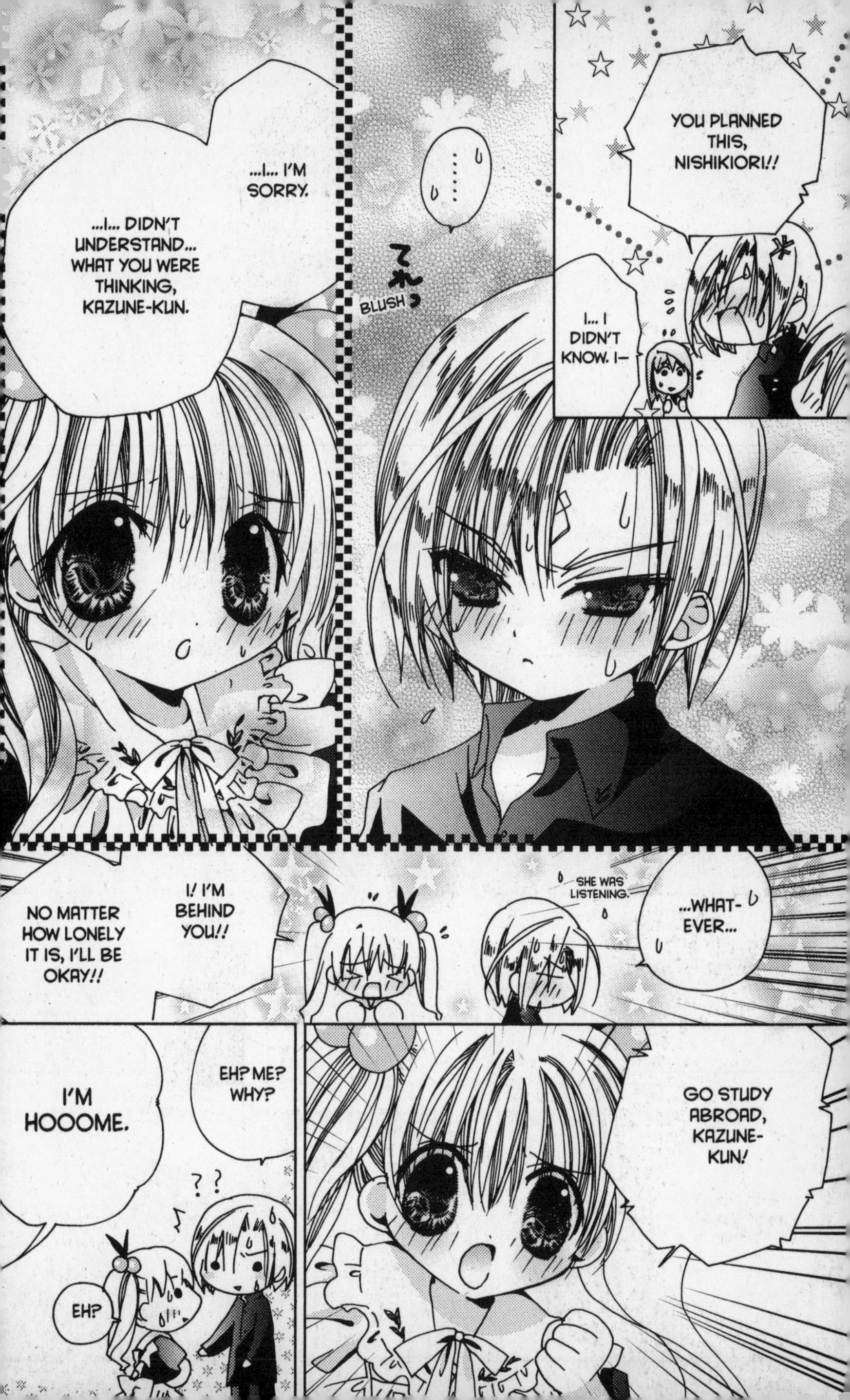
YOU PLANNED THIS, NISHIKIORI!!
I... I DIDN'T KNOW. I—
......
てれ
BLUSH
...I... I'M SORRY.
...I... DIDN'T UNDERSTAND... WHAT YOU WERE THINKING, KAZUNE-KUN.
...WHAT-EVER...
SHE WAS LISTENING.
I! I'M BEHIND YOU!!
NO MATTER HOW LONELY IT IS, I'LL BE OKAY!!
GO STUDY ABROAD, KAZUNE-KUN!
EH? ME? WHY?
I'M HOOOME.
EH?

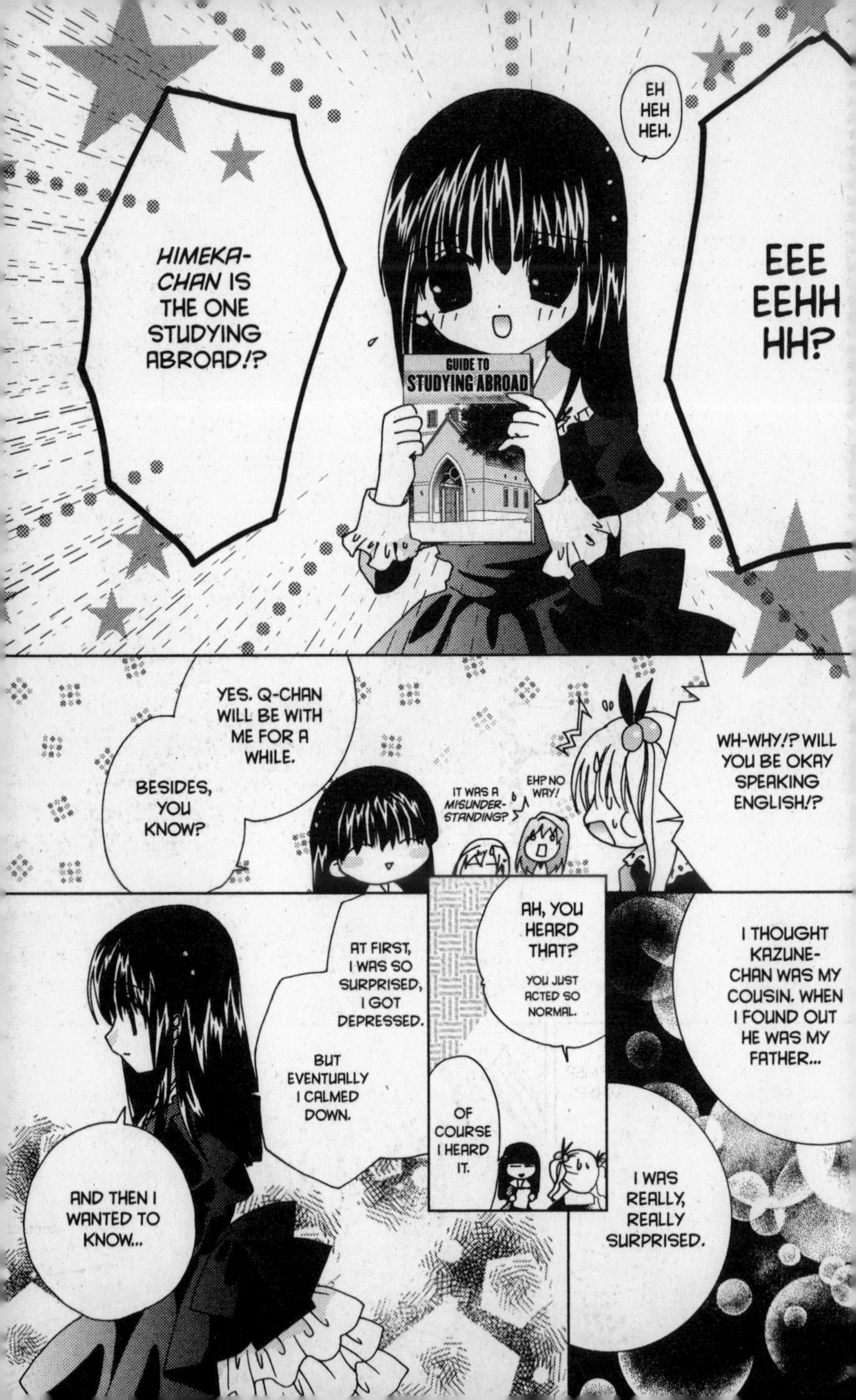
EEE EEHH HH?
EH HEH HEH.
GUIDE TO STUDYING ABROAD
HIMEKA-CHAN IS THE ONE STUDYING ABROAD!?
WH-WHY!? WILL YOU BE OKAY SPEAKING ENGLISH!?
EH? NO WAY!
IT WAS A MISUNDERSTANDING?
YES. Q-CHAN WILL BE WITH ME FOR A WHILE.
BESIDES, YOU KNOW?
I THOUGHT KAZUNE-CHAN WAS MY COUSIN. WHEN I FOUND OUT HE WAS MY FATHER...
I WAS REALLY, REALLY SURPRISED.
AH, YOU HEARD THAT?
YOU JUST ACTED SO NORMAL.
OF COURSE I HEARD IT.
AT FIRST, I WAS SO SURPRISED, I GOT DEPRESSED.
BUT EVENTUALLY I CALMED DOWN.
AND THEN I WANTED TO KNOW...

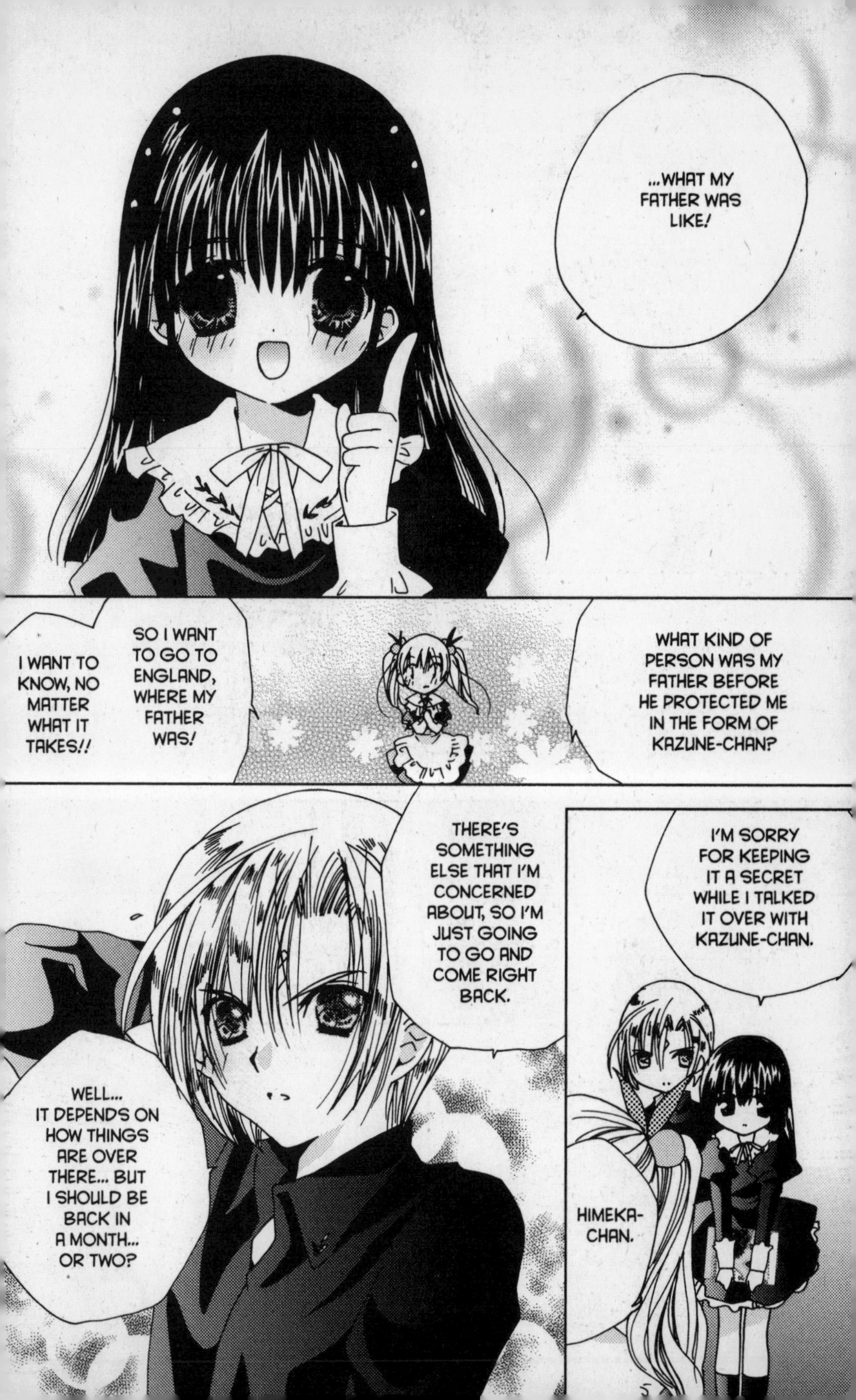
...WHAT MY FATHER WAS LIKE!
WHAT KIND OF PERSON WAS MY FATHER BEFORE HE PROTECTED ME IN THE FORM OF KAZUNE-CHAN?
SO I WANT TO GO TO ENGLAND, WHERE MY FATHER WAS!
I WANT TO KNOW, NO MATTER WHAT IT TAKES!!
I'M SORRY FOR KEEPING IT A SECRET WHILE I TALKED IT OVER WITH KAZUNE-CHAN.
HIMEKA-CHAN.
THERE'S SOMETHING ELSE THAT I'M CONCERNED ABOUT, SO I'M JUST GOING TO GO AND COME RIGHT BACK.
WELL... IT DEPENDS ON HOW THINGS ARE OVER THERE... BUT I SHOULD BE BACK IN A MONTH... OR TWO?

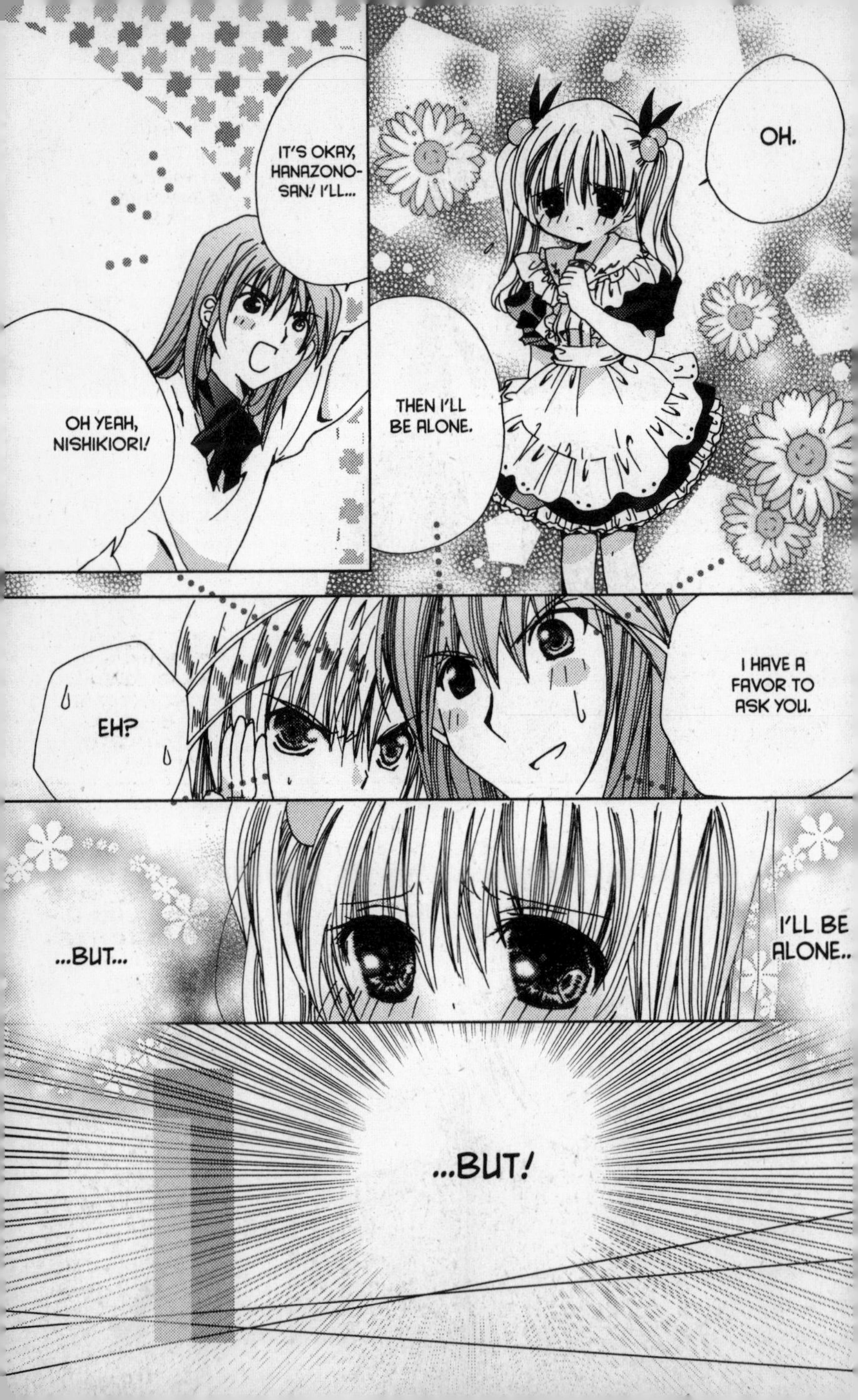
OH.
THEN I'LL BE ALONE.
IT'S OKAY, HANAZONO-SAN! I'LL...
OH YEAH, NISHIKIORI!
I HAVE A FAVOR TO ASK YOU.
EH?
I'LL BE ALONE..
...BUT...
...BUT!

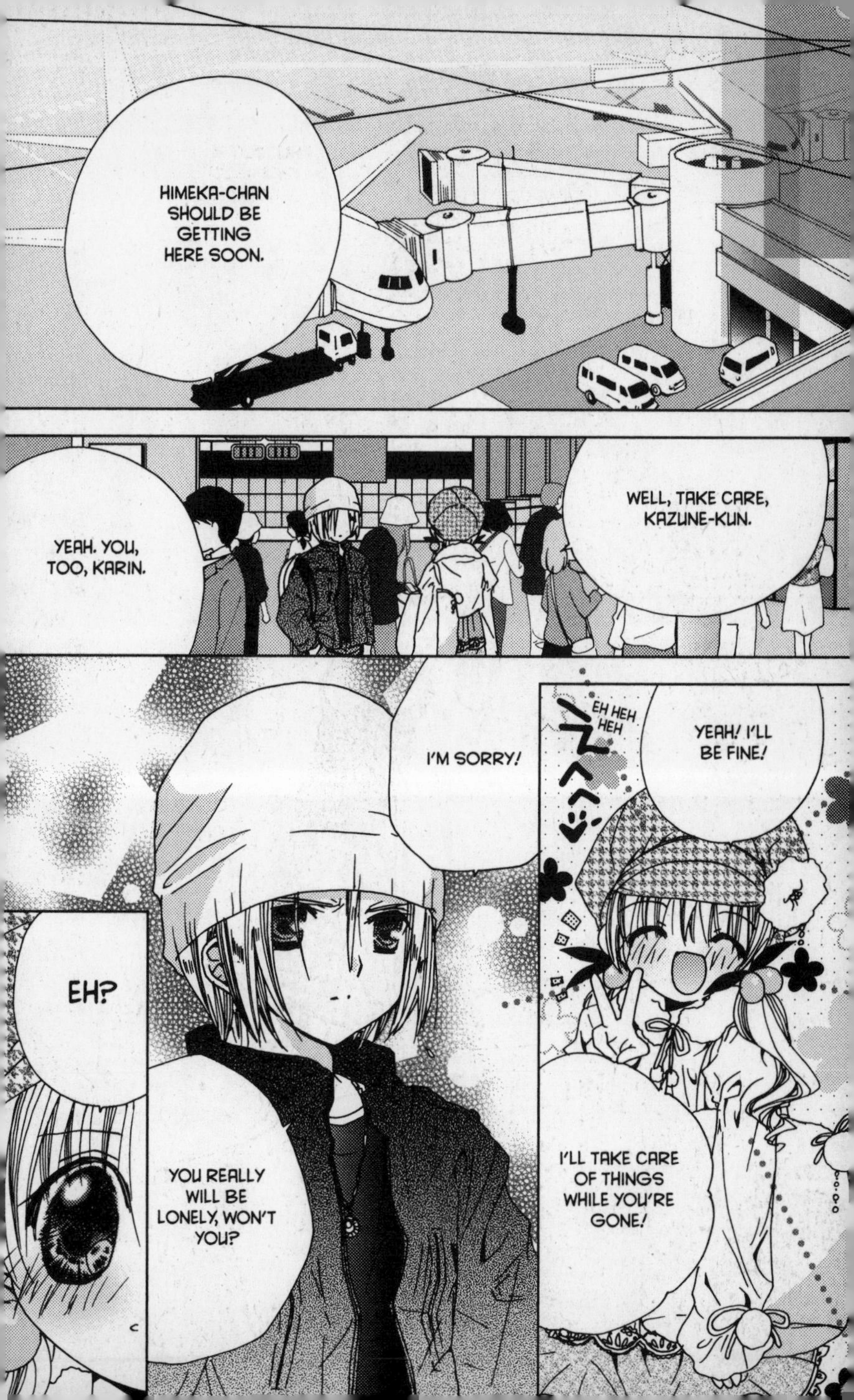
HIMEKA-CHAN SHOULD BE GETTING HERE SOON.
WELL, TAKE CARE, KAZUNE-KUN.
YEAH. YOU, TOO, KARIN.
YEAH! I'LL BE FINE!
EH HEH HEH
I'LL TAKE CARE OF THINGS WHILE YOU'RE GONE!
I'M SORRY!
YOU REALLY WILL BE LONELY, WON'T YOU?
EH?

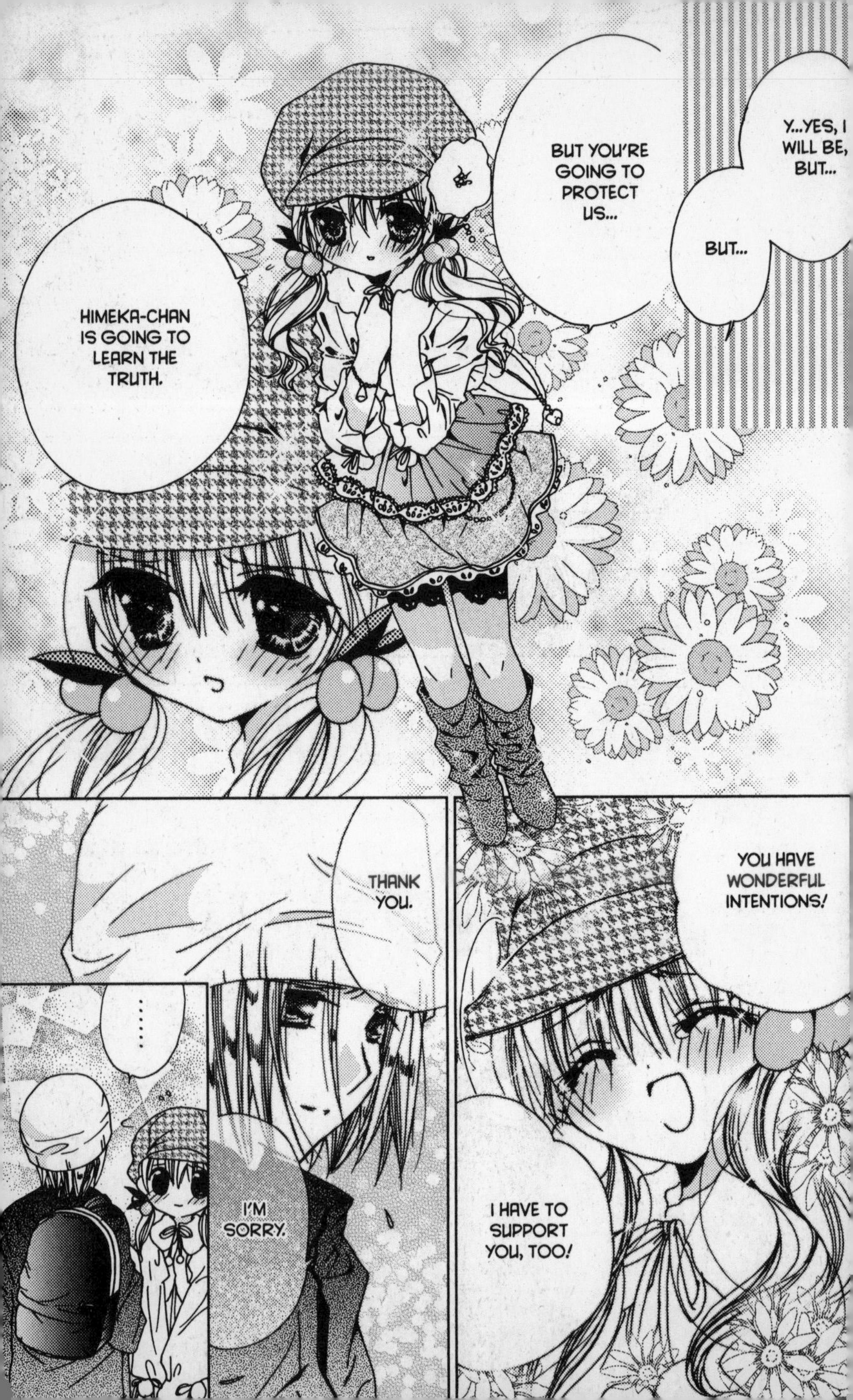

Y...YES, I WILL BE, BUT...
BUT...
BUT YOU'RE GOING TO PROTECT US...
HIMEKA-CHAN IS GOING TO LEARN THE TRUTH.
YOU HAVE WONDERFUL INTENTIONS!
I HAVE TO SUPPORT YOU, TOO!
THANK YOU.
......
I'M SORRY.

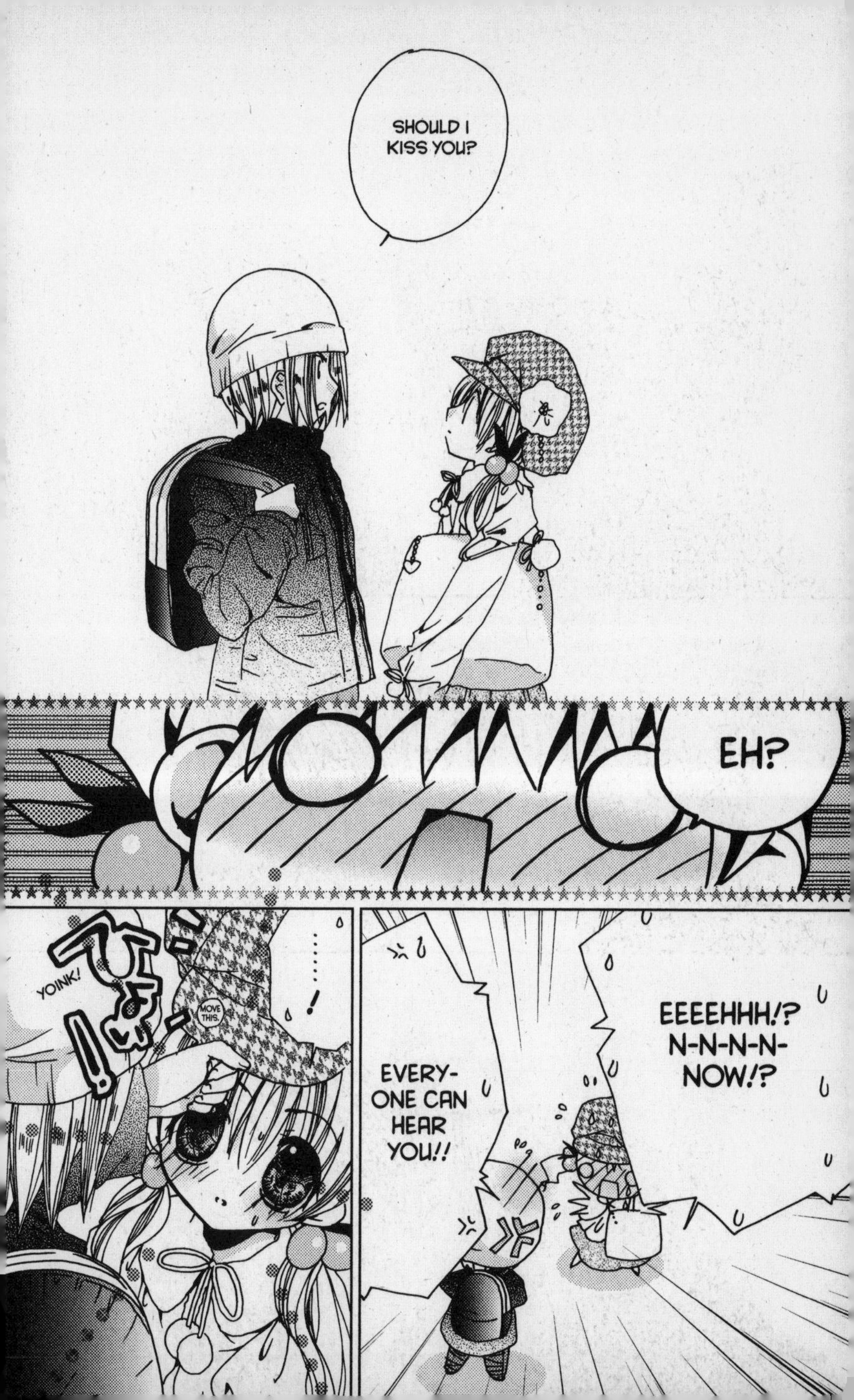
SHOULD I KISS YOU?
EH?
EEEEHHH!? N-N-N-N-NOW!?
EVERY-ONE CAN HEAR YOU!!
......!
MOVE THIS.
YOINK!

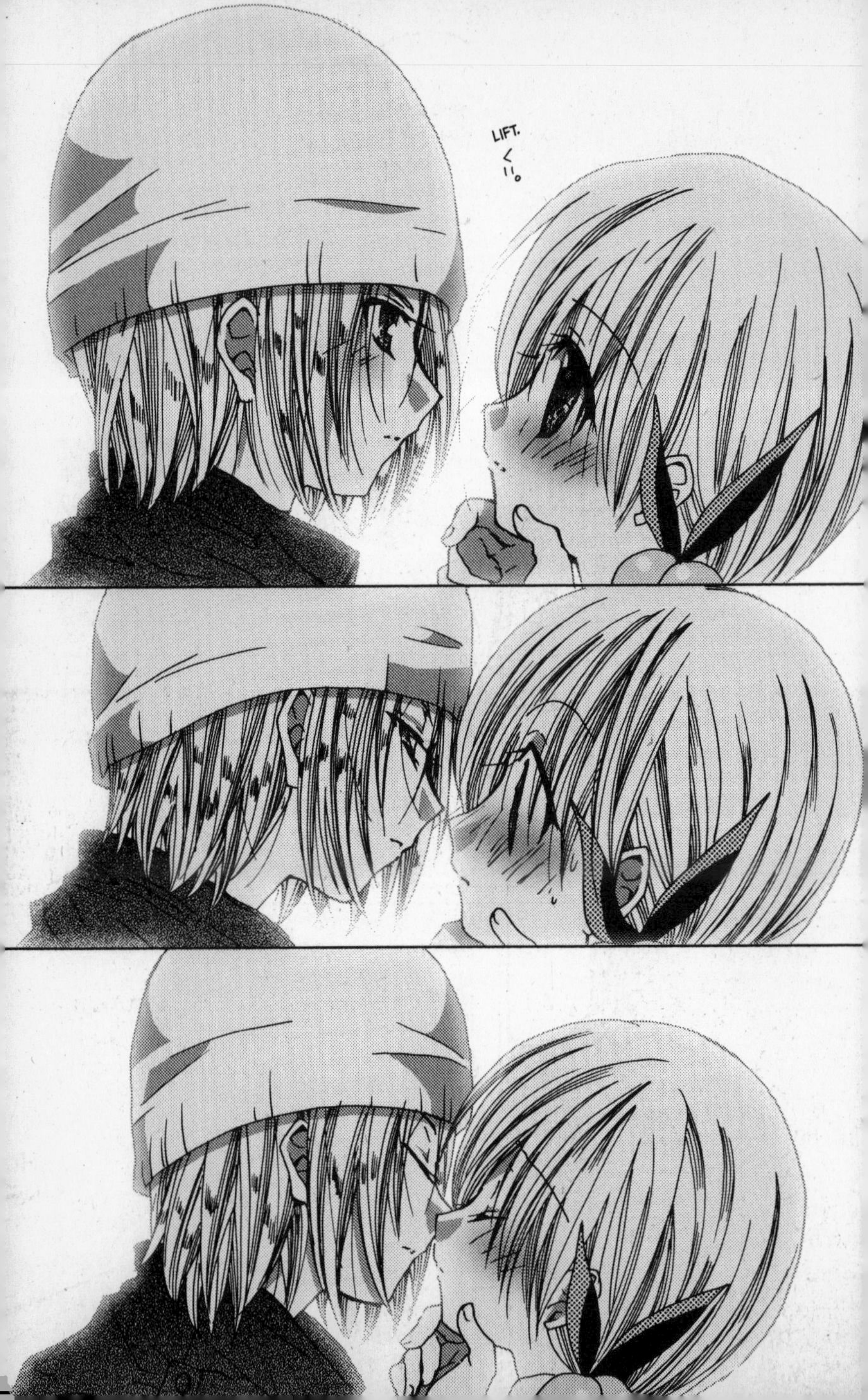
LIFT.
くい。

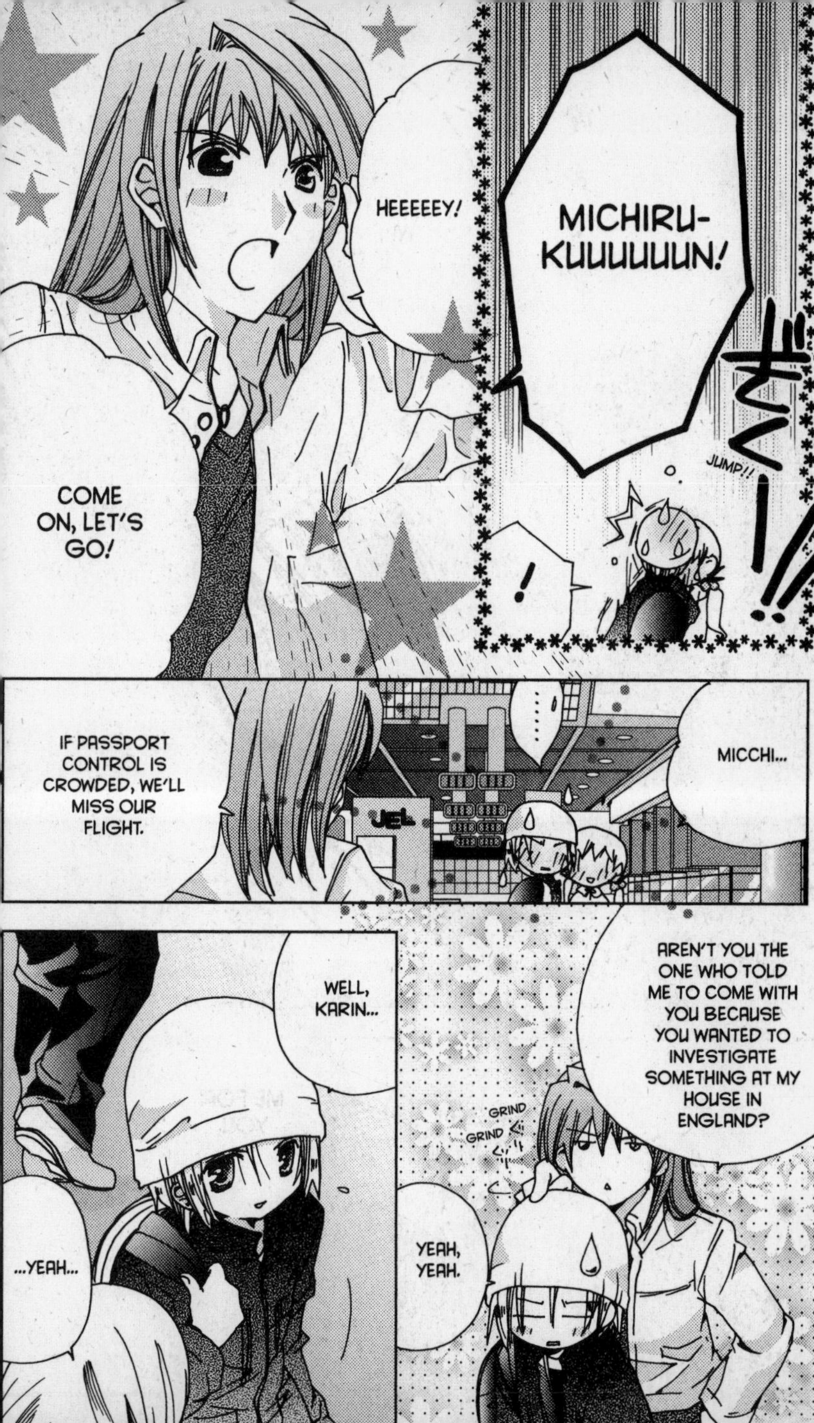
MICHIRU-KUUUUUUN!
JUMP!!
!
HEEEEEY!
COME ON, LET'S GO!
MICCHI...
......
IF PASSPORT CONTROL IS CROWDED, WE'LL MISS OUR FLIGHT.
AREN'T YOU THE ONE WHO TOLD ME TO COME WITH YOU BECAUSE YOU WANTED TO INVESTIGATE SOMETHING AT MY HOUSE IN ENGLAND?
GRIND GRIND
YEAH, YEAH.
WELL, KARIN...
...YEAH...

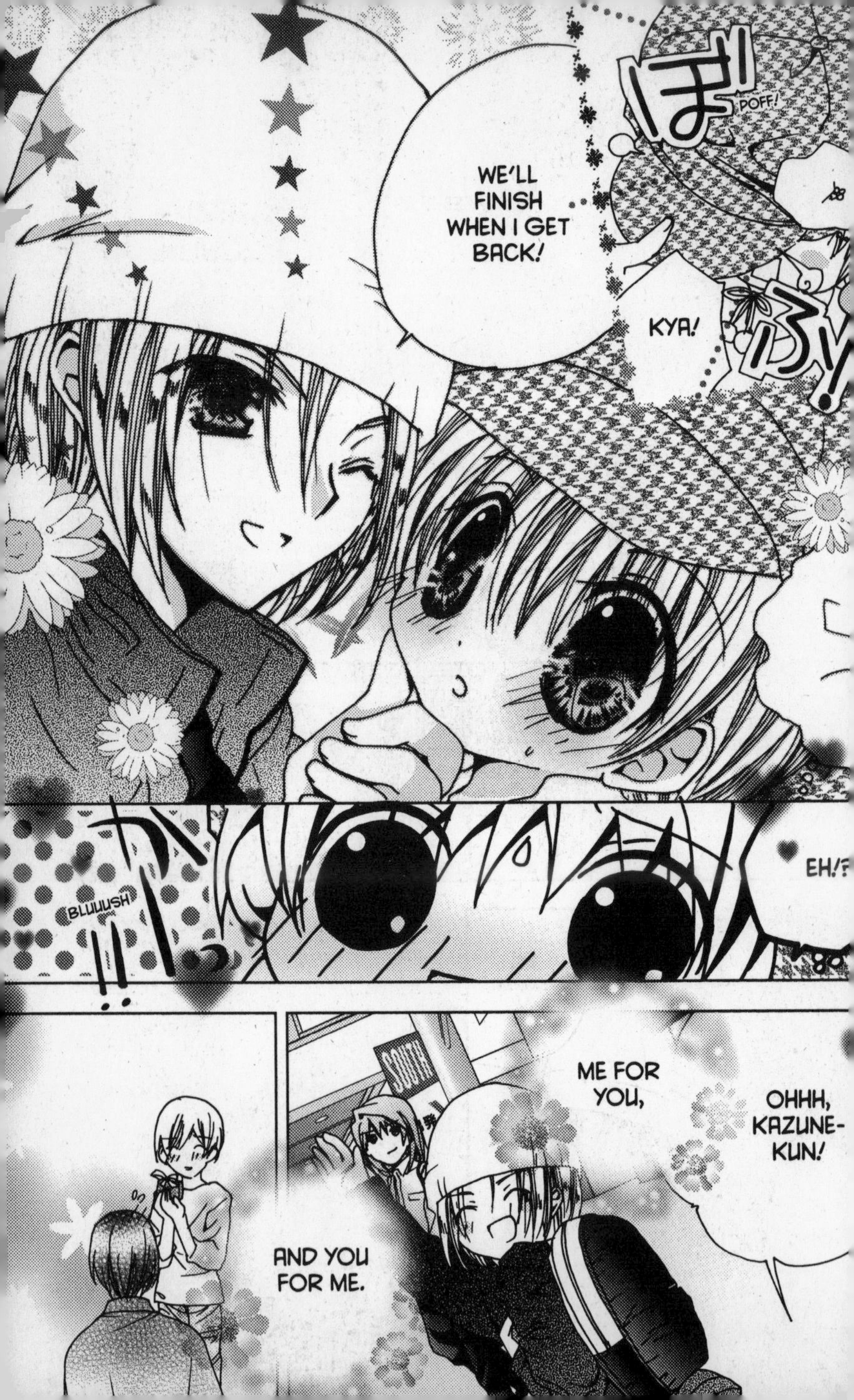
POFF!
WE'LL FINISH WHEN I GET BACK!
KYA!
EH!?
BLUUUSH
OHHH, KAZUNE-KUN!
ME FOR YOU,
AND YOU FOR ME.

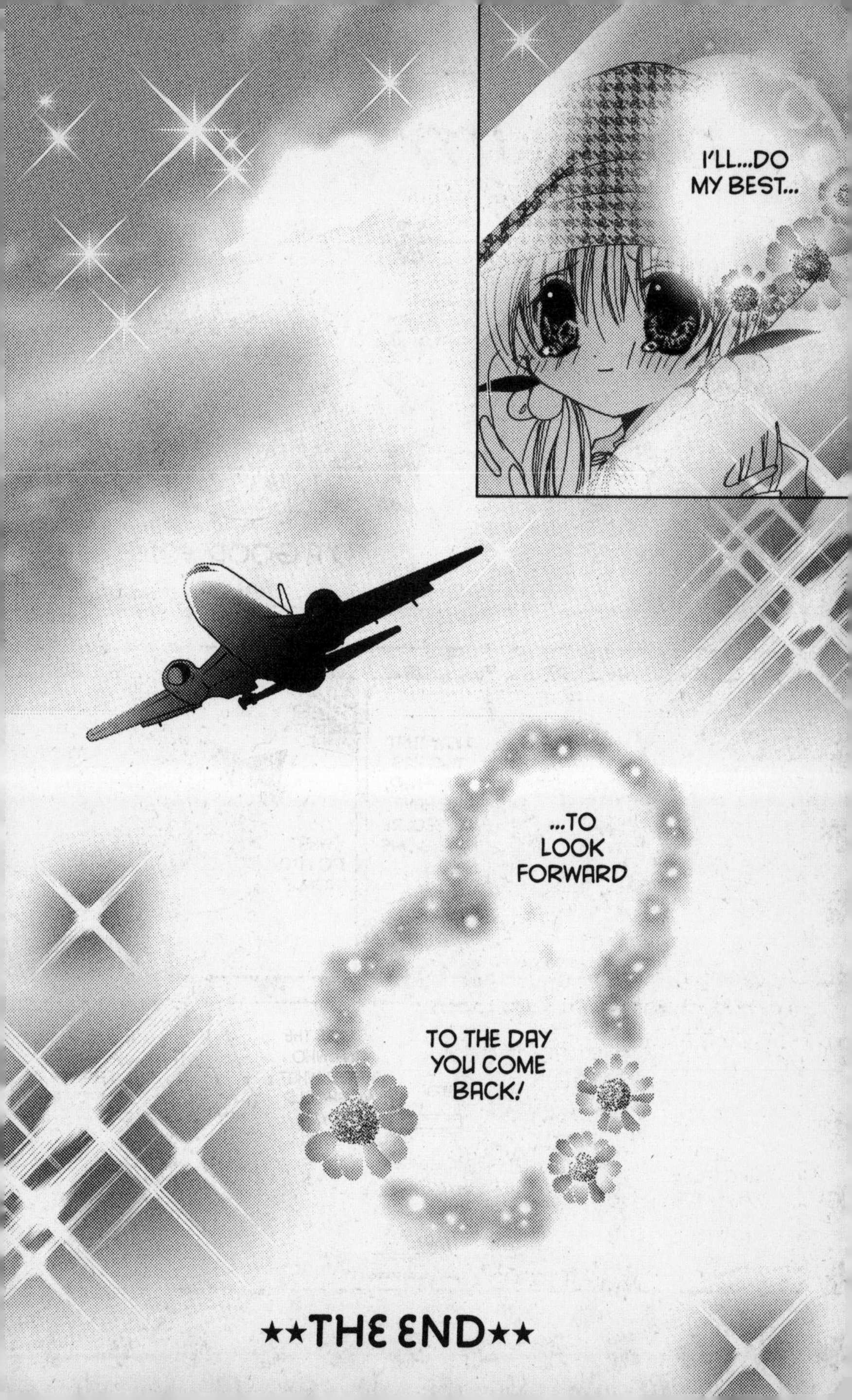
I'LL...DO MY BEST...
...TO LOOK FORWARD
TO THE DAY YOU COME BACK!
★★THE END★★

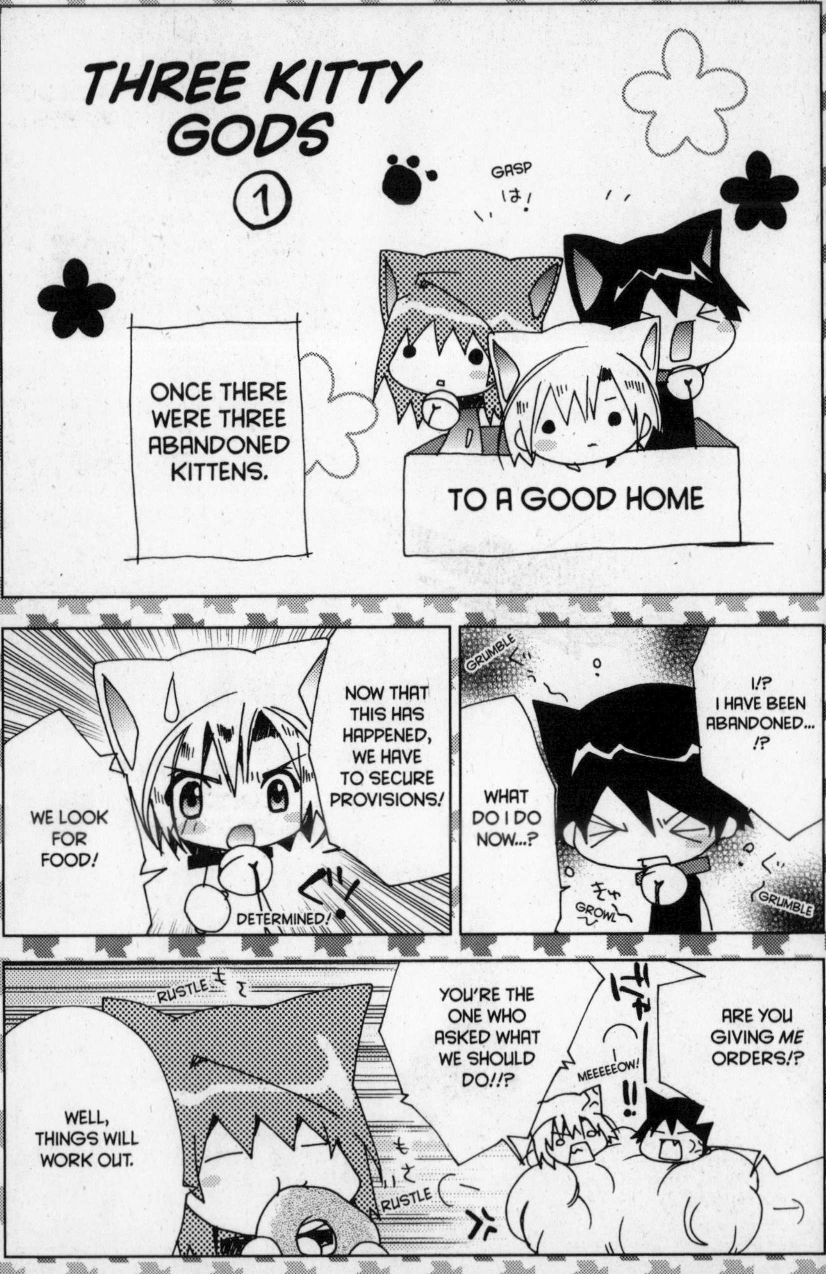
THREE KITTY GODS
1
GASP
は!
TO A GOOD HOME
ONCE THERE WERE THREE ABANDONED KITTENS.
GRUMBLE
I!? I HAVE BEEN ABANDONED... !?
WHAT DO I DO NOW...?
GROWL
GRUMBLE
NOW THAT THIS HAS HAPPENED, WE HAVE TO SECURE PROVISIONS!
WE LOOK FOR FOOD!
DETERMINED!
ARE YOU GIVING *ME* ORDERS!?
MEEEEEOW!
YOU'RE THE ONE WHO ASKED WHAT WE SHOULD DO!!?
RUSTLE
WELL, THINGS WILL WORK OUT.
RUSTLE

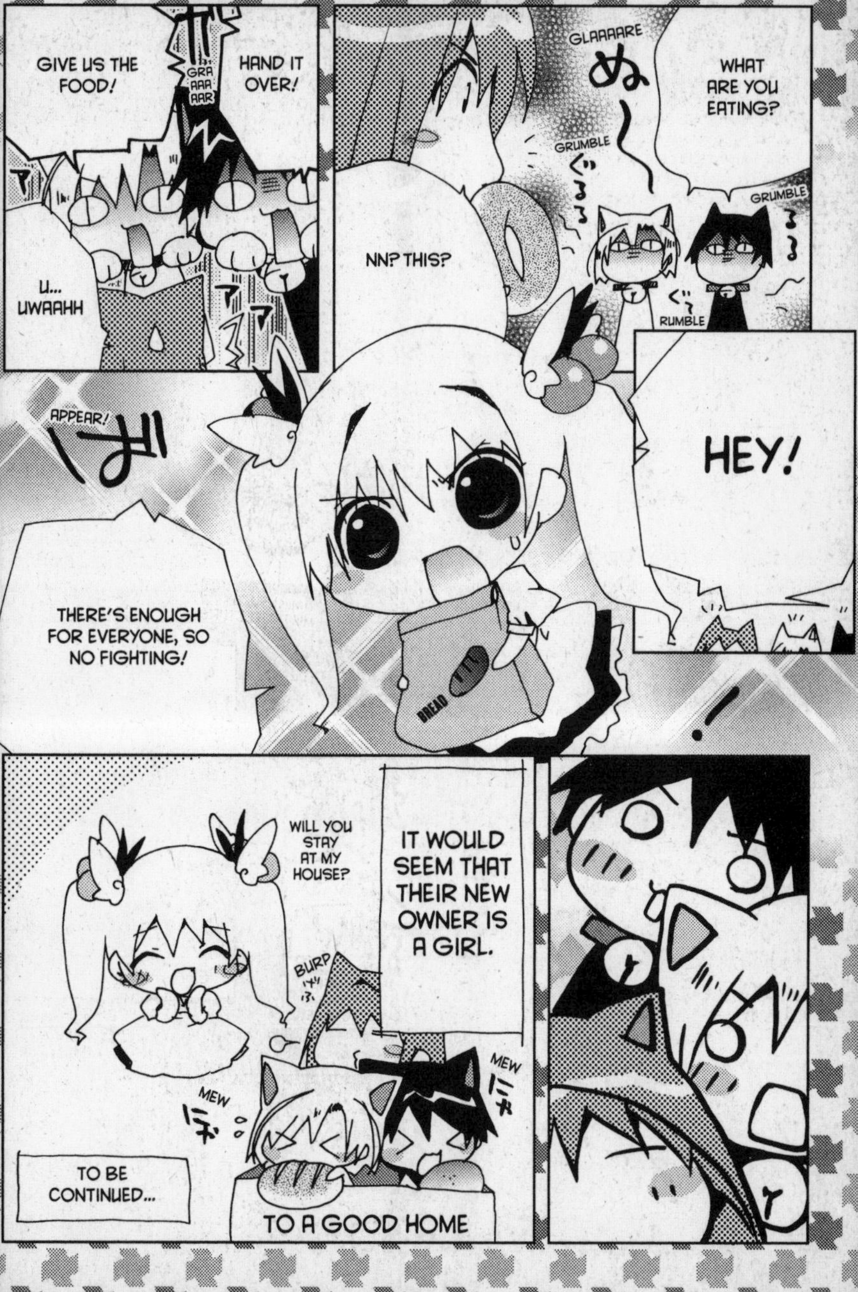
WHAT ARE YOU EATING?
GLAAAARE
ぬ～
GRUMBLE
ぐるる
GRUMBLE
るる
RUMBLE
ぐ
NN? THIS?
HAND IT OVER!
GRA AAA AAR
GIVE US THE FOOD!
U... UWAAHH
HEY!
APPEAR!
ぱ
THERE'S ENOUGH FOR EVERYONE, SO NO FIGHTING!
BREAD
IT WOULD SEEM THAT THEIR NEW OWNER IS A GIRL.
WILL YOU STAY AT MY HOUSE?
BURP
げふ
MEW
にゃ
MEW
にゃ
TO A GOOD HOME
TO BE CONTINUED...

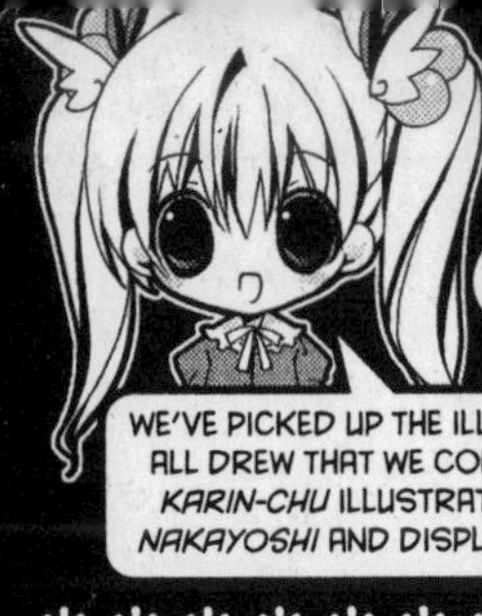

COMIC KAMICHAMA KARIN CHU

SPECIAL

ILLUSTRATION GALLERY

WE'VE PICKED UP THE ILLUSTRATIONS YOU ALL DREW THAT WE COULDN'T FIT IN THE *KARIN-CHU* ILLUSTRATION CORNER IN *NAKAYOSHI* AND DISPLAYED THEM HERE!

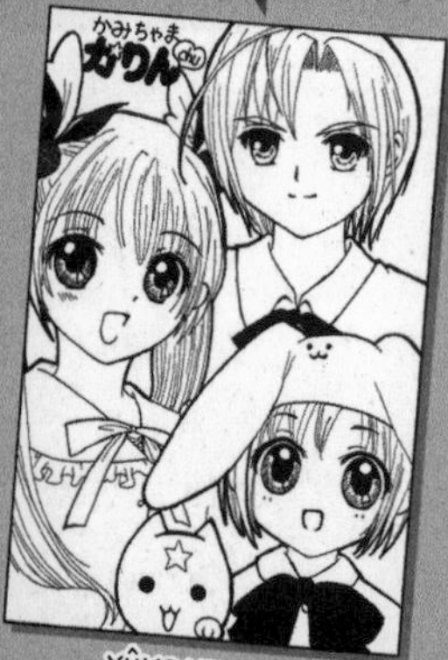
かみちゃま
かりん chu

YÛKO YANASE, AICHI PREFECTURE

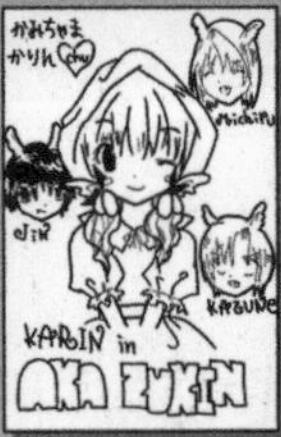
KARIN in
AKA ZUKIN

YURIKA ABE, SAITAMA PREFECTURE

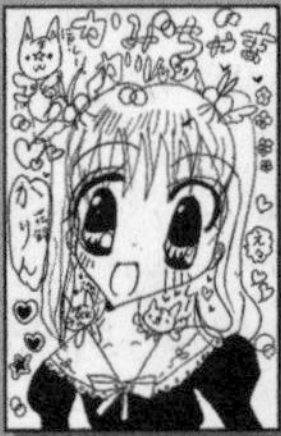

AMANE SAKAI, SAITAMA PREFECTURE

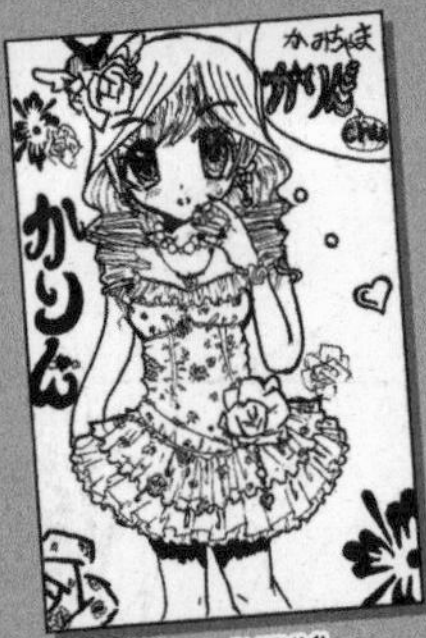
かみちゃま
かりん
chu

MIKI SUZUKI, MIE PREFECTURE

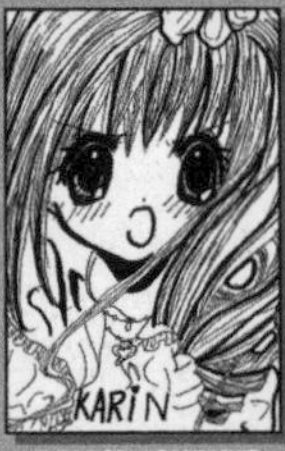
KARIN

ASUKA TSURUTA, KAGOSHIMA PREFECTURE

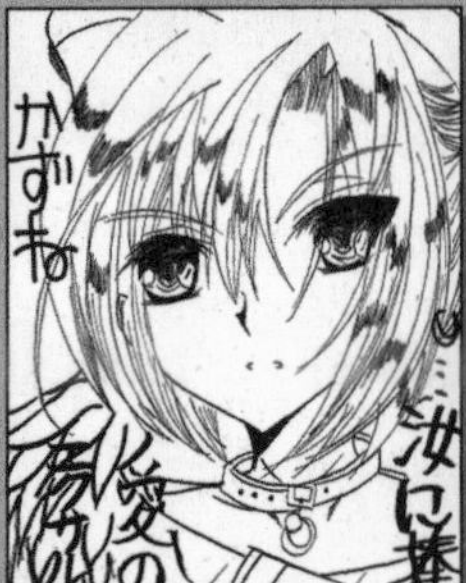

MIHO HORIKAWA, OSAKA

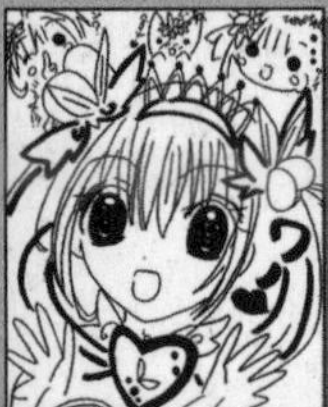
かみちゃま

ISAKI SAWAMURA, KOUCHI PREFECTURE

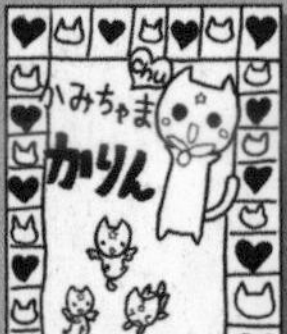
かみちゃま
chu
かりん
しーちゃんと
子ネコ3びき

MIYUKI AZUMOTO, OSAKA

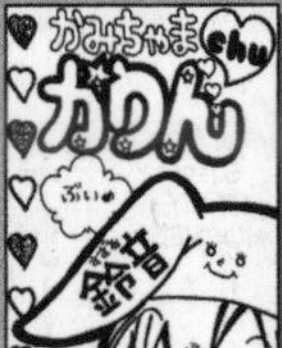
かみちゃま
chu
かりん

SAKI NAKAO, TOTTORI PREFECTURE

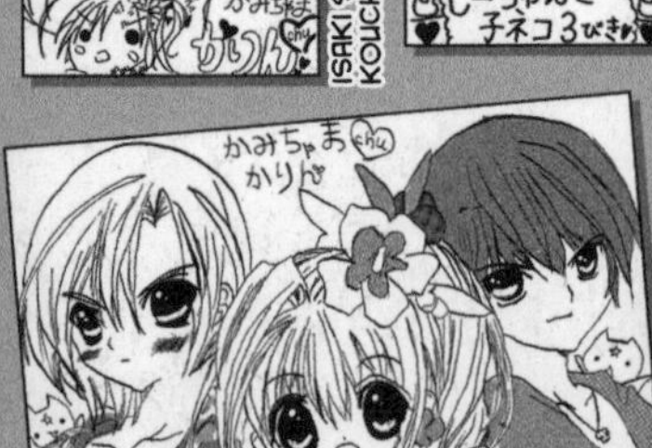
かみちゃま chu
かりん

AOI ÔTEKI, SHIGA PREFECTURE

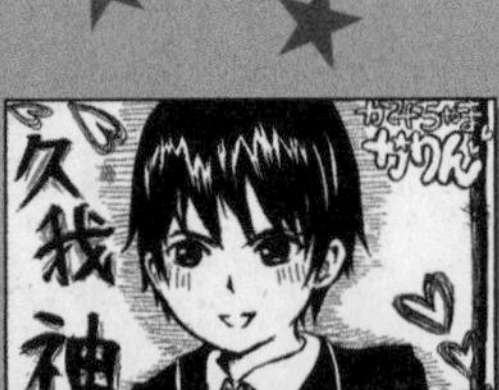
久我神

ASANA FUJITA, SHIZUOKA PREFECTURE

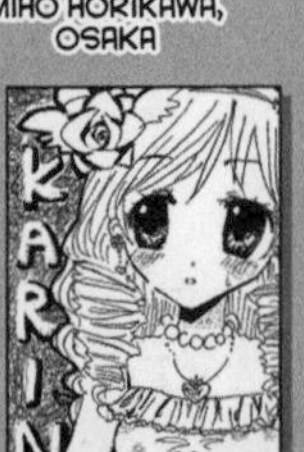
KARIN

NARUMI TANAKA, MIYAZAKI PREFECTURE

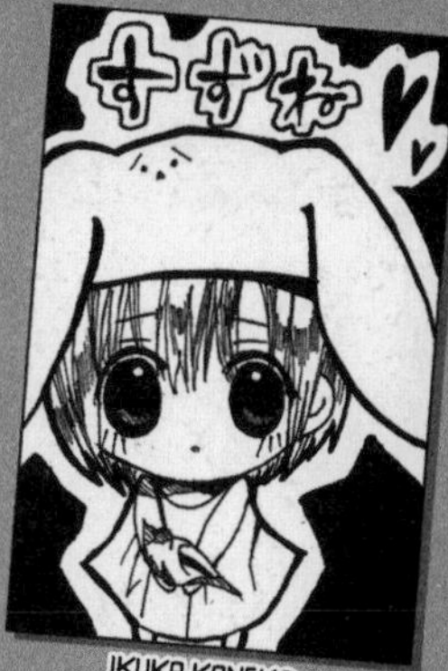
すずね
Ikuka Kaneko, Aichi Prefecture

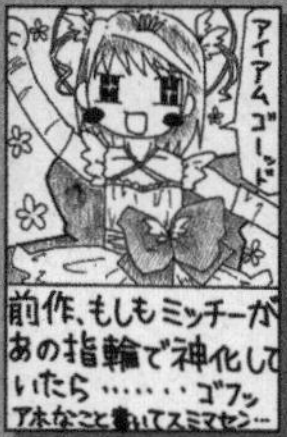
アイアムゴッド
前作、もしもミッチーがあの指輪で神化していたら……ゴフッ
アホなこと書いてスミマセン…
Haruka Suzuki, Ibaraki Prefecture

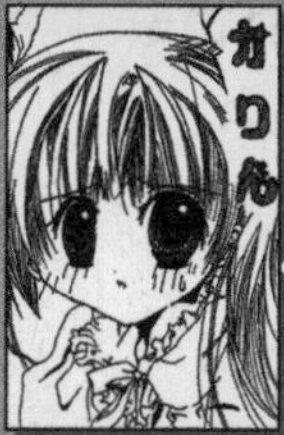
かりん
Ayumi Satô, Yamaguchi Prefecture

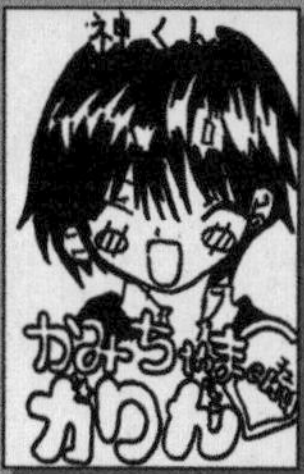
神くん
かりん
Yûka Takagi, Yamaguchi Prefecture

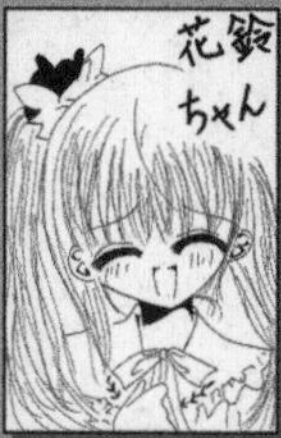
花鈴ちゃん
Michiho Nakamichi, Hyôgo Prefecture

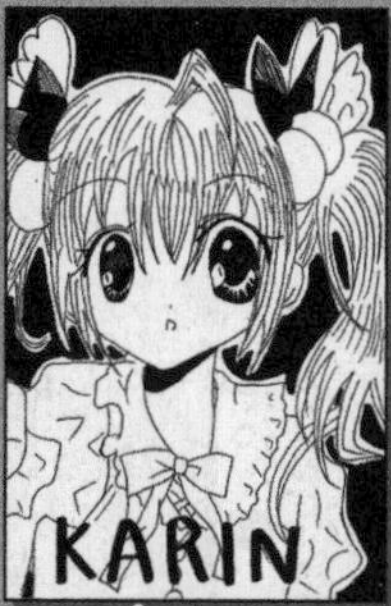
KARIN
Shôko Kimura, Saitama Prefecture

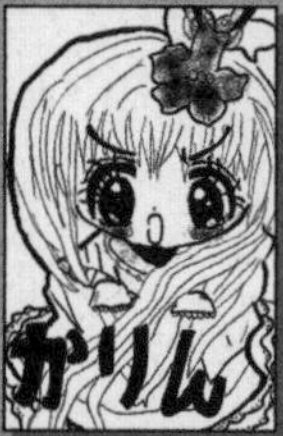
かりん
Mai Okude, Tokyo

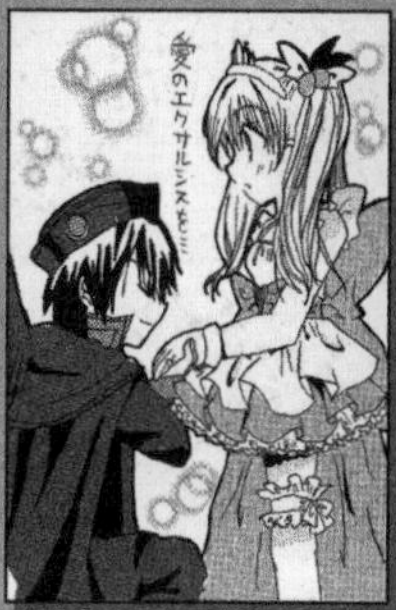
愛のエクサルシスを…
Kahoko Takahashi, Niigata Prefecture

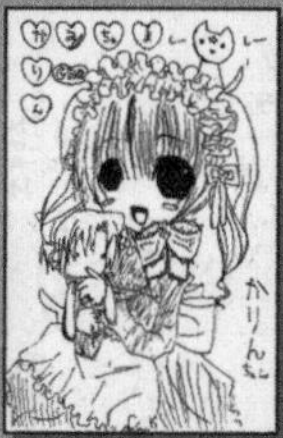
かりんちゃん
Maki Nishiuchi, Kouchi Prefecture

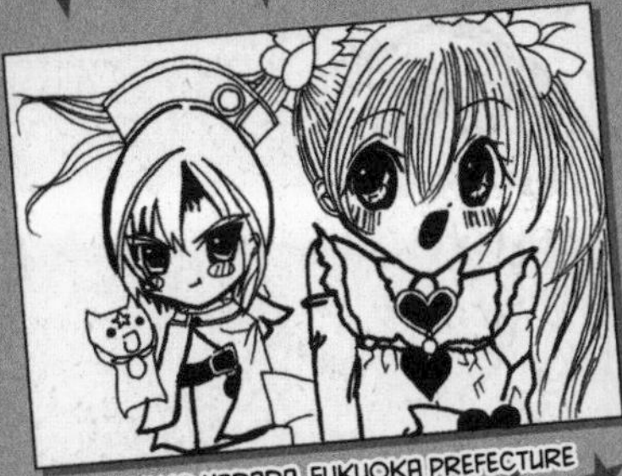
Naoko Harada, Fukuoka Prefecture

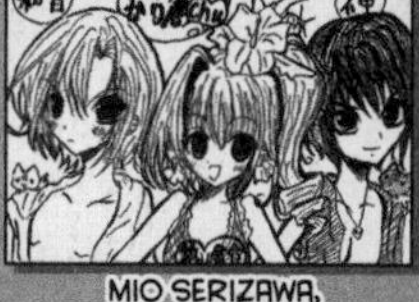
和音
神
Mio Serizawa, Shizuoka Prefecture

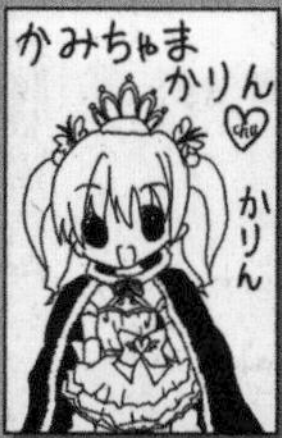
かみちゃま
かりん
chu
かりん
Saori Kawaguchi, Yamaguchi Prefecture

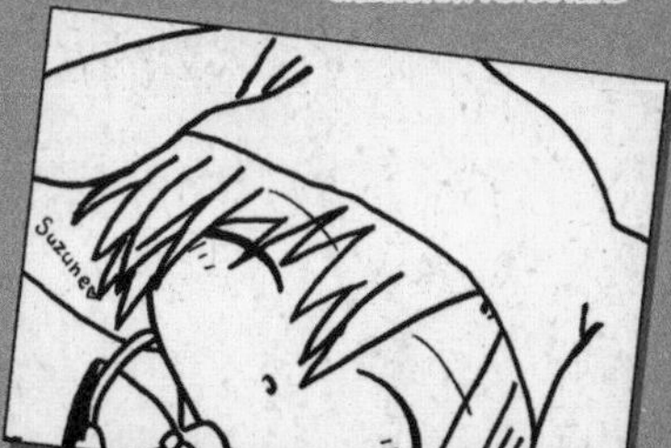
Suzune
Haruna Muramoto, Nara Prefecture

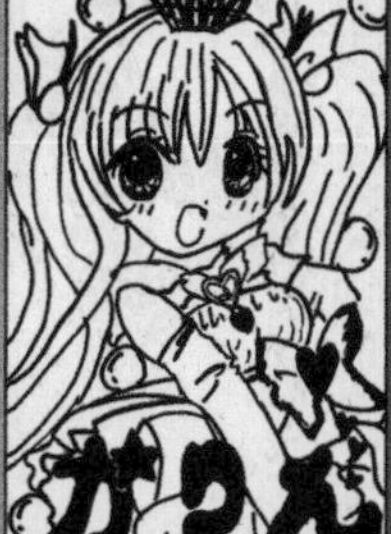
かりん
Ayano Umeda, Miyazaki Prefecture

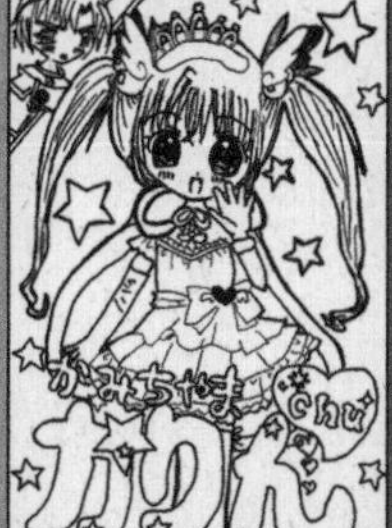
かみちゃま
chu
かりん
Megumi Nakama, Kanagawa Prefecture

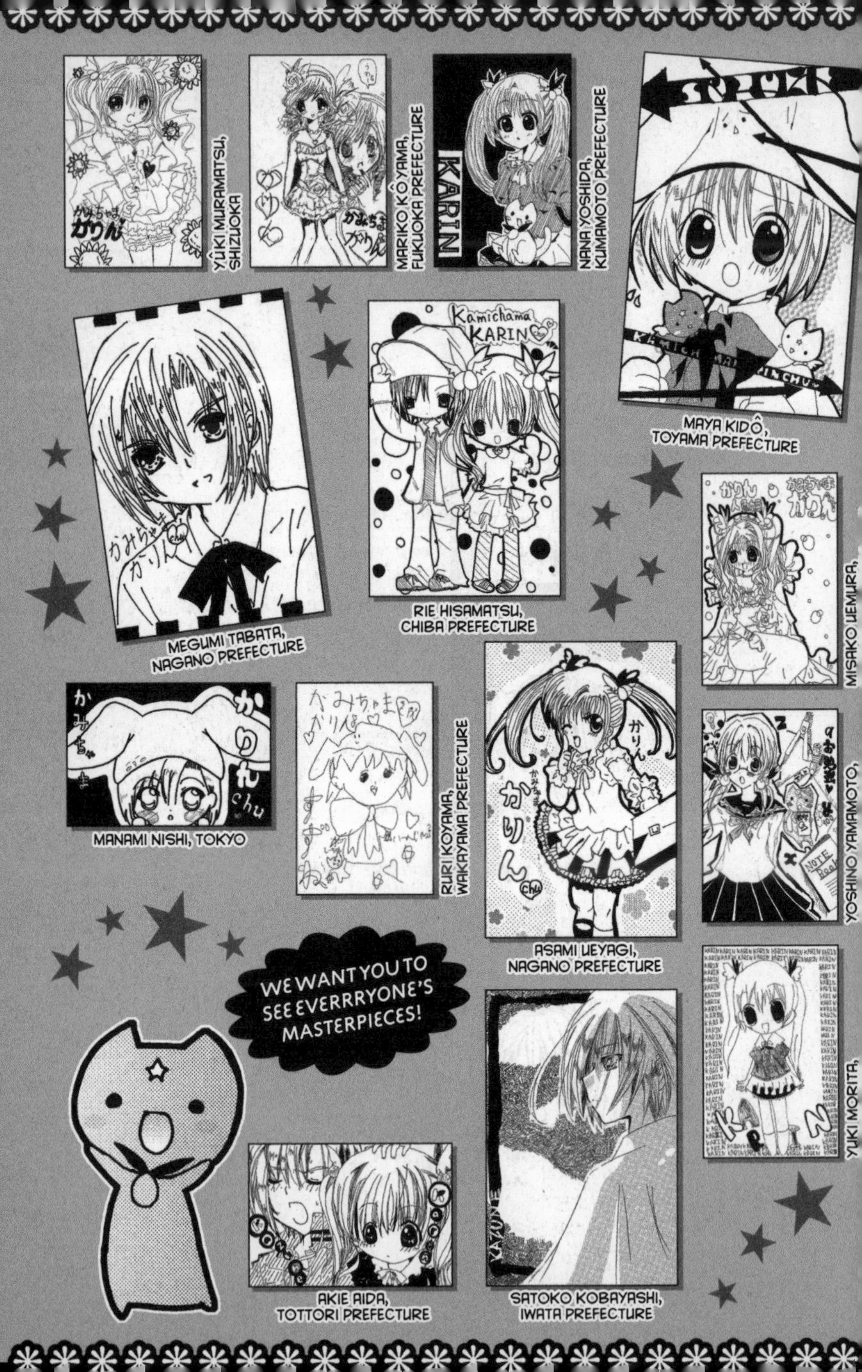
YÛKI MURAMATSU, SHIZUOKA
MARIKO KÔYAMA, FUKUOKA PREFECTURE
NANA YOSHIDA, KUMAMOTO PREFECTURE
MAYA KIDÔ, TOYAMA PREFECTURE
MEGUMI TABATA, NAGANO PREFECTURE
RIE HISAMATSU, CHIBA PREFECTURE
MISAKO UEMURA,
MANAMI NISHI, TOKYO
RURI KOYAMA, WAKAYAMA PREFECTURE
ASAMI UEYAGI, NAGANO PREFECTURE
YOSHINO YAMAMOTO,
YUKI MORITA,
WE WANT YOU TO SEE EVERRRYONE'S MASTERPIECES!
AKIE AIDA, TOTTORI PREFECTURE
SATOKO KOBAYASHI, IWATA PREFECTURE

About the Creator

Koge-Donbo, Kamichama Karin Chu

Koge-Donbo, who also creates under the pen name Kokoro Koharuno, chose this unusual pseudonym in honor of Akira Toriyama's cat! This popular and prolific creator is currently working on several manga series, including *Di Gi Charat* and *Kamichama Karin Chu*.

Born on February 27, Koge-Donbo is a Pisces with blood type A. She loves traditional Japanese culture. She was a member of her college's aikido club and is now studying the art of Noh drama. Koge-Donbo is also fond of traveling and eating curry, ramen, and *okonomiyaki*.

Current Works

Di Gi Charat
Kon Kon Kokon
Kamichama Karin Chu
Sumo Ou
Princess Concerto
Aquarian Age

Completed Works

Pita-Ten
Tiny Snow Fairy Sugar
Kamichama Karin
Koihime Soshi
Yoki Koto Kiku

I'M SO HAPPY!

Translation Notes

Japanese is a tricky language for most Westerners, and translation is often more an art than a science. For your edification and reading pleasure, here are notes on some of the places where we could have gone in a different direction or where a Japanese cultural reference is used.

Kamichama Karin chu

Kami is the Japanese word for god. A great, powerful god would normally be referred to as *kami-sama*, because *-sama* is used to confer great respect. In Kazune's opinion, however, Karin is not great enough to be called *kami-sama*, at least at first. So he says she's more like a *kami-chama*, because *-chama* is a baby-talk version of *-sama* and conveys her cute childishness as a goddess. *Chu* is a Japanese pronunciation of the English "two," and it's also the sound a kiss makes, very fitting for this sequel to *Kamichama Karin.* ❤

Okonomiyaki

Loosely translated as "fried to your liking," an *okonomiyaki* is a pizzalike pancake fried with various ingredients—whatever you like.

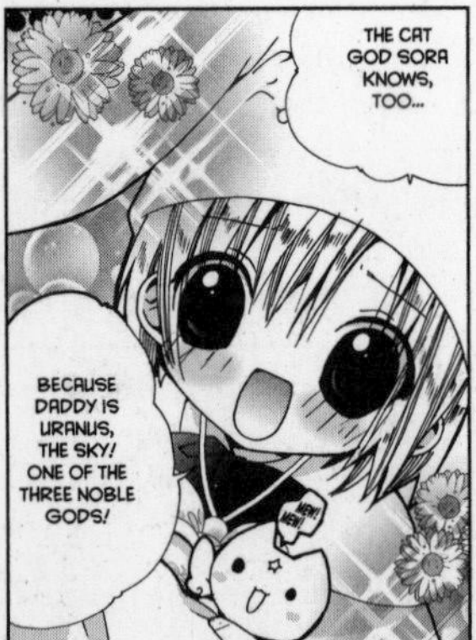
THE CAT GOD SORA KNOWS, TOO...
BECAUSE DADDY IS URANUS, THE SKY! ONE OF THE THREE NOBLE GODS!
MEW! MEW!

Uranus and cat god Sora, page 30

In Greek mythology, Ouranos is Father Heaven. Uranus is his Roman name. It's appropriate that his familiar would be named Sora, the Japanese word for sky.

Suzune, page 31

Suzune is a combination of Karin and Kazune's names. *Suzu* is another way to read the Chinese character for *rin* in Karin, and the *ne*, of course, comes from Kazune's *ne*.

Abeshi and *hidebu*, page 36

In order to make it past the rabid fangirls, Kazune gets ready to fight by dressing up as Kenshiro, the main character from the Japanese manga and anime *Fist of the North Star,* by Tetsuo Hara and Buronson. One of the things this series is famous for is the unusual grunts made by the bad guys as Kenshiro beats them to a pulp, and *abeshi* and *hidebu* are the most famous. They're basically different ways of saying "ow."

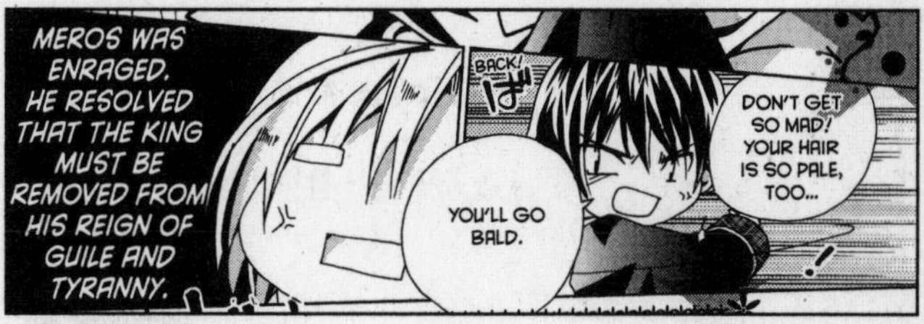
MEROS WAS ENRAGED. HE RESOLVED THAT THE KING MUST BE REMOVED FROM HIS REIGN OF GUILE AND TYRANNY.
DON'T GET SO MAD! YOUR HAIR IS SO PALE, TOO...
BACK!
YOU'LL GO BALD.

Meros was enraged, page 56

This is an excerpt from *Hashire Meros* (*Run, Meros!*), a short story by Japanese author Osamu Dazai. Kazune feels much like Meros—he is enraged and determined to take Jin off his high horse.

Chronos clock, page 60

Chronos is the Greek god of time, so of course if you're going to use a divine clock, you would want to use his.

Sake bath, page 104

Sake is Japanese rice wine. Adding sake to a hot bath has various positive health effects. It's good for the skin and helps the body cleanse itself. Unfortunately, the sake in the steam has the usual negative alcoholic effects on Kazune's state of mind.

Xavier, page 126

Francisco Xavier is the Jesuit missionary known for bringing Christianity to Japan.

minima!

BY MACHIKO SAKURAI

A LITTLE LIVING DOLL!

What would you do if your favorite toy came to life and became your best friend? Well, that's just what happens to Ame Oikawa, a shy schoolgirl. Nicori is a super-cute doll with a mind of its own—and a plan to make Ame's dreams come true!

Special extras in each volume! Read them all!

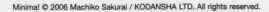

STOP

TOMARƐ!

You're going the wrong way!

MANGA IS A COMPLETELY DIFFERENT TYPE
OF READING EXPERIENCE.

TO START AT THE *BEGINNING*,
GO TO THE *END*!

THA

Authentic manga i̶s̶ from right to left, exactly the *opposite* o̶f̶ ̶American books are read. It's easy to follow: Just go to the other end of the book, and read each page—and each panel—from right side to left side, starting at the top right. Now you're experiencing manga as it was meant to be!